A Guide to Child Health

Michaela Glöckler and
Wolfgang Goebel

A Guide to
Child Health

Translated by Catherine Creeger

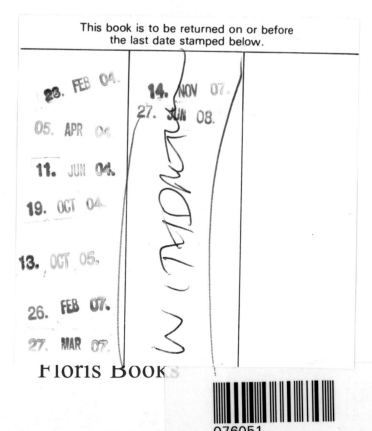

Floris Books

Edited by Christopher J Moore

Originally published in German under the title
Kindersprechstunde by Verlag Urachhaus in 1984.
First published in English in 1990 by Floris Books, Edinburgh

This edition published in 2003, translated from the fourteenth German edition of 2001

British Library CIP data available

ISBN 0-86315-390-9

Printed in Poland

Contents Overview

1
2
3
4
5
6
7
8
9
10
11
12
13
14
15
16
17
18
19
20
21
22
23
24
25
26
27
28
A

Detailed Contents

The Foundations of Healthy Development

Health through Education

Appendix

Preface to the Second Edition

This book is aimed especially at young parents who need help to gain confidence in dealing with their child in sickness and in health. It is also aimed at childcare and health-care workers and at therapists and physicians actively grappling with the connection between medical and educational issues. In recent decades, salutogenic research — that is, investigation into the origins of health — has made it clear that loving, age-appropriate interactions with caregivers have profound effects on children's physical and mental health, while child-rearing efforts can be actively supported by a medical science that views illnesses as developmental opportunities rather than as mere disturbances in the natural course of events. In addition to heredity and environment (the two old, familiar factors influencing individual development), a third decisive factor has long been recognized, namely, the quality and uniqueness of interpersonal relationships. Hence, in addition to suggesting ways of strengthening the child's personality at different age levels in order to develop social skills, this book is intended to encourage families to cultivate an atmosphere imbued with central human values such as honesty, shared responsibility, and mutual respect, an atmosphere that allows the child to feel accepted as an individual.

The first part of this book is devoted to recognizing specific problems and appropriate therapeutic measures in common illnesses. Our aim is to help parents who are observing and supporting sick children to determine for themselves when a visit to the doctor is either absolutely necessary or advisable as a precautionary measure. For the most part, we have limited our therapeutic recommendations to very general measures to avoid impinging on the physician's freedom to decide what is best in each individual case.

The second part of the book outlines the phases of growth and maturation and includes pointers on fostering each child's unique development and on self-education for the adults in a child's life. The importance of rhythm for physical and mental health is discussed, as are suggestions for age-appropriate play, sensory stimulation, nutrition, clothing, and healthy sleep.

The third part is devoted to education and its therapeutic possibilities. In our time, we need a new culture of family, education, and development, a culture that once again acknowledges the relationship between education and the healing arts. Admittedly, in order to develop such a culture, we will first need to foster a concept of the human being that encompasses both the findings of natural science and the insights of modern psychology and spiritual research made possible by Rudolf Steiner's anthroposophy and the efforts of other modern holistic systems of knowledge.

The Guide to Child Health owed its original appearance to requests from the publisher, Johannes M. Mayer of Urachhaus Publishers in Stuttgart, and from parents who repeatedly expressed the wish for a reference work that would review the advice they received in consultations in our pediatric practices. The first edition appeared in 1984 and the book has now gone to its fourteenth edition in Germany, on which this second English edition is based. We extend our sincerest thanks to all who supported us personally and professionally during the writing of the book. Special thanks are due to the staff of Urachhaus Verlag for their excellent work, for their consistently positive and receptive attitude, and their patience in incorporating all the changes, additions, and corrections that a new edition requires (in this case, especially the chapter on immunization and many important references to events, problems, and questions of topical interest that may influence child development).

At the beginning of this new century, we see ever-intensifying conflicts between rich and poor, and between exploitation and conscious stewardship of the natural world. The challenges we will confront in the years to come are becoming all too obvious: we must learn the true meaning of healing and what constitutes individual and social health and, in a world where it is especially endangered, we must cultivate human empathy and dignity.

Herdecke, Germany and Dornach, Switzerland
August 2003
Michaela Glöckler
Wolfgang Goebel

Symptoms of Illness in Childhood

Pleasure is a gift of destiny
that reveals its value in the present,
while suffering is a source of insight
whose significance will become evident in the future.
Rudolf Steiner

1. Pain Due to Illness or Injury

The younger the child, the more difficult it is to find out where it hurts. For this reason, common pain-causing ailments and injuries will all be discussed in one chapter to show to what extent parents can recognize what is causing the pain. We will begin with two very general examples that suggest how to deal with children's pain:

A little girl falls and scrapes her hands and knees badly. Gritting her teeth, she totters away from her playmates and heads for home, picking up speed as she nears home. As soon as she sees her mother's face, she begins wailing at the top of her lungs, literally pouring out her pent-up emotions.

All day, a five-month-old baby is somewhat restless and reluctant to nurse, and at bedtime he begins to cry inconsolably. His mother, perplexed because he always goes to sleep without a fuss, picks him up again for one final burp. It doesn't help. She has already changed his nappy, and his bowel movements were perfectly normal all day. He doesn't feel hot, but just to make sure he has no fever, she checks his temperature rectally. It's a little over 38°C/100.5°F. As soon as she puts him down again, the little boy begins screaming louder than ever. Now his mother begins to get anxious. Is he still thirsty? He refuses a bottle of sweetened herb tea. She picks him up and rocks him in her arms, but even that doesn't help any more. She bounces him a bit, which he usually enjoys, but his crying becomes unbearable.

Alarmed, his mother decides to take him to the doctor's office (surgery), where she reluctantly hands over her little screaming bundle of misery. No chance of examining him in this state, so the only thing the doctor can do is to hold the baby and walk up and down the room, very slowly, almost one step per breath. Gradually both the mother and the baby calm down, and the screaming subsides. All that pent-up air escapes in one great burp, and the baby's little head sinks back in exhaustion. After a couple of gasping sobs and a deep sigh, he calms down. He doesn't flinch in pain as the doctor carefully palpates his abdomen. His ears look fine, too. A quick examination of any other organs that might be involved reveals nothing unusual, but there's a swollen spot on the jaw behind his lower lip. (A more experienced parent would probably have checked there immediately.) Finally his mother realizes what's going on!

The screaming is repeated twice more in the night, but now the baby's mother remains calm. They both sleep a bit later in the morning. At changing time, everything is back to normal, except that Mum is pleased to see his very first tooth peeking through.

Both of these examples show that children's reactions to pain depend in part on the circumstances that surround them. As adults, we are called upon to support our children by responding with composure and confidence. If we ourselves can face the situation calmly, our children will tolerate pain differently from if we panic. Children pick up on our agitation, anxiety, or longwinded expressions of sympathy, which simply intensify their experience of pain.

1.1 Headache

With a rising fever

A frequent scenario: In the morning, a child complains of headache and not feeling well; by evening, she has a fever of 39.5°C/103°F. Headache is a common, transitory symptom at the onset of a fever due to a cold, flu, or other illness; it usually disappears once the fever peaks. It may be accompanied by chills, muscle aches, stomach ache, or nausea.

Meningeal irritation
(meningismus) and meningitis

If a headache persists after the fever peaks, and if it is accompanied by nausea or vomiting, then perform these tests:
- Ask your child to lift her arms while sitting on the bed with legs

outstretched. Does she have to support herself from behind? (See Figures 1 and 2).
- In a sitting position, can she kiss her knee by bending her neck and flexing her knee until she can touch it with her mouth? (See Figure 3).

Being able to perform both of these movements virtually rules out the possibility of *meningitis.* Call your doctor if your child is too young for such tests or fails either one of them. (Be aware, though, that a child may balk, start to cry, and appear unable to perform if parents seem unduly anxious or over-explain their request.) When in doubt, take your child to see a doctor, who will decide whether meningitis is a possibility. Similar symptoms can also occur if there is myogelosis, or muscular contraction or inflammation of the lymph nodes located deep in the neck.

Viral meningitis (caused by mumps, for example) is generally harmless, although certainly unpleasant for the child.* But if *bacterial* (septic) *meningitis* is suspected, waste no time in getting your child to a hospital or clinic where a lumbar puncture (using a fine needle to extract spinal fluid for further testing) can be performed. Prompt antibiotic treatment very often prevents permanent damage from bacterial meningitis, but this condition and its treatment require hospitalization.

If the possibility of meningitis has been ruled out, offer your child sips of herb tea sweetened with sugar or glucose and continue to follow the recommendations for treating fever (see Section 2.2). *Always consult your doctor if a headache or vomiting persists for more than eight hours with no sign of improvement.*

Migraine

Recurrent headaches not accompanied by fever can mean many things; the cause must be determined by a physician in each individual case. Intermittent, attack-like episodes of

* *Viral meningitis:* Viruses are minute parasites visible only under electron microscopy. They cannot reproduce outside of living cells.
  Bacterial meningitis: Bacteria are tiny living organisms, visible under a light microscope, that can be cultured on an organic medium. Some bacteria cause suppurative (pus producing) infections in other living organisms. Antibiotics are effective only in bacterial infections; viral infections do not respond to antibiotic treatment.

headache with or without nausea and vomiting may indicate childhood migraine. Treatment should be prescribed by a physician and will vary among individuals, depending on their overall constitution. The following general guidelines, however, have proved helpful.

- The child's regular diet should include easily digestible unsaturated fats, not too much protein, and plenty of vegetables and salads. Sweets should be limited.
- Four or five small meals are better than three large ones.
- Regular sleeping habits and getting up at the same time each day are important. No sleeping in on Sunday!
- Make sure the child gets enough fresh air and physical activity.
- Your child should sleep off a migraine attack in a darkened room. During the time of sever headache do not give her anything to eat, or at most a few fat-free crackers and herb tea with a bit of lemon. Patience and rest will help the pain ease.
- Medications we have found helpful include Kephalodoron (or Bidor) 5% tablets. Taking two tablets twice a day (before breakfast and lunch) for at least three months often reduces the frequency and severity of migraine attacks. These tablets contain no painkillers but only specially processed homeopathic quartz and iron sulphate, so there is no danger of dependency; acute treatment with more frequent doses (for example, two tablets every half hour)

during an attack is perfectly safe The most effective therapy, however, is prophylactic — taking the tablets regularly, even in pain-free intervals. The same is true of another time-tested remedy, Ferrum/Sulfur comp. globules (five to seven three times a day).

In defective vision

If headache occurs only while reading, a visit to the optometrist is advised. Such headaches are usually due to nearsightedness, farsightedness, or other vision problems.

At school

If your child complains of headaches before, after, or during school, talk to your child's teacher or — if the problem persists — with your doctor. Headaches and stomach aches at school are quite common in children, especially between the ages of nine and twelve.

Possible causes include reluctance to go to school, noise, poor ventilation, unrecognized hunger (for example, skipping breakfast or eating it in a hurry), lack of sleep, stress from academic pressures, and so forth. Also, a child's circulation may be temporarily destabilized during periods of rapid growth, resulting in inadequate supplies of blood to the head or stomach. Fresh air and movement are often helpful in such cases, as is a snack (an apple, half a sandwich, or yoghurt), or lying down for a short rest.

At home on the weekend

Take a look at your family situation if your child's headaches occur mainly at home and especially on the weekend. Is something unpleasant troubling the child or making him afraid? Is the daily rhythm of getting up, eating, being active, and going to bed abandoned at weekends? In headaches of this type, following a regular schedule, even at weekends, has often proved helpful. Avoiding sweets between meals is especially important. Regular bowel habits are also important, and flatulence (wind), if present, should be treated. On another level, it is also important, to avoid focusing the entire family's attention on a child who complains of headache. Instead, he should experience being put to bed — "sidelined," so to speak. If having a headache is made too attractive, he will learn to project any lack of enthusiasm for the activity of the moment into his head and to enlist adult family members to keep him company.

Needless to say, *never* dole out your neighbour's leftover painkillers without your physician's approval!

When an infant is put to bed

Expressions of pain and general crankiness when an infant is put down suggest *teething pains, earache,* or *headache* made worse by the increased volume of blood in the head veins in the lying position. The first two diagnoses can be confirmed by examining the baby; headache is presumed to be the cause of pain when all other possible causes have been ruled out. Fever may accompany all three causes and is often present in middle-ear infections.

1.2 Teething pains

Teething pains (ruled out if the mucous membranes along the gum line are consistently pale in color) are a likely cause of pain if gum swelling, reddening, or sensitivity to pressure is present, and of course if the tooth is already visible beneath the skin. Giving the baby a piece of orris root to chew on can be helpful, as can massaging the gums with Wala liquid mouth balm diluted 1:20 with water, or a 1:100 dilution of either Weleda mouthwash concentrate or rhatany root tincture. In South Africa, Weleda Teething Remedy (Chamomilla/Millefolium comp.) drops are available.

Teeth often erupt in the alphabetical order indicated schematically below:

G E F C B   B C F E G
———————————————————————
G E G D A   A D F E G

A and B are the central incisors, C and D the lateral incisors, F the canine teeth, and E and G molars. With regard to some questions that emerge later in life, physicians interested in their patients' overall development may find it important to know which tooth emerged at what age and whether anomalies of shape or location were present.

1.3 Earache

Earache is confirmed in an infant or toddler if, when you press on the tragus, the small projection in front of the external opening of the ear, the child turns away from the pressure and expresses acute discomfort (so-called tragus pain, see Figure 4). A child who frequently rubs her ear, however, is more likely to have pain in her mouth than an earache. A middle-ear infection (otitis media) is often preceded by a cold. Otitis as a viral infection is especially painful due to rapidly developing blisters on the eardrum. When these blisters burst, they release a few drops of fluid that may be tinted with blood. The pain lasts for approximately one day. With suppurative otitis media, some ten to twenty percent of affected eardrums discharge into the outer ear, after which the pain disappears quickly. When the affected eardrum does not discharge, the pain usually disappears after one or two days. If it lasts longer, the second ear often becomes infected after the first.

In all of these above-mentioned cases, holding a little pack of chopped onion or warmed dried chamomile flowers against the affected ear offers pain relief (see page 422).

Fever should ease significantly within three days. If it persists, your doctor should examine the child again to rule out complications. Fever suppressants do not help the healing process. Discharge from suppurative middle-ear infections usually continues for five to ten days and may persist even longer without causing permanent hearing damage, although of course regular monitoring is needed. (*In infants,* ear discharge may develop suddenly, with no preliminary warning signs, and disappear just as suddenly. Here, too, thorough follow-up examinations are in order. Warm clothing and bonnets or caps are recommended, since infants can become very sick with a relapse unless care is taken.)

In our experience, myringotomy (puncturing the eardrum to draw off pus) is rarely necessary. An ear that is dried out too quickly is more prone to recurrence of the illness, especially when a crust forms and pus is trapped behind it. In such cases, the child's temperature usually rises above 38°C (100.5°F) again, and you should consult your doctor.

A perforation in the eardrum generally heals well by itself. Congenital weakness of the mucous membranes is almost always present in the exceptional instances when chronic ear discharge develops. Based on the literature (see Bibliography) and our own experience, otitis media is an illness that only rarely requires antibiotic treatment. If suitable means are used to help the body actively come to grips with the infection, the general strengthening that results means that relapses become less frequent.

Therapy
Treating a middle-ear infection is always a job for a physician, who can simultaneously treat upper respiratory infections, rhinitis, or enlarged adenoids or tonsillitis, as needed.

In our experience, uncomplicated middle-ear infections generally respond well to any one of the following:
- Levisticum Rh 3X 10 drops every hour;
- Erysidoron I (Apis 3X and Belladonna 3X), five to ten drops (depending on age) diluted in water, four to six times a day; or, alternatively,
- Apis/Levisticum 3X/4X, five globules every hour.

For chronic cases, a longer course of treatment with Levisticum root

(Levistici radix) is recommended. Pour one cup of boiling water over a teaspoon of the crushed root and allow to steep for five minutes. The daily dosage is one cup of this tea, drunk one sip at a time throughout the day.

Many other time-tested treatments are also available.

Harmless ear discharge can occur when water enters the auditory canal, softening earwax so that it runs out and looks like pus. Similarly, a brownish "bloody" spot on the pillow is often only a softened plug of earwax.

Vomiting is not typical of simple otitis media; consult your doctor if it occurs in conjunction with earache.

When cleaning a child's ears, be careful to touch only the earlobe and the visible part of the auditory canal with the swab. Deeper penetration disrupts self-cleaning of the auditory canal's epithelium, which naturally moves away from the eardrum toward the outside as it grows, carrying old earwax with it. If earwax becomes too dense, a daily drop of olive oil in the auditory canal (administered with the child lying on her side) is generally enough to soften it.

1.4 Eye pain: Conjunctivitis

Conjunctivitis, one of the most common eye problems, typically does not involve severe pain and does not require examination by a doctor. *(Do consult a doctor, however, whenever severe pain occurs in one or both eyes.)* The symptoms of conjunctivitis are: reddening of the conjunctiva (the mucous membrane covering the white part of the eye and the inner surface of the eyelid), avoidance of light, the sensation of a foreign object in the eye, and (sometimes) itching. Severe pain is not typical of conjunctivitis and constitutes grounds for an immediate visit to the doctor. The causes of conjunctivitis are many: cold wind, allergies, infections, measles, etc. The use of a drop of silver nitrate solution (now widely replaced by antibiotic drops) in each eye at birth to prevent gonorrhea can also cause irritation that persists for several days.

When evaluating eye irritation at home, it is important to distinguish among the following forms.

Suppurative inflammation in newborn babies involving one or both eyes.
Treatment: Calendula D4 eye drops, used under a doctor's supervision.

Persistent watery eye is caused by blockage of the tear ducts draining into the nose. Droplets of pus often appear in the corners of the eyes closest to the nose.

Treatment: Calendula D4 eye drops and carefully massaging the area of the nasal tear duct, using gentle pressure and a clean little finger, sometimes help. An eye doctor can probe this delicate duct to clear it, but this measure is usually unnecessary.

Reddening and suppuration in both eyes in the post-newborn stage, accompanied by significant reddening of the conjunctiva and avoidance of light; eyelids tend to stick together.

Treatment: Clean the lids with a sterile cotton swab and boiled water cooled to lukewarm (or better still, 0.9% sterile saline solution from the pharmacy). Because of the risk of allergic reactions and irritation from suspended particles, *do not* use chamomile tea! Calendula D4 or Echinacea/Quartz comp. eye drops, three to four drops in each eye once an hour (to "rinse out" the infection). If no improvement is noted in two or three days, take the child to the doctor.

Reddening and watering of both eyes, without suppuration: Usually due to sensitivity to wind, dust, or smoke or a symptom of hay fever.

Treatment: Euphrasia eye drops, dosage as above. In hay fever, Gencydo 0.1% or Euphrasia eye drops, one drop several times a day.

Reddening of one eye with or without suppuration: Caution is in order, since these symptoms may be due to either a foreign object in the eye or an inflammation of the cornea. It is best to go straight to the doctor.

1.5 Sore throat and neck pain

A feverish toddler is lying teary-eyed in bed. Asked where it hurts, she points to her stomach. She ate nothing today and drank only a few sips of tea.

Whenever pain is associated with refusing food, check first your child's stomach and then her mouth and throat, to the extent that you are confident in your ability to do so. (By pressing quickly and firmly on the back part of your child's tongue with a spoon handle or a tongue depressor, you can take advantage of the gag reflex to see your child's throat and tonsils. Just make sure to release the pressure quickly!) Sore throats are children's most common reason for refusing food. The appearance of the throat and the course of the illness vary, depending on the cause.

In *viral tonsillitis,* the most frequent finding is glassy red spots (like fine grains of tapioca) along the gums. The tonsils are somewhat red and the tongue is coated. The child has a high fever (up to 40°C/104°F) and may vomit. These infections are usually harmless.

In *strep throat* or *septic sore throat,* the tonsils and the back of the gums are bright red, possibly spotted with white. Usually, the bacterial responsible for this condition are streptococci. Fortunately, the course of this disease is generally much milder now than it was in the past. Possible complications include middle-ear infections (see Section 1.3), impetigo (see Section 5.13), and (rarely) inflammation of the kidney (glomerulonephritis). Rheumatic fever (whose symptoms include acute polyarthritis and myocarditis) is a very infrequent complication (see also scarlet fever, Section 7.3). For most physicians, the possibility of such severe complications constitutes grounds for insisting on the use of antibiotics and viewing any decision not to use them as an error in professional judgment. It goes without saying, therefore, that a physician must always be consulted in such cases and that the physician and the parents must be in agreement if treatment is not to include antibiotics.

A point to consider, however, is that the sore throat that precedes the development of these rare streptococcal complications is often minor or even totally absent and that complications may occur in spite of early and thorough antibiotic treatment. (Reports from the US confirm that rheumatic complications can develop in spite of penicillin therapy.) In ten years of treating strep throat, the one patient we saw who developed myocarditis had already received antibiotic therapy. Furthermore, it has been shown that many people who are neither ill nor contagious have streptococci on their tonsils. For example, swabbing the throats of healthy kindergarten children produced 5 to 30% positive cultures for streptococcus. Given the fact that children have frequent contact with playmates, siblings, and the many adults in their immediate surroundings, the possibility of streptococci recolonizing the tonsils shortly after the conclusion of antibiotic treatment is high. It becomes obvious that even the widest possible use of penicillin cannot prevent the appearance of streptococcal complications with any degree of certainty.

We personally urge parents and physicians to arrive at mutually acceptable decisions for or against the use of antibiotics on a case-by-case basis. Regardless of the decision, a strep throat patient requires careful treatment: bed rest until at least three days after the fever abates, contact with your physician every two or three days until the child is fever-free, a check-up two or three weeks after symptoms have disappeared or at any point if recovery is unsatisfactory. The majority of the patients we treated did not require antibiotics.

When the tonsils are thickly coated and bright red, a doctor should be consulted immediately to determine the cause, which may be *infectious mononucleosis* (Section 7.7). *Diphtheria* (Section 7.6) is a rare but possible cause of these symptoms.

Thrush (a fungus infection in the mouth) affects the mucous membranes of the inside of the cheeks more than the throat and does not cause pain (see Section 5.12; see also trench mouth, Section 7.9).

Home treatments for sore throats include hot or cool lemon-juice compresses applied around the neck (see page 423f) for the early stages of *viral tonsillitis,* as well as other acute sore throats. Alternatively, make a poultice with lemon slices (page 424). In addition, the patient should sip well-warmed sage tea with honey and lemon and gargle with strong sage tea. A sweat pack (see page 435) is sometimes helpful. Chemical disinfection of the mouth is useless, but Wala's Echinacea Mouth and Throat Spray® or gargling with Weleda's Bolus Eucalypti comp.® are time-tested remedies that offer some relief. In NZ, Weleda mouthwash, or Ratanhia Mouthwash, is available. Internal medications depend on the specific diagnosis and should be prescribed by a physician. If no holistically-oriented doctor is available, we rec-

ommend over-the-counter treatments such as Cinnabar comp. (one saltspoonful four times a day) or Apis/Belladonna c. Mercurio (five to seven pillules five times a day). For *chronic tonsillitis* or recurrent colds with sore throat, a two-week course of treatment with mustard footbaths has proved very helpful (see page 432)

Other types of throat and neck pain
Abscesses behind or under the tonsils occur occasionally in the context of a sore throat. The patient feels terrible, has a high but often fluctuating fever, and cannot open his mouth fully. Tonsillar abscesses require prompt treatment by a physician.

Treating *lymphadenitis* (lymph gland inflammation) is less urgent; it is safe to wait and observe how the illness progresses. At the side of the neck below the jawbone, a lumpy, outward-facing, pressure-sensitive swelling is evident to the touch. (For throat poultices, see page 422f) The illness takes one of two possible courses. Often, the swelling slowly recedes, although the lymph nodes may remain palpable for months as they gradually shrink. In other cases, parents will notice that the painful nodes grow noticeably bigger and harder each day. In both courses, the body itself actively insures that healing occurs. As a result, most children who have had such abscesses enjoy good resistance to suppurative infections for the rest of childhood. In our experience, therefore, it is worth avoiding antibiotic therapy while the illness is being overcome, although hospitalization may be required in some cases.

In almost every child, *smaller lymph node swellings* (swollen glands) can be detected during harmless infections or sometimes without any other sign of illness. Take your child to the doctor only if the painless swelling increases over several weeks.

Pains at the back and side of the neck may also be due to muscular spasm or stiff neck. Symptoms persist for several days and are significantly relieved by heat. Use circulation-enhancing ointments or warm oil compresses covered with a wool cloth. For the compresses, use either pure sunflower or olive oil or 10% lavender oil (see below).

1.6 Chest pains

Painful *breathing or coughing* usually means that the mucous membranes lining the airways are irritated. Steam inhalation, honey-sweetened cough-relieving herbal teas, and oil compresses on the chest (see page 427) relieve this irritation. Time-tested oils for chest compresses are 10% lavender and eucalyptus oils. You can make either of these oils yourself by diluting the pure etheric oil with nine parts of olive oil.

Pains in the *chest wall* occur when the muscles are irritated locally, rather like muscular rheumatism, during a respiratory infection or influenza. The patient cannot breathe deeply but gets enough air and does not cough. When the irritation is close to the heart, the patient may describe the pain as heart

pains. This type of pain, which is usually sharp and of sudden onset, can be treated with a warm oil compress.

Another type of *left-sided pain* is due to accumulation of air in the intestine under the left dome of the diaphragm. In this case, too, the patient has difficulty in breathing deeply, and between breaths there is a dull pressure on the left side near the heart. Caraway tea and other carminatives bring relief. Rubbing the area with a clockwise motion (make sure your hand is warm!) may also get the trapped air moving. Sometimes the patient herself can relieve the pain by pressing on her abdomen.

Pains that originate in the heart are extremely unusual in children. Chest pains associated with a current or prior serious illness, racing pulse, or curling up in the fetal position are signs that something is seriously wrong; consult a physician.

Pains in the ribcage accompanied by high fever and jerky, interrupted exhalation are infrequent but clear signs of *pleurisy.* This condition, which is usually preceded by pneumonia, will require a visit to the doctor for a chest X-ray and possible hospitalization for treatment.

A *stitch in the side* is usually caused by cramping of the lateral muscles of the abdominal wall and occurs while walking with a full stomach. To relieve a stitch, instruct the child to hold his breath and press on his upper abdomen with his forearms while moving into a squatting position.

1.7 Abdominal pain

Many different observations lead the parents of infants to suspect abdominal pain:

"My baby is all cramped up."

"He cries for a while, then he's quiet, then he starts screaming again."

"Her stomach is all tight and hard."

"He looks so pale."

"Her stomach is gurgling."

"He's vomited twice."

"She doesn't want to eat."

"He didn't have a bowel movement yesterday."

Questions about symptoms such as these often bring parents to the doctor with their infants. But if parents are calm enough to perform some simple examinations themselves, they can often learn to distinguish harmless symptoms from dangerous ones and help their children feel better at home.

Flatulence (gas or wind)

Example: An infant some weeks old cries after every meal but usually not while nursing. Did he get too much or too little to drink? Was his formula too cold or maybe too thick for the nipple (dummie)? Did he manage a big burp afterward? Other than these circumstances, the most likely cause of the crying is either flatulence or strong intestinal peristalsis. Symptoms that may accompany flatulence include: minor spitting up, a somewhat tight abdomen, and straining to pass hard, normal, or loose stools. (The classic "cranky hour" in the late afternoon or evening has nothing to do with flatulence.)

For reasons that remain incompletely explained, infants often cry in the late afternoon or evening without seeming to be hungry or tired, and their crying is different from cries of pain. Air swallowed while crying, however, may cause stomach aches. Carrying your infant in a sling is the best way of calming her at this time of day. It is vital that inexperienced parents learn that disciplining an infant will not make her be quiet. Most brain injuries in this age group occur in babies shaken by parents desperate to stop their crying.

Not typical of windy pains are: vomiting (meaning more than a couple of mouthfuls), a pale face, a tight abdomen, diarrhea (multiple loose bowel movements between meals), failure to gain weight, or sudden screaming indicative of intense pain. Take your child to a doctor to determine the cause of these symptoms.

Breastfed infants frequently suffer from wind when their mothers eat a lot of whole-grain bread, beans, or vegetables such as cauliflower or cabbage. Babies who are not breastfed may benefit from a change in formula; ask your doctor first (see also Section 14.3).

Some soothing and calming measures:

- Warmth. Try a heated cloth or warm, moist abdominal compress made with chamomile, yarrow, or lemon balm tea (see also pages 429f). Also effective is rubbing the baby's abdomen in a clockwise direction with oil infused with lemon balm or chamomile or with 10% caraway oil, diluted 1:2 if needed. Wool undershirts that cover the abdomen, warmer diapering, and perhaps a hot water bottle (better still, a warmed bag of cherry stones) are recommended. Keep the baby's knees warm, too.
- Internally, a few spoonfuls of well-warmed fennel tea right before meals may help. (So-called carminatives, available as drops, don't work any better than fennel tea.)
- Carry the baby in a sling for ten minutes after burping her. Another tried-and-true method to soothe the baby after nursing is to hold her on your upper thigh with her back to your chest and lightly massage her feet, ankles, and calves (one foot with each hand). Letting her kicking feet encounter the resistance of your hand is often enough to calm a restless infant.
- Monitor how much your child is eating (see Section 14.1)
- If you're breastfeeding, watch your own consumption of whole-grain bread and raw rolled oats. Stone fruits such as cherries and peaches are reputed to cause gas, but you needn't avoid them. Raw whole grains are much more of a problem.
- Your infant's symptoms will be worse if you yourself are stressed by a busy day or by impending exams, eat in a hurry, or are constantly distracted or unhappy.

If it is any consolation, this type of abdominal pain will disappear by itself when your baby is eight to twelve weeks old.

Appendicitis

In toddlers and older children, the typical sign of appendicitis is continuous, increasing pain that develops slowly over a period of hours and gradually becomes concentrated in the right lower abdomen. The abdominal pain is usually accompanied by lack of energy, nausea, coated tongue, and pain while walking and hopping. A hot water bottle does not bring relief and is generally rejected by the patient.

What to do

Do not give your child anything to eat or drink.

Check his temperature both under the arm (leave the thermometer in place for five minutes, making sure that it is correctly positioned, and with a blanket over his shoulders and arms) and rectally (one and a half minutes); record both results and note the difference (see Section 2.2 on *Taking your child's temperature*).

Take your child to the doctor.

In toddlers, appendicitis may be difficult to recognize because symptoms are mild or uncharacteristic or because they immediately resemble acute abdominal disease (see page 36).

Even for doctors, diagnosis is often not straightforward, and of course where possible we would want to avoid surgery. However, we advise strongly against treating this condition simply with topical remedies and medication.

Colic (intestinal spasms)

Colic (intestinal spasms) shows as sudden pains, often in the area of the navel, severe enough that the child willingly goes to bed. The pain is generally gone within an hour but recurrences are likely. Children with intestinal spasms look pale, but there is no localized sensitivity to pressure anywhere in the abdominal area. This diagnosis, however, is one that can be made only by a doctor after excluding all other possible causes (see also page 36 and Section 4.1, acetonemic (ketonic) vomiting, and page 241, lactose deficiency). If the diagnosis is correct, the symptoms are harmless although unpleasant, and a course of treatment with warm abdominal compresses after the midday and evening meals for four to six weeks is usually helpful (see page 429).

Worms

Threadworms (oxyuris) are fragile, threadlike little creatures, one to two centimetres in length, that live in the rectum and lay their eggs outside the anus at night. They cause itching and sometimes eczema on the anus, which children scratch. The infection is then transmitted to other children via fingernails and towels. The presence of eggs is easily confirmed by picking them off the unwashed anus in the morning with transparent tape, which is then stuck on a microscope slide for examination.

Roundworms (ascaris), which may cause abdominal pain, are much less common now than they once were.

They are approximately 20 cm (8 in.) long, but males are significantly smaller than females. They are transmitted on salads and other raw vegetables that have been fertilized with human excrement. The larvae develop inside the eggs for 30 to 40 days after ingestion. From the intestines, they travel by way of the portal vein, liver, and heart to the lungs, where they break out of the pulmonary alveoli after about a week. Via the bronchi and the pharynx, they find their way back to the intestines, where they mature. Many different symptoms, including allergic reactions, may develop during this complicated journey. Worm eggs appear in the stools only after this developmental cycle is completed.

Therapy

For threadworms, we have had success with oral administration of Weleda's Allium/Cuprum sulfuricum compositum, three times a day, five to ten drops (depending on the age of the child) in addition to careful hygiene (washing hands with soap and a nail brush; no sharing of hand towels). For roundworms, Quartz 50% (less than $^1/_3$ tsp. three times a day) is also worth trying. The success of the treatment is confirmed if microscopic clinical examination of a stool sample reveals no worm eggs after about three weeks.

Most parents today prefer a one-day chemical treatment.

Urinary tract infections

Abdominal or back pain (with or without fever, pallor, generalized weakness and loss of appetite), wetting accidents, and a burning sensation on urinating are all possible signs of a urinary tract infection, which may be either a bladder infection or pyelitis (inflammation of the lining of the renal pelvis). The burning is sometimes so bad that children hold their urine to avoid it. It is important to know that the burning disappears sooner than the infection. Urine analysis is called for whenever such symptoms appear, although contamination or external infections in the genital area may produce false positives. Serious kidney damage is possible when urinary tract infections occur frequently or become chronic. For this reason, diagnosing and treating this group of diseases is always a job for a physician. In addition to medical treatment, warm compresses over the bladder are recommended (see page 430)

Inguinal hernia

A hernia is discovered by observing and palpating the child's groin, where a protrusion develops (see Figure 6). This bulging hernial sac, which may be as small as a nut or as large as an orange, usually incloses part of the intestine or, in girls, one of the ovaries. In boys, the hernia may extend into the scrotum. *Any painful swelling in this part of the body requires prompt medical evaluation.*

The neck of the hernial sac may constrict, making it impossible to return the inclosed body parts to their normal position ("incarcerated hernia"). Torsion or inflammation of a testicle may also occur. Pushing the contents of a hernial sac back into position is fairly difficult; ask a doctor to show you how. Hernias in the area of the navel usually heal spontaneously even without bandaging, but inguinal hernias are rarely healed without surgery. (See also hydrocele, Section 1.9)

Acute abdominal disease

Colic-like or constant severe abdominal pain accompanied by vomiting along with pallor and palpable abdominal changes (usually a painful tightening of the abdominal wall that makes the child's abdomen feel "stiff as a board") are signs of possibly life-threatening acute abdominal disease. Sudden severe pain with no apparent cause, crying indicative of extreme pain, or vomiting that is not associated with a hard abdomen and showing no sign of improvement within hours is also reason to suspect intussusception (the slipping of a length of intestine into an adjacent portion).

It is imperative that children with these symptoms be evaluated by a qualified physician. It's best to go straight to a pediatric hospital where surgery can be performed if needed.

Parents who have not yet experienced the much less dangerous ketonic or acetonemic vomiting (see page 82) may confuse it with the symptoms of acute abdominal disease.

Abdominal pain with influenza

Abdominal pain, in addition to chills, lethargy, headache, and body ache, may mark the beginning of the flu. Vomiting may also appear during this stage. The initial abdominal pain usually disappears once the typical sharp rise in fever occurs. This type of pain is distinct from appendicitis in that there is no localized sensitivity to pressure on the abdomen, and the difference in temperatures measured rectally and under the arm is not more than 0.5°C/1°F (tenths of a degree are indicated by the shorter lines on the thermometer). A fever that rises rapidly above 38.5°C/101.5°F is not typical of appendicitis. Cool arms and legs indicate that the child's temperature is still rising. A hot water bottle on her abdomen is intolerable to a child with appendicitis (see page 34) but feels good to a child with the flu.

Other causes of abdominal pain

Sore abdominal muscles caused by overexertion while playing or engaging in sports.

Abdominal pain associated with *diarrhea* (see Section 4.1).

When your young child complains of a stomachache, it is also worth checking his mouth for *inflamed tonsils.* Children often interpret pain as coming from the stomach, or the pain may be due to the early stages of fever or to swollen abdominal lymph nodes.

Colic-like abdominal pains may appear several hours to half a day before the onset of acetonemic vomiting (see Section 4.1). In this case, warm abdominal compresses made with oxalis essence or yarrow tea are helpful (see page 429); applications may be repeated daily for several days or weeks, if needed.

Unusual thirst and increased urination for several days, with or without abdominal pain, are signs of possible **diabetes mellitus.**

Stomach aches before or during school suggest **mental overexertion** or psychological stress factors that should be discussed with the child's teacher. Your doctor may also be able to help explain the problem or suggest harmless helpful measures. As a rule, chemical sedatives or analgesics are not indicated.

Other causes may include **birthday parties** with all that cake and excitement, bacterial food poisoning, experiencing outbursts of anger by a parent or teacher, nervous anticipation, or the child's own ambition, jealousy, etc.

We also recommend reviewing your child's day with an eye to how you yourself may be contributing to the development of stomach aches. Two examples illustrate the possibilities:

Mother: I have to feed Stevie now.
   Child: Mummy, can I have an apple?
   Mother: You know, you don't always

have to eat just because Stevie's eating.
   Child: Mummy, you were going to read me the rest of the story.
   Mother: Please leave me alone now; I have to finish feeding Stevie and put him down for his nap.
   Child: Mummy, my tummy hurts ...
   Mother: Oh, for heaven's sake, not again ...

Mother: I can't believe this little guy is hungry again. He's a bottomless pit. Claudia, can you bring me Stevie's bottle? It's in the warmer. [Claudia brings the bottle.] And I peeled an apple for you. It's in the kitchen. Can you find it? [Claudia happily returns with the apple.]
   Mother, singing to herself: Now it's time to eat ...
   The baby drinks while Claudia eats her apple.
   Mother: How's your apple? Can I have a taste? Yum ... When Stevie's done, I need to run to the store quickly.
   Claudia: I want to go too.
   Mother: Not this time. It's already really late. But I'll let you watch Stevie for me for a moment; you can make sure the sun doesn't shine right in his face. I'll just ring Mrs Hopper to ask her to come over while I'm out. And I'll finish telling you that story as soon as I get back. [Claudia is proud to be big enough to be entrusted with her baby brother and is glad that he's quiet and not screaming.]

In the first example, the mother can't fully identify with what she's doing. She's struggling to keep up with everything she needs to do and can't manage to gain any leeway. She is probably overtired and may have been hearing criticism from a relative. Her relationships to the two children are like psychological puppet strings that allow the children to manipulate her.

In case the situation has already deteriorated to the point where your child is complaining of a stomach ache, here's a tip for regaining control:

Child: Mummy, my tummy hurts.

Mother: Your tummy hurts? Go and lie down on your bed. I'll make a hot water bottle for you and come and check on you as soon as I'm done here.

A little later.

Mother: Don't you look comfy! Are you feeling better? I'm just going to ask Mrs Hopper to come round and keep an eye on the two of you while I run to the store ...

This time the mother attempts to reestablish limits by responding to her daughter's complaint with an initiative of her own. Unless the symptoms are legitimate, Mum should not allow herself to be distracted from her original intention. Keep in mind that children who complain of stomach ache often mean something else, such as:

"You haven't paid any attention to me today."

"You're so busy working and it's no fun."

"I can't think of anything to do."

Or even, "You're putting up a wall between us."

Unlike the first mother, the second approaches the situation with initiative and imagination, reaching out to her child and creating a sense of comfort and security that goes beyond physical concerns. When the first mother is ready to learn something from her daughter's stomach ache, she begins with physical warmth and imbues it with emotional warmth and closeness. The hot water bottle soon becomes superfluous.

Is this child "pretending" to have a stomach ache? Not unless she has been exposed to examples of dishonest behavior from an early age. Because children experience their surroundings with great intensity, anything emotionally "indigestible" that exceeds their level of tolerance has immediate physical effects. Whether they take advantage of the symptoms, either more or less consciously, to achieve their own ends depends on the context in which the problems occur. In any case, these symptoms should not be interpreted in moral terms.

1.8 Musculoskeletal pain

The causes and manifestations of this type of pain are so variable that few generalizations are possible. Regardless of whether an accident has occurred or the pain appears spontaneously, it is essential for parents to attempt to get as complete a picture as possible of what led up to the pain. Take your child's temperature before you go to the doctor. Is there any new or temporary swelling or unusual warmth in the painful area? It may be helpful for the doctor to know about these signs and when they first appeared, since they may indicate serious underlying illnesses such as rheumatic disorders, osteomyelitis (an inflammatory bone disease), and other diseases that we will not discuss here. Fortunately, they are rather uncommon, and in any case they always require thorough medical investigation.

Broken collarbone in newborn babies

A newborn baby with a broken collarbone (a relatively common birth injury) will show signs of pain when he is laid down or when his shoulders are moved. The break may be missed when the doctor examines the child after delivery; later, however, swelling around the break makes it obvious later. This type of fracture always heals without intervention, and symptoms disappear after a few days. A baby with a broken collarbone may prefer to keep his head turned to one side or the other; to avoid a skull deformity. Be careful to alternate head positions when you lay him down (see page 197).

Muscular torticollis (wryneck)

When an infant always holds her head tilted to one side with her chin pointing slightly in the other direction, muscular torticollis is most often the cause. A slight swelling in the sternocleidomastoid muscle on the side in question will allow your doctor to recognize this condition, which is caused by slight rupturing of the muscle during delivery. Any excessive stretching of the muscle causes pain. A program of careful stretching, implemented by a physician or physical therapist, usually restores the balance. Untreated, this condition causes deformation of the head (page 197).

Limping in toddlers

Before consulting your doctor, examine the soles of your child's feet yourself. You may find a callus, a spot where a shoe pinches, or an injury from stepping on a tack or the like. Be aware that if a family member or acquaintance limps, your child may be copying this behavior. Muscle soreness after unaccustomed exertion can also cause limping.

Contusions, strains, sprains

In the case of a bad fall or accident, the child should be seen by a doctor to insure there are no torn ligaments or bone fractures. Applying arnica or calendula compresses or ointments helps relieve painful symptoms. (Note that some children may be allergic to arnica.)

1.9 Phimosis, hydrocele, undescended testicle

These conditions involving the male genitals seldom cause pain, but we will cover them here because they sometimes require surgical intervention.

Phimosis (constriction of the foreskin)

In 70% of all male babies, the foreskin is tight at birth and will not slide over the glans. According to Danish statistics, the condition persists in only 4% at puberty if left untreated. Hence the best approach is to do nothing except when boys develop recurrent painful infections in the foreskin, which in turn cause further constriction due to formation of scar tissue. Constriction due to scarring may also result if the foreskin is inexpertly stretched or subject to subtle but chronic irritation. In such cases, surgical shortening of the foreskin (circumcision) under general anesthesia is recommended. In case of referral, ask the pediatric surgeon or urologist for details of the procedure.

Retention of smegma* and subsequent suppurative inflammation may occur when part of the foreskin sticks to the glans. The foreskin often frees itself spontaneously, or a physician can free it with a bulb-headed probe. This condition may persist for years, however, without causing problems, in which case no intervention is needed. We recommend beginning routine cleaning of the glans only at puberty or whenever significant amounts of smegma accumulate.

With or without phimosis, occasional erections may occur, beginning in infancy. Little boys sometimes report pain or a sensation of tightness associated with their erections. Juvenile erections are not a sign that the child is masturbating. They are especially likely to occur during sleep, in the early morning hours.

Hydrocele

A hydrocele is a fluid-filled sac located above or beside a testicle. When the gonads descend from the abdominal cavity through the inguinal canal into the scrotum, they pull the peritoneum (the smooth lining of the inside of the

---

* Smegma: white, crumbly deposits of cast-off epithelial cells that accumulate between the foreskin and the glans.

abdominal cavity) with them. A "wandering" testicle can move up and down within this enclosure. Before this projection of the peritoneum closes completely, blister-like remnants may persist and may be filled with fluid when irritation occurs.

These so-called hydroceles usually disappear spontaneously in infancy. As a rule, they should be left alone; don't press on them while diapering the baby. If they persist in preschool children, surgery is often performed, especially if an inguinal hernia also requires correction.

Undescended testicle

In this condition, no testicle is evident in the palpated scrotum. A "retractile" testicle, which descends when the child is sitting in a warm bath and slips up again in the course of bathing or under cooler conditions, does not require surgery. All other forms often do require surgery and should be evaluated by a physician.

Some pediatricians and surgeons recommend hormone treatment before surgery. Because these hormones cause stimulation of the reproductive organs similar to the natural stimulation of prepuberty, they also cause emotional shifts that may lead to aggressive personality changes. While hormone treatment does promote testicular descent (at least in the absence of mechanical obstructions), the descent is often not permanent and the need for surgery is not eliminated. Loosening of the tissues also occurs, which some surgeons view as desirable because it makes surgery easier, should it prove necessary. In most cases, the little boy's penis becomes somewhat larger and does not return to its original size when treatment is stopped.

We do not recommend hormone treatment. It disrupts a child's hormone levels unnecessarily and has adverse effects on his physical and emotional makeup. Instead, we recommend trying constitutional therapy with anthroposophical or homeopathic medicines before resorting to surgery. If these medications do not produce the desired effect, the option of surgery remains open.

Here are some of the current arguments for and against surgery: On the basis of animal experiments and examinations of semen and tissues from human testes, pediatric surgeons maintain that a true undescended testicle should be surgically corrected before the age of two years. Delaying the operation presumably entails the risk of hypofunction not only of the undescended testicle(s) but also of the descended testis if only one is affected. On the other hand, early surgery also has impacts on the child's bodily and emotional makeup, and the consequences of such intervention are unpredictable. Furthermore, the studies mentioned above cannot predict the success of the operation in individual cases.

With this reservation, we recommend surgery as a general rule if constitutional therapy has not produced success by the time the child is two years old.

1.10 First Aid and accident prevention

General comments about accidents

Most accidents involving toddlers happen when the children are driven by the joy of discovery. The child recovers most quickly from the shock of the event in the presence an adult who can rationally survey the situation. Quick action and calm behavior are the most important prerequisites for being truly helpful; scolding or exaggerated expressions of sympathy make the situation more difficult for the child and are also not appropriate when inattention (or even premeditation) on the part of an older child precipitates an emergency situation.

The advice we can offer here is no substitute for a course in first aid, and we urge all of our readers to take such a course.

Acute life-threatening events (ALTE)

If a baby is lying pale and motionless in bed and is not breathing visibly, move her as quickly as possible to a hard surface (table, bench, floor).

- Check her mouth for vomit or tough phlegm that may be blocking the airways. Immediately wipe out her mouth and throat with your little finger.
- Immediately begin cardiopulmonary resuscitation. Perform cardiac massage by applying five short strokes of firm pressure to the breastbone (approximately two strokes per second), using either the ball of your hand or both thumbs; adapt the pressure to the elasticity of the infant ribcage. The next step is mouth-to-mouth resuscitation. Tilt the child's chin upward, cover her open mouth and nose with your own lips and blow twice, carefully, so that the ribcage rises and falls twice. Then apply five more strokes of cardiac massage, two more breaths, etc. These measures will be effective only if the respiratory arrest has been brief. As soon as you feel a heartbeat or pulse, stop the cardiac massage and continue mouth-to-mouth resuscitation until the child is breathing on her own again.
- Have someone else call the emergency medical service, making sure to provide your name, the exact address, and the child's location in the building.

See Section 11.2 on causes.

Resuscitation

Resuscitation attempts are easier if one person performs the heart massage and another the mouth-to-mouth resuscitation. Of course these techniques are most effective if performed by someone who has received training in a first-aid course. Nonetheless, an untrained person should also immedi-

Emergency resuscitation

Artificial respiration

1. Check the child's breathing and remove any obvious obstacles to breathing.
2. Lay the child on its back and tip the head back by pressing on the forehead and lifting the chin.
3. Take a deep breath and blow gently into the child's mouth and nose until its chest rises. With an older child, pinch the nose and breath into the mouth only.
4. Remove your mouth to take another breath. The child's chest will fall.
5. Repeat three or four times rapidly. Check for pulse in the child's neck.
6. Continue at a rate which is like slightly fast breathing. Keep up the artificial respiration until the child breathes normally.
7. Make sure the child has medical attention.

Heart massage

1. Feel for the child's pulse in the carotid artery at the side of the neck. If the pulse has stopped, the child will be pale in color, perhaps gray or blue, and the pupils will be dilated. Do not attempt heart massage if there is still a pulse.
2. Lay the child on its back and check the airways.
3. Push down lightly on the lower breastbone, keeping your arm straight. With a baby, press about twice per second. With an older child, press about once per second.
4. After fifteen compressions, give artificial respiration (see above).
5. If there is still no pulse, repeat steps 3 and 4.
6. Insure the child gets medical attention as soon as possible.

ately attempt to implement these measures because they are the only chance of bringing the child back to life. Those present in situations of extreme danger must do whatever they can to help, and on their own responsibility.

A possible complication of resuscitation attempts is that the stomach also inflates because of air blown into the oesophagus. If this happens, periodically attempt to press the air out of the child's abdomen with your hand.

Other complications may result if excessive force is used either in inflating the lungs (pulmonary rupturing) or applying cardiac massage (broken ribs). The possibility of such complications must not deter anyone from attempting resuscitation if there is no prospect of emergency medical personnel reaching the scene immediately.

If the child is still breathing but is gasping for breath or breathing at irregular intervals, try clapping on his cheeks, back, and the side of the ribcage to see if the situation improves. In any case (even if the child recovers rapidly and returns to normal), get professional advice as soon as possible.

Suffocation, acute respiratory distress

Some examples:
Aspiration of vomit into the windpipe, which usually occurs only in very young infants or children who are not fully conscious.

A piece of a **nut** or a part of a **toy** "goes down the wrong way," that is, is inhaled rather than swallowed. This happens mainly to toddlers, but infants are also at risk when their siblings play at "feeding" them.

Treatment
If the child is not getting any air, cannot cough, and turns dark blue, and if the object inhaled is round (not pointed!):

Place an infant or toddler face down on your forearm with your hand supporting his head (see below). Place an older child face up over your knee, with one hand supporting his head; head and torso should tilt downward. With your free hand, thrust on the sternum or upper abdomen. Carefully

search his mouth for the object, either allowing it to fall out or removing it with a spoon.

If the child is coughing and getting some air and turns blue only briefly or not at all:

Calm the child and have him hold his arms over his head, then administer a few claps on the back.

If the child is still breathing heavily after several hours, or if there are unusual breathing sounds:

Take him to the nearest hospital, where a bronchoscopy can be carried out. This procedure usually reveals a deep-seated object that must be removed with specialized instruments.

Prevention
Grind nuts for toddlers; do not allow them to eat larger pieces. Children under the age of five should not be given whole nuts or allowed to play with marbles or toys with small parts that can be removed or bitten off. Avoid too much silliness and joking around at meal times. Choking can be dangerous.

Be aware that small children can accidentally strangle themselves on cords or chains, especially where these are stretched across a pram or bed. Plastic bags are not toys; they can cause suffocation. Insure that bars on a gate or playpen are spaced less than 20 cm (4 in.) apart, to prevent a child's head from passing between them.

Important: Remember that prohibitions and warnings simply incite children to do the forbidden. Keep alert yourself and make sure that your children's surroundings are safe.

Drowning

Lower the head so the water can run out. If the victim does not begin to breath again immediately, however, don't waste time on this step. Begin mouth-to-mouth resuscitation immediately and provide pure oxygen as soon as possible. Perform cardiac massage if needed (take a first-aid course to learn the technique).

Traffic accidents

If the injured person is still breathing, *speaking,* or moving, lay her on her side, cover her warmly, and stay with her until help arrives.

If the person is **unconscious** but still breathing, do not move her away from the scene of the accident until trained help arrives. Cover her warmly; stay with her, if possible.

Give mouth-to-mouth resuscitation immediately if the injured person is *not breathing.* If she has no pulse or heartbeat, administer cardiac massage to the best of your ability.

Cover a *heavily bleeding wound* (spurting blood or a steady flow) with the cleanest cloth available and apply pressure. Do not apply a tourniquet. Slight bleeding will stop by itself.

Do not change the position of severely painful body parts (especially important for back pain). Moving the victim can cause further damage.

If a child is slightly injured, the quickest way to find out where she is hurt is to ask her to move each limb by herself; help her very carefully.

Call an ambulance in all of these cases.

Fainting

Standing for a long time (especially in a stuffy atmosphere), viral infections, pain, or the sight of blood can trigger fainting. Lay the unconscious child on the ground, loosen tight clothing and belts, and elevate his legs. A whiff of an aromatic substance or sponging his face with cool water may help. Where narrow rows of seats make lying down impossible, leave the child sitting but tilt his upper body forward so that his head is as low as possible. This posture allows more blood to flow to the heart and then to the head. Wait for a few minutes after the child regains consciousness before helping him to walk (one person on either side).

Breath-holding attacks
(affective respiratory spasm)

Sudden screams of pain or anger may be followed by momentary loss of consciousness (affective respiratory spasm). When this occurs, wiping the child's face with a cold washcloth usually helps. It is important to remain calm and avoid panicking. The more upset adults become, the more likely it is that the incident will be repeated, because children instinctively sense the impact of their condition on adults. Brief mouth-to-mouth resuscitation may be needed in some cases. Consult a physician if more than a few such incidents occur.

Toxic and corrosive substances

Eye injuries from acids or bases: First rinse the affected eye under running water for approximately ten minutes, making sure the eye is fully opened. Then take the child to the nearest hospital.

Skin burns caused by corrosive substances: Remove clothing quickly. Rinse the affected area thoroughly under running water, then treat as for burns (see opposite).

Swallowing acids or bases: Do not induce vomiting, which would expose the oesophagus to the corrosive substance again. Also do not induce vomiting if the child has swallowed polish, spray cleaner, gasoline, or any corrosive cleaning fluid. Instead, immediately give the child plenty of water or tea to dilute the poison.

Swallowing pills, alcohol, or non-corrosive poisons: Induce vomiting as quickly as possible. Do it at home if you can't get to the nearest hospital quickly. The recommended procedure is:

- Give the child 2 to 4 cups of water to drink (add fruit juice, if readily available, to improve the taste).
- Hold a small child over your knee; a bigger child should lie on her side.
- With one hand, press the child's cheeks in between opened teeth. With the index finger of the other hand, touch the back of the throat (or insert the handle of a spoon into the throat) until vomiting begins.

Unusual drowsiness or excitability may be a sign of poisoning! If you suspect poisoning, it is best to head straight for the hospital casualty department or at least call your doctor. Make sure you know the number of your regional poison advice center.

In any case of suspected poisoning, search the child's surroundings for empty or unsealed packages of medication, bottles of solvents, unfamiliar plant parts, etc. Take this and any vomit (induced or spontaneous) with you to the hospital.

Prevention: Keep all domestic fluids, poisons, and medicines locked up out of reach of children. Health center posters or local authority advice on poisons and stings should be kept at hand, as well. National Poisons Information Centers can be found in local telephone directories.

Burns and scalds

Immediately pour cold water over the affected areas (including through clothing and into shoes, if necessary!). Hold the area under cold (preferably running) water for several minutes until the pain lessens. Then undress the child and find the damaged areas. If you're lucky and act quickly, cold water can prevent blistering and necrosis (destruction of tissue) from scalds.

A child with burns covering more than 5% of the body's surface must be hospitalized for observation, because generalized symptoms can develop over the next few days. (As a point of reference, the surface of a child's hand is approximately 1% of his body surface.) Cover any blisters with a clean (preferably sterile, e.g. freshly ironed) cloth and consult a physician.

Smaller burns can be treated at home by keeping the wound constantly moist with Combudoron® or Wala burns essence or gel. After a day or two, allow the burn to air-dry and cover it with a dry bandage.

Minor injuries, accidents, and shocks

Falling off the bed or changing table: When to worry about concussion? What to do if your infant rolls off a low bed on to a carpeted floor? He cries immediately and does not vomit; when you feel his head (straightaway, and again half an hour later), you do not find any flat, cushion-like swellings on his skull. As soon as he recovers from the shock, the child is quite lively again. In this case, there is no need for a doctor to examine him.

It's a different matter if your child falls off the changing table (or off a high stool or out of his highchair) and hits his head on a hard floor. If this happens, always have him examined by a doctor as a precautionary measure. If he loses consciousness (even if only briefly), vomits (a sign of concussion), or has a flat swelling on his skull (possible skull fracture), take him immediately to the nearest hospital.

Contusions (bruises) on the scalp: Quickly press the ball of your hand against the affected area and then apply a cold washcloth for five minutes.

Crushed finger: When a finger has been crushed in a door, etc., hold it under cold running water for three to five minutes. Depending on the severity of the injury, either apply a moist arnica bandage or consult a physician immediately. (Note that some children may be allergic to arnica.)

Nosebleeds: Have your child sit leaning against the back of a chair but with her head bent slightly forward. Press with two fingers against both sides of her nose (where no bone gets in the way) to close both nostrils. After five minutes (time it!), let go, ask her to blow her nose, and wait to see if bleeding recurs. Repeat the process if needed. Call your physician if the bleeding does not stop within ten minutes, if it was caused by a fall, if the bridge of the nose swells, or if the nose appears deformed.

Tooth knocked out completely: Take both the child *and* the tooth to a dentist immediately.

Small, bleeding cuts should be allowed to bleed for a few minutes before applying a sterile adhesive or gauze bandage.

Scrapes (abrasions) on the knees should be carefully cleaned using cooled, boiled water and sterile gauze or an ironed cloth. Before cleaning the scrape, wash your hands and dry them on a clean towel. Scrapes should be allowed to air-dry before applying a thick layer of a mild medicated powder. A bandage is usually necessary to prevent further injury and to protect the scrape from rubbing against clothing. The bandage does not need to be changed more often than two or three times a week unless it chafes or gets smelly or the scrape oozes or shows signs of infection, in which case the bandage should be changed once or twice a day.

Slightly oozing wounds can also be treated with powder, but treat *heavily oozing wounds* twice daily with a thick layer of ointment to prevent them from sticking to the bandage.

Remove *splinters, thorns,* and *ticks* from the skin as soon as possible. To remove a tick, lift it out of the skin carefully with a needle, or with a pair of tick tweezers (available from your pharmacy), using a counterclockwise twisting motion as you pull it out. If part of the tick remains in the skin, consult your physician (see Secion 10.18, Tick-borne encephalitis vaccination, and Section 7.14, Lyme disease).

Gaping wounds, puncture wounds, and *animal bites (especially human bites!)* that puncture the skin require immediate medical attention.

Insect bites in the throat or back of the mouth: Give your child a cold drink to sip or ice to suck on and see a doctor immediately.

Tetanus prophylaxis is indicated when unvaccinated children receive dirty wounds or are stung by a wasp or other insect that is in frequent contact with the ground. For more information, see Section 10.6, Tetanus inoculation.

Swallowing a foreign object such as a marble, coin, or pin: Search the stools carefully afterwards by breaking them up in the water of the toilet bowl. Objects larger than 2 cm ($^3/_4$ in.) in diameter often get stuck, usually in the oesophagus. X-rays may be indicated in this case or if the object has not appeared in the stools within 48 hours. Small batteries contain corrosives and may cause serious stomach damage if swallowed;

immediate medical attention is required.

Skin reactions to plants may occur on summer days out of doors, through inadvertently touching poisonous plants or grasses. The skin may become red and blistered very like a burn. Treat as for sunburn (see Section 5.16). A minor case of nettle rash can be treated at home with soothing powder or with Combudoron lotion. Children should learn to recognize the characteristic leaves of plants such as poison ivy or other local varieties, and avoid contact. The itch from poison ivy can be terrible. Wash the skin well with soap as soon as possible. For relief, try Combudoron ointment or compresses with Combudoron liquid or jelly. In more severe cases, you may need to seek a doctor's help (see also Section 5.19, Allergic contact dermatitis).

Accidents at school or in kindergarten may involve formalities related to insurance regulations. In reporting what happened, adults who witness such accidents should handle the incidents calmly and objectively, without making accusations. A measure of self-control is helpful for the children involved and sets a good example.

1.11 Emotional pain

Children experience many different types of emotional pain, which mark the beginning of the part of a child's biography that is the shadow side of the good and happy experiences. Children may demonstrate any of the following behaviors: they may cry bitterly or become anxious when they know their parents plan to go out in the evening; they may feel unjustly treated or react emotionally to corporal punishment at the hands of their parents or caregivers; they may feel themselves caught in conflicts between their parents; they may become outsiders in school or kindergarten, be excluded from their classmates' friendships and cliques, or even be subjected to bullying; they may be teased because of their clothes, appearance, or disabilities; they may be subject, if they are older, to pangs of conscience or feelings of shame, profound grief, hopelessness, or despair.

Emotional pain is always an indication of separation, a sign that the psyche has been prevented from participating harmoniously in its surroundings or revealing itself freely and gladly to its companions. Such pain has a much more profound effect on children than on adults, in spite of the fact that some adults tend to imagine that children have no real problems at all. Adults, after all, can distance themselves from problems by processing them and thinking them through, while children cannot. The younger they are, the more direct the effect of events around them. Their suffering is uniquely intense because they do not really understand it and cannot let go of it. For them, the only immediate help is to forget or to be distracted.

Conversation with an adult can help an older child process emotional pain, but a great deal depends on the adult's response to the event that triggered it. One-sided expressions of sympathy or tirades against the event do not help. It is helpful, however, if the adult can convey to the child (either with or without words) that his deep suffering has been perceived and taken seriously. (See also Section 11.1, Chronically ill children).

Before the age of ten, children are not yet able to objectively process emotional crises, but if they experience that an adult is dealing with the problem, acknowledging it rather than suppressing it, they have a vague sense that their pain does have some kind of meaning and points to some kind of task, so to speak. They experience that although bad things do happen, they happen within a larger, living, breathing context and are familiar and manageable to adults. For example, if a child tormented by anxiety experiences an adult who has achieved a profound trust in destiny, the longing to do likewise is implanted, consciously or unconsciously, in the child's soul. Later on, this child will more easily learn to overcome her anxious approach to the world.

Something we have already noted with regard to dealing with physical pain is also true of emotional pain. It is up to adults to consciously carry, process, and overcome that part of the burden that a child cannot yet come to grips with. Ultimately, the universal remedy for all types of emotional pain is warm, authentic interest in the person affected by it — or in other words, our own understanding and love.

1.12 Children in hospital

The younger the children, the more essential it is for them to be accompanied by a parent or other trusted, familiar adult when they are hospitalized. For this reason, many hospitals now accommodate parents who wish to spend the night with their child. Where special accommodations are not available, parents should do everything they can to insure that one of them is allowed to stay with the child. For preschool children, the constant presence of a parent should be seen as an essential part of medical care. We sincerely hope that in future all pediatric wards will be designed to allow parents to stay with their children.

While illness removes a child from his accustomed daily rhythm, hospitalization also tears him out of familiar surroundings. Under these unusual circumstances, all impressions have a greater than normal impact on a child's soul. The greatest possible love and attention are needed to insure that hospitalization is not a damaging experience. Physicians, nurses, and parents should do everything they can to insure that children have good memories of periods in hospital.

When a parent cannot (or, in the case of an older child, need not) be admitted along with the child, flexible visiting hours are essential so that children can see their closest relatives at any time. When children are hospitalized for longer periods, it is important to provide stimuli for age-appropriate play and learning. Hospitals do not always have occupational therapists available, or even a play group or hospital class, so parents need to take the initiative here.

Adults need to be sensitive to whether (and when) children hospitalized with serious or life-threatening illnesses want to talk about their condition. Taking children's signals seriously requires good cooperation between parents and nurses in particular. Not only are nurses primarily responsible for most of the children's care, but their daily contact with young patients also often means that they are in the best position to understand certain questions or interpret a state of suppressed despair.

A fundamental principle of dealing with hospitalized children is to minimize special treatment and sentimental expressions of sympathy in handling the issue of illness. Children are often grateful if their parents, instead of talking about the illness, distract them by reading aloud and generally behave as normally as possible.

To entertain hospitalized children, we recommend anything that gives them pleasure and stimulates independent activity and reflection. We do *not* recommend the use of acoustic or visual media, which hinder rather than support both the recovery process and the child's development as an individual. In contrast, the effects of human interest and involvement and independent activity (such as illustrating a fairy tale or story in a nice bound booklet) are always positive.

2. Fever and Its Treatment

The warmth of a fever arises from increased metabolic activity in all muscles of the body. The actual increase in body temperature, however, is due to reduced skin perfusion. As a result, a child in the early stages of fever is pale and cold; in an extreme case, they may shiver all over until the fever reaches its target level. In many illnesses, fever is a decisive aid to overcoming and processing bodily challenges. Other functions and activities such as eating, digestion, sensory perception, interest in one's surroundings, play, and so forth take second place to the body's efforts to produce a fever. But before going into detail about fever's significance for the child's body, we will first describe the course of some typical fevers and discuss how to evaluate and treat fevers and so-called febrile seizures at home.

2.1 Typical fevers

A four-year-old has been playing outside all day. As his mother takes his jacket off in the evening, she notices that he has cool hands and looks a bit pale. He eats little at suppertime and is unusually willing to go to bed. He falls asleep around 9:00 and sleeps restlessly, tossing and turning in bed. When his parents check on him around 11:00, they notice that he's "burning hot." He even talks in his sleep, but he wakes up quickly and seems surprised to be moved to his parents' big, cool bed. The thermometer quickly climbs to 40°C/104°F. There is something a little different about how he answers his parents' *questions, as if he had become a bit older and more mature. His voice is pleasant, but thinner than usual and a bit vibrating. His parents are familiar with this state and know that he may also begin to fantasize. They go through the usual procedures — cool compresses on his calves, a little tea — and then everyone goes to bed. The boy falls asleep immediately. In the best-case scenario, the worst of the fever is over by morning.*

A little girl has been whining and not feeling well all day. She feels chilly and vomits once, several hours after reluctantly eating her lunch. Now she has a headache and body aches and spontaneously asks for a hot water bottle on her stomach. After sleeping a little, she wakes up with a temperature of 38.5°C/101.5°F, but she feels somewhat better and is no longer cold. She takes a few sips of herb tea but doesn't want anything else to eat or drink. The next day, her temperature is 39°C/ 102°F. At the doctor, her mother recalls that she has been somewhat out of sorts for three days. The doctor discovers some minor inflammation in her throat and decides that no fever reducers or antibiotics are necessary. The fever lasts another two days, and the little girl goes back to kindergarten the next week (see page 65).

Another child has been coughing more and more for the past two days; on the third day, his temperature rises rapidly. He is short of breath, his lips are slightly blue, and his nostrils flare with each breath. The doctor listens to his chest, discusses the options with his parents, and prescribes a few medications. The prognosis is good; perhaps they'll be able to avoid antibiotics this time. Toward the end of the feverish period, which lasts another two to five days, the little boy coughs up a lot of phlegm. After that he begins to recover visibly. This illness will always stand out in his memory as a major event in his life. His parents, however, are quite worn out from keeping up with his medications and applying all those compresses to his chest and calves. His chart at the doctor reads "broncho-pneumonia."

The fourth child suddenly begins having abdominal spasms at almost regular intervals. Then she starts vomiting, which continues for a day before giving way to a high fever. Now she keeps down the sweetened tea she is offered and looks a bit more lively. This is a viral infection with acetonemic (ketonic) vomiting (see page 82).

These examples demonstrate the course of several common types of fever. There are two more examples in Section 2.3.

Now, what to do when your child has a fever? First of all, you must have confidence in your own ability to assess the situation, and this confidence comes with practice. Lack of confidence leads to anxiety, which is never helpful for your child, so it is always best to consult your physician if you feel unsure. One of the most satisfying experiences for a doctor is to see parents' confidence grow so that they have less and less need of a physician's advice.

In the sections that follow, we will summarize the most important practical rules and points to remember in treating a child's fever.

2.2 Taking your child's temperature; evaluating and treating a fever

The most convenient and effective way to take the temperature of an infant or small child is rectally. Make sure that the child is lying comfortably on his side and that the tip of the thermometer disappears completely into the rectum.

Take an infant's or toddler's temperature with the child lying on her back. Grasp both ankles firmly with one hand and use the other hand to insert the thermometer, holding it like a spoon and bracing your hand against the baby's buttock with your little finger (see Figure 11). This grip stabilizes the thermometer so that any inadvertent movement will not hurt the baby. Leave the thermometer in place for one to two minutes.

If an inflammatory abdominal disease such as appendicitis is suspected, take the child's temperature both rectally and *under the arm* as well and note the difference between the two readings. Make sure that the tip of the thermometer is centered in the armpit and that the child's upper arm is pressed against his chest. Cover his arm and shoulder. It takes five minutes for the temperature to register using this method; even so, these readings are less reliable. As a rule, true body temperature is 0.5°C/1°F higher than the underarm reading, and in appendicitis the difference is usually greater.

Since adults generally prefer to take their temperature *orally,* we rec-

ommend separate thermometers for these two uses. Timing and accuracy of oral readings are the same as for rectal measurements. We recommend mercury-free liquid thermomenters. All other methods, including infrared thermometers are not always reliable, or subject to error, as well as not being environmentally-friendly.

Elevated body temperature can occur due to overheating when the body cannot give off enough heat to compensate for excess heat entering from outside. In infants, this type of temperature quickly disappears when the baby's bonnet and leggings are removed. Vigorous movement can also cause body temperature to rise above 38°C/100.5°F. In such cases, check again after the baby has been lying still for half an hour.

How *high* a temperature is safe? There is no hard-and-fast rule. Any newborn baby who has had a temperature of over 38°C/100.5°F for several hours should be seen by a doctor; do not delay if the baby is not drinking or

Temperatures up to 37.5°C/99.5°F are considered normal

A temperature between 37.5°C and 38°C / 99.5°F and 100.5°F is elevated but subfebrile

A temperature of 38°C/100.5°F or higher is considered a fever.

If your child has cool skin but a fever over 40°C/104°F or if he has a seizure, call your doctor immediately. If you cannot reach a doctor, administer a fever-reducing suppository containing an age-appropriate dose of paracetamol/ acetaminophen and take the child to the hospital (call ahead first).

seems unwell. Any fever that is higher than 40.5°C/105°F or fluctuates by more than 1.5°C/2.5°F should also be evaluated by a physician. In all other cases, the decision of whether or not to consult your doctor should be based on factors other than the fever itself.

Signs of fever; treating fevers

If your child seems different or you "don't like how she looks," more detailed observation is in order. How is she moving? Is she imitating others the way she normally does? Check her eyes, nostrils, and breathing; feel the warmth on her forehead, neck, torso, and limbs. Touch her abdomen and note any signs of pain. Take her temperature as described above. If you are unfamiliar with or concerned about the symptoms you observe, call your doctor, who will ask a few more questions about her appetite, bowel movements, vomiting, etc.

If the skin on her arms and legs (especially her calves) *feels cool* and the thermometer indicates approxi-

mately 38.5°C/101.5°F, you can be sure that her temperature will continue to rise because her body is not yet giving off heat through the extremities. Her calves and feet will feel hot only when the fever has stopped rising and her body is actively attempting to eliminate excess heat. *Do not,* under any circumstances, apply cool compresses to her calves during the initial chill stage, but applying "hot" compresses made with arnica essence (see page 431) to the wrists and ankles is helpful. In addition, cover the child warmly and give her some hot herb tea. (Note that some children may be allergic to arnica.)

If her skin feels hot all the way to the calves, apply *leg compresses* if her temperature is over 39°C/102°F (see page 432). *Cool sponging* can also be used, but only if it feels comfortable to the child. These measures support the body's efforts to eliminate excess heat through the skin. At this stage in a fever, it is important not to obstruct the escape of heat. In cooler climates, keep your child covered, but not as warmly as when the fever was rising. Non-chemical fever suppositories such as Weleda Chamomilla comp., Wala Aconit/China comp., or Heel Viburcol will help your child feel better and can be used even if her extremities are not yet hot.

If your child has a *febrile seizure* and his skin is *hot,* cool him by wrapping him in a damp towel (the water should be at room temperature). Otherwise, proceed as below and see Section 2.3.

A child with a *rising fever* feels unwell and vomits readily. She may have a headache or stomachache that will lessen when the fever peaks. Do not force her to eat, but give her warm herb tea if she asks for something to drink.

Feeding a child with a high fever but no diarrhea: Give her plenty of fluids (slightly sweetened herb tea, or milk diluted with the same amount of water, or cool or lukewarm diluted fruit juice (cherry, blackcurrant, pear or lemon; in South Africa Schlehen elixir). A bland diet is required with no potatoes and little fat or protein; no nuts, chocolate, etc. Do not try to maintain weight in a child with a fever; she will quickly gain it back after the illness is over.

Clothing and *bedding* must be carefully adapted to the temperature of the room and the stage of the child's fever.

Here are some general guidelines: Fresh air but no drafts. In cooler climates, if the window is open, your child should stay well covered and wear a bonnet and sweater if needed. Even in the heat of the summer, keep him covered, at least with a sheet. In any case, your child's limbs should stay warm and he should feel comfortable.

A restless child may refuse to stay covered and want to get up and run around in spite of a fever. He needs the calming presence of an adult who will sing, hum, tell stories, or engage in some other quiet activity.

It's useful to have a *portable cot* that you can move around the house so the child can accompany you as you work (see Figure 26). Provide simple toys that leave room for the imagination (see Section 13.7).

2.3 How dangerous are febrile seizures?

A child's first incident of seizure-like loss of consciousness, with or without convulsions, is always reason to call your doctor. If the seizure continues, take your child to the doctor or to the hospital as quickly as possible (see also First Aid Section, page 45f, on fainting and affective respiratory spasms).

The examples and discussion that follows applies only to convulsions related to infections.
A little boy is playing outside as usual. Perhaps the wind changes, or perhaps he is not dressed warmly enough. On the way home with his mother, he suddenly turns pale, stiffens, and loses consciousness. His

concerned mother observes a few twitching motions of his mouth. He is no longer stiff but still strikingly pale. She quickly carries him into the house, where he soon regains consciousness. He seems cold; well covered, he promptly falls asleep in his bed. On the telephone, his mother tells their family doctor that he was cold and therefore couldn't possibly have a fever. Advised to check anyway, she is surprised to see the thermometer go up to 39°C/102°F (see Section 2.2). The little boy falls asleep in the car on the way to the doctor. An examination reveals nothing serious. The doctor calls it a "febrile seizure" and wants to see the child again the next day after he's had a good sleep. The seizure is unlikely to recur, but an anticonvulsant medication is prescribed to keep on hand just in case. If there had been any sign of meningitis, the little boy would have been hospitalized. Two weeks later, the doctor orders an EEG (see below). When the seizure occurred, the boy's temperature was probably only 38–38.5°C/100.5–101.5°F.

A little girl has a fever of over 40°C/104°F when her face suddenly begins to twitch. In a few seconds, the twitching spreads to her whole body and she loses consciousness — a terrifying sight for her mother. If the seizure stops by itself in one to five minutes or within another five minutes with the help of medication, her parents can breathe a sigh of relief. If it doesn't stop, they should take her to the hospital as quickly as possible.

Febrile seizures are common in the first few years of life because the immature brain has a lower convulsion threshold than the adult brain — that is, it reacts to elevated temperatures with much greater sensitivity. Although an EEG performed immediately after a febrile seizure may reveal mild to moderate pathological changes, these signs disappear completely within two weeks. In most cases, febrile seizures are not serious (see also Section 2.4). Only two out of every hundred children who have febrile seizures go on to develop a convulsive disorder. **Febrile seizures do not "cause" epilepsy,** although they may be the first sign of it in children predisposed to convulsions. We must make it quite clear that in such children, the fever-suppressants prescribed to prevent febrile seizures *cannot* prevent the development of a lasting seizure disorder. For this reason, we do not routinely recommend fever-suppressing suppositories or tablets, even for seizure-prone children. But we do recommend individualized, constitutional, preventive treatment both for children who tend to have febrile seizures and for children with true seizure disorders.

If your child has experienced an uncomplicated febrile seizure, we recommend asking your doctor about using appropriate constitutional remedies (anthroposophical or homeopathic) to address any imbalances in the body's reactive status. In addition, take these precautionary measures in subsequent feverish infections:

- Make sure that your child is dressed warmly enough to avoid precipitating or exacerbating the initial chill stage of the fever.
- Avoid worrying or exciting a child

with a high fever, and cool his head (the first part of the body to become hot) with a wet washcloth. Otherwise, follow the recommendations outlined in pages 56f.

2.4 The purpose and meaning of fever

Before concluding this chapter, we would like to say a few words about the use and misuse of fever-suppressants.

How great is the chance that your child will experience a febrile seizure? Before childhood is over, approximately five in every hundred children will have febrile seizures. In all, these one hundred children will have perhaps five hundred infections with high fevers. This means that five hundred cases of illness must be chemically manipulated in order to prevent approximately five febrile seizures. And as we saw in the first example above, the fever is often detected only after the convulsion occurs — too late for suppositories to do any good.

In treating childhood illnesses, it is always important to keep each child's individual developmental situation in mind. Anyone who takes this approach will neither administer fever-reducing suppositories indiscriminately nor totally avoid their use as a matter of principle. One child may "need" an elevated temperature to enhance her metabolic activity so

she can "remodel" her bodily constitution, while another needs to avoid being weakened by an excessive feverish reaction. When a child has had an initial febrile seizure, it is a pleasure to see his family regain confidence in the child's own forces as he "learns" to deal with fever and makes it through his next feverish infection without convulsions. We hope that thoughtful parent-physician collaboration that focuses on each child as an individual will once again gain ground.

Fever is a crisis-like change in the body's warmth system. Its causes are varied. For a child, even a birthday party, a long trip, a sudden change in the weather, overcooling, or an erupting tooth may overburden the body, leaving it susceptible to colonization by germs. Animal experiments have shown that viruses and bacteria reproduce best and are thus most likely to cause damage at temperatures of 32–35°C/90–95°F — that is, below normal body temperatures. Hence the expression "to catch cold" is quite justified. On the other hand, fevers provide optimum temperatures (generally 39–40°C/102–104°F) for killing or preventing the proliferation of the viruses or bacteria that affect the body.[1]

Fever is a natural weapon in the body's defense against germs. In the process of activating endogenous defenses, many important reactions are set in motion only by fever. Antibiotics interfere with these independent efforts and should therefore be administered only when the body cannot hold its own against a bacterial infection. And in any case, antibiotics are ineffective against viruses, which are implicated in more infections than bacteria.

Thermoregulation and fever also have a soul-spiritual aspect. Heat is more than just a quantitative factor measured with a thermometer. As such, warmth also manifests in the activity of the human soul and spirit. We "feel warm inside" when we meet a good friend or revisit the familiar landscape of our childhood. When we have a good idea or wax enthusiastic about an ideal, warmth can literally shoot into our limbs. Conversely, fear, anger, or great sorrow, or even hate, envy, or discontent in our surroundings, makes our blood "run cold." We may speak of an icy mood, frosty silence, or a cold refusal, or we may say, "That leaves me cold." Just as a comfortable body temperature of 37°C/98.5°F supports the activities of body, soul, and spirit, so too a joyful experience, inner concentration, or meditative

work can have harmonizing effects on how the body is pervaded with warmth. Blood circulation and the supply of blood to the organs are sensitive not only to the body's movement and nutrition but also to our emotions and thoughts. We quite rightly relate warmth to the soul and spirit as well as to the body. At all three levels, the same warmth is at work, although it is sometimes more inwardly and sometimes more outwardly active.

The unified nature of warmth allows us to experience ourselves as self-contained physical and soul-spiritual beings. Hence we can say that the body's warmth organization as a whole is the physical vehicle of the self, the human "I." Every illness is accompanied by a change in this warmth system and thus affects and involves the I in a very direct way.

We owe thanks to Rudolf Steiner's research into the human constitution for recognizing this connection and making it bear fruit in education and medicine. We change our attitude toward illness when we see it as related to a child's own activity and volition — that is, to his or her I. Hence the individual differences — the child who "never" runs a fever, the one whose fevers remain slight and rise slowly, the one who gets brief attacks of high fever. We meet whole families of children who are always the first to be flat on their backs while the neighbour's kids are still splashing in the puddles. Then they switch roles, and the last one to catch cold may have the longest struggle with the infection. Other individual differences become evident in adults. A person who enjoys her work and works long and hard but rhythmically may be much less susceptible to colds and flu than someone who takes a lot of time off to "relax." When we enjoy our work, when the I is heavily involved in it, our warmth system is stimulated, "immunizing" us against illness. Psychoneuroimmunological research has confirmed that positive emotions like courage, enthusiasm, trust, and love stimulate the human immune system while stress, anger, fear, lethargy, and depression weaken it.[2] Hence, when we confront the high fevers of childhood infectious diseases, we must ask about the purpose of each fever. Is it an attempt to temporarily strengthen the soul-spiritual element's ability to intervene in the body? Or to create a substitute for a lack of soul activity? We can make many interesting observations that help to answer these questions.

Here is a very telling example: Relatives who initially say a newborn baby "looks just like his grandfather" may later change their minds and decide that he looks more like his mother. But after he undergoes a feverish illness, his parents discover a new trait not found among his relatives and are pleased to see his own unique personality emerging. Fever helps a child's I adapt its inherited body to its own purposes, making it a more suitable vehicle for self-expression. Predisposition to diseases such as eczema or asthma in infancy has been known to improve after serious fever-

ish illnesses. A possible physiological explanation for this phenomenon, as suggested by the immunological and genetic research of the last two decades, is that a person's genetic material is not a fixed entity as was previously assumed but rather a dynamic one that may manifest differently under different circumstances. It has long been known that genes and their functions are influenced not only by the immune system but also by soul-spiritual and psycho-social processes throughout the person's lifetime.[3]

From a purely outer perspective, the rapid regaining of weight lost during a feverish illness is an indication that the body is being organically remodeled. The child has deconstructed some aspect of her inherited body and is rebuilding it under the independent direction of her own warmth organization. In our own pediatric practices, we have experienced repeatedly that flu with a high fever, a carefully managed case of pneumonia, or even measles may introduce a new, more stable phase in a child's development. Less frequently, longer bouts of repeated illness indicate a task that remains to be accomplished.

Fever's effect on the body can be compared to good educational methods — under both circumstances, the child learns something through her own efforts. Constantly telling children "Do this; don't do that; you're not allowed to do that" is generally considered poor educational practice. Unfortunately, this is exactly what happens in many feverish infections. As soon as a child's temperature exceeds 38.5°C/101.5°F, she is given a suppository, and if infection is confirmed antibiotics are prescribed too, leaving her body with little chance for independent involvement. Furthermore, a body thus treated loses an opportunity to practice the "flexibility" it will need to confront tasks more serious and more important than overcoming the feverish infections of childhood.[4]

Of course we know that dramatic and extreme reactions such as febrile seizures can occur and that permanent damage is possible. To counteract these reactions in a timely way is the appropriate function of the medical profession. Because complications, although infrequent, must be caught in time, childhood feverish illnesses do require a doctor's attention.

3. Respiratory Diseases

The location of the respiratory problem is the decisive factor in identifying and treating such ailments. The first group discussed here includes diseases of the upper respiratory tract (between the nose and the throat) and irritations of the upper respiratory mucous membranes. The second group encompasses diseases of the lower respiratory tract from the epiglottis through the trachea and bronchi to the pulmonary alveoli, where gaseous exchange occurs. Characteristic signs of lower respiratory illnesses are listed in Section 3.5.

3.1 Nasal congestion

Nasal congestion in very young infants is not harmless and must be monitored and treated by a physician. In the first three to four weeks of life, a baby has not yet learned to breathe through her mouth, so when her nose is blocked she gets air only when she cries. Nasal blockage can cause serious oxygen shortage of air, up to and including cyanosis (turning blue), a problem that is especially evident when the baby is nursing. She takes a few hungry gulps, chokes on nasal discharge or makes unsuccessful attempts to breathe, releases the nipple, cries until she turns pink, grasps the nipple again, and so on until she is exhausted. The importance of keeping her nasal passages clear is obvious.

Treatment
Fresh, steam-moistened air prevents drying of the mucous membranes and softens nasal discharge, making it easier for the motions of sneezing and swallowing to loosen it and remove it from the narrow nasal passages. If you have central heating or radiant floor heating, hang damp cloths in the room, rewetting them frequently, or use a vaporizer. We recommend the simplest kind without motor or fan but just two metal plates which heat the water and produce sterile steam noiselessly.

Fresh air from an open window can be very comforting to a stuffy nose. In cool climates, your baby should be warmly dressed in soft wool and well covered (a hot water bottle at his feet is good, too).

Only *water-based medications* should be applied to the mucous membranes inside the nose. 1% sodium chloride solution (physiological saline), carefully inserted into the nose one drop at a time, is often the only medication needed. You can buy this solution in your pharmacy or make it at home by adding one teaspoon of table salt (about 4.5 grams) to half a litre (two cups) of water. Bring the solution to the boil, and then pour some of it into a clean glass jar. It keeps for about two days, but sterilize the dropper in boiling water once a day. Decongestant nose drops are sometimes avoidable, but if you must use them, make sure that the brand is intended for use in infants and does not contain ephedrine, and never use the drops for more than a few days. Oil-based nose drops and ointments should be used only at the nostril openings, not inserted into the nose.

There is less reason to recommend decongestant drops or sprays for older children. Nasal discharge serves a purpose; a cold is a self-limiting condition that should be allowed to run its course unhindered. Decongestants constrict the blood vessels of the mucous membranes; the alternation between this constriction and subsequent dilation when the medication wears off disrupts the natural course of healing. Frequent use can also dry out and damage the nasal mucous membranes, which in turn may eventually lead to ozaena, a chronic nasal disease characterized by fetid discharge and atrophic structural changes. Instead of decongestants, we recommend inhaling steam from chamomile tea (see page 436) during acute nasal congestion. A treatment that older children may find helpful consists of sniffing a lukewarm 2% salt solution (approximately 2 g table salt in 100 ml boiled water, or 1 teaspoon per cup) up through the nose out of a cup and spitting it out through the mouth. (Since the concentration of salt is higher in the solution than it is in nasal discharge, this treatment is a natural means of reducing swelling in the mucous membranes and clearing the entrances to the paranasal sinuses.) This procedure, although not exactly pleasant, is extremely effective. If your child has dry, red mucous membranes at the entrance to his nose, apply a specially formulated nasal cream available from your pharmacy.

Sniffling and *snoring* sometimes persist for months after an infant's first cold but will disappear in time. No treatment is needed as long as the baby can breathe freely. You may be able to avoid many colds by keeping your baby's head and ears covered with a bonnet (see pages 197 and 438).

Sneezing removes bits of solid matter from the nose. In infants, it generally does not indicate the beginning of a cold. Crusts in a baby's nose are more likely to be caused by dry, heated air than by inflamed mucous membranes.

3.2 Viral infections: colds and flu

A runny nose and other cold symptoms usually appear at the beginning of (or during) a respiratory infection and may be accompanied by inflammation and discharge in the air cavities of the skull, which include the *ethmoid, maxillary,* and *frontal sinuses* (the frontal sinuses do not develop until children are of school age) and the tympanic cavity or middle ear. Inflammation occasionally also occurs in the petrosal bone that surrounds the inner ear. Always involved are the pharynx and its "lymphatic apparatus" — like the adenoids. These lymphatic organs are the most important point in the interplay between the body and its environment. The tracheal and bronchial mucous membranes also often become inflamed. Hoarseness develops when the larynx (the entrance to the trachea) is involved, coughing when deeper air passages are affected. A moderate to high fever that persists for three days is typical of these infections.

Often no distinction is clear between a "cold" and a "flu," but an illness that begins with headache and body ache is generally called "flu." This type of illness sometimes displays the double fever peaks typical of viral infections. A brief, often unnoticed rise in temperature occurs in the first two days; after a pause, it is followed by another, higher increase in fever that lasts for about three days. Any fever over 38.5°C/101.5°F that lasts for more than three days suggests

that the original infection has paved the way for a more serious illness, so it is essential to consult your doctor at this point.

True cases of influenza (not to be confused with Haemophilus influenzae type B or Hib infections; see Section 10.8) are difficult to recognize among the many viral infections of childhood, although they are sometimes distinguished by their slightly greater severity (see also flu shots, Section 10.17). Parents need to realize that children who are well cared for generally recover spontaneously from the great majority of flu-type infections within a few days and without developing complications. Symptom-suppressing treatments such as fever reducers, cough suppressants, decongestants, and antibiotics to prevent bacterial infection simply impose additional, unnecessary burdens on the body. A child who is otherwise healthy will overcome such infections without help and acquire at least temporary immunity (see also page 60).

Parents of children who have just entered kindergarten typically lament that their kids spend no more than a couple of days at school before they're sick and homebound again. If it is any consolation, you can expect this pattern to persist for one or at most two winters, after which your child will learn to handle these frequent infections and ward them off as her immune system grows stronger. In other words, her body goes through a learning process that leads to a more stable state of health.

In this "forest" of minor infections, the familiar childhood diseases stick out like a few towering trees. In some instances, they seem to put an end to a long string of infections. If there are younger siblings at home, they may be infected, too, which gives parents cause for concern because babies' immune systems are still undeveloped. In fact, however, as anyone who has three or more children can confirm, the youngest ones who go through the classic childhood illnesses at an early age are actually healthiest later on because they have had to struggle so intensely with these infections.

But we must not assume that immature immune systems and the possibility of contagion are the only factors in the development of infections. Children's illnesses often begin the day after a fall down the stairs, a birthday party, a long car trip, or going to a movie. In the first instance, parents are understandably concerned that the fall and the illness may be related, and of course a physician needs to rule out unexpected consequences of a head injury. In most cases, however, the illness is simply the young body's response to being overwhelmed by some unaccustomed event, and "catching" an illness restores the balance.

Keeping this in mind, we can develop an image that makes many of childhood's phenomena more understandable. Normally, a small child is intensely involved with his immediate surroundings and identifies strongly with it. As a result, any of the above listed events, or perhaps an outburst of parental anger or immoderate corporal punishment, tends to throw the child back in on himself in a way that is actively painful. Through such incidents, the soul's experience of itself in the body is both taxed and constrained, producing an emotional "chill" that the child's immature constitution is not ready to deal with. In these situations, both physical and emotional warmth are healing. Anything we can do to help the child feel comfortable in his body supports his sympathetic relationship with his surroundings, and love and attention warm and strengthen the body. From this perspective, we can approach the treatment of infections differently, soothing the child's way through illness rather than suppressing symptoms with medication. We see the illness and the triggering event as an opportunity to strengthen and harmonize the child's constitution.

Helpful external treatments for upper respiratory infections

- Provide fresh air that is not too dry. If necessary, use a vaporizer.
- Spread a little eucalyptus oil or Olbas oil on a cloth or saucer and set it on a heat source.
- For nasal congestion, have your child inhale steam (see page 436).
- Apply chest compresses with oils (see page 427).
- Rub your child's chest with 10% lavender or mallow oil. For coughs, use chest rubs (see page 428) with or without hot, moist compresses.

• If your child is shivering, keep him warmly covered. If needed, give hot tea to drink and pile on extra covers to induce sweating. Afterwards, take him to your own pleasantly cool bed.

A sick child should be allowed to sleep a lot. Avoid exciting her or giving her mechanical toys to play with (see also Section 13.7). A little doll or a dwarf who peeks out from under the covers or climbs pillow mountains will provide hours of amusement. For how to treat fevers, see Section 2.2, pages 56f).

Many families have a favourite home remedy for viral infections (usually a combination of herbal or homeopathic ingredients). Ask your family doctor about the many different options available.

3.3 Enlarged adenoids and tonsillitis

In childhood, chronic obstruction of the airways in the back of the nose is generally due to proliferation of lymphatic tissue at the back of the pharynx. The presence of growths can be confirmed by X-rays, but we recommend avoiding exposing your child to this amount of radiation. In any case, the clinical signs are unmistakable. A child with a pronounced case has a characteristically sleepy expression and nasal congestion; her mouth is open all the time and her hearing is often impaired — sure signs that her symptoms are due to enlarged adenoids.

Although both lymphatic growths and enlarged palatine tonsils tend to shrink by themselves, they often prevent the child from achieving the stabilized state of health and resistance to infection that most youngsters develop by age five. A constantly open mouth and poor air circulation in the affected area are constant invitations to infection, and a child with enlarged adenoids endures repeated bouts of middle-ear infections, paranasal sinusitis, and bronchitis. A growth that displaces the entrance to the Eustachian tube may impair hearing by preventing air circulation in the tympanic cavity. This hearing impairment may also delay the development of speech.

It is always worth trying a conservative approach to adenoidal conditions. Home treatment consists of two or three salt-water baths a week, two sessions of steam inhalation a day, and drinking three cups of horsetail tea a day. Mustard poultices are applied to the soles of the feet once daily, but be careful with children with sensitive skin. To make the poultices, mix ground mustard with water to form a paste and apply it to the soles of the feet (arches only) on scraps of cloth about the size of the palm of your hand (for more details, see also page 433). Leave the poultices in place until your child feels a burning sensation, then remove them and have your child put on warm wool socks. Lots of singing and humming is also recommended.

If you see no improvement after four to six weeks of home treatments, it is time to consult a doctor. In severe cases, surgical removal of the pharyngeal tonsils may be unavoidable, and this operation (often performed on an outpatient basis) is always indicated if the symptoms are impacting on your child's physical and emotional wellbeing. Unfortunately, adenoids frequently grow back. The *palatine tonsils* are important organs in the body's defense against infection and should be removed only in truly urgent cases; a few bouts of tonsillitis do not warrant this procedure and are no cause for alarm.

3.4 Hay fever

Hay fever is usually an allergy to pollen from grasses, trees, or flowers. Other common allergens that irritate the mucous membranes of the eyes and nose include animal dander and dust mite excrement in house dust. Certain bacteria and fungi can also cause the same symptoms. Hay fever, especially if accompanied by asthmatic symptoms, is often a tremendous burden, and allergy sufferers are always in search of treatments with lasting effects. The beneficial effects of allergen-poor sea air are well known, and repeated periods by the seaside have cumulative and generally strengthening effects.

Three treatment options
Desensitization consists of a series of injections of specially produced allergen extracts. After testing to identify the patient's allergies, gradually increasing doses are injected into the surface of the skin. This approach is very effective for those allergic only to single, specific plants but less effective for people who have multiple allergies or are allergic to house dust, which is almost impossible to avoid. One disadvantage of this treat-

3

ment, which must be continued for at least three years, is the need for frequent shots. There is also always the chance that a shot may provoke a severe allergic reaction. Many people also find that they become sensitive to other allergens either during or after successful desensitization to the original allergen; that is, their symptoms return because they have become allergic to something else.

Another option is *eating* a daily spoonful of local *honey* (preferably raw, from natural beeswax honeycomb). This treatment must be continued throughout the year.

Regular *injections* or *inhalation* treatments with an extract of lemon and quince (commercially available as Gencydo 0.1% and Citrus e. fruct./Cydonia e. fruct. 2X/2X) are a third option. Topical applications of Gencydo 0.1% drops (in both the nose and the eyes) are also effective. This treatment is usually accompanied by medications tailored to the patient's individual constitution. Many patients are well satisfied with this treatment and return the following year to consolidate the gains they have made. This therapy, like the other two, must be administered consistently and at regular intervals. For autumn allergies, Gencydo treatments should be begun in the spring, to prevent symptoms before they start.

We recommend the second and third types of treatment. In severe cases, anti-cistaminica can be added by the doctor.

3.5 Diseases of the Lower Respiratory Tract

We will begin this section by describing abnormal breathing sounds and their causes, as an aid to understanding and identifying lower respiratory ailments.

Cough

Coughing is a protective reaction to accumulation of mucus, irritation due to inflammation in the trachea or bronchi, or — more rarely — an inhaled foreign object (see First Aid Section, page 48).

Barking cough
A cough that sounds like a dog's bark, accompanied by respiratory distress and a harsh, rasping sound (stridor) during inhalation, is due to swelling around the vocal cords and suggests croup (see pages 71f).

Hoarseness or loss of voice

Inflammation and irritation of the vocal cords may also result from overuse of the voice. Chronic hoarseness may be caused by nodules on the vocal cords and is diagnosed by an ENT (ear-nose-throat) specialist.

Inhalation with stridor, respiratory distress, *intercostal retraction (inward movement of the muscles between the ribs) and retraction at the neck above the breastbone (suprasternal notch)*

After a choking incident, these symptoms mean that bits of food are causing reflexive closing of the vocal cords. Calm the child and place him face up over your knee, with one hand supporting his head; head and torso should tilt downward. With your free hand, thrust on the sternum or upper abdomen.

Croup (see pages 71f).

Calcium deficiency (rickets) occasionally produces these symptoms in children between the ages of three and eighteen months. See rachitic tetany, Section 10.2. Consult your doctor immediately.

Muffled sound and obstructed air entry when breathing

In a child who feels terrible, who has increasing difficulty in breathing and speaking, often accompanied by increased salivation, and who has blue lips and nails, and a high fever, these are signs of *epiglottitis.* Refusing food due to pain is sometimes an early sign of this condition. **Due to the danger of suffocation, this is a medical emergency. Take the child to the nearest hospital immediately.** On the way to the hospital, allow the child to sit up if it helps her breathe better.

Snoring sound while inhaling

This sound occurs when the child's tongue is relaxed and resting on the lower pharynx. It disappears when the child is turned on his side.

Hawking, rasping or rattling sounds while inhaling

Unless accompanied by high fever and flaring nostrils, these sounds indicate simply that mucus has accumulated somewhere in the pharynx, and are harmless.

Subtle singing or "whistling" sound while exhaling

When exhalation takes longer than inhalation, this sound is a sign of obstructive or asthmatic bronchitis (see page 73).

Flaring nostrils (the sides of the lower part of the nose move in and out as the child breathes)

Flaring nostrils indicate that the child is not getting enough air, either because the airways are partially blocked or because portions of the lungs are not functioning due to illness. When accompanied by heavy breathing, high fever, coughing, and dark lips but no unusual respiratory sounds, flaring nostrils are often a sign of pneumonia (see page 75).

Significantly reduced movement on one side of the ribcage during breathing
The focus of the illness lies on the side that moves less. When accompanied by high fever and flaring nostrils, this symptom suggests pneumonia (or pleurisy, especially if exhalation is jerky). An inhaled foreign object can also cause decreased breathing motions on one side. Regardless of the cause, this symptom requires treatment by a physician.

Different manifestations of cough

See Section 3.2 for how to treat uncomplicated bronchitis due to a viral infection. It most cases, it is quite normal for a cough to persist for a week or two after the acute stage of this illness; simply continue treatment as before. We do not recommend cough suppressants, but cough-relieving teas are fine.

A cough that lasts longer than two weeks should be watched carefully. Take your child's temperature each morning and evening for a week, and then consult your physician if the cough persists.

Increasing bouts of coughing that last approximately half a minute and occur more than half an hour apart suggest whooping cough (see Section 7.11).

Cough, nasal discharge, and a slight temperature ten to fourteen days after *exposure to measles* suggest that your child is also coming down with the measles. Unless their parents give explicit consent, avoid exposing other children who might contract the disease (see page 114; call ahead before taking a child with measles to your doctor's office/surgery).

Coughing that continues for hours (often only at night) with no other signs of discomfort is often simply due to minor irritation of the airways. Treat it by humidifying the air in the child's room (see Section 3.1) and as for viral infections (see Section 3.2). Children are often much less bothered by their own coughing than the adults whose sleep they disturb.

A *sudden bout of coughing,* especially if it occurs during the day with no warning signs and is accompanied by gagging, respiratory distress, rasping sounds during inhalation and exhalation, and spasmodic "whistling," especially while exhaling, suggest that the child has inhaled a foreign object, often a chunk of peanut, a bead, or a plastic part from a toy. Small marbles are especially dangerous because they can block the trachea completely (see First Aid Section, page 48). The measures described on those pages are not only useless but dangerous if a child has swallowed a thin, sharp object such as a pin, but they are always worth trying for pieces of nut and the like. Always call the nearest children's hospital if you suspect that your child has inhaled a foreign object into her lungs.

Croup (acute laryngitis)

If your child has a respiratory infection, then a loud barking cough and rasping inhalation (stridor) are sure signs of an inflammatory swelling of the mucous membranes around the vocal cords.

The characteristic croup cough typically begins when the child is asleep (generally between 11:00 pm and 1:00 am). It is less likely to start during the day. Croup may be preceded by a walk in an easterly wind, excitement, or a change in weather. Croup cases increase markedly in late autumn (November). The children just learning to talk are most frequently affected, which makes sense in view of the heavy demands placed on their organs of speech.

A child with croup is often afraid of suffocating, so the first thing to do is to pick her up and comfort her.

If you are already familiar with this condition, check the severity of your child's respiratory distress immediately and again approximately ten minutes later. If two adults are available, one should fetch the vaporizer or, alternatively, a couple of damp cloths to hang around the child's bed and a pot of hot water to put close by in a safe place on the floor. Meanwhile, turning on the hot shower in the bathroom is a quick way to produce hot, moist air for your child to inhale. Then take her temperature and administer any medication your doctor has provided for such cases. If prescribed by your doctor, an epinephrine inhaler or nebulizer may be used. After that, offer your child some tea or diluted juice and put her back to bed. That night, an adult should sleep in the child's room or in the next room with the door open.

If this is your first experience with croup, *you should take your child to the nearest hospital or to your doctor immediately,* where you will learn to recognize the different degrees of severity of the illness in case the croup recurs.

Stage 1: Barking cough

Stage 2: Stridor (see above) is slight when the child is at rest, more severe with movement or excitement.

Stage 3: More severe stridor at rest, flaring nostrils, retractions of the suprasternal notch (the base of neck above the breastbone) and between the ribs, tension in the auxiliary breathing muscles in neck and shoulder.

Stage 4: Symptoms from the previous stages increase. The child is very restless and has blue lips and fingernails, and her pulse rate increases to 150 per minute or higher. She may lose consciousness.

Experienced parents should not hesitate to deal with Stages 1 and 2 at home. (Consult your doctor, however, if your child has a high fever.) If Stage 3 lasts more than ten minutes or turns into Stage 4, always take your child straight to the nearest hospital, where more intensive measures often produce improvement and an intubation can be performed if the child's condition continues to worsen. In this procedure, performed under anesthesia, a plastic tube is inserted through the nose or mouth into the trachea to prevent further narrowing. If the epiglottis is inflamed (see page 70), the risk of suffocation is high and this procedure is always performed immediately.

About treating croup

Of course the choice of drug treatment is up to your family doctor and will be based on his or her understanding and experience. The epinephrine inhaler mentioned above is a great help in emergency treatment because it works in just a few minutes, reducing and (in our experience) almost always eliminating the need for corticosteroids.

Never give chemical sedatives to a child with croup. They can mask the severity of the condition by suppressing the restlessness that is a sign of Stage 4.

To calm a child with croup, it is important to keep her surroundings as calm and business-like as possible.

Due to the alarming nature of this illness, we would not recommend consulting with your doctor by telephone. On the other hand, an experienced doctor can recognize a dangerous condition by listening to the child breathe and cough over the phone, and if your description of other aspects of the illness completes the picture adequately, you may be able avoid a long car ride in the middle of the night, in which case a phone call is certainly worth trying. In all probability, however, only a very experienced doctor who already knows the young patient will agree to a telephone consultation under these circumstances. It is also essential to rule out the possibility of rachitic tetany (see Section 10.2).

Does my child have asthma or obstructive bronchitis?

Because this question is commonly heard in a doctor's office whenever a child coughs a lot or has frequent bouts of bronchitis, we will discuss obstructive bronchitis and asthma in greater detail.

A child with obstructive bronchitis exhales slowly and with difficulty. He is exhausted and his chest and nostrils are distended. If you listen close to his nose, you can hear a combination of quiet "whistling" and gentle bubbling sounds (reminiscent of the sound of simmering water or the asthmatic breathing of older people) as he exhales. This illness (which may or may not be accompanied by fever) develops when swelling of the mucous membranes displaces the bronchi and obstructs respiration. Tough phlegm develops, and in toddlers and older children, cramping of the bronchial musculature occurs. This condition is usually triggered by a harmless upper respiratory infection that begins as a cold or pharyngitis and moves downward into the airways. It is important to know that by no means all children who develop obstructive bronchitis on the heels of a bronchial infection later become asthmatic. Fat infants are most susceptible to obstructive bronchitis, especially in winter and during the change of seasons. This susceptibility disappears in later years.

The first time you experience these symptoms in your child, consult your physician, who will help you learn to evaluate your child's condition. Mild forms of the illness have very little effect on children's sense of wellbeing; infants are alert and enjoy joking around. In other cases, however, their breathing is labored and whistling; nursing is difficult, and they look slightly blue in the face. These children must be treated by a physician, or even hospitalized in severe cases.

The *most important home remedy* for obstructive bronchitis is a chest poultice made with ground ginger or mustard. Once you have experienced its soothing effects, you will know that it is worth the effort to make it. It is a very strong treatment and should be used only if you have mastered the technique and only on the advice of the child's doctor. Never apply one of these poultices to a child who is less than four months old, has overly sensitive skin, or is allergy-prone. Ginger or mustard poultices work by increasing perfusion in the skin over the ribcage, which stimulates breathing, makes secretions more fluid (allowing them to be coughed up more easily), and relaxes cramped bronchial muscles. Ginger is somewhat milder and more warming than mustard. (For how to make these poultices, see pages 425f). Fresh air is important during the treatment, and you can even apply the poultice outside the house if you wrap your child up warmly and watch him carefully.

Although the symptoms of **asthma** are quite similar to those of obstructive bronchitis, asthma can be triggered not only by infections but also (most commonly) by external aller-gens (such as pollen, animal dander, or dust mite excrement in house dust), by physical exertion in cold air, or by stress and emotional issues. At the beginning of an attack, the patient often has a sensation of heaviness in the chest. This is quickly followed by breathing problems as the connection between internal and external air spaces is reduced by inflammatory allergic swelling in the bronchi and tension in the smooth muscle fibers. Occasionally, asthma disappears spontaneously during adolescence. (See also Sections 3.6 and 6.1).

About treating asthma

Drug therapy, whether short or long-term, must be prescribed by your physician, who will decide whether to use the allopathic medications typically prescribed in pediatric asthma (bronchodilators, cortisone, and others) and/or homeopathic or anthroposophical medications. Overmedication is not uncommon in asthma cases and may cause hormonal side effects or chronic circulatory problems. In some cases, parents or children downplay the severity of the symptoms out of concern over possible side effects.

In recent years, asthma education has begun to play a major role in treatment. Asthmatic children and their parents learn to assess symptom severity and the appropriate treatment. The goal is to minimize the impact of the illness and allow the patient to enjoy a normally active life. Whether in individual conversations with the child's physician or in a group session, learning to deal with anxiety is one of the most important elements in asthma education and is especially applicable to the child's immediate surroundings. Either emotional upheaval or a cold can trigger an asthma attack, and calming a young child or — in the case of an older child — breathing and relaxation exercises that she has learned to perform independently can significantly reduce the severity of the attack. The inner "victory" of accepting and learning to deal with her condition is a significant step toward lessening her symptoms.

In our experience, effective *adjunct therapies* that often reduce the need for medication include:

- Ground mustard or grated ginger poultices, especially for attacks triggered by infections. For asthma attacks due to other causes, try lavender oil wraps (made, if needed, with hot, moist compresses) or hot horsetail wraps (see pages 428).
- During an attack, give plenty of fluids (herb tea or mineral water).
- Massage is very effective during an attack if done properly.
- Many children are helped by a course of copper ointment compresses applied to the kidneys every evening (Cuprum metallicum praep. 0.1% ointment or red copper ointment, see page 430).
- Drinking astringent oak bark or sage tea in the morning and bitter veronica tea in the evening as constitutional aids to waking up and falling asleep is also effective in the

long term. A young child will readily imitate Mum if she drinks the tea, too, making a joke out of shuddering as she swallows it. (Admittedly, the tea needs to be made quite weak to begin with.) Many little ones learn to like these teas.

Pneumonia

When a child with an upper respiratory infection or bronchitis still has a high fever after three days, looks worse, is short of breath, and has flaring nostrils and dark red lips, pneumonia is almost always the cause. This diagnosis is still very frightening for many parents, although in most cases the course of the illness is not especially dangerous in kindergarten-age or even older children. Greater caution is advised in the case of infants or in older children weakened by other acute or chronic illness.

Pneumonia must be diagnosed and treated by your family doctor or pediatrician. For children at risk or when the quality of care cannot be guaranteed at home, your physician will recommend hospitalization. A doctor experienced in complementary medicine may be able to avoid using antibiotics. For many years, we have not prescribed antibiotics for either ambulatory or hospitalized patients except in high-risk or unusually severe cases or on the family's request. In our experience, one of the advantages of antibiotic-free treatment is that the pneumonia very rarely recurs. The purpose of such treatment is to help the organism learn to respond more flexibly to environmental influences and to achieve a new level of stability by coming to grips with the illness. Immediately administering antibiotics blocks the normal course of the disease and denies the organism an opportunity to exercise its own forces of resistance and strengthen them to fight future infections. On occasion, the body makes a second attempt at the same illness at a later date. If we view illness only as something to be eliminated as quickly as possible, of course we will prefer antibiotic treatment, but if we acknowledge it as an opportunity for the body to learn — that is, as a process that the body itself seeks out in order to apply its own forces and exercise its defenses — we will attempt to support and soothe the patient without immediately opting for suppressive therapies. This supportive approach respects the quality of the patient's future health and the individuality of the child whose forces and assets act in concert with the treatment we provide.

Treating pneumonia at home involves the same measures described in the section on viral infections, adapted as needed to the child's weakened condition. When cough is the dominant symptom, especially in children who are quite thin, rubbing the chest with 10% lavender oil (mentioned already in several different contexts) or with ointments containing etheric oils of camphor, eucalyptus, or the like have proved effective. For significant fluid accumulation in the bronchi or on the lungs, apply warm damp compresses made with horsetail (Equisetum) tea or thick Quark (fermented skimmed milk; see pages 428f). For respiratory spasms (as described in the preceding sections), use chest poultices made with ground mustard or ginger.

For general treatment measures, please review Section 2.2 on fever treatment.

3.6 Respiration as an expression of psychological activity

Even in infants and toddlers, the emphasis of respiration clearly shifts from expansive exhalation and relaxation during sleep to deep inhalation in the waking state. The various states we observe in children's daily lives — the contraction of pain and the expansive release of joy, hopeful sighs of relief, limp resignation, nimble activity, and sudden cessation of movement — are all accompanied by their own respiratory rhythms that adapt dynamically to the subtlest stirrings of the child's soul. Nothing is more informative about another person's momentary emotional state than observing their breathing. In the waking state, the soul is drawn in — "inhaled" — into the body, ready to sense and move, to experience and act, to love and hate. In sleep, the soul leaves behind a peacefully resting "remnant"; the body lies tired and heavy in bed, and the gentle ebb and flow of the breath belongs completely to the body's life processes. The soul no longer supports conscious activity and conveys no expressions of emotion.

If we consider the possibilities for abnormal changes in respiration as described in previous sections, we note that disturbances in the ability to move air hinder the soul's free interaction with its environment. This phenomenon is most evident in asthma (see page 73f).

But other disturbances also influence breathing — for example, slight acidosis or alkalosis of the blood, usually related to heart, lung, or kidney diseases. Damage to the nervous system may also change the character of respiration, as do certain drugs such as barbiturates, which depress respiration.

Just as we spoke of a warmth-body in connection with the activity of the human I, we can also see the air-body (regulated by respiration) as directly related to the life of the human soul. On the one hand, this air-body is connected to the entire metabolism through gaseous exchange and assorted buffer systems in the blood. On the other hand, it enables the activity of a human soul to express itself in a body. After all, the very nature of emotional experience is rhythmical alternation between attempts to be self-contained and becoming receptive to the concerns of one's surroundings. The laws of soul activity (sympathy and antipathy, the dynamics of pleasure and pain, laughing and crying) correspond to the inherent laws and dynamics of air: pressure and suction, concentration and dilution, the ability to expand in all directions yet become concentrated again under appropriate conditions of pressure. Thus healthy breathing supports the soul's ability to express itself freely. Conversely, positive emotional input or restful, comforting experiences can help restore order to disturbed respiration.

The alternation between waking and sleeping is repeated in miniature in each breath we take — sleeping corresponds to the outpouring of exhalation, while waking (which isolates a certain amount of air from the environment, as it were) corresponds to inhalation. The great transformations of birth and death are also linked to breathing. With a baby's first breath, the soul activity that supports consciousness pervades the child's body, which moments before was still heavy, dark, newly born. At the same instant, the baby's skin turns pink, his eyes open, and he utters his first cry. And in a dying person's last unutterably long and gentle exhalation, we experience their final exit from a body that has become unusable.

4. Vomiting, Diarrhea, and Constipation

In Chapter 1, we discussed the abdominal disorders characterized first and foremost by pain, and the chapter on nutrition includes a few constitutional digestive disorders, which usually require examination by a physician. In terms of assessing digestive disturbances at home, vomiting, diarrhea, and constipation are the most important symptoms to consider. Of these three cardinal symptoms, two — vomiting and diarrhea — are often important attempts at self-healing. Their purpose is to protect the body from harmful influences, but because they entail losses of fluids and salts, the cause of the disturbance must be recognized and treated promptly. On the other hand, constipation — whether pathological, organic, or functional — always burdens the body rather than relieving it, and chronic constipation may also affect a child's moods and emotions.

For the sake of clarity, we will begin by defining a few basic terms:

Vomiting: At least one-fourth of the last meal comes up again.

Spitting up: One or two mouthfuls are regurgitated.

Diarrhea: Here, not only the *frequency* (for example, six to ten times a day), but also the *quantity* (a few squirts or a cupful), *color* (yellow, gray, green, brown, black, bloody, etc.), and *consistency* (watery, runny, loose, mushy) are important. Two soft stools in one day, for example, do not constitute diarrhea.

Fever: Fever means a temperature of over 38°C/100.5°F, taken orally or rectally.

4.1 Vomiting and diarrhea

Occasional vomiting in infants

Occasional vomiting may be due to too much to eat, too much air in the stomach, food that has gone slightly bad, a cold, irritation of the throat or palate, teething, etc. Try to find out what caused it. If you are not breastfeeding, give your baby only herb tea with 5% glucose.

Other, more worrying, causes of vomiting include:

Pyloric stenosis in the first three months

Pyloric stenosis (hypertrophy and spasm of the pyloric sphincter) generally appears from the third week of life and is characterized by projectile vomiting, that is not accompanied by diarrhea or fever. Symptoms tend to increase over several days, and weight loss may occur in severe cases. What should a mother do? Check the baby's weight two or three times a week. Give him more frequent, smaller meals, and take your time burping him.

A doctor should examine the baby if he stops gaining or loses weight. A hot water bottle or warm abdominal compresses made with chamomile tea, lemon balm tea, or oxalis essence may be enough to ease the symptoms in some children, while others will need medication or perhaps even surgery (fortunately, the operation is not very invasive).

Gastro-oesophageal reflux

Gastro-oesophageal reflux occurs when the valve at the entrance to the stomach does not close completely, allowing peristaltic movements of the stomach to force food back up into the baby's oesophagus. In infants, signs of this condition include frequent dribbly vomiting or spitting up in a broad stream, especially while nursing. What to do about this condition? Take plenty of time burping him, and keep his stomach warm. Your physician may advise you to raise the head of the baby's cradle or crib so that she lies on an incline with her head higher than her legs. Also try thickening her feedings with rice cereal, arrowroot or similar. Brownish threads of blood in the vomit should be reported to your doctor immediately, because they indicate that gastric juices are damaging the oesophagus. Medication to reduce the acidity of the stomach or surgery is seldom necessary.

Simple gastrointestinal infections

Often a gastrointestinal infection will begin with vomiting. Sometimes the child is pale and not well some hours beforehand. Sometimes diarrhea begins after one or two days. Some children will vomit without having diarrhea (acetonemic vomiting). A light to high fever and stomachache may develop.

Possible causes of diarrhea include milk that has been standing around too long, other foods that are slightly "off," localized or general overcooling, viral infections, and bacterial infections (especially *E. coli* or *Salmonella)*. The body expels these "foreign irritants" by vomiting.

The overall impression is important. Does your child seem merely irritated by these symptoms, or is he totally different than usual?

Warning signs which require an immediate visit to the doctor or hospital:

- Noticeably quiet and weakened child showing apathy
- Rings around his eyes, dry tongue, hard abdomen when touched, infrequent urination
- High fever around 40°C/104°F
- Blood mixed with the stools.

Depending on the circumstances the doctor will decide whether further treatment at home is possible, or whether he needs intravenous infusion.

Diarrhea

Replacing fluids and diet during acute diarrhea

Fennel tea is best in this case. Young infants can also have very dilute chamomile, rosehip, blackberry-leaf tea or tea made with dried apples.

Add about a teaspoon of glucose in 250 ml or one cup of tea and a few grains of salt.

Continue feeding **breastfed infants** as usual, perhaps adding a little fennel tea.

For **formula-fed infants** dilute the feed to about half the concentration. Fennel tea can be also be given. With more severe diarrhea give your baby only fennel tea (with glucose and salt added as above) for one or two meals. Then continue with formula feed, but diluted to half the concentration.

Some parents have had success using thin cream of rice (3–4 g rice powder in 100 ml / 1 tsp in half a cup of water, with a teaspoon of glucose and a pinch of salt.)

If your baby is more than three months old, on the second day he can also have mixed puréed carrots in the bottle, again adding about 5% glucose.

On day 2, the vomiting should have stopped and the stools become less frequent. The carrots, although they should make the stools somewhat more solid, typically look the same "coming out as going in." Without carrots, the stools generally remain loose, stringy, and without much volume — typical "hunger stools."

Toddlers and school age children

1. If vomiting is frequent, do not give any food or drink for 2 to 4 hours after being sick.
2. The best and easiest to digest is the above herbal tea with glucose and salt. It is important to give this in tiny doses — begin with a teaspoonful, progressing to small sipls. Too great a quantity cannot be absorbed by the stomach .

Some children prefer cold tea or

still water instead. Only add juice or milk in tiny quantities to give an "optical inducement."

A commercial rehydration mixture from your pharmacy has the best posible ingredients for replacing lost salt and minerals. However, they taste sweet-salty and many children do not like them.

3. If all is going well, offer rusk, salty sticks, lightly salted rice or oat porridge.
4. After 2–3 days vomiting should have stopped. Now puréed carrots, grated apple, mashed banana, white bread or rolls, toast or crackers, or mashed potatoes can be taken.
5. After 4–5 days the diarrhea should be also better. Now low-fat foods can be added: diluted milk, yoghurt, thinly spread butter.

To support recovery, your doctor may recommend medications such as Geum urbanum RH 3–5X (5–10 drops 3–5 times a day) or Veratrum album radice 6X (5 drops 3–5 times a day, diluted).

Acetonemic (ketonic) vomiting

The abdominal wall is soft and not painful to the touch, but severe colic-like abdominal pains may appear, sometimes several hours before the actual attacks of vomiting begin. For unknown reasons, some children between the ages of two and ten are susceptible to disruptions in fat breakdown, which cause the production of acetone and similar compounds. People with an acute sense of smell

notice the apple-like odour as soon as they enter the child's room.

Treatment: If this is your child's first bout of acetonemic vomiting, consult your doctor. In future episodes, you will be able to assess the situation yourself. It's essential to provide sugar and fluids to restore metabolic balance. Every ten minutes, give your child a sip of herb tea with 5% glucose added (that is, 1 teaspoon per 100 ml / half a cup). The sugar in the tea is the remedy for acetonemic vomiting. Fennel or chamomile tea are suitable; acidic teas such as mallow or peppermint are not as good. Apply a warm chamomile or oxalis compress (see external applications, pages 430) to the child's abdomen.

Don't worry if your child vomits several more times after drinking the tea. Reassure him and tell him he'll feel better soon, and urge him to take the next sip of tea slowly. He'll keep down at least some of it. After an hour or two, slowly increase the amounts you give him to drink until he can keep down a cup of sweetened tea at a time. Instead of straight sweetened tea, you may give him either still mineral water with glucose or a commercial rehydration mixture from your pharmacy, which has the advantage of replacing lost salt and minerals. Although children who have been vomiting are often given Coca-Cola and salted crisps, we do not recommend this practice. Coke, which contains phosphates and caffeine, is a stimulant and therefore not a suitable drink for children, especially those prone to acetonemic vomiting, whose vegetative functions are less stable than normal.

Carefully palpate your child's abdomen from time to time to make sure that it remains soft. Once the vomiting has stopped, you can give him some dry rusk in addition to the tea, but nothing else for the rest of the day. The next day, his diet should be bland and fat-free. Low-fat foods should be continued on days 3 and 4.

If the vomiting persists for more than a few hours in spite of these measures, it is advisable to consult your doctor. You should certainly do so if your child develops a dry tongue and rings around his eyes, as there *may be a need for an immediate intravenous infusion.*

Other causes of vomiting
If your child ***vomits after a head injury,*** take her to the emergency room.

For ***vomiting after a sudden fright or upset,*** calm your child and keep her warm. If the shock seems serious, have her examined by a doctor.

If ***occasional vomiting*** occurs at increasingly frequent intervals and is usually accompanied by headache, ask your physician to perform a neurological examination.

4.2 Chronic constipation

Nursing infants almost never develop constipation severe enough to require treatment (see Section 12.5). In infants who are no longer nursing, the dietary measures described on Section 14.3 should counteract any tendency toward diarrhea. If dietary measures fail, your physician must determine the cause of the problem. Even in toddlers, chronic constipation is often due to painful anal fissures. Constitutional (or, less frequently, organic) and emotional reasons must also be explored, so a visit to the doctor is definitely in order if your child repeatedly retains her stools for longer periods of time, with or without soiling her pants.

Treatment guidelines for constipation due to disrupted bowel habits (as on a trip, for example) or unaccustomed diet:

The first step is to make a few sensible dietary changes. Sometimes it is enough to replace a couple of servings of milk with peppermint tea and a piece of bread with honey. If your child becomes constipated on oat cereals and whole-grain bread, try reducing the amount of fiber in her diet, especially if wind and stomach aches are frequent problems. On the other hand, a child who would quite happily subsist on pasta, white bread, and chocolate may need to be encouraged to eat fiber-rich foods. *Binding foods* include cocoa, bananas, apples, black tea, blueberries, and milk; *laxative foods* include rhubarb, stewed prunes, figs, buttermilk, yoghurt, sour milk, mineral water, and flaxseed. Flaxseed meal is especially useful for treating constipation in children because it can be mixed with almost anything. Try giving your child a teaspoon of ground flaxseed twice a day before meals, mixed with yoghurt or soup or a little honey and three drops of lemon juice. It is also important to drink plenty.

Next, with persistent constipation, it is important to realize that the entire large intestine is packed full and must be emptied. Suppositories can be used, but their stool-softening effects are often inadequate. It is important to empty the entire large intestine, not just the rectum. Here it would be advisable to check with your doctor on the best course to take. Your doctor may feel that the most effective and least uncomfortable course would be to administer an enema of warm water. Repeated use of enemas and suppositories can lead to dependency, so it is a good idea to talk to your doctor about how often they should be used.

Don't forget that the family situation can be an important factor in treating constipation. If constipation is an old, familiar problem for the older generation, a child's first missed bowel movement will have a very different impact than it does if her parents are not already sensitized to the issue. Regardless of family history, however, it is indisputably true that nothing is more constipating than worrying about bowel movements. In contrast, lively interest in one's surroundings has a laxative effect. If your child tends to be constipated, make sure that every day includes something exciting to look forward to, even if it is just a little surprise he prepares for someone else. This is also true of infants and toddlers, but in their case the element of anticipation and surprise must be provided through how you relate to them.

4.3 Learning to digest

Earth who gives to us this food,
Sun who makes it ripe and good,
Dear Sun, dear Earth,
By you we live,
Our loving thanks to you we give.

Christian Morgenstern

The fact that a baby's gastrointestinal tract is especially susceptible to disturbances indicates that the ability to digest is acquired gradually. What do the digestive organs have to "learn?" What does digestion actually accomplish? The purpose of digestion is to destroy everything that makes a food identifiable; in other words, the better the digestion, the less an ingested bit of fish or radish remains as it was. Foods can be used to build up human substance only after being broken down completely. As products of the outer world, they must "die" in order to serve the development of human forces. If any trace of undigested protein from a different species enters the blood stream, it triggers an acute reaction in the form of fever or allergic symptoms. The appearance of food intolerances (to gluten, milk protein, or specific sugars) means that the body is no longer adequately able to transform that particular bit of the outside world into human substance.

Any dietary plan should progress from the most easily digested foods to the least digestible. Some illnesses may make it necessary to eliminate certain foods temporarily. Ideally, however, the goal should be to again learn to digest foods that once had to be avoided. The more our metabolism is able to transform all foods into human substance, the stronger and more determined we can be.

It is astonishing to realize that the bodily work of digestion is the polar opposite of how the human soul and spirit process the outer world. Healthy digestion transforms mineral, plant, and animal matter into human bodies, while healthy soul-spiritual digestion accomplishes just the opposite. Our attempts at recognition and understanding succeed only to the extent that we are able to submit to that which we hope to understand, to transforming ourselves into it, so to speak, and seeing it from the inside. In understanding and recognizing something other than ourselves, we become one with the outer world. We must overcome our personal feelings, opinions, and preferences if they are "wrong," i.e., not in line with the reality that we are attempting to understand. In digestion, the world communicates with humans on a bodily level; that is, the world is transformed into human matter and human forces, sacrificing itself so that human beings can exist. In our mental efforts, however, we communicate with the surrounding world on a soul-spiritual level, learning to understand it on its own terms, as it actually is, by overcoming ourselves and "sacrificing" personal perspectives or erroneous opinions. These two ways of processing the outer world support each other, but they reveal the full scope of human nourishment only when seen together. Both spiritual and physical nourishment always involve a transformation that allows development to occur. Understandably, therefore, in the Christian religion with its focus on evolution and development, the process of nourishment appears in its true and sacred significance in the Christian rite of Holy Communion.

Rudolf Steiner expressed this reality in a grace that children also enjoy saying:

The plant-seeds are quickened in the night of the Earth,
The green herbs sprouting through the might of the Air,
And all fruits are ripened by the power of the Sun.
So quickens the soul in the shrine of the Heart,
So blossoms Spirit-power in the light of the World,
So ripens Man's strength in the glory of God.[5]

5. Skin Diseases and Rashes

In this chapter, we will discuss the most important skin diseases other than rashes due to the classic childhood diseases. The surface of the skin reflects the entire body's state of health. Skin symptoms vary greatly, and many different causative factors — nutrition, hydration, circulation, liver, kidneys, adrenals, the thyroid gland, and the nervous system — may be involved. Skin symptoms more or less directly reveal the activity of the living body or the person's soul and spirit. It is well known, for example, that itching can be caused by deposition of uric acid and bilirubin in the skin during metabolic disturbances of the kidneys and liver. Even more familiar are the phenomena of turning pale with fright or anxiety and blushing with shame, or the more subtle blush of pleasurable excitement.

The discussion of symptoms and diseases in this chapter will help parents judge whether or not a visit to the doctor is warranted. We will also provide general guidelines for skin care and home treatment of skin diseases.

5.1 Birthmarks in infants

Stork's beak marks (or salmon patches) are flat, superficially reddened areas of skin appearing at birth. They are caused by harmless dilation of delicate blood vessels in the skin. If located centrally (in the middle of the forehead or neck) or symmetrically (on both eyelids or eyebrows, for example), they usually disappear in the baby's first year. One-sided marks, however, tend to remain.

Strawberry marks (naevi, or *haemangioma)* are soft, red, round, elevated areas of skin. They generally appear (and grow larger) during the first year of life and then gradually disappear.

Café-au-lait spots are usually inconspicuous, several centimetres in diameter, irregular in shape, and permanent. If your baby has more than five such spots, or if they cover large areas of skin, ask your doctor about them.

Dark pigmented spots (port wine stains) with or without hairs, are permanent. They vary so greatly in size and shape that no generalizations are possible. Pigmented spots that grow or change should be examined by your doctor or a skin specialist.

5.2 Yellow skin coloration / jaundice

In infants, yellow skin coloration that does not also involve the whites of the eyes usually comes from eating large amounts of carrots and is totally harmless.

In *jaundice,* the whites of the eyes are also yellow. Jaundice is present to a greater or lesser extent in almost all newborn babies as long as the liver is still breaking down fetal blood pigment. Jaundice is much less evident in infants whose beds are close to windows, and *light therapy* is used if the jaundice is pronounced. In serious cases, therapy is administered in the hospital throughout the night using special lamps. *Exchange transfusions* are almost never necessary except when cases of *Rh incompatibility* between mother and child cause very high bilirubin levels in the newborn.

After discharge of the blackish meconium, an infant's stools should turn yellow. If instead they turn grayish white and the normally almost colorless urine turns a stronger shade of yellow, *cholestasis* (reduction or cessation of bile flow) is the cause. Jaundice after the newborn stage usually suggests *liver disease.* Both cases should be diagnosed by a physician without delay.

5.3 Milia (whiteheads)

Milia (whiteheads) are firm, white pimples the size of pinheads on a newborn baby's skin, usually around the eyes. They are caused by retention of keratin in oil gland ducts. Whiteheads disappear by themselves, as do the yellowish, somewhat larger spots that parents sometimes discover in the baby's mouth on the jaws or at the junction of the hard and soft palates. These larger spots are sometimes confused with thrush (see Section 5.12, page 97).

5.4 Seborrheic dermatitis (cradle cap)

Cradle cap is the name given to the greasy, adherent crusts that appear on the skull and eyebrows of infants only during the first few months. Cradle cap can be softened with oil and then carefully pried off with a fine-toothed comb. (Don't worry, you won't damage the baby's fontanelle in the process!). Like cradle cap, rough *pimples on the cheeks* in the first few weeks of a baby's life are common manifestations of so-called seborrheic dermatitis (see below); like adolescent acne, these skin symptoms reflect hormonal changes. Pimples in infants are filled with sebum rather than pus, however. This rash is not contagious, and a mild, fat-based skin-care cream from your pharmacy is usually enough to take care of them. (For pimples that appear later in childhood, see eczema, Section 5.5.)

Seborrheic dermatitis, which has no common name in English, is an inflammatory skin disease due to irregular flow of sebum. In this con-dition, the skin's vegetative activity is too strong, resulting in increased fat production and the development of greasy scales. In seborrheic dermatitis, the firm pimples described above become irritated. An inflammatory rash appears first in the diaper area, in folds of the skin, or in the navel. It spreads slowly but may eventually cover the baby's entire body. In generalized seborrheic dermatitis, very thorough skin care is important so that the raw spots do not become infected. There is no itching, and affected babies are generally happy and do not appear irritated by the condition. It is not always easy for physicians to distinguish seborrheic dermatitis from fungal infections, especially since the two conditions may overlap. Seborrheic dermatitis often disappears by the time the baby is four months old. Oil baths are a suitable treatment. (For crusts on the scalp, see cradle cap, above.)

5.5 Chronic endogenous eczema, atopic dermatitis, or neurodermatitis

These three names refer to one and the same condition, namely, constitutional susceptibility to eczema. Half of all children with this condition have a family history of eczema. Many have food or milk allergies or other allergic symptoms, and there are also genetic connections to hay fever and asthma. This syndrome has become increasingly common in recent decades. Contributing factors include not only hereditary predisposition and individual environmental pollutants and food allergens but also general changes in human lifestyles and habits (see Section 6.1).

The most obvious symptom of this type of eczema is itching, often so severe that children scratch themselves bloody. Eczema usually affects the skin of the head and shoulders in infants, the torso and limbs of somewhat older children, and finally the folds of the large joints and the backs of the hands. The skin of eczema patients is usually uniformly dry. The rash typically consists of firm, itching nodules, which may appear in groups, forming raised patches. The rash may ooze or look raw; if scratched, it may be covered with crusty scabs.

In many cases, certain foods exacerbate the condition. Many nursing mothers eliminate certain foods from their own diets when they notice that these foods make their infants' eczema worse. If a mother has eczema herself, she may decide to eliminate cows' milk and dairy products as a precaution while nursing. Premature weaning is not necessary except in occasional very severe cases. Eczema often appears in infants only when cows' milk is introduced, but as a rule these symptoms disappear in a few days. If your baby has persistent but mild symptoms, it is up to you to decide whether you would rather live with them and continue giving the child cows' milk (perhaps in the form of mild yoghurt) or switch to a soy-based formula or the more expensive mares' or goats' milk/yoghurt. If you find a source of mares' or goats' milk, we recommend asking the producer how the animals are housed and fed.

If an infant with a family history of eczema is given cows' milk as a temporary measure in the first few days of her life, great care should be taken when reintroducing cows' milk at a later date. Ideally, she should either have a blood test for cows' milk antibodies or be given only one drop at a time under a doctor's supervision. An allergic shock reaction is possible in a child previously exposed in this way.

We advise against constantly experimenting with changes in your baby's staple foods. You can expect diet-related eczema to improve spontaneously and significantly in the child's second year of life.

5

Nonetheless, many eczema patients remain sensitive to citrus fruits and other acidic foods as well as nuts and sometimes fish and eggs. Fermented milk products are often tolerated even when fresh milk still triggers eczema. Honey and sweets may make eczema symptoms worse, but true allergic reactions are not involved in this case. Hence, if a child with eczema has a bout of vomiting and diarrhea, do not hesitate to give him the glucose sweetened herbal tea he so urgently needs, even if his eczema gets a bit worse.

Treatment for eczema should be adapted to the child's individual condition and situation. We do not recommend cortisone ointments and use them only when either the parents or the child cannot afford the extra time required for alternative therapies. The suggestions that follow are intended as aids in the interim until individualized treatment is decided upon.

An ointment consisting of these ingredients has proved helpful for *dry skin:*
Equisetum Oleum 10% (Weleda) 50.0
Distilled water 75.0
Eucerin/Aquaphor (Eucerinum anhydricum) ad 200.0

This ointment is helpful for *severe itching:*
Decoctum aquos. Equiseti 10% 100.00
Eucerin/Aquaphor (Eucerinum anhydricum) ad 200.00

For *acute attacks of itching,* we recommend a warm bath with horsetail tea (boil one handful of dried horsetail herb in one litre/quart of water for ten minutes and strain it into the bath). Reapply ointment after bathing.

For *severely oozing eczema,* apply wet, *cool* compresses made with horsetail tea (see page 435).

Keep the itching areas of skin covered with cotton underwear or with a one-piece coverall that also incloses the hands. You can make this yourself by adapting the size of the pattern on page 439. Your child will love this outfit because "Mummy made it." Embroider it with sun, moon, and stars or paint friendly little faces on the hands. Your child will play with her "puppets" for hours and will not be able to scratch.

It's important for parents to remain as calm and objective as possible. Often, a child's severe itching tests the strength of the entire family. Mum is on the verge of despair and at the end of her tether because she never gets a good night's sleep. A child with eczema soon learns to use scratching as a way to get what he wants, refusing to sleep in his own bed and always demanding the opposite of what anyone else wants. Once the family pet, he soon becomes the family tyrant. The only way to prevent this is to treat a child with eczema as "normally" as possible. Implement the treatments listed above as matter-of-factly as you can, and then return to your daily routine without showering the child with further attention.

Psychological considerations: On the one hand, the dry skin of an eczema patient seems less alive and more of a barrier than normal; on the other hand, it reacts with greater sensitivity, and exudative eczema is *too* alive and open. You can help your child shift her emotional focus from her body to her surroundings not only by providing a protective covering of topical medications (ointments or compresses) and suitable clothing but also by fostering her interest in what is going on around her. If you also allow her to experience clear limits (that is, if you as parents are sure of what you want and of what needs to be done at the moment), her personality will grow stronger and she will be able to redefine her relationship to the world. This approach has positive effects on the illness and goes a long way toward alleviating skin symptoms.

5.6 Marbling of the skin

Either blue coloration of the lips, fingernails, or feet or marbling of the skin (mixed red and blue coloring over entire parts of the body) may mean that the child is or has been too cold. Such spots are sometimes also observed during a period of rising fever, and children who have just eaten big meals are also more susceptible. Depending on the situation, dress your child in woolen underwear or wrap her up warmly.

If blue skin coloration is associated with rapid breathing, a weak or rapid pulse, and general weakness, it may be a sign of lung or heart disease, so consult your physician in such cases.

Chilblains can occur in toddlers who have been out in the cold and immobile for too long. The reddish, doughy swollen spots are very painful and are especially common around the joints of the fingers and toes. Applying too much heat from outside is just as bad as the outdated practice of rubbing the spots with snow. It is best to give your child some hot herb tea with honey and cover him warmly with wool blankets or down comforters.

5

5.7 Red cheeks

Red cheeks can be caused by many factors: fever, teething, scarlet fever, fresh air, excitement. Occasionally, they are the result of overexposure to cold during a walk in the wind. Especially in round-cheeked six-month-olds, slightly frozen spots may remain visible for weeks. The rather dark red spots on the cheeks cover areas of tissue that feel hard to the touch. These spots remain hypersensitive to cold for a long time and need extra protection in the form of dollops of fat-based ointment, covered with gauze dressings if needed.

One-sided, painful swellings that increase in size require prompt medical treatment.

5.8 Pallor

Facial pallor is not a sign of anemia as long as your child's lips, earlobes, fingernails, and the mucous membranes lining the eyelids are normally rosy. Consult your physician, however, if these parts of the body are also pale or if a pale child is also unenergetic and listless. Iron supplementation is indicated only in confirmed cases of iron-deficiency anemia.

5.9 Inflamed navel

In the third week after birth, a newborn baby's navel may still be moist or even bleed slightly. There's no hurry if you see only a few little pimples around the navel, but if the skin is red and swollen, your doctor should examine the baby immediately. This inflammation is usually a so-called umbilical granuloma, which is nothing more than the "proud flesh" commonly seen in slowly healing wounds. (In this case, the wound is simply the 2–3 mm spot where the umbilical cord was attached.) Your physician will simply dab the spot with a silver nitrate "pencil." Follow your physician's instructions for after-care at home, or proceed as follows. Clean the spot once or twice a day with 70% alcohol or other skin disinfectant, pat dry or allow to air-dry, and apply powder (Wecesin, for example). The navel is usually not bandaged because clean nappies or diapers are just as hygienic and get changed more often. Under this treatment, the little pimples around your baby's navel will also disappear. Disinfectants and alcohol may start to cause irritation after three or four days, so don't use them for longer than that. If the navel is still spotting at that time, your doctor may need to treat it with silver nitrate again. Use baby oil for any further aftercare.

As a rule, mothers are wary about poking around in their babies' navels, but in fact the fear of breaking through into the interior of the abdomen is unfounded. Secretions, scabs, and remnants of powder in the navel can cause irritation and sometimes even a bit of bleeding. After about three weeks, do not hesitate to clean your baby's navel energetically with a swab dipped in baby oil.

5.10 Pustules and blisters in young infants

The nodules of a seborrheic skin rash on the cheeks are generally pointed, firm, and yellowish. In contrast, pustules or blisters that are somewhat flat, usually a few millimetres in diameter, and greenish yellow in color contain actual pus and colonies of staphylococcus bacteria. These pustules occur either singly or in groups and usually appear on the skin of the head, armpits, or nappy area, although they may also appear anywhere else on the body. In infrequent cases, pus-filled blisters one centimetre or more (half an inch) in diameter develop in a matter of hours. Take your baby straight to the doctor if this happens. Seek medical care for smaller pustules, too, but as long as the baby seems otherwise well and has no fever, the situation is not as urgent. Until you can see the doctor, do whatever you can to minimize the spread of germs. Change the baby's clothes and sheets completely once a day, and those of everyone else in the family. Also wash all bath and hand towels. Clean out the bag that holds your baby-care supplies. You may need to throw out the supplies and buy new ones; squeeze ointments on to disposable applicators instead of your fingers. Thoroughly wash your hands with soap and scrub with a fingernail brush before and after washing the baby.

It is not true that staph infections appear only when hygiene is inadequate. They also appear in families who overuse disinfectants, which destroy the normal skin flora, resulting in increased susceptibility to colonization by germs. It is important to know that these infections can be easily transmitted to other young infants whose immune systems are still immature. To avoid possible mammary gland infections in nursing mothers, parents should keep their fingernails short to allow thorough cleaning. Also, avoid letting your hair touch the infant, because it can harbour bacteria. Under medical supervision, staph infections can usually be treated effectively with topical disinfectants and measures to keep the skin dry.

5.11 What to do about diaper/nappy rash?

In common parlance, "nappy rash" or "diaper rash" means any and all inflammatory skin symptoms in the nappy area (see Figure 7). Frequent causes of simple nappy rash (sudden, bright redness of the skin around the anus, usually not extending beyond the folds in the buttocks) include leaving stools in the nappy for too long, unusually irritating stools (for example, after giving your baby orange juice or apples), mild digestive disturbances (more frequent during teething), or the beginnings of diarrhea.

Treatment
Clean the rash first with water, then with oil. Dry the area thoroughly and apply a fat-based ointment that adheres well (for example, zinc oxide ointment with cod-liver oil). Change nappies frequently.

Little red pimples with thin rings of white scales around the edges suggest *thrush,* a fungal infection. Often they appear first around the anus or genitals, but they may eventually merge and spread to cover the entire nappy area all the way to the navel (see Figure 8). Ultimately, the rash becomes a uniformly red, firm surface that tends to ooze (see Thrush, Section 5.12).

We do not need to discuss *ammonia dermatitis* here, since we're sure our readers change their babies' diapers often enough. This type of diaper rash develops when the breakdown of urine produces ammonia, which irritates the skin.

Seborrheic dermatitis, discussed in Section 5.4, may also appear in the diaper area. Apply both the fat-based cream recommended for general seborrheic dermatitis pimples and an additional coating of zinc oxide ointment. In this case, too, clean the area with oil if possible.

During the first weeks of life, *skin irritation in the folds of the groin* may be due to either inadequate or overly rough cleaning of these sensitive areas of skin. Care for these areas by dabbing them clean with generous amounts of oil; treat the patches with a fat-based, additive-free ointment. Don't use powder, which can form crumbs and cause further irritation. After a while, firm, grayish areas of thickened skin may appear along the fold of the groin. In this case, the outer layer of skin has combined with skin-care products to form a crust. Bathing and oiling should remove these deposits within a week.

Stripes of irritated skin may develop *at navel level or around the thighs,* where disposable plastic-covered diapers rub. Treat this irritation with drying ointments, and change your diapering technique (see also Section 12.6).

During the first few weeks of a baby's life, a relatively *dense rash of pimples or blisters* may appear, extending beyond the nappy area to the upper body. Such rashes are not always clearly either bacterial or fungal in origin. Experience shows that they disappear quickly if you simply eliminate fabric softeners and give each washload an extra rinse. As a preventive measure, we always recommend washing nappies with ordinary laundry detergents without softeners, and you should certainly make the switch if your baby develops skin irritations. (We are all familiar with the results of large double-blind studies of laundry detergents, but our unblinded experience continues to suggest that this recommendation is valid. Try it for yourself! There is an obvious difference in the absorbency of terry towels washed with and without fabric softeners, for example.) In addition, it is sometimes necessary to put nappies through an extra rinse cycle or even rinse them by hand if your washing machine uses too little water.

5.12 Fungus infections

Some fungal skin diseases have increased dramatically since the victory of synthetics over natural-fiber clothing, while others owe their spread to antibiotic suppression of bacterial infections. In any case, diseases formerly limited to specific occupations with heavy moisture exposure, populations with poor hygiene, or exceptionally weakened patients have become familiar (although not a popular topic of

Meningitis

Figure 1. This child definitely does not have meningitis. He can sit with his arms extended, bending forward from the hips with legs outstretched, without feeling pain.

Figure 2. Meningitis is probable in this case. When asked to sit up and keep her knees straight, this girl supports herself from behind and keeps her head bent somewhat backward. She cannot extend her arms forward without pain.

Figure 3. Pain and neck stiffness also prevent her from raising her knee to her chin or kissing it, even when she uses her arms to help. If your child cannot perform this gesture, meningitis or at least meningeal irritation is even more probable, and prompt examination by a doctor is advised.

Ear infections

Figure 4. Testing for ear infections. When a baby or toddler has a fever, you can determine whether they also have an earache by applying brief pressure to the tragus (the small projection in front of the external opening of the ear). A child with an earache will wince or turn her head away; an infant will start to cry. The photograph shows an obviously older child who could just tell you where it hurts!

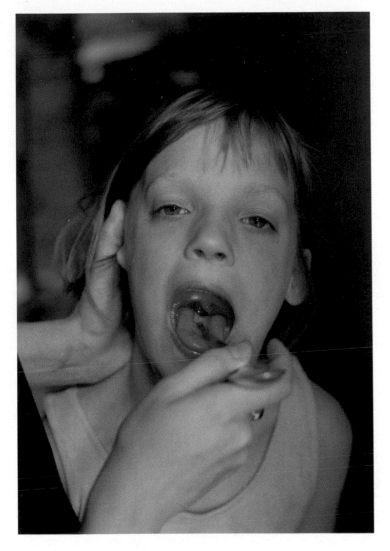

Looking at the throat.

Figure 5. Looking at the throat. Before calling the doctor, parents can check a feverish child's mouth and throat by themselves. Is her tongue coated? Do you see spots, blisters, or a film coating the mucous membranes? Finally, ask her to say "ah" or, with a spoon handle, apply brief pressure to the tongue approximately two-thirds of the way back. The momentary gag reflex will expose the tonsils and the rear wall of the throat. Are they red? Covered with an opaque coating? Or simply mucus-covered? If the child has lost her voice, is having trouble breathing, or is seriously ill, a physician should perform this examination. (We highly recommend looking at your child's throat once in a while when she is healthy, to learn what a child's normal throat looks like.)

Hernia

Figure 6. Inguinal hernia. Note the
bulge on the right side of the child's
groin.

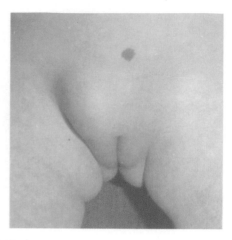

Nappy Rash

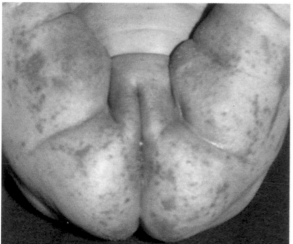

Figure 7. A fairly
advanced case of nappy
(diaper) rash.

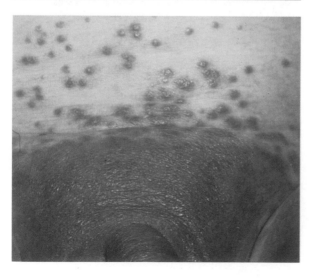

Figure 8. Scaly nappy
(diaper) rash suggests
thrush, a fungus infesta-
tion. Spreading and merg-
ing of the individual spots
is typical.

Measles

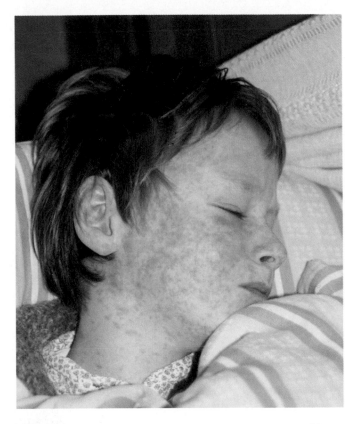

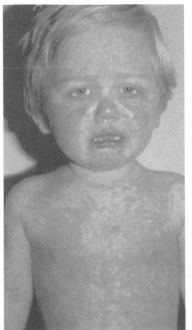

Figs. 9 and 10. Measles is characterized by irregular spots that tend to merge; they appear first on the head and rapidly spread downward. The rash is preceded by conjunctivitis, runny nose, and cough. The highest fever occurs together with the rash.

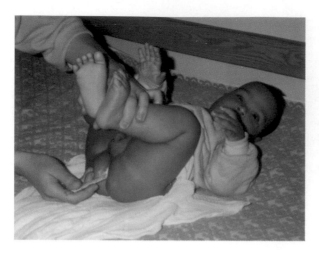

Taking temperature

Figure 11. Taking your baby's temperature when fever is suspected. Rest your hand against the child's buttocks so that unexpected movements will not cause the thermometer to shift.

Scarlet fever

Figure 12. The typical scarlet fever rash consists of small spots that look like red pimples. The rash, which often appears only very briefly, tends to be concentrated in the groin area.

Figure 13. The first sign of scarlet fever is a thick, white coating on the tongue, which disappears after two days and leaves behind a raspberry-red surface of raised dots. The palate and tonsils are often bright red with inflammation, and white dots or coatings also often appear on the tonsils. The cheeks are red, but a triangle around the mouth remains pale.

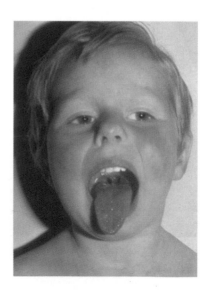

Chicken pox

Figure 14. Within two or three days, the skin develops a pattern of various-sized spots not unlike an astronomical chart. Early-stage red nodules are accompanied by new blisters and older scabs. The scalp is also affected, and the rash often also appears on the mucous membranes of alimentary canal and genitals.

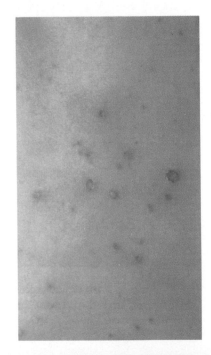

Figure 15. Chickenpox at this age is generally mild and unproblematic. If your child's immune system is compromised or if she has serious eczema, however, consult your physician as a precautionary measure.

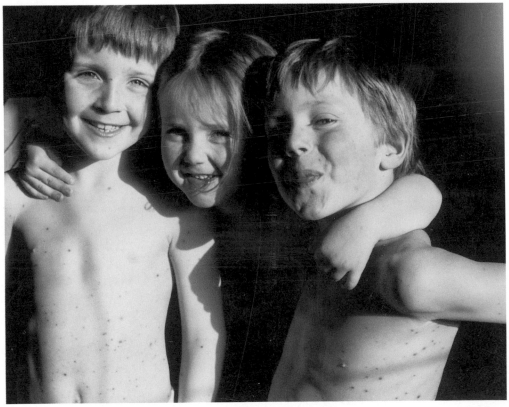

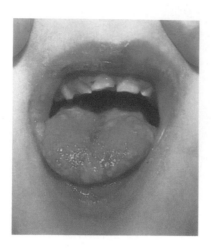

Herpetic stomatitis

Figure 16. Many painful ulcers (aphthae) *appear on the reddened mucous membranes of the mouth.*

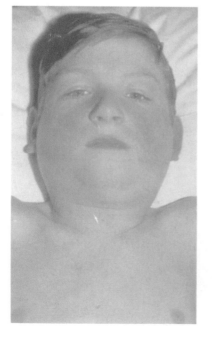

Mumps

Figure 17. The swelling (painful to the touch) affects the back part of the cheeks and the area under the ears. As a result, the lower portions of the earlobes protrude.

conversation) in every family. Increasing use of antifungal antibiotics throughout the world is an indication of the scope of the effort to control fungal diseases. Whether our current habits promote or suppress fungi, they are definitely on the rise.

Thrush in the mouth and diaper area

Thrush in the mouth is a white network or crumbly layer that may be either fine-textured or coarse. Patches are most likely to appear on the insides of the cheeks and on the tongue, but the layer of fungus sometimes extends all the way to the lips. A white coating on the tongue without involvement of the mucous membranes of the cheeks, however, is not necessarily a sign of thrush.

Initially, thrush around the anus manifests as dotlike, often oozing nodules, but these nodules spread rapidly and merge at least partially, developing thin rings of scales at their edges (see Figure 8). The infection usually begins in the mouth and migrates through the digestive tract to the anal area. At this stage, it can be detected in the stools. In severely weakened children or those receiving concurrent treatment with broad-specturm antibiotics, intestinal thrush is extremely persistent. In such cases, the stools smell like yeast.

Treatment

In general, even in cases previously treated with antimycotic drugs (usually either nystatin or miconazole) with only temporary success, you can count on the efficacy of local treatment of the mouth and buttocks if you are willing to be patient. The principle is simple: in the mouth, the mucous membranes are stabilized by "brushing" them with swabs dipped in diluted natural mouthwash or mouth balsam or, in South Africa, Gentian violet 1%, which also removes some of the fungal layer. The fungus does not disappear as quickly as it does under antimycotic treatment, but this is not necessarily a disadvantage since recurrences are less likely.

For fungal infections in the nappy area, it is important to know that fungi grow in places that are damp and dark. (Some grow better with more heat, while others require coolness.) They also cannot grow in oil, especially if it contains etheric oils, so you can figure out for yourself what you need to do. Wash the skin with water, but follow up by washing it again with plain sunflower seed oil. (Use sunflower oil simply because in the amounts you need, it is significantly less expensive than commercial baby oil.) Then apply an oil that contains an appropriate etheric oil, such as 10% lavender oil, calendula oil, or a mixture of the two. (Thyme oil and eucalyptus oil are too irritating.) Then apply a protective layer of skin cream.

If your baby has thrush, change her nappies as often as possible, including once or twice during the night. Dampness and breakdown products from urine can undo all your therapeutic efforts. We recommend gauze nappies covered with wool "soakers" made of heavy, minimally processed sheep's wool (for knitting instructions, see page 437). During this time, sponge-bathe your baby. If you must give her a bath, keep it short so that her skin doesn't soften, which allows the fungus to penetrate deeper.

Whenever her skin gets wet for any reason, it must be thoroughly dried. You can even use a hair dryer, if needed, on a low setting. After drying, apply plenty of oil as outlined above. You can expect to see improvement after three or four days, although a few new patches may appear. Complete healing, however, takes two or three weeks.

If improvement does not occur, ask your doctor to reconfirm the diagnosis. In any case, a more radical approach that will eventually work is to keep the baby naked. Fasten a thin batten or wooden rod over the middle of the cradle and hang a blanket over it to keep the space below as warm as possible. (Make sure the baby can't dislodge the blanket.) Dress the baby only from the waist up and lay her in the space beneath the blanket with her bottom resting on several layers of diapers. You will need to keep her room very warm, or perhaps place a hot water bottle under the mattress, to keep her from getting too cold.

Athlete's foot

Athlete's foot *(tinea pedis)* is characterized by crumbly or scaly peeling of the skin between the toes or on the callused portions of the soles of the feet.

Treatment principles: As much air and as little water and soap as possible (but as much as necessary, to avoid social isolation due to odour!). After a quicker-than-usual shower or a short footbath in sage or oak bark tea, dry (or blow-dry) the affected areas and surrounding skin very thoroughly. Then rub the skin either with one of the oils listed above or with massage oil that contains only natural etheric oils (no irritating additives). Have your child go barefoot, walk around the house in his sock feet, or wear open sandals as often as possible. Instead of socks made with synthetic fibers, choose wool or cotton socks and change them daily. Make sure your child doesn't wear rubber boots or shoes with synthetic linings for any longer than is absolutely necessary.

5.13 Purulent skin infections

Erysipelas

If your child has a fever, feels exhausted, and has a rash consisting of raised but irregularly bounded, bright-red spots that rapidly spread to cover larger areas of skin, have a physician examine her immediately. It is hardly ever possible to treat this condition without antibiotics.

Impetigo

The disease begins with isolated itching pustules that rapidly spread and are usually covered with thick yellow scabs. Scratching spreads the infection. Irritated areas of skin (such as under the nose during a cold) are usually affected first. Impetigo appears mainly in toddlers and in summer. It is very contagious and is difficult to control without disinfectant treatment; fortunately, mercury-containing medications are no longer used. If your child experiences repeated cases of impetigo, consider the sandbox as a possible source of infection. How long has that old sand been there?

Folliculitis (infection of the hair follicles)

Folliculitis is characterized by small pustules, sometimes with hairs in the centers. Contributing factors include oily skin, increased perspiration, too much fat in the diet (especially pork and sausage), digestive irregularities with constipation, inadequate or inappropriate skin hygiene, and puberty. It's best to simply wait out puberty, but take steps to reduce the other factors.

Boils, furuncles and carbuncles

Boils or furuncles are pus-forming inflammations that are somewhat larger and sit somewhat deeper in the skin than pimples; very large ones are called carbuncles. If such abscesses occur in the armpits, they are usually inflamed sweat glands.

Treatment of all pus-forming infections is the same as for lymph node abscesses in the throat or groin, which are discussed in the section on throat infections, where the advantages of lancing (performed by a physician once pus has begun to form) over antibiotic treatment are also described.

If your child has several boils at the same time or if they appear repeatedly (more likely in toddlers and school-age children than in infants), constitutional treatment is indicated. In inflammations of this sort, the body itself builds up a protective wall to contain the pus. In infrequent cases, no barrier forms and the inflammation spreads to surrounding tissue. This infection (called a phlegmon) requires prompt treatment and hospitalization.

Infections on the hand

Cracks or wounds on the fingers or on the palm of the hand give easy access to deeper layers and lead to pus-forming infections. If your child has a progressive, throbbing infection on a finger, consult a doctor as soon as possible. Even a day's delay can cause permanent damage or even the loss of the finger. Take the same precaution if a so-called hangnail worsens.

Minor nail bed infections (*whitlows*) develop easily in young infants, either spontaneously or because their fingernails are cut too soon. An infection of this type usually heals well when kept covered in medicated ointment, but get your doctor to take a look at it if the inflammation spreads to encompass the entire first joint of the finger. Bandage it like this: Apply a dollop of medicated ointment to the affected finger, and then cover all the fingers with a piece of gauze fastened at the wrist. Cover the gauze with a mitten-like sack knotted loosely at the wrist. Change the entire bandage once or twice a day. Do not use an adhesive bandage or tape on infants; it might cut off circulation in a finger, or the baby might choke on it if it comes off. Even for older children, adhesive bandages are usually not the most effective way to cover infected spots.

5.14 "Blood poisoning"

More correctly described as purulent inflammation of the lymph vessels *(lymphangitis),* "blood-poisoning" is well known and rightly feared, since it can be dangerous if not treated immediately. It usually appears after a minor injury that may even be overlooked, or after such an injury has been scratched open again. Red stripes appear suddenly, running up or down the inside of an arm or leg, for example, and the lymph nodes in the armpit or groin quickly swell and become painful. Immediate medical attention is required. In most cases, the affected limb is immobilized with a splint and wrapped in compresses moistened with a disinfectant. A tetanus booster shot is often recommended. Special caution is needed if the child also has a fever.

5.15 Fever blisters (cold sores, herpes simplex)

Fever blisters appear mostly on the lips. They do not contain pus. They are caused by the virus HSV-1 (see also Section 7.9). Do not expect your doctor to be able to get rid of them as if by magic. They can be treated either with a drying cream or with one containing lemon balm (melissa) extract (such as Lomaherpan, Herpalieve, or Herpilyn). Normally with treatment the blisters form crusts in 2-4 days and heal in 5-7 days. Calendula ointment (Weleda) or Mercurialis ointment are other available treatments. Virostatic creams shorten the duration of symptoms but do not prevent recurrences.

5.16 Sunburn

Sunburn can be treated with the same diluted solutions described in the section on burns, including Combudoron (nettle and arnica) gel or Vitamin E cream. Note that some children may be allergic to arnica (see page 47). In serious cases, apply wet compresses and change them often. An alternative is to frequently dab the affected areas of skin with the solution. Where available, Quark (fermented skimmed milk) or live yoghurt poultices are also soothing and help speed healing, but do not use them on children with eczema who are allergic to cows' milk.

Do everything you can to prevent sunburn (and overexposure to light) before it occurs. Children at play outside should wear sunhats and T-shirts, even when swimming. A good sunblock should be applied. Due to thinning of the ozone layer in the stratosphere, the threshold dose for sunburn is reached more quickly today than it used to be, a particular concern in the mountains and at high latitudes (southern Australia, New Zealand, northern Europe). Excessive exposure to light (like any other ordinarily healing influence) can cause damage. *Children's skin is more sensitive to sun than that of adults,* and it is possible for them to get an overdose of sun on their skin even before sunburn is evident. This overdose may cause symptoms of sunstroke. That night or the next day, the child develops chills, a fever of up to 40°C/104°F, headache, and vomiting. If these symptoms appear, *always consult a physician.* While waiting for medical attention, keep the child cool or in the shade, and apply a cool compress to the forehead to remove excess heat. Most dermatologists warn against overexposure to sun in childhood and adolescence because it increases the risk of skin malignancies later in life.

Recommendations: Always protect your baby's brain and spinal cord by dressing her in a shirt and brimmed hat when the sun is strong. Never let her fall asleep in the sun; bring her into the shade when she gets tired. It is much healthier to expose children to the sun for shorter periods over several weeks. Always remember that too much sun dulls mental activity. Recently, mineral micro-pigments (titanium dioxide, zinc oxide), which are non-allergenic and have purely physical effects, have been recommended over the chemical UV filters formerly used in sunscreen lotions.

5.17 Insect bites and skin parasites

Bee and wasp stings: When your child is stung by a bee, promptly remove the stinger with a pin or the point of a knife. Do not squeeze it out! If available, press a freshly cut onion on the sting. Alternatively, use moist compresses made with diluted nettle/arnica extract (Combudoron). If a systemic reaction develops (because the stinger hits a blood vessel or because your child is allergic), take your child to a doctor immediately. Consider a tetanus shot if the sting is from a wasp (see Section 10.6).

Mosquito bites occur only on uncovered parts of the body. Some people find that dabbing them with saliva or with water (with or without soap) helps the itching. Here, too, Combudoron gel is helpful, or if the itching is severe, use diluted Combudoron lotion. Watery emulsions of etheric oils (Zedan insect repellent, etc.) are available from your pharmacy or natural health store and will repel insects for several hours. In areas where mosquitoes are numerous at night, it is a good idea to hang mosquito netting over the bed.

Scabies is caused by mites and characterized by inflamed areas of skin in which millimetre-long tunnels may be visible. The parasites themselves are almost never seen. If a child has scabies, other members of the family are usually affected as well. Eczema caused by traces of mite excrement may persist for a week. Clothing must be boiled, dry-cleaned, or hung outside for four days. Your doctor will prescribe medication.

Flea bites are rare nowadays because the species of flea specific to humans is said to be extinct in some countries. Sometimes, however, fleas may migrate from domestic or wild animals to humans. Bites arranged in rows (along the waistband, for example) are reason to suspect fleas. If you have fleas indoors, spray with natural pyrethrum, which is relatively harmless. Used bedding and clothing that has already been worn should be shaken out over a full bathtub before spraying.

Head lice

These have become very common, and with school-age children routine checkups by the school nurse will usually identify when there is a problem. An itchy scalp makes the victim aware of them. With a little experience, it is easy to find the nits and often also the surprisingly agile adults, which vary in size. If a child has head lice, it is best to treat the entire family.

Treatment

Unfortunately, natural pyrethrum extracts are no longer reliably effective, and in many countries resistance to permethrin (a synthetic pyrethrum derivative) has also been reported. Alternatives currently attracting inter-

est include neem oil products (widely available through the internet).*

Lice can be treated with neem-based shampoos followed by applying a neem-based cream to the hair and scalp. Apply the product to all infected and hairy parts of the body. This is left overnight and washed out in the morning. Before washing, use a flea comb to remove the dead lice and sterile eggs. Remove remaining nits with tweezers or a fine comb. Repeat the treatment in 7 to 10 days.

If pyrethrum extract is used, treatment involves a week of daily hair washing and searching for nits, but the same schedule of hairwashing with vinegar added to the wash water is also effective if combined with daily searches and cutting out individual hairs with attached nits. In Australia, NZ and South Africa an available product is Lice-B-Gone, manufactured in the USA. Another method, effective over two weeks, is to wash the child's hair with rosemary shampoo and conditioner then use a fine-tooth comb while the hair is still wet with conditioner. Clean the comb of lice between strokes. The child can be standing in the bath or on a towel. Repeat every 3-4 days if lice are found.

After treating as directed and

---

* Experts from the German Federal Department of the Environment and the Institute for Consumer Protection, in a drug advisory dated June 2000, reject synthetic pyrethrins and continue to hold up pyrethrum extract as the gold standard. Some neem products have proved effective in individual cases but their general effectiveness against lice has not yet been confirmed by clinical studies.

thorough hair drying, all family members are searched again for nits. New infestations are found approximately 1 cm ($\frac{1}{2}$ in.) above the scalp. If they are more than 3 cm (1 in.) up, you can be certain that they are old, i.e., empty. (When in doubt, viable nits can be identified under the microscope.) Because of the location of new nits, it is important to begin combing very close to the scalp if you use a nit comb, which is available from your pharmacy. A less uncomfortable approach is to cut out individual nit-infested hairs at the base.

Do not let embarrassment prevent you from informing your child's teacher and other parents as soon as you discover a lice infestation. Lice are very social creatures and are extremely fond of certain individuals. They are *not* a sign of inadequate hygiene! Full disclosure is the only way to prevent both the spread of lice and reinfestations. Depending on the type of treatment they received, your children (although no longer contagious themselves) may easily bring a louse home from school or kindergarten again the very next day. Reinfestation can also come from their own beds or clothing if these have not been completely changed and kept in an overheated room for two days. (In the heat and without a host, any larvae that have emerged rapidly exhaust themselves and die.)

Make sure you are aware of any local regulations excluding louse-infested individuals from school or public events. Children should return to school only when no more nits can be found on their heads. (They may still have a few empty or dead nits in their hair even after they are completely free of lice, but without examining the nits under a microscope, you will not be able to tell whether they are old or new ones.

5.18 Warts

Warts may be raised (on the fingers) or flat (plantar warts on the feet). They are caused by a communicable virus and often spread through public swimming pools. They can be "iced" away with dry ice or surgically removed. Corn-softening adhesive bandages do not help, but strong solutions (which require a prescription) do. We prefer an ointment containing bismuth and antimony. Most warts respond to this treatment, although patience is required, since it takes one to three months. Some people also attempt a cure by magic or incantation. We have no personal experience with this approach.

Molluscum contagiosum is characterized by multiple firm, pinhead-sized, keratinous nodules with central openings. They generally develop on more delicate areas of skin. Treatment options include squeezing out the con-tents, abrasion, or using the above-mentioned salve, or tea-tree oil. They eventually resolve spontaneously. They are spread through contact or in swimming pools.

5.19 Allergic skin reactions

The many different chemicals found in cleaning supplies, laundry soften-ers, hand creams, cosmetics, textile treatments, etc., have produced a mul-titude of allergic skin reactions whose manifestations vary so greatly that we might almost say that there is no skin ailment that cannot be mimicked by an allergic episode (see also Chapter 6). If an allergy is suspected, experiment with avoiding specific substances to see if the symptoms recede. Foods such as strawberries and medicinal herbs such as arnica also occasionally cause allergic skin reactions. Certain modern drugs (especially sulpha drugs and antibiotics) trigger skin allergies in some individuals; symptoms are often severe enough to prevent the use of the medication. Allergic reactions to germs are also possible; in such cases, a rash develops during a flu or other infection. Here, too, the mani-festations are very diverse (spots may be tiny or medium-sized, or some-times even large raised patches like hives). The skin anywhere on the body may be affected.

Treatment
Baths containing horsetail tea (see page 436) have proven effective for all allergic skin rashes.

After the bath, apply a moisturizing ointment if the skin is dry. This for-mula is one possibility:
Urtica dioica 10% infus. 80.0
Eucerinum anhydricum (wool alcohol
 ointment) ad 200.0

If the skin is normal or oily, use a soothing powder instead of ointment.

Depending on the overall allergic picture, constitutional remedies may be used to stimulate liver or kidney activity or other metabolic functions.

Allergic contact dermatitis

In summer, walks or working in the open can sometimes lead to in-advertent contact with plants of all kinds that cause skin reactions and rashes. In some areas, contact with poison ivy can cause severe itching and redness of the skin. Other plants which give contact dermatitis are yarrow, primula, sumac and poison oak. In the North America, cow parsnip, a *Heracleum* species, causes photodermatitis, a rash very similar to a burn, with reddening and blistering of the skin. Treatment is the same as for sunburn. Children should be taught to recognize these plants in their locality and avoid contact if possible.

Hives (urticaria)

Most people have endured rashes caused by nettles or horsefly bites, and are therefore familiar with the skin symptoms known as "hives." Hives are swollen areas that are either pale against a red background or reddened against a background of normal skin. They are irregularly distributed and highly irregular in shape. Although they cause severe itching, patients tend to rub the spots rather than scratch them. Duration of symptoms is also variable; they may be gone the next day or persist for weeks. In most cases the cause is unknown; hives are not caused by allergies in the strict sense. Milder cases can be treated at home with a soothing powder. For generalized symptoms, consult your physician.

Papular urticaria

This rash, which tends to occur instead of hives in toddlers, feels similar to the touch to hives but the raised, reddish or pale spots are only a few millimetres in diameter. As with hives, the causative mechanism is uncertain.

Rash in newborn babies

Newborns often develop a rash of yellowish, irregular distributed, pinhead-sized nodules surrounded by relatively large, irregularly bounded reddened areas. Individual spots disappear and new ones appear in a matter of hours, and the entire rash disappears on its own within a few days. Here, too, the cause is unknown.

6. Allergic Sensitivity and Modern Civilization

6.1 Immune response as a learning process

Many parents wonder why allergies have increased so significantly in recent decades. Undoubtedly, part of this increase is due to new chemical irritants in the environment. But why the immune systems of many children and adults are no longer able to adapt adequately to new allergens is a different question. What influences weaken the immune system and its functions? How can immunological learning be supported?

A brief definition of "allergy," a term coined at the beginning of the twentieth century by pediatrician Clemens von Pirquet, is "increased reactivity." When *allergens* (allergy-triggering foreign substances) are ingested (in food or medications), inhaled, or touched (certain plants or animal hair), the body's endogenous defenses are strongly activated. Instead of learning to deal with certain substances, the body resists them. This resistance causes skin rashes, itching, swelling of the mucous membranes,

diarrhea, or other symptoms. Specific (and often non-specific) *antibodies* to these allergens are formed in the blood or on cell surfaces. Since the blood stream carries antibodies throughout the body, merely touching an allergy-triggering food with one hand may be enough to cause swollen lips and a red face.

Antibody formation is the basis of immunity. With regard to infectious diseases, it is highly desirable. It often occurs unnoticed, in "silent" or sub-clinical infections. In allergies, however, it becomes a problem. Excessive antibody production interacts with other processes to produce allergic symptoms.

In some cases, however, allergy-prone bodies do learn to deal with allergens over a number of years. A change of climate may encourage this process, since it forces the body to change, adapt, and generally become more flexible. Similar results are sometimes noted after childhood illnesses accompanied by high fever, which place heavy demands on the entire immune system and may ultimately also make it stronger and more functional. This is also the goal (not always accomplished) of yearlong constitutional treatment with homeopathic medications. Other than food allergies, the most frequent allergic illnesses of childhood are chronic eczema (see Section 5.5), asthma (Section 3.5, page 73), hay fever (Section 3.4), and hives (Section 5.19) Bee or wasp stings (see Section 5.17) may occasionally cause allergic (anaphylactic) shock.

It is more than a mere analogy that medicine tends to describe immunological processes in terms corresponding to different stages of learning: "perceiving" or "recognizing" damaging substances, distinguishing between "self" and "non-self", immunological "memory," and the like.

The ability to learn as a preventive measure

One of Rudolf Steiner's most pertinent discoveries was that the body's self-healing forces (and thus also immunoregulation) are related to the activity of thinking. Steiner describes two polar aspects of the etheric body: on the one hand, it is the vehicle of heredity, reproduction, growth, and regeneration; on the other hand, the vehicle of a person's thought processes (see Section 15.4). Thus immunological functions depend not only on heredity but also on a person's soul-spiritual

productivity and enthusiasm (see Section 2.4). From the medical and scientific perspective, this connection has been confirmed by the results of psychosomatic research. For example, oncologists have discovered that cancer patients' immune systems are more effective in overcoming the illness if the patients are in a position to process conflicts in their lives in a meaningful way, thus achieving a stronger sense of identity and a better understanding of their current situation. We also know that individuals whose lives are imbued with real ideals are better equipped, immunologically speaking, to overcome illness.

From this perspective, what kind of accompaniment and support do the learning processes of the human body, soul, and spirit need in order to enhance the immune system? And what factors prevent them from doing so?

On the bodily level, immunizations and antibiotic therapy deprive the body of much of the active work of coming to grips with germs. Our food now contains many more artificial additives than it once did, which can place excessive demands on the body. Processed, preserved, and overcooked foods (such as white rice, white flour, canned or frozen foods, etc.) are refined and denatured, often making them easier to digest. As a result, there is less reason for the body to exert itself.

On the *soul level,* much of modern life involves little real emotional participation. Affluence, a superabundance of toys, inadequate attention, and disregard for children's needs prevent strong identification and processing from occurring on this level, too. In addition, the mass media offer age-inappropriate stimuli that persist as "indigestible" foreign elements in a child's consciousness.

On the *spiritual level,* modern life is characterized by lack of idealism and reduced ability to find meaning and direction in life. Children are exposed to unmanageable and unassimilated helplessness, doubt, indifference, haste, lack of communication, social and political apathy, resignation, and depression on the part of the adults around them.

On all three levels, many necessary learning processes are eliminated, and children are prevented from acquiring abilities central to a healthy sense of identity.

Conversely, the *immunocompetence is enhanced* if children enjoy learning from the very beginning. Joy in learning, the willingness to see old, familiar things from ever new perspectives, and the ability to process negative experiences in positive ways are much easier for children to achieve if these attitudes are modeled at home and practiced in kindergarten and at school.

An obvious objection to this line of thinking is that allergic illnesses such as asthma (or neurodermatitis, which appears in infancy) are primarily hereditary; that is, they predate any upbringing and education that might prevent them.

In response, we must point out that even inherited allergic sensitivities have developed over time and continue to develop. Individuals today come from a background of three or four generations that have experienced and suffered from the spread of a materialistic worldview that encompasses fear of living and dying, doubt in the very meaning of existence, and horror in the face of increasing mass misery. All of these factors weaken an individual's self-acceptance and sense of identity and foster allergic illnesses that are on the increase worldwide. The etheric body, as the vehicle of heredity along with thought processes and life processes, experiences this lack of coherent identity, imprints it on an individual's genetic makeup, and passes it on to the next generation in the form of allergic predisposition. Our efforts to cultivate a lifestyle that would prevent this predisposition from manifesting can begin with rethinking and overcoming materialistic attitudes and searching for a spiritual identity that is the source of true humanity.

Practical measures and influences

- loving identification with the child,
- promoting the child's sense of identification — for example, through a limited number of toys that permit many different experiences,
- supporting his attentiveness by cultivating sensory impressions (see Section 13.8)
- creating a sense of security and trust through a regular, rhythmical daily routine and by cultivating religious values,
- setting clear limits. On the bodily level, an allergic child cannot

distinguish between self and non-self in the way that a normal child does. Learning to make this distinction on the soul level works back on bodily functions. Either excessive permissiveness or excessive discipline ignore the child's need for healthy limits on the soul level.

- decisiveness on the part of adults, accompanied by loving willingness to adapt to and take direction from life's concrete situations, is especially helpful in supporting an allergic child.
- healthy, simple food.

7. The "Childhood Illnesses" and Other Diseases

Almost all parents face their first child's first illness with uncertainty and anxiety. Suddenly, the child is different, changed — sensitive, irritable, cranky, or unusually serious and quiet — and hot with fever.

Our level of trust in a child's own healing forces depends on what we experience in dealing with his first few infections. We all know that we cannot expect childhood to be free of tests such as infections, spiking fevers, and childhood illnesses. Hence, we need to see childhood illnesses not only as problems but also as factors contributing to the development of a later, more stable state of health.

In contrast to the allergic illnesses we have just described, each infectious disease leads to recovery through a surprisingly regular, predictable series of interactions between "offensive" and "defensive" processes. Because of this predictability, these infections are also called "self-limiting" diseases. Their main visible symptoms — fever, rashes, swollen lymph nodes, or vomiting — are usually signs of the body's struggle to overcome the infection. They are part and parcel of the body's response to the illness and pave the way for overcoming it — that is, for achieving a new state of equilibrium on a higher level of immunity. This difference between infectious and allergic illnesses may explain why the latter sometimes improve after young patients undergo classic children's illnesses and why asthma is less prevalent in parts of the world where small children experience many infections.

Many of today's adults still owe the strength and flexibility of their immune systems to the fact that as children, they were allowed to learn to cope with germs; that is, they survived symptoms of acute illness without being given fever suppressants, antibiotics, or vaccines. It remains to be seen how future generations of adults will fare, since their childhood has not been shaped by the same degree of experience with illness. Is there some connection between the suppression of infections and worldwide epidemic increases in weakness and functional disorders of the immune system, as expressed in many different allergies due to hypersensitivity of the surface organs (skin, lungs, intestines)? Today, too, we can no longer speak convincingly of "childhood illnesses," because both the possibility of immunization and the increasing isolation of people in the industrialized world has produced a temporal shift in infectious illnesses once considered typical of childhood. The incidence of measles and chicken pox, for example, is now greatest in adolescents and adults.

The following sections are intended to give a concrete overview of the symptoms, risks, and complications of the major infectious diseases and to alleviate unfounded anxieties about them. Which illnesses a child must come to grips with and how he or she does so are not matters of coincidence but part of the child's individual destiny. Hence we will attempt to describe the acute symptoms of childhood illnesses in a way that enables parents to support their sick children with as much confidence as possible.* For the same reason, we have added a chapter on the purpose and meaning of these symptoms (see Chapter 9).

Chapter 10 on preventing illness provides the basic information needed for making individualized, well-considered choices with regard to available immunizations (ssummarized in Section 10.19).

7.1 Measles

Symptoms: Measles begins with a runny nose, cough, reddened eyes, and moderate fever, between ten and thirteen days after exposure. From day 12 to day 14, white dots and "spider webs" (so-called Koplik's spots) appear on the mucous membranes lining the cheeks. A second period of fever begins on day 14, accompanied by the emergence of fine spots that appear first behind the ears and quickly spread over the head, torso, and limbs, merging into a red rash covering large areas (see Figures 9 and 10). The patient feels very ill.

Diarrhea is not uncommon. With the exception of the cough, which persists longer, symptoms subside within five days after the rash appears.

Incubation period (the interval between exposure and the first signs of illness): 10 to 12 days.

Communicability: Very high from day 9 after exposure until the fourth day after the rash appears. The virus is spread by airborne droplets that are propelled many metres through coughing and sneezing.

Immunity: Lifelong after a case of measles. An infant whose mother has had measles is fully protected by her antibodies for four months and par-

---

* Practices vary in some countries. For New Zealand a useful webpage is http://www.imac.auckland.ac.nz

tially protected for several more. If the mother has only been vaccinated, passive immunity is unreliable.

Concomitant illnesses and complications: Otitis media (inflammation of the middle ear), sinusitis, and pneumonia are not uncommon. Encephalitis with dangerous complications is a rare after-effect (see below).

Treatment: Bed rest; quiet, darkened room, primarily liquid diet for fever.

The combined symptoms of measles have considerable impact. A child with measles feels exhausted and avoids light, peering out from under the covers with reddened eyes that are reduced to barely visible slits in his bloated, red-speckled face. His attempts to speak may produce only a deep, mucus-y attack of coughing. Four days earlier, the illness began as a seemingly harmless cold with a slight fever. Yesterday at the doctor's office, he seemed better already, but the doctor looked in his mouth and discovered small white spots and lines on the mucous membranes of the cheeks — the first sign of measles. That afternoon, the boy's limbs began to feel cold; by evening he developed a high fever, and single spots of up to one centimetre in diameter began to appear, first behind his ears and on his head and then rapidly merging and spreading downward until his arms and legs were also covered.

Daily contact with your physician is important during this phase, when the child feels very ill. Several times a day, note his pulse rate and respiratory rate, check for flaring nostrils, and record his temperature. Significant improvement in symptoms should be evident around the third day after the beginning of the rash. The cough will persist for a week or longer.

Earache (see Figure 4) indicates the beginning of a middle-ear infection; flaring nostrils are signs of pneumonia. A series of seizures or a further period of rising fever accompanied by convulsions indicates encephalitis. An isolated febrile seizure early in the illness, however, is usually harmless.

During the acute phase, have your physician examine the child at home if at all possible. If you cannot avoid moving him — for example, if you have to take him to the hospital — make sure he remains lying down at all times.

A diagnosis of measles should always be confirmed by a doctor. We do not recommend antipyretics (fever suppressants), but see Section 2.2 for recommendations for treating fever.

During the entire illness, it is important to insure that your child gets the rest so urgently needed. Young patients should not have to look into the light or at brightly patterned wallpaper. *Above all, they should not be constantly exposed to radio or television in the background.*

It is important to know that a child's immune forces may be depleted for several weeks after a case of measles, depending on the severity of the illness. Allow for adequate recovery time, preferably in consultation with your physician.

Children who have been in contact

with the patient during the contagious period (see above) have already been infected, so there is no point in avoiding further contact. *To avoid inadvertent exposure of other children, however, call ahead before taking a child who may have measles to the doctor.* On the other hand, some parents of unvaccinated toddlers would be glad to have their children come down with measles, since the disease is less severe at that age than in older, school-age children, while successfully vaccinated children have the chance to get a booster without further vaccination. See the section on immunization for information on vaccination and adult measles (see Section 10.13).

In developed nations, *complications* are seldom a problem if children with measles are given extra rest and careful treatment, although caution is advised and experience in dealing with the illness is helpful. Severe pneumonia during measles is a rare but possible complication that can be fatal even in developed countries. In the tropics and in countries that are less developed with regard to hygiene, standard of living, and health care, the danger of measles is incomparably greater. In these countries, take local experience into account when deciding on prevention and treatment. One empirical report from Africa, however, seems significant: mortality from measles was greatly reduced during one epidemic simply because no fever suppressants were administered.[6]

Vaccination recommendations set the incidence of encephalitis due to measles at 1:1000 to 1:2000 — clearly too high. Empirical results from practising physicians suggest an incidence of approximately 1 in every 10,000 cases of measles, and one expert calculates that only 1 in every 15,000 toddlers with measles gets encephalitis. The possibility cannot be ruled out, however, that routine use of fever suppressants is contributing to the increasing frequency of encephalitis as a complication of viral infections (see Section 2.4, and Endnote 28). According to current knowledge, measles encephalitis is fatal in approximately one-sixth of pediatric cases, and one-fourth are left with permanent and sometimes serious neurological damage. In 1960 the prognosis was generally still considered good.[7] Children who have gained experience in dealing with infectious illness by being allowed to ride out previous infections without suppressive medication generally also make it through measles better than children who have not. If encephalitis develops nonetheless, a combination of the continuous supportive presence of a parent in the hospital, drug therapy for cerebral oedema, and complementary medical treatment may positively influence the course of the illness.[8]

7.2 German measles (rubella)

Symptoms: Rash of fine red spots, palpably enlarged lymph nodes on both sides of the neck, fever.

Incubation period: Rash appears two to three weeks after exposure.

Communicability: Less communicable than measles, for example. Transmission occurs through viruses in airborne droplets. Immunity frequently develops as a result of "silent" infections with no visible signs of illness. The disease is said to be contagious from one week before to ten days after the appearance of the rash, but this contagious period is questioned.

Immunity: Lifelong, after a clear case of the illness.

Complications: In childhood, none. Rheumatic diseases may develop after German measles in adolescents and adults. Birth defects or stillbirths are known to occur when women contract German measles during the first four months of pregnancy. (Approximately 25–35%, or at most 50%, of the affected fetuses are harmed by the illness, although all are infected.) For vaccination possibilities, see Section 10.11.

Treatment: Bed rest as long as fever persists.

This illness, harmless in itself to the child, causes a rash that appears two to three weeks after infection. On first glance, the rash resembles measles, but the spots are more evenly distributed and are concentrated on the torso; they rarely merge. The fever that accompanies the rash may be high but is unproblematic. Swollen lymph nodes in the throat, neck, or back of the head are typical.

7.3 Scarlet fever (scarlatina)

Symptoms: Rapidly rising fever, possibly with chills, headache, and vomiting that does not repeat. The dense, reddish rash of very fine spots looks like red goose bumps, appears primarily in the groin and armpits (see Figure 12), and may be visible only briefly. The cheeks are red but a triangle around the mouth remains pale.

Pain on swallowing, varying degrees of redness and swelling of the back of the palate, uvula, and tonsils. A white coating develops on the tongue but comes off by day 3, revealing a bright red, raspberry-like surface (see Figure 13). Swollen lymph nodes in the throat.

Fever recedes immediately with

antibiotic treatment but only between days 4 and 7 without it. Occasionally, a second phase of the illness develops at the end of the second week, with another rise in fever and more pronounced swelling of the lymph nodes. The rash flakes off beginning in the second week and large areas of skin on the palms and soles may peel during the third week.

Incubation period: two to five (maximum seven) days.

Communicability: varies widely. Only approximately 10% of all individuals contract scarlatina one or more times during their life. Infants are not susceptible; most susceptible are children between the ages of three and eight years.

Transmission: Through secretions, direct contact, or contact with contaminated objects or air, but usually only through close contact (sharing a room or dwelling). The pathogens are various haemolytic strains of *Streptococcus pyogenes* (B-hemolytic group A). Patients are contagious as long as they have even the slightest symptoms.

Immunity: Recurrences are possible within a few months, frequent after a year, and are most likely after antibiotic treatment.

Concomitant illnesses and complications: Otitis media (especially during the second stage), impetigo, fissures at the corners of the mouth, or inflammation of the nasal mucosa or entrance to the nose. *Glomerulonephritis* (kidney inflammation) is an infrequent complication that may develop one to three weeks after scar-

let fever or strep throat (see Section 1.5) Its symptoms include scanty, bloody urine; pallor, edema, and in some cases an increase in blood pressure. This complication, which cannot be prevented by antibiotic treatment, is now rare in the developed world. Recovery is usually complete. *Rheumatic fever* has also become a very rare complication, but it is greatly feared because it frequently involves inflammation of the heart and subsequent heart defects. It is much more frequent in less affluent circumstances, especially in Third World countries. Most cases of rheumatic fever today, however, are triggered by undiagnosed cases of strep throat rather than by scarlet fever.

Treatment and quarantine

Because of the possibility of complications, scarlet fever should always be treated by a doctor.

Antibiotic treatment begun on the third or fourth day of the illness is reputed to reduce the possibility of recurrence without increasing complications. The patient should not attend public events until they have been treated for at least 48 hours and are symptom-free. Family members, even when symptom-free, should take a doctor's advice on attending public events.

Treatment without antibiotics is acceptable only when the parents and the doctor are in agreement. Depending on the course of the illness, scarlet fever is treated with mandatory bed rest and complementary medications. Children not treated with antibiotics should not return to school or other public activities until they are symptom-free and at least three weeks have elapsed since the beginning of the illness. It makes sense to keep siblings who have been exposed away from the sick child; wait a few days to see whether they develop symptoms.

In the past forty years, manifestations of scarlatina have become much milder, often almost unrecognisable.

A high fever that persists past day 4 of the illness is sometimes due to so-called Kawasaki disease, which is unrelated to scarlet fever and must be treated differently.

Although thorough examination by a doctor reveals no particular cause, children may still look pale and seem weak for a number of weeks after even mild cases of scarlet fever because the disease is accompanied by strong breakdown processes that may affect or even damage organs. For this reason, we recommend that children who have had scarlet fever (even if treated with antibiotics) be allowed a long convalescent period (at least three weeks before resuming their normal activities). They should be examined again by a physician if old symptoms persist or new ones (such as earaches) develop. A urine analysis should be performed and the patients should be checked for heart damage at a final examination after three weeks.

In our pediatric practices, we meet many parents who want to avoid antibiotic treatment, especially when their children have already received penicillin several times for scarlatina.

In our experience, this is usually possible if good parent-physician cooperation can be maintained. Treatment that avoids antibiotics is our first choice, although we leave the decision up to the parents as long as the family situation allows the parents to respond adequately to their child's illness. Avoiding antibiotics is not a safe option in situations where many people are living together (in group homes or refugee camps) or in underdeveloped countries.

As a rule, family members are infected within a week, although whether or not they actually develop scarlet fever is another question. If a family member needs to avoid contagion, it is best for him or her to stay with relatives or friends for the duration. Isolating the patient and preventive measures such as hand washing and wearing protective clothing in the sickroom may not be effective in preventing the spread of the disease to other family members, although they are worth trying. Vigorous gargling with Bolus Eucalypti comp. or Olbas oil is recommended for people exposed to scarlet fever, especially adults who could infect other children through their work. Adults in this situation should be treated by a physician if they develop a sore throat. Prophylactic penicillin treatment for the entire family often does not prevent the rapid return of scarlet fever.

We have known many parents who report positive changes in their children after successful recovery from scarlet fever: a characteristic facial feature becomes more prominent, or a new ability, new interests, or a more stable state of health may develop. For example, a five-year-old girl's drawings of her house suddenly acquired greater detail, and she felt "all grown up" and stopped wetting her bed. A nine-year-old was amazed to discover after her second bout with scarlet fever that "the whole world looks like it is just been washed." All of a sudden, she perceived colors with much greater intensity than before. Such observations are easy to overlook, of course, but attentive parents who cultivate a positive attitude toward children's illnesses will be pleased with these little discoveries.

7.4 Roseola (three-day fever, exanthema subitum)

Symptoms: Rapidly rising fever, not infrequently accompanied by febrile seizures. Three days of high fever (up to 40°C/104°F) that does not fluctuate greatly, after which a rash of fine red spots develops as the fever rapidly falls.

Incubation period: one to two weeks.

Susceptibility: Slight, but greatest from the seventh month of life to the end of the second year.

Transmission: by airborne droplets containing herpes type-6 viruses (HHV-6). The path of contagion is almost always unknown.

Complications: generally none.

Unlike the childhood diseases described above, "three-day fever" is characterized by a rash that develops only at the end of the illness. Because the fever is high and its onset sudden, febrile seizures may easily develop, but they are harmless in most cases. Chemical fever suppressants are effective only for a few hours at a time and are not recommended because they force the child to expend energy repeatedly to reestablish the targeted high temperature.

7.5 Other infections with red skin rashes

A rash of fine spots may also develop at the end of other influenza-like illnesses. This telephone call to the doctor is typical: "Two days ago, he had a fever and a runny nose. He was better yesterday, but today he has a rash but no fever." If, as is usually the case, there are no other symptoms to report, there is no need for this mother to bring her child in to be examined. The rash signals the end of the illness, so to speak. Germs in the herpes virus group are involved in many of these infections.

7

7.6 Diphtheria

Symptoms: The patient has a relatively low fever but feels moderately to severely ill. Pharyngitis and tonsillitis and/or rhinitis and laryngitis (see *Croup*, page 71). A dirty white, sweet-smelling coating on the tonsils may spread to the palate as the disease progresses but is often absent in cases today. Swelling of the lymph nodes in the throat.

Incubation period: Two to five days.

Susceptibility: In epidemics prior to the introduction of vaccines, 5 to 10% of the population.

Transmission: Bacteria are spread through airborne droplets or surface contamination. Healthy people, including individuals who have been vaccinated, can spread the disease.

Immunity: Recurrences are possible.

Complications: Heart and kidney failure due to bacterial toxaemia. Temporary paralysis of the soft palate. Diphtherial croup.

Treatment: Hospitalization is required. Penicillin is effective against the bacteria but not against the dangerous toxin that may already have been produced. In addition, we recommend Cinnabar comp. and Argentum met. prep. 30X.

In the first third of the nineteenth century, diphtheria was considered one of the most dangerous childhood diseases and mortality rates were high. For approximately fifty years, however, the disease has been very uncommon in affluent countries, and almost no physicians have any experience with it. In eastern Europe (especially the former Soviet republics), a diphtheria epidemic in 1987–90 affected mainly adults who, with few exceptions, had not been completely immunized. Infection rates in Germany did not rise during this time. Since 1995, the disease has been effectively controlled by rigorous vaccination programs. In the UK, the vaccine is administered as part of a triple vaccine (DPT) along with whooping cough and tetanus.

Diphtherial croup is much more life-threatening than viral croup.

Diphtheria is remarkable among serious contagious diseases for the extent to which a full-blown case suppresses the patient's endogenous forces. Although the patient does not develop a high fever, he looks pale and his pulse is rapid and weak, and his blood pressure tends to be low. The disease is characterized by internal toxaemia that affects the circulatory and nervous systems in particular.

7.7 Glandular fever (infectious mononucleosis, Epstein-Barr virus)

Symptoms: Fever and tonsillitis, usually with extensive white coatings that do not extend to the palate. Swelling of the lymph nodes. Occasional minor rash.

Incubation period: 10 to 14 (maximum 50) days.

Susceptibility/Transmission: Only through close bodily contact — hence the common name "kissing disease" — so even roommates may be unaffected. The illness is usually milder in toddlers and may even go unnoticed.

Communicability: The disease can still be transmitted through intimate contact for several months after initial symptoms appear.

Immunity is usually lasting except in individuals with weakened immune systems.

Swelling occurs not only in the lymph nodes but also in the spleen and liver. *Complications* are unusual in children. Acute symptoms may be preceded and followed by longer periods of fatigue. Individuals who have had glandular fever should avoid immunizations for the next four months until the immune system is fully functional again.

Treatment

No special treatment is required. Archangelica ointment may be used externally for easing the swelling of the lymph nodes.

7.8 Chicken pox (varicella)

Symptoms: Itching, scattered blisters appear in succession and form scabs. Fever is usually mild and brief. The illness lasts five to ten days.

Within a few days, irregularly distributed spots appear in succession, rapidly developing into fluid-filled blisters that form scabs before healing. Because spots at all stages of development are present at the same time, the rash is reminiscent of an astronomical chart with "stars" of different sizes (see Figures 14 and 15). The blisters also appear on the scalp and the palms of the hands, on the genitals, and in the mouth. In some cases, abdominal pain indicates that the intestinal mucous membranes are also affected. The pain may be acute and may be confused with appendicitis.

Bed rest is indicated only if the child has a fever. Treatment is usually limited to applying a soothing powder to the itching areas of skin. In the evening, a lukewarm bath containing chamomile tea or spruce-needle extract may help relieve itching. Do not use these products if the blisters become infected.

Infected blisters may leave small scars as they heal, but these usually disappear with time.

Incubation period: 11 to 21 days.

Susceptibility: very high. Casual exposure, through an open door or window is sufficient. Development of immunity through "silent" (asymptomatic) infection is unusual.

Transmission: Through viruses in airborne droplets. The contagious period begins one to two days before symptoms appear and ends when the last blisters have dried up.

Immunity: The virus may be reactivated and reappear later in life in the form of shingles. Infants are immune for the first several months of life if their mothers have had chicken pox.

Complications: Infrequent. Symptoms are more severe in individuals predisposed to neurodermatitis. The disease is dangerous in those with weakened immune systems and in infants whose mothers contract the disease around the time of their birth (see below).

As such, this disease is harmless, but it is dreaded in hospitals because it can be transmitted through air-conditioning systems and endangers patients with weakened immunity.

Recently, very rare but serious complications involving streptococcal infections that affect connective tissue, muscles, and bones have been reported after cases of chicken pox. For this reason, a case of chicken pox accompanied by high fever or symptoms of serious illness requires prompt hospitalization.

Some people who have had chicken pox are susceptible to shingles (herpes zoster) later in life during times of stress or immunological weakness. This condition is characterized by firm blisters that penetrate the skin and appear only in one specific area corresponding to a major nerve. Neuralgic pain may be severe, and the patient may have a high, persistent fever. Children who contract the virus from a grandmother, for instance, who has shingles, develop chicken pox rather than shingles.

7.9 Mouth ulcers (Herpes simplex stomatitis)

Symptoms: Pronounced bad breath, *many painful blisters and ulcers (aphthae)* in the mouth, often accompanied by high fever and swollen lymph nodes. Duration: seven to nine days. Children between the ages of ten months and three years are most susceptible.

Incubation period: two to six (maximum twelve) days

Susceptibility: to the acute form, slight. Silent infections often result in immunity, and milder cases with few aphthae are possible. Transmission occurs through bodily contact or airborne droplets.

Immunity: Only partial. Lifelong recurrences of cold sores (fever blisters) are possible, but may appear in some people only during a serious illness such as pneumonia.

Complications: In patients with neurodermatitis, the disease may be serious and large areas of skin are affected.

Aphthae are flat, grayish, painful craters (up to the size of lentils) that develop in the mucous membranes of the mouth (see Figure 16). In herpetic stomatitis, aphthae develop in large numbers and may also appear on the skin around the mouth. Children with herpetic stomatitis often refuse to eat, and it is difficult to persuade them to drink enough to prevent dehydration. Hospitalization is required in severe cases involving dehydration.

Home treatment: Diluted Weleda mouthwash, Cinnabar comp. (one salt-spoonful five times a day) or mouth balsam (Wala Mundbalsam gel) relieve symptoms somewhat in children old enough to tolerate rinsing their own mouths. In South Africa, Wala Echinacea comp. mouthspray is available. All orally administered medications must be diluted with water to reduce the alcohol concentration to less than 1%. Taking Apis/Belladonna cum Mercurio (five globules five times a day) assists treatment. Weight lost during herpetic stomatitis is rapidly regained.

Single aphthae (ulcers) that persist for a few days or weeks have nothing in common with herpetic stomatitis except the pain they cause. They are most likely to appear as a result of specific sensitivities to infrequently eaten foods such as Christmas cake or pudding.

7

7.10 Mumps (epidemic parotitis)

Symptoms: Fever (usually high) and painful swelling of the parotid glands (salivary glands located below each ear), which makes the ear lobes protrude (see Figure 17). Duration: up to one week.

Incubation period: two to three weeks.

Susceptibility: Silent infections often result in immunity. Infants are usually not susceptible.

Transmission: By airborne droplets. The contagious period probably extends from twenty-four hours before the appearance of symptoms to three days after. In some cases, however, viruses have been isolated from the saliva as early as a week before and as late as nine days after the beginning of symptoms.

Immunity: Most effectively acquired by having the illness; recurrences are rare.

Complications: Inflammation of the testes is possible in adolescent and adult males with mumps. Hearing impairment, although infrequent and usually one-sided, is generally permanent. *Mumps meningitis (or meningo-* *encephalitis),* a common condition without consequences and not to be confused with encephalitis, is a very rare complication (see Section 1.1).

Symptoms and their severity vary considerably, but hamster-like swelling of the cheeks and around the ears is typical (see Figure 17). Most patients have a high fever and feel very ill. In some children, the pancreas is involved and vomiting and colic-like abdominal pain may occur. In others, one or both cheeks may swell briefly, with recurrent swelling with or without fever a few days later. Still others develop severe, persistent headaches and do not want to sit up in bed; in most such cases the meninges are affected and these symptoms are due to the above-mentioned *mumps meningitis.* This condition may go unrecognized; fortunately, it is almost always harmless in children. It is often possible to avoid hospitalization, and lumbar puncture is almost never necessary in mumps meningitis. Antibiotic treatment is useless, since mumps is a viral infection. For help in recognizing this complication, see also the chapter on headaches (Section 1.1).

Usually one-sided, very painful testicular inflammation, which often develops in post-pubescent and adult males with mumps, may reduce the viability of the semen, although no one becomes sterile as a result of mumps, not even if both sides are affected. Comparable inflammation of the ovaries is possible in females but is generally harmless.

Infrequently, mumps causes hearing loss (the incidence is said to be one in every ten to fifteen thousand cases).

The incidence of true encephalitis is even less. Data on the frequency of such complications needs to be evaluated critically, since they are influenced by geographical, cultural, and individual constitutional factors and may also reflect epidemics or inadequate treatment. (For information on vaccination, see Section 10.12.) Complications may appear as late as two weeks after the beginning of the illness.

Home treatment: Apply archangelica ointment or warm compresses made with sunflower or olive oil to the cheeks (not the skull). For abdominal pain, apply warm, moist compresses made with chamomile or yarrow tea. The patient's diet should be fat-free. Do not attempt to reduce the fever, even if it is high, except on the advice of your physician. As noted earlier, fever may lessen the possibility of complications by reducing viral activity.

Parents report again and again that their children develop new independence after having mumps.

7.11 Whooping cough (pertussis)

Symptoms: Runny nose, cough, and elevated temperature for a period of one to two weeks, followed by increasing attacks of coughing, especially at night. The attacks, which occur more or less at one hour intervals, last approximately half a minute and often end in vomiting. Total duration of the illness is six to ten weeks.

Incubation period: Approximately seven to fourteen days.

Susceptibility: Highest in the youngest children; *infants are not protected by maternal antibodies!* Symptoms are less characteristic in adults, and the illness may go undiagnosed.

Transmission: In airborne droplets for a distance of about two metres. Bacteria are present in exhaled air even when the patient is not coughing. The contagious period begins seven to ten days after infection and lasts until four weeks after the beginning of the paroxysmal stage.

Immunity: Generally good in those who have had the disease, but apparent recurrences are possible because other germs mimic the symptoms of whooping cough.

Complications: Pneumonia. In infants in the first three months of life, respiratory failure, convulsions, and one particular type of encephalitis are possible. Today, some cases of sudden infant death (SIDS) are being linked to undiagnosed pertussis infections (see Section 11.2).

If a physician's receptionist hears a barking, spasmodic cough in the waiting room, the mother of the child in question will be astonished at how quickly they are escorted into an isolation room (see Section 10.9).

The *typical coughing attacks of pertussis* most frequently occur at night, triggered by the gradual accumulation of tough, glassy phlegm in the bronchi, which is then removed through strong, loud, harsh, staccato coughing. The child has no time to catch his breath between coughs, and repeated coughing drives all the air out of his lungs. His tongue is bent tube-like around the stream of air; his face swells and turns somewhat blue. After a few seconds (which always seem much too long to concerned onlookers), a slow, crowing intake of breath occurs between cramped vocal cords. The whole coughing sequence repeats once or twice more, after which the child vomits up the phlegm (and possibly also his last meal.) The child is exhausted and quickly falls asleep, but before he does you can give him some kind of liquefied food. It will be at least half an hour before the next paroxysm of coughing

occurs, and by that time the liquid will have been absorbed by the intestines.

When your child has an attack of coughing, do not clap him on the back, pull him out of bed, or show other signs of excitement. This does nothing to shorten the attack and will only make the situation worse for an already upset child. To help him inhale, support his forehead lightly and accompany the coughing with soothing words, such as "Go ahead, cough it all up. Good. Now take a breath and cough again," to let him know that everything is as it should be and there is no need to panic. Your calm presence is often the only help he needs. Little children who lie on their stomachs may raise themselves up on their arms until the coughing fit is over and then lie down again. Ideally, one parent should sleep on an extra bed in the child's room, so that someone is available to clean up vomit if needed and replace the protective covering on the child's bed.

Fever is not typical of the paroxysmal stage of pertussis, so consult your physician if your child develops a fever.

Prevention: In babies less than three months old, whooping cough is dangerous because young infants have difficulty coughing effectively. Brain complications are not infrequent.

All parents-to-be must know how to prevent infection in their newborn or young infant: Adults or children who are coughing or fighting infections should avoid the infant's room; if the parents themselves are affected, they should wear masks. Whooping cough in a kindergarten or neighbourhood is a risk to infant siblings of older children who have not had the disease, and their mothers should be alerted if a case occurs. Your doctor can take necessary measures if you suspect your infant has been infected. Administering a narrow-spectrum antibiotic can prevent the infection from developing in newly infected infants.

If your young infant is infected: Susceptibility to pertussis is almost 100% in newborns, even among breastfed babies. If you suspect that your infant has been exposed, monitor her constantly and consult your physician. The baby should be hospitalized as soon as symptoms appear, and the prognosis is better if one parent is admitted along with the child.

Infants between the ages of three and six months still become seriously ill with pertussis, but in most cases they are able to cough more effectively. Depending on the circumstances and the experience of parents and physician, antibiotic prophylaxis may still be advisable. In children older than one year, complications are rare except in situations of neglect, and antibiotic prophylaxis is no longer needed. We have often been able to dispense with it in otherwise healthy children over the age of three months.

Whooping cough is significantly more dangerous in children who have rickets or whose diet is low in calcium. For this reason, we always recommend examination by a physician when the paroxysmal stage of whooping cough becomes evident in a child less than one year old.

Paroxysmal coughing can recur months later, whenever the child contracts a new infection, even though she is no longer contagious. It has long been known that whooping cough rarely leads to asthma or allergies and has nothing to do with recent increases in these diseases.

Parents often note that children who were formerly picky eaters develop very robust appetites after having had whooping cough.

Medical treatment: Not only in infancy but also later, pertussis is more dangerous if chemical sedatives and cough suppressants are administered because these drugs reduce the frequency and intensity of coughing. As a result, phlegm is more likely to remain in the lungs, where it can contribute to the development of pneumonia and oxygen deficiency in the brain. In view of this situation, homeopathic or anthroposophical treatment seems the more rational and less dangerous approach.

It is sometimes possible to reduce the severity of nightly coughing attacks by giving the child a good warm bath in the evening, followed by brief application of a damp, cool compress to the throat or chest. (The compress should not cover the spinal cord.)

Antibiotic treatment is indicated only to prevent infection in an infant or in weakened children who also have pneumonia. Antibiotics lessen the duration and severity of symptoms only when administered in the early stages of the disease, and they may prevent the development of effective immunity.

7.12 Infectious hepatitis, type A

Of the various types of liver infection, hepatitis A is the most common and least dangerous in children. Experts emphasize that it never causes permanent damage (cirrhosis). In the early stages of the illness, patients are tired and have no appetite; nausea or vomiting, abdominal pain, diarrhea, and fever may also be present. When jaundice appears (as it does in only about one-third of patients), these symptoms usually improve, but the patient's urine becomes abnormally dark and her stools lose color. Transmission generally occurs through the stools and can be significantly reduced by good bathroom hygiene. Fifteen to fifty days elapse between the time of infection and the appearance of symptoms, but the virus begins to be eliminated in the stools (that is, the patient is contagious) a week or two earlier. In any case of jaundice, a physician should determine the cause. (For problems with prophylactic treatment, see Section 10.15.) Any case of viral hepatitis must be reported to your local health authorities.

Treatment consists of bed rest, warm yarrow tea compresses applied to the liver area (see page 430), and an easily digestible diet. In addition, we recommend Fragaria/vitis comp. (Hepatadoron) tablets (made from strawberry and grape leaves) to strengthen the liver (an organ that is overburdened by modern lifestyles) as well as Taraxacum planta tota Rh 3X drops or globules and Taraxacum Stanno cultum Rh 3X.

7.13 Infectious hepatitis, type B

There is little difference in the acute symptoms of hepatitis B and hepatitis A, but the incubation period of hepatitis B is longer — one and a half to six months. It is estimated that only one-quarter to one-third of those infected develop visible symptoms. The younger the patient, the less apparent the illness but the greater the chance of it becoming chronic. The relationship between this virus species and humans is unique in that some of those infected never manage to overcome the virus; it persists in their blood and they may remain able to infect others for a long time. Infections due to blood transfusions — which are no longer a significant means of transmission — allowed this type of liver infection to be distinguished from others. At present, sexual contact is the most frequent source of infection, and the incidence of the disease is highest in big cities where promiscuity and drug addiction are prevalent. Very infrequently, the disease is transmitted between family members — for example, when children are adopted from foreign countries with epidemic rates of hepatitis B. The risk of infection in kindergarten is very low. Carriers can shelter the virus for years with no signs of illness before they either overcome it or develop a chronic liver infection that leads to cirrhosis.

Of the other forms of liver infections, hepatitis C is the most common, constituting 10-15% of reported cases. 60-80% of hepatitis C cases are chronic.

7.14 Lyme disease (borreliosis)

The bacterial pathogens involved in Lyme disease *(Borrelia burgdorferi)* are transmitted by tick bites. Sometimes a red rash develops around a bite (the bite itself often goes unnoticed), spreading outward over several weeks while the center turns pale, forming a red ring. The rash may be accompanied by flu-like symptoms, which persist for several weeks. People used to simply wait out the symptoms, but now we know that untreated infections can become chronic, causing serious consequences (arthritis, neuritis, encephalitis, or chronically inflamed and atrophied patches of skin) weeks, months, or even years after the acute symptoms subside. (Tick-borne encephalitis, see Section 10.18).

Vaccines have recently been developed and may be available in some countries, and the germs respond to antibiotic treatment. Since the severity of later symptoms is unpredictable, infected individuals who develop the characteristic rash are generally treated with antibiotics as a precaution. In the 25% who do not develop the rash, later symptoms can be diagnosed as complications of Lyme disease only if Borrelia antibodies are present in their blood. For people who are frequently bitten by ticks, taking antibiotics after every bite is not a practical solution.

8. The Meaning and Purpose of Illness

8.1 What is the Purpose of Childhood Illnesses?

During their children's visits to the doctor, parents sometimes ask questions that are part of a larger context and deserve lengthy answers. Among these are questions about the meaning or purpose of specific diseases. In this chapter, we will tackle this issue with regard to the classic childhood illnesses.

Meaning and development

The experience of pain and suffering can enrich human lives or point to new developmental possibilities. This is not true of animals. Because the behavior of mature animals is almost perfectly adapted to their circumstances, undergoing illness or suffering pain cannot make a lion more perfectly lion-like or a dog more dog-like. In contrast, the pain and suffering encountered on life's journey can alert human beings to new opportunities for development, and we can continue to become "more human" as long as we live.

Therefore, although it has been the custom since ancient times to put suffering animals out of their misery if we are unable to help them quickly, the growing acceptance of assisted suicide for humans on supposedly humanitarian grounds is much more questionable. The concept of euthanasia or "mercy killing" testifies to a profound misunderstanding of the spiritual nature of the human being and the role of pain and suffering in human biographies (see also Section 11.1). Although the physician's task is to do everything possible to relieve suffering and bring about healing, enduring painful experiences is an essential part of human existence.

Because different illnesses affect different parts and processes of the human body and produce different experiences for the individual soul-spiritual being occupying that body, it makes sense to reflect on the specific meaning and purpose of different types of illness.

Illness and the members of the human constitution

The human I is active in the element of warmth, while our emotions work in the element of air within the human body. Similarly, vegetative life processes take place in the fluid element, and the individually configured physical body manifests in the solid element. The laws governing solids, liquids, and gases — that is, the states of matter — and heat, which pervades them all, offer the human being differentiated possibilities of expression. Rudolf Steiner called these four different complexes of laws, which interact in a unique way in each person, the four members of the human constitution. The following overview summarizes what he said about them:

- The complex of laws governing **solid structures — "physical body"** — mediates the emergence of form and structure.
- The complex of laws governing **functions active in fluids — "life body"** or **"ether body"** — mediates the appearance of life processes and temporal connections and sequences.
- The complex of laws governing **functions active in air — "soul body"** or **"astral body"** — mediates the expression of emotions, mobility, and consciousness.
- The complex of laws governing **functions active in warmth — "I-organization"** — mediates the development of intentionality as the vehicle of the individual human spirit.

The significance of these members for the life of the human soul and spirit is addressed in other parts of this book. In this chapter, we will emphasize the bodily aspects of their influence because in childhood a soul-spiritual being focuses on "incarnating" into the body and learning to feel at home there. The more suitable the body (or the more suitable it becomes as the child develops), the easier this process is. How many people today feel like strangers to themselves because they are not totally comfortable in their bodies or cannot express themselves through them? The role of medicine and education is to create conditions that permit the healthiest possible incarnation process. The so-called childhood illnesses play an important part in working through and individualizing specific parts of the body.

Illnesses with *high fevers* are primarily an indication that the I and its warmth activity are intervening in vegetative functions, influencing metabolic processes more strongly than usual and triggering fever-induced immune processes. A child with *whooping cough,* on the other hand, takes possession of his body's respiratory organs and functions in a new way. Diseases that involve significant *swelling of lymph nodes or glands,* allow children to get a new grip on their vegetative processes. The water-filled blisters of *chicken pox* contain endogenous matter that needs to be eliminated from the domain of life. These blisters and the subsequent development of small scars subtly alter the child's physical form. The thrust of the symptoms of childhood diseases may be directed either outward (as in skin symptoms) or inward (in the diseases involving the blood or individual organs). This difference is most evident in the contrast between smallpox (now eradicated) and diphtheria.

The body's response to each illness is a one-sided or unbalanced activity summoned up by the child's I in an effort to alter the interaction among the members of his or her constitution. If we attribute symptoms exclusively to germs and recovery to the disappearance of pathogens, the most important questions remain unanswered. What is the relationship between a particular illness and the being of this patient? Why does the illness affect someone else differently or not at all? What is the relationship between the pathogen and the essential nature of the illness? The medical histories of different individuals are never exactly the same. One had a bad case of measles but a mild case of scarlet fever, the other the opposite. One person never contracted whooping cough, another never had mumps. Individual differences of this sort reveal something about the being of the person in question, something we ordinarily fail to consider. But how do we develop susceptibility to a particular illness? Because Rudolf Steiner's spiritual scientific research, which provides some insight into this question, also encompassed life after death and the law of reincarnation, we will also briefly discuss their relationship to illness.

Life after death

As Rudolf Steiner describes the process, the physical body is laid aside at death, and during the next three days and nights (when the wake is held in some parts of the world) the life body gradually also detaches from the other members of the deceased person's constitution. Since the life body is thought-like in character (see also page 270) and encompasses the entire scope of the person's development from conception to last breath, its release is experienced as a grandiose tableau of memories that spans the entire earthly life that has just ended. All the details of the person's life are revealed again. After three days and nights, the ether body is absorbed into the general thought-substance of the universe, just as the substances in the corpse are absorbed into the totality of the material world. All superficial or non-binding aspects of the overview disappear; what remains is like an extract of everything the person was truly able to unite with his or her being during life.

The next step is the release of the soul body. This process takes longer, approximately one-third as long as the person's elapsed life (that is, as long as the total amount of time that he or she spent sleeping). In literature and in many religious texts, this period of life after death is described as "purgatory" or purification. Here we relive all of our past life's soul experiences, but not as we underwent them during life. Instead, we experience what *others* went through because of us. (We have similar experiences unconsciously every night as we sleep.) For example, instead of re-experiencing his own satisfaction and "righteous" indignation, a person who publicly exposed someone else's wrongdoing now experiences all the details of what the other person felt during this event. Our experiences during the period of purification not only objectify our past soul experiences but also serve as a starting point for shaping our destiny in the next earthly life. If in our past life we wronged someone else as a result of not knowing all the facts of the matter, we resolve to balance out this action. As our next life's destiny develops, it incorporates the possibility of doing good when we meet that person again.

This aspect of how destiny develops also has consequences for our future predisposition to specific illnesses. For example, a person who did not develop loving relationships during her last life feels this as a deficit after death. The experience of how her behavior affected others and caused them pain is imprinted deeply on her being. Although she had certain reasons for her reticence during earthly life, she now sees it in a different, objective light and realizes the limitations and inadequacy of her self-centered earthly perspective. (Religious traditions refer to this process as "judgment" or seeing past events from the right perspective.) On her journey between death and rebirth, the new understanding that imprints itself on her being may predispose her to a specific illness.

Health and the ability to love

We have said that being healthy means being able to confront the world's phenomena freely and with interest. Two aberrations are possible here — on the one hand, withdrawing from the world in order to brood and believing that the truth that will change the world can be found only within ourselves; on the other hand, succumbing completely to the allure of daily life, increasingly renouncing self-assertion, and being driven by events like a leaf in the wind. Inner integrity in the first instance and self-sacrifice in the second — both positive attributes unless taken to extremes — become unbalanced. Being healthy means being able to make flexible use of our options as the situation demands, a quality that Schiller called "play." We can speak of illness only when people lose self-control or are so fixed within themselves that they can no longer alter their situation by themselves. Their relationship to the world is so seriously disturbed that they find themselves unable to take the world seriously enough (in the first case) or themselves seriously enough (in the second case). Both the self-sacrificer and the egotistical loner lose the ability to love. This ability, however, is the inner foundation of human health. On the one hand, it means being able to take part in the world's affairs with interest, allowing the people and events in our surroundings to become alive in our own souls; on the other, it means holding back and allowing others to be free.

In Christianity, love as the goal of human development is called a new commandment (John 13:34). The many possibilities of illness that we are exposed to show us how difficult it is to obey this commandment and how far we still have to go to reach this goal. The human soul in search of its own humanity oscillates unceasingly between the dangers of egocentricity and self-sacrifice. When we first experience this fateful fact, we may question to what extent we can be held responsible for our strayings from the path: "Aren't we forced to be what we are and to act as we do?" "We can't escape from our own skin, can we?" At this point, the issue of human freedom moves into the foreground. There are many advantages to blaming our inability and problems on circumstances, constitutional weakness, or other people — that is, on anyone and anything except ourselves.

Freedom and necessity in destiny

Freedom to do something or to refrain from doing it is closely linked to our ability to do it. Freedom applies when we are choosing between options, not when we are laboriously acquiring capabilities. We all feel "unfree" when we have to learn something. How much lack of freedom, for instance, is involved in preparing for an exam? Did anyone ever learn to do arithmetic without obeying mathematical laws?

Once we have passed the exam or learned arithmetic, however, our freedom increases in that our ability to act has been expanded. The same is true with any necessity of destiny. It simply defines the circumstances necessary for acquiring a specific ability. Once that ability has been acquired, however, we achieve a new level of freedom that makes us more mature and more complete. Hence individual freedom presupposes "individual necessities," that is, a personal destiny made up of specific conditions. Recognizing this fact is a central concern of Christianity, the essence of which can be summed up as the merging of the two ideals of *freedom* (as the result of learning processes) and *love* (as the result of interest in and receptivity to others) as if in a single focal point. From this perspective, every illness also represents a necessity, a condition under which we can acquire an ability that we will later be able to use freely. Similarly, illness can be seen as a "private lesson" from the lord and companion of our destiny, that is, God Himself. The first rule of treating illness, therefore, is to do everything possible so that the patient can reap the benefits of the experience and (if at all possible) be led toward healing. After all, the only possible meaning and purpose of illness is to become healthy again — healthy in body, soul, and spirit, with new consciousness and enhanced capabilities. Our task is to support this process.

8.2 AIDS — A Challenge

AIDS, or acquired immune deficiency syndrome, was first recognized in the early 1980s. Even if HIV (human immune deficiency virus) is responsible for the infection, it is nonetheless true (in this instance as in infectious diseases in general) that pathogens are not the only factor in the development of the disease. Another important factor is prior damage to or weakening of the immune system, which makes the body susceptible to the pathogens. Especially at risk of AIDS, therefore, are individuals whose endogenous defenses have been weakened or — as is the case in newborn babies — have not yet developed adequately. An individual's response to the virus is always unique, and additional factors (called co-factors) must always be present before the disease finally manifests. To date, no single effective therapy or vaccine has been developed, but there are several medications that have positive effects on the course of the disease and concomitant illnesses that result from the underlying immuno-deficiency.

For more information on the emergence of the disease, its distribution, manifestations and treatment, see the *Bibliography* at the end of the book. With regard to treatment, see the recommendations for strengthening the immune system in various parts of this book. Especially recommended, however, is the use of the curative eurythmy exercises that have been empirically developed in many therapeutic sessions over the last decade (see Useful Organizations on page 453). Curative eurythmy, which can be begun in infancy, strengthens the child's constitution so that it confronts the disease more effectively.

Here we will emphasize a single aspect that is helpful for managing the illness, especially when dealing with children who contracted the disease at birth or hemophiliacs infected through transfusions. How can we understand and support such a destiny? How can we help as much as possible? Supporting AIDS children is a great challenge for parents and teachers. To accompany children on their life's journey if they have already been branded by death requires us to expand our consciousness beyond the threshold of death (see Section 11.3) To allow these children to grow up in an atmosphere of complete acceptance and understanding, we must also grasp the meaning and purpose of this particular illness.

The task of this illness and its purpose

The healthy human body is truly what Genesis calls an "image of God." The healthy human being — standing upright, moving freely, with all the body's possibilities available — is a sovereign being and reveals the comprehensive developmental options and abilities of the human body. Illness, however, always imposes limitations on this perfection. Just as we can say that the healthy body is the image of the future, god-like human being, so too each illness can be said to reflect a task that the body must perform as it struggles to approach the health of the divine image through its own efforts.

Healthy individuals may also notice how little their own efforts have achieved in the pursuit of this divine image. We may walk free and upright, but are we really free and upright? The true inner freedom of overcoming thousands of dependencies and true uprightness — that is, "righteousness" — are both tremendously difficult to achieve. Healthy individuals, however, are free to become conscious of their own imperfections and to set goals for their own development. It is up to them whether or not they choose to take steps in this direction. It is different for people who are ill. Their freedom is already limited; their illness assigns a clear task for them to work on (see also our discussions of freedom and necessity in destiny, page 133).

What task, what element in perfecting the image of God, does AIDS reflect? On the physical level, AIDS is characterized by all kinds of symptoms related to weakening of the immune system. Where endogenous defenses, self-protection, and the preservation of biological identity once prevailed, we now encounter progressive failure of these abilities to the point of losing one's biological identity and the ability to preserve it. As the disease pro-gresses, the body's structures break down as the result of infections, ulcerations, tumours, and disturbances in neurological functioning. It becomes less and less possible for a human personality to express itself appropriately in such a body, even if consciousness is fully preserved. The body becomes an image, as it were, of physical self-renunciation or "selflessness."

Is this illness an image of a task that confronts our time more than any other? Today, both individuals and societies are egocentric to an extent that is unprecedented in human evolution. Our politics and economics disregard natural habitats and the lifestyles and cultures of entire ethnic groups. This is the "big picture" aspect of a phenomenon — also evident on a smaller scale, right down into family relationships — namely, an almost overwhelming tendency to give free rein to our capacity for egocentricity, ambition and power-striving, and to invest ever more time and money in increasingly rarefied forms of consumption. Here, at the height of personal and societal egocentricity, there suddenly appears an illness that is the exact opposite in that it presents a physical image of openness and sacrifice of the human personality. This illness shows us what the whole world needs to learn if our culture is to take a decisive step forward. Those suffering from AIDS experience and express, on the bodily level, a task that belongs to all of us: to work toward overcoming egocentricity. From this perspective, AIDS patients are representatives of all of us. AIDS is a "representative" disease. All who suffer from it experience overcoming egocentricity — that is, the essence of selflessness — on the bodily level. On this level, they are forced to learn what our modern culture must learn of its own free will. For AIDS patients, dying of this illness means approaching the ideal of selflessness, the most important ideal for modern humanity, on the physical level, i.e., unconsciously. They will bring this capacity with them into their next life as an unconscious but informative factor that cultivates the potential for an altruistic attitude toward life and great interest in world affairs.

In their next life, AIDS patients will encounter a materialistic culture increasingly impregnated with egotism. Their current life is preparing them to help counteract this culture in positive ways.

Illness as unconscious spiritual experience

Anyone who has followed our train of thought thus far must now confront the question of how closely the experience of illness and pain is linked to spiritual development and to the spiritual progress of humankind. What is accomplished on the bodily level is also significant for spiritual development, and vice versa. From this perspective, illness is a physical projection of spiritual experience, or, as Rudolf Steiner once formulated it, *the physical imagination* (image) *of spiritual life.*[9] How are we to understand this statement? What does it mean with regard to how we view the development of an illness? How does a syndrome like AIDS develop? Is an illness actually a reflection of something else on a different level? If so, how does that happen?

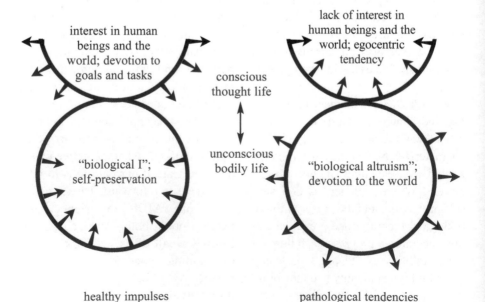

healthy impulses   pathological tendencies

The key to understanding this complicated line of questioning lies in the unique features of the etheric body (see pages 130 and 270) and its interaction with the other members of the human constitution, which is graphically represented opposite.

The healthy body appears as the image of the all-uniting, all-harmonizing divinity. The sick body presents in visible form the tasks and challenges of the spiritual development of the individual and of humankind. In this respect, illness appears as an unconscious initiation process; its importance in the sequence of repeated earthly lives is thus revealed (see page 175). Nothing that a human individual undergoes and experiences is ever lost; it forms part of their further development. The unfree experience of suffering through illness in one earthly life manifests in a future life as an inborn soul-spiritual talent, which — if consciously cultivated — will enhance the person's self-awareness and experience of freedom.

Dealing with AIDS

Avoiding situations that could lead to infection is one outer means of preventing AIDS, a means based solely on the fear of contagion. Hence it protects the individual without in any way helping to change our society's egocentric attitude toward life. But as we saw earlier, this is exactly what our society needs — to strengthen its inherent defenses by working on a new approach to life that considers the well-being of the entire planet instead of pursuing personal profit and personal advantages.

We hope that the viewpoints we have presented here have made it clear that AIDS is not a disease specific to marginal groups in our society. Rather, it is a problem that we all must identify with. Those who actually contract the disease endure the symptoms of a suffering that is common to all of us. They are our representatives, they suffer on our behalf, and they challenge us to do everything possible to help in this situation. Thus our natural human responsibility is to insure that the AIDS patients around us sense this reality. It is important for children with AIDS to be lovingly cared for and welcomed in schools and kindergartens. Again and again we hear of parents' fear that their own children will be infected. This fear is objectively unfounded and must be counteracted by concerted efforts on the part of physicians, teachers, and parents.

9. Preventing Illness and Promoting Health

Issues of preventive medicine that doctors expect to cover with parents during their children's regular medical checkups include recommended schedules for immunizations and dental checkups, rickets prevention, the basics of nutrition, and general hygienic measures. Above and beyond these issues, however, lies the whole field of research into what health is and how it can be promoted. Towards the end of the twentieth century, this new, health-oriented approach to medicine — dubbed *salutogenesis* — began to elicit increasing discussion.* For example, one question it raised was whether research should not focus more on how the body stays healthy, rather than on factors that contribute to illness. In this sense, anthroposophical medicine and education have always taken a consistently salutogenic approach. As early as 1919, Rudolf Steiner made the teachers of the Stuttgart Waldorf School aware of the impact of many hours of daily instruction on growing children.[10] In this developmental phase, when the physical body is being built up, any external stimuli that must be processed (whether on the level of body, soul, or spirit) has either health-giving or damaging effects on the interaction of the members of the child's constitution (see also Chapter 17, Health through Education).

In this context, it is informative to note the findings of a Swedish study on health differences between Waldorf and state school students.[11] The Waldorf children received few immunizations, had significantly fewer allergies, and were treated with antibiotics significantly less often than the control group. 61% of the Waldorf children had contracted measles in comparison to only 1% of the control group, 93% of whom had been vaccinated. This study leaves unanswered the question of how much Waldorf educational methods contributed to these results. It will prove important to develop methodologies that will allow such questions to be researched scientifically.

---

* *Salutogenesis:* from the Latin *salus,* health; *genesis,* creation.

9.1 How does health develop?

During a flu epidemic that affects only 30% of the population, some people attribute their illness to infection, while others wonder why they came down with the flu when 70% of those around them remained healthy in spite of similar exposure. Studies of disease and health will complement each other meaningfully only when we supplement our current reductionist view of illness (i.e., the infectious model of disease) with both an equally justified dispositional model and research into the causes of health — that is, with a holistic perspective. Serious studies of how health develops and persists in spite of stress must take the whole human being, including social surroundings, as the starting point. Pathogens then yield center stage to the question of which bodily, psychological, or spiritual factors can ultimately be held responsible for the immunological weakness that allows predisposition or susceptibility to illness to develop. Among others, these factors include:

- On the bodily level: genetic causes, inadequate or inappropriate nutrition, too little sleep or exercise, excessive exposure to cold.
- On the soul level: stress, anxiety, boredom, unhappiness, depression, relationship problems.
- On the spiritual level: deficiencies of idealism, motivation, spiritual nourishment, or stimulation.[12]

Medical sociologist Aaron Antonovsky lists three main causes of the development and persistence of health.[13] His three primary factors involve the ability to successfully come to grips with resistance, whether on the level of the body, the soul, or the spirit:

- Overcoming metabolic imbalances resulting from nutrition, movement, rest, climate change, and other disturbances. Each body, organ, and individual cell is located somewhere on a continuum of health and illness. New health develops constantly as disruptive factors and pathological tendencies are overcome.
- Building up the so-called "sense of coherence" during childhood and adolescence. Antonovsky also uses the German word *Weltanschauung* (or view of the world) in this context. What he means is the possibility of processing everything we encounter in a meaningful way and integrating it into a personal sense of our own life and understanding of our environment. The more meaningfully the different levels of experience (as well as each new experience) can be incorporated into an evolving overall picture, the healthier the person and the more resilient and inspiring their *Weltanschauung*.
- Using "resistance resources" to come to grips with the stresses and adversities of life. Resistance resources represent an individual's

sum total of compensation and coping strategies for positively overcoming problems and worries in life and work. These resources help prevent people from completely breaking down under overwork, anxiety, stress, loss, and social marginalization or exclusion or under extreme circumstances such as imprisonment and torture.

Those in special education refer to "resilience research," the study of factors that make children resistant and able to grow up healthy in spite of domestic situations marked by chaos, alcoholism, violence, or other stress factors.[14] Decisive factors that preserve and enhance resistance include:

- Being loved by another person
- Believing in God
- Trusting in progress and in the future
- Being able to find meaning in one's own destiny by processing problems and conflicts and integrating them into one's life.
- Outer security and a high standard of living
- A stable social network.

If health is the body's ability to balance out one-sided stress factors and counteract possible disease tendencies, there must be as many different forms of "health" as there are of illness. Individuals face unique and specific challenges in regulating body heat, ensuring adequate supplies of oxygen and nutrients, and establishing a fragile state of balance between breakdown and regeneration processes in the body. These efforts require just as much care and support as children's emotional and mental ability to process events.

Health is also the orderly interaction of bodily, emotional, and mental functions and activities. How is it possible that good thoughts actually have healing effects? How do peaceful feelings promote sleep and ease physical pain? Why is a positive attitude toward life refreshing and appetite-stimulating? These effects have been confirmed by comprehensive psycho-neuro-immunological research (see Section 2.4, and Endnote 2) and documented by salutogenic research. A concrete understanding of these phenomena will continue to elude us, however, until we stop restricting ourselves to natural-scientific approaches and become interested in the reality of the laws of soul and spirit and their relationships to bodily functions.

9.2 Promoting health of the soul and spirit

Motivation and meditation

In the second and third parts of this book, we will offer many practical suggestions for promoting health in children and adolescents. At this point, we would like to give examples of what adults can do both for themselves and — indirectly, by modelling health-promoting behaviors — for their children.

The most important and readily available means of preventing illness is to enjoy your work. It generates emotional warmth that keeps the body healthy (see Section 2.4). Thus it is essential to organize or approach your daily work in ways that make it possible for you to enjoy it.

Anger, discord, hurry, stress, and lack of overview are destructive and depleting and work against the preservation of health. If these influences accompany us into sleep for long periods of time because we cannot resolve them, our sleep loses its ability to restore us. We "break down" and become more susceptible to infections.

Almost everyone is aware of this type of "emotional pathology" from direct personal experience. "Psychosocial stress" — that is, the combination of personal and social problems — can be effectively dealt with only by deciding to pursue either a path of self-development or conflict resolution methods. Psychotherapy, biography work, and pastoral counseling offer many different options. Anthroposophical meditative training also offers techniques for meditation, concentration, and relaxation. Although their *raison d'être* is the search for self-knowledge and a spiritual understanding of the world rather than the preservation of health, these techniques, like all other sincere spiritual efforts, have direct positive effects on health. For example, the beneficial ordering effects of Steiner's verbal meditations are immediately apparent on reading them. It is helpful to recall and reflect on words and themes of this sort now and again in the course of the day or before important or difficult events.[15]

We are fully justified in thinking of hygiene not only as regular bathing, clean clothes, and appropriate living conditions but also in terms of emotional and mental hygiene. Do we cultivate our life of soul and spirit as carefully as we care for our bodies? Couldn't a brief session of meditation or concentration exercises each morning and evening become just as much of a need as brushing our teeth?

Rudolf Steiner's discussions of nervousness and the human I and of practical training in thought offer a series of very effective exercises for schooling attentiveness, memory, perception and concentration.[16] Other central issues of emotional hygiene include how we think and feel about other people and realizing that our thoughts and feelings can be either destructive or constructive for ourselves and for others. How we think and feel contributes to the "climate" in our homes, which is also experienced and judged by our children and teenagers.

The effect of art

Artistic activity is a very gratifying way of promoting health. The third part of this book will describe art's contribution to stabilizing health in childhood and adolescence, so at this point we will mention only the basics and refer you to the Bibliography. Again, we have Steiner's research to thank for providing an exact scientific basis for this field. The creative activity of modeling, sculpting, and carving directly stimulates and regulates the sculptural, formative functioning of the etheric body, to which it corresponds. Musical laws and their relationship to air (as the vehicle of sound) corresponds to the activity of the astral body, which is also musical in character. Every detail of the human body is structured according to specific proportions and numbers, not only with regard to the body's shape but also the rhythms and relative proportions of its physiological functions. In his book *Harmony of the Human Body,* Armin Husemann makes a first attempt at a comprehensive understanding of the musical laws governing the human body. Singing and other musical activity (but also working with different color "tones" and moods in painting) has harmonizing effects on the astral body's activity. The result is a sense of emotional harmony that works back on bodily functions.

Through artistic speech and speech therapy, the I-organization is directly activated. After all, we express ourselves in the truest sense of the word when we say something about ourselves or how we understand the world.

Eurythmy and curative eurythmy, which together constitute an art form that combines the governing principles of sculpture, music, and speech and applies them to bodily movement, have comprehensive effects on bodily functions and regulate the interaction of the different members of the human constitution (see also the section on curative eurythmy, Section 22.4).

9

9.3 Hygienic measures

In the bacteriological sense, hygiene includes isolating contagious patients, disinfecting rooms and objects, wearing protective clothing (including gloves, masks, and goggles if needed) and ensuring the safety of water and food. Without consistent implementation of such hygienic measures, the successes of modern surgery and epidemic control would have been impossible, and rates of infant and maternal mortality in hospitals would still be at nineteenth-century levels. Nonetheless, every mother knows that her well-protected baby on the changing table will soon be crawling around on floors dirtied by other people's street shoes.

In the long term, is it more prophylactic to avoid germs or to learn to cope with them? A logical extension of this question is, should every illness be treated with antibiotics or only those that a child is unable to overcome without such help? Experience shows that first children are seldom ill as babies because they grow up alone and catch infections only from their parents. When they enter kindergarten, however, we can expect at least two winters of frequent colds. First children bring home almost every infection that is going around; they seem to spend more time at home than in kindergarten. Second children have similar experiences, but by the time third children come along, they constantly catch upper respiratory infections from their older siblings and may also come down with alarmingly severe cases of the classic childhood diseases at very early ages. These third children, however, are often the sturdiest and healthiest later on. This typical experience speaks for itself and may be some consolation for families with many children.

9.4 Observing and cultivating healthy rhythms

Why is it so important to cultivate daily rhythms, especially in early childhood? For one thing, all life processes are linked to specific rhythms and time sequences. For another, an infant's ability to regulate rhythmic functions is still undeveloped and needs support and stimulation.

Another consideration is that human autonomous, rational activity isolates us from our natural surroundings and allows us to disregard life-supporting rhythms to a considerable extent. Years or decades of disregarding the body's rhythmical functions may exceed the system's limit of flexibility and cause its collapse, resulting in a number of different illnesses or weakened states. In contrast, consciously cultivating the most important rhythms increases the body's stress tolerance and prepares it to encounter life's challenges.

What is so special about rhythmical sequences?

- Rhythm is the repetition of similar processes under comparable circumstances. In respiration, the archetypal rhythm, no breath is exactly as deep or as long as any other, if measured exactly, and yet each breath is similar to the last.
- Every rhythm balances out polarities. Wherever contrasting elements collide in nature, rhythms mediate between them. For example, rhythmically structured fleecy clouds appear in the sky where high and low pressure systems meet. Rhythmical wave patterns line the shore, where movable water encounters solid ground. The breathing process mentioned above rhythmically balances the polarities of movement and rest.
- Rhythms form the basis of every adaptive process. Because rhythmical repetitions are never exactly the same but represent subtle fluctuation around an average value, flexible adaptation is an attribute of rhythmical processes, whereas a strict tempo is totally inflexible and has no capacity for balancing out or integrating differences.

- Rhythm substitutes for strength. Any rhythmically repeated action takes less exertion and energy than a one-time action performed at an unusual time or under unusual circumstances.
- Regular, rhythmical activities foster the development of habits, which are the structure underlying personality and character. Learning to observe regular times for eating and sleeping and to structure the day in a way that balances work and recreation, tension and relaxation, allows us to face the demands of daily life reliably and productively. In contrast, when we pay no attention to our internal clocks and become heavily dependent on outer circumstances or on our own momentary inclinations, we risk exhausting ourselves because we overestimate what we can accomplish. We lack the flexibility to adapt, the strength to persevere, and a sense of healthy limits.
- Every consciously repeated action strengthens the will and thus also our ability to act.
- Rhythms link nature and humans to the change of seasons, the sequence of day and night, and the many different movements of the planets against the background of the fixed stars. All of the rhythms and proportions that regulate the courses of the planets in our solar system are reflected in the life processes of plants, animals, and humans and reveal the common origin and connected life of all known creation.[17]

Only in the twentieth century did research on biological rhythms and time structures become a recognized branch of science. The sections that follow provide an overview of the essential rhythms that underlie and support life processes. Our suggestions on daily, weekly, monthly, and yearly rhythms are intended to stimulate a new family culture that once again takes these rhythms into account. Healthier, more adaptable children are our reward for our efforts.[18]

Cultivating daily rhythms

All of the functions of the adult body that are so beautifully regular and synchronized with the sun (such as the twenty-four hour rhythm of body temperature — 0.5°C/1°F lower in the morning than in the evening — daily fluctuations in blood sugar levels, various hormones, and blood salts, and other metabolic processes) are arhythmical and unsynchronized in newborn babies, who have not yet learned to develop typical maximums and minimums in the alternation between day and night.

The later structure, elasticity, and adaptability of a person's rhythmic system depend on how it is imprinted in infancy with all of daily life's little actions related to eating, bathing, playing, and sleeping. All organs, especially the large organs of metabolism and digestion, must coordinate their functions and learn how to work together optimally. Alternations between eating and not eating, activity

and sleep, are essential in fostering this learning. To encourage your infant to develop a twenty-four hour rhythm, it is helpful to pay special attention to getting up in the morning and going to bed at night (always at approximately the same time, if possible). In the morning, this process is supported by a morning song and looking out of the window together. From the very beginning, an infant's bedtime ritual can include lighting a candle, singing a few notes (possibly accompanied by a simple children's harp or lyre — preferably tuned to a pentatonic scale), and a short evening prayer before saying good night.*

The more clearly a baby's day takes shape in the course of the first weeks and months — mornings at home while Mum does housework, afternoons spent outside being carried in a sling — the more strongly he will experience the course of the day and the difference between day and night and be able to respond with his entire body.

The weekly rhythm

The names of the days of the week reflect the fact that they were once associated with the planets — including the Sun and Moon — that moved across the background of fixed stars.

---

* Pentatonic scales are five-note scales with no half steps, such as the series D-E-G-A-B. Pentatonic melodies have a light, open character and can end on any note of the scale. In Waldorf and curative education, the pentatonic instruments most commonly used are flutes (recorders), lyres, and children's harps.

Sunday – Sun
Monday – Moon (French *lundi)*
Tuesday – Mars (French *mardi)*
Wednesday – Mercury (French *mercredi)*
Thursday – Jupiter (French *jeudi)*
Friday – Venus (French *vendredi)*
Saturday – Saturn

The planets in the sky are very different in their individual manifestations — distant, indistinct Saturn; brightly shining Jupiter; red flickering Mars; the warm radiance of Venus in the morning or evening sky; elusive Mercury, only briefly visible for a few days shortly before sunrise or after sunset; the Moon with its constantly changing illuminated shape; and the Sun, towering over all the others and shedding its light everywhere. With practice, we can become aware that the days of the week are equally different in character. Research on rhythms has shown that the seven-day rhythm is the essential rhythm underlying responsive processes, including adaptation and healing. Acknowledging the rhythmic character of the course of the week is a way to support and stabilize the seven-day rhythm as the basis for flexible reactions to stresses and injuries of all kinds.

For example, Sunday can assume a more festive character, with a more leisurely breakfast preceded or followed by some singing or reading aloud. All the other days of the week can also have their special morning songs or specific activities. Regular obligations distributed throughout the week can be anticipated with pleasure and set the tone for each day. The same is true of little cultural habits — visiting friends or relatives or receiving visitors at home, looking at pictures, or making music. In the past few centuries, human beings have become increasingly emancipated from weekly, monthly, and yearly rhythms. Increasingly prevalent symptoms of burn-out indicate how severely this lack of rhythm undermines health. "Having enough time" begins with consciously cultivating time, that is, by shaping its rhythm, sequence and intervals through the alternation of activities and pauses (see also pages 293f). The same is true of fostering religious and meditative life. The secret to acquiring and developing inner forces and abilities is to distribute inner work over daily or longer rhythms. We should not omit to mention here that from the chronobiological perspective, a six-day school week for children is preferable to a five-day week.*

* In this context, we would like to point in particular to the eight-fold path of the Buddha as formulated for modern human beings by Rudolf Steiner. It includes a specific exercise for each day of the week:
Saturday – attention to one's conceptual activity
Sunday – work on right judgment
Monday – consciously cultivating conversation and choice of words
Tuesday – paying attention to one's actions ("right deed")
Wednesday – finding the right perspective in life
Thursday – correctly assessing one's own strength and ability to work
Friday – attempting to learn as much as possible from life.[19]

The monthly rhythm

From the science of climatotherapy, we know that the restorative value of a four-week cure is significantly greater than that of a two or three-week cure. And when someone is truly exhausted, two to three months of recuperation are needed; a four-week vacation is not enough. The monthly rhythm is the rhythm of profound recuperation, habit development, and stabilization. It takes at least four weeks for a new habit to take hold. Waldorf Schools take advantage of this fact by dividing instruction into four-week subject blocks whenever possible.

Activities that cultivate monthly rhythms include looking at calendar pictures, singing songs about the months, and observing seasonally changing natural processes and related farm and garden work. The type of clothing we wear also changes as the months go by.

In planning your vacations, we urge you to consider the four-week rhythm whenever possible. We advise against short vacations when rest and relaxation are the goal. Short breaks may be a stimulating change of pace for adults, but they are more likely to be a strain on children, who often come down with infections during or after a short vacation trip.

The yearly rhythm

It takes nine months of gestation plus the first three months after birth for infants' physical bodies to mature to the point where they can focus their eyes and grasp with their hands. It takes another year for them to learn to walk, another to learn to speak, and still another year until independent thinking begins. The physical body continues to develop in yearly rhythms, and seasonal changes in weather and light stimulate bodily changes. Similarly, each childhood illness has specific years of life in which cases are most and least likely to occur.

Long-term adaptation also follows yearly rhythms. When we have lived for more than one year in the same place — that is, when we experience one season of the year for the second time — we feel at home there. When we have lived there for more than seven years, we feel like "locals." It is a good tradition to celebrate the anniversaries of historical events, just as we celebrate birthdays and yearly seasonal holidays (see also Section 24.3).

10. Prevention and Immunization

10.1 Fluorides and tooth decay

Experience has shown that dental caries are almost unknown in volcanic areas where the water contains high levels of fluorides. But even in other areas, cavities became common only when consumption of refined sugar increased, as the Swiss physician Adolf Roos graphically describes in his account of how eating habits changed in a remote mountain valley when the area was opened up to development.[20]

Especially likely to promote cavities are sugary candies and sodas, and even constantly sucking on a bottle of sweetened herb tea or fruit juice. Fluorides deposited on the tooth surfaces have been proven to make them more resistant to acids. The acids that develop in dental plaque when sugar is broken down by oral bacteria are especially damaging. It is hoped that in addition to its surface effects, fluoride supplementation during tooth development will make the entire structure of the tooth enamel more durable.

The American Academy of Pediatrics recommends fluoride tablets only when the fluoride content of tap water is less than 0.3 ppm (part per million), which is approximately 0.3 mg per litre or quart, and only after the age of six months. Fluoride overdose can sometimes be recognized later when tooth discoloration (whitish spots) develops. Your local water treatment board can tell you the fluoride content of your drinking water.

It is interesting to note that nature doles out fluorides very sparingly to breastfed babies. Mother's milk contains extremely little fluoride (0.01 mg per litre as compared to 0.2 mg per litre in drinking water.[21] In other words, the mother's body protects the baby against high levels of fluoride. Since mother's milk has always been considered the ultimate food for infants, we believe that these proportions are meaningful and provide a natural standard for fluoride consumption in the first few years of life.

We recommend a balanced diet that largely avoids refined foods such as processed sugar and white flour. Clean your child's teeth with a small-headed toothbrush using a gentle but firm circular motion on the vertical surfaces (which will also thoroughly clean the gumline) and a back-and-forth motion on the chewing surfaces. At least rinsing the mouth after between-meal snacks (which should not include sweets) is a good idea. It is also important for kindergartens and schools to provide opportunities for toothbrushing after meals. If you use fluoridated toothpaste, use it no more than twice a day.

10.2 Preventing rickets

Rickets is a disease due to light deficiency. Since it appears primarily in industrial areas in the temperate zones, it can also be considered an illness caused by civilization. Light deficiency causes disorders in calcium and phosphate metabolism, which if left untreated can lead to serious bone deformities, inadequately mineralized teeth, inhibited growth, and reduced resistance to infection. Serious forms of the disease are seen today only in cases of severe neglect or congenital metabolic disorders. Any child, however, can suffer from rickets if nothing is done to compensate for lack of light. Infants in their first winter are most at risk and most often affected. In the early industrial era of the 1800s, living conditions for the elderly were so catastrophically bad that this age group was also at risk for rickets (known as osteomalacia in adults).

The term rickets derives from *rachitis* which actually means inflammation of the spinal column, and its general use is based on confusion of several different syndromes. This name has become so entrenched, however, that it has not been replaced. A more accurate term would be "light deficiency disease." In rachitis, calcium deficiencies in the blood may become so acute that spasms may result (rachitic tetany). Current interest in the disease focuses on this complication, since severe bone deformation has become very rare.

Diagnosis: The first sign of early-stage rickets is usually *increased perspiration* over a period of weeks without other visible reasons such as fever, increased drinking, or overly warm clothing. Dampness typically appears at the back of the head and on the palms and soles. An early sign of *calcium deficiency* is marked, increasing, and unexplained *restlessness* during the day or at night, up to and including startling at the slightest noise. These early signs of tetany should be investigated immediately by your doctor. A thorough medical examination will readily determine the cause.

Prevention: The simplest method consists of routinely giving your baby 500 IU (international units) of vitamin D_3 four times a week, for a total of 2,000 IU per week. This supplementation should continue through the child's second winter. This dose, which is less than the amount that was recommended for years in Europe, has a long history of successful use in other countries. Formula-fed babies usually need no additional vitamin D, since a litre of prepared formula contains approximately 400 IU. This dosage is adequate if administered consistently and if the baby does not already show signs of the beginnings of rickets or calcium deficiency. If you use 500 IU tablets, put them directly into your baby's mouth, or dissolve in a teaspoon of water.

Until recently, fish-liver oil capsules that supplied similar amounts of vitamin D could also be used to prevent rickets. In Europe, most physicians no longer recommend cod-liver oil because of possible contamination with mercury and pesticides. Irradiation therapy with ultraviolet light has also been largely abandoned.

Parents who wish to avoid vitamin D supplementation — for reasons we will discuss shortly — may attempt to do so under the following conditions:

- Monthly checkups with a physician experienced in alternatives to supplementation.
- Expose your baby's head to the blue sky as often as possible (see pages 194f). When the baby is three weeks old, begin with ten to fifteen minutes at a time, gradually increasing to two hours a day or longer. If the weather is good and you do not live in a city with dense smog, this amount of time is certainly enough to prevent rickets. Make sure that your baby's forehead is not covered and that nothing (bedding, cradle veil, window glass, balcony roof) comes between her face and the clear blue sky, preferably near the zenith. (The sky near the horizon contains more moisture and does not allow ultraviolet light to pass through.) In industrialized areas, you do not need to be afraid — at least not yet — of exposing your baby to too much ultraviolet light because of the dwindling ozone layer. In high latitudes as well as in the mountains and at the seashore, however, it is always important to avoid too much exposure to the sun and to ultraviolet rays. Never leave your baby unattended directly in the sun.
- Breastfeed your baby for at least six months, longer if possible (see Section 14.1). Nursing babies almost never get rickets, and if they do, the symptoms are not severe. We have never seen a case of tetany (spasms due to low blood levels of calcium) in a baby who was exclusively breastfed. Rickets and tetany both become possible, however, when breastfed babies are weaned.
- Be especially careful not to overfeed or underfeed your baby if you are using a non-dairy formula. Over-

nourished children are more susceptible to rickets because the need for vitamin D increases with body weight, while underfed infants are more susceptible to tetany. *Do not experiment indiscriminately with milk-free or low calcium diets.* If your baby drinks more than 500 ml (2 cups) or significantly less than 350 ml ($1^1/_2$ cups) of cow's milk per day over long periods, we recommend adjusting this amount to somewhere between 400 and 500 ml ($1^2/_3$–2 cups) per day (see Section 14.3). If the only dairy product in your baby's diet is butter or if he eats no dairy products at all, you *must* pay particular attention to his calcium intake to prevent deficiency.

- Maternal attention. Take time to play with your baby and "irradiate" her with your love. Loving human attention is also a source of light, albeit the internal, soul-warming kind. We see early-stage rickets much more frequently in babies whose mothers work or when neither parent stays at home. The statement "I take her outside everyday" can conceal a multitude of sins in terms of how parents expose their babies to heat, wind, light, noise, and other sensory perceptions. For example, blazing sun on the patio at midday, a January snowstorm with wind blowing from the east, or a ride in the baby carriage with the canopy up are not healthy outdoor experiences.
- If needed, a prescription for a homeopathic or anthroposophical constitutional remedy to stimulate

light metabolism. Internal medications as well as external applications such as therapeutic baths may also be prescribed prophylactically. These measures seldom fail if the physician is experienced.

- If you cannot fulfill all of these conditions, your baby's risk of rickets increases and extra caution is advised. Be especially alert to the possibility of rickets and be ready to fall back on vitamin D if necessary, in consultation with your doctor.

Problems associated with conventional rickets prophylaxis: In the 1920s, the discovery that the compound known as vitamin D could be synthesized by irradiating ergosterol yielded a highly effective therapy for children with rickets. At that time, it became the standard practice to administer massive-dose therapy of 5 to 15 mg. of vitamin D (one milligram is 40,000 IU) three times in the first year of life. In spite of early warnings from the anthroposophical pediatrician Dr Wilhelm zur Linden, this sclerosis-promoting measure was implemented until the 1960s, when it was suddenly abandoned because it was shown to cause vascular damage.[22] It was replaced with a recommended intake of 1,000 IU a day for two years. It took another thirty years for physicians to realize that 2,000 IU a week is an adequate dose for light-deprived children.

In spite of these advances in understanding, we fully support parents who prefer exclusively natural methods of prevention. Parents must be able to abide by the conditions listed above, however. They must also know that rachitic spasms are very rare in infants who have shown no previous signs of rickets or tetany. Early signs of calcium deficiency include involuntary pursing of the lips, involuntary paw-like hand gestures (flexed wrists with extended fingers), inspiratory wheeze (stridor) without signs of infection. These signs call for immediate clinical diagnosis and treatment.

Another consideration in preventing rickets is that phytin, a substance occurring naturally in all grains and especially abundant in oats, makes some of the calcium in foods insoluble so that it is excreted in the stools. Milk-based formulas do not contain phytin and are also supplemented with 400 to 600 IU of vitamin D_3 per litre (400 IU is the same as 1 µg, that is, one microgram.) If your baby gets either enough light or enough vitamin D, phytin does no harm because cow's milk contains more calcium than phytin can bind, and the amount absorbed is enough to prevent rickets. When a baby does not get enough light, however, phytin can make the situation worse.

10

10.3 Vitamin K prophylaxis: Preventing serious clotting disorders in infants

Very infrequently, severe cerebral hemorrhaging occurs in newborn babies, premature babies, and infants in the first two (or at most three) months of life. Exclusively breastfed babies are most often affected. In some cases, congenital defects in the digestion and absorption of fats in the intestine are at fault, but often the cause is not apparent and the problem is attributed to deficiency of vitamin K, which is necessary for the production of clotting factors in the liver. Vitamin K is present in breast milk in quantities that are minute but sufficient for most children.

In international conferences on this problem, it has become evident that the rate of infantile cerebral hemorrhage decreases significantly in countries where high doses of vitamin K are administered prophylactically to all newborns and infants. The initial method of administration (intramuscular injection) has been largely abandoned, although the suspicion that this practice triggered malignancies has not been confirmed.

In a number of countries, almost all midwives and obstetric clinics are required to administer vitamin K prophylaxis immediately after birth. In

UK and South Africa, 1 mg intramuscular injection is given to all newborn babies. In the UK an alternative option is 2 mg of Konakion given orally at birth, followed by 2 mg on days 4–7 followed by a third dose at one month.

In any case, have your baby examined by a doctor immediately if you notice bleeding from the navel or nose, blood in stools or vomit, or blood spots under the skin. Cholestasis (failure of bile flow) can cause protracted, greenish jaundice in newborns. This disorder is associated with a similar risk of hemorrhage and also requires prompt investigation.

10.4 General remarks about vaccinations

Almost all countries of the world either recommend or require vaccination of all children against the following diseases during the first two years of life: tetanus, whooping cough, diphtheria, Hib (Haemophilus Influenzae), measles, mumps, and German measles. Some countries also require tuberculosis immunization, and sometimes even chickenpox vaccinations are recommended. Wherever laws permit parents to decide which immunizations their children should receive, the risks and benefits of currently recommended inoculations are openly debated, along with their possible indirect effects on the development of immunity. Ideally, parents (in consultation with their doctors) should be free to decide whether and when their children will be vaccinated and which vaccines they will receive.

We hope to provide our readers with a basis for making sound decisions on these serious issues. If you have read the section on the meaning and ethical aspects of illness, you will not be surprised to find that our approach to vaccination is quite different from what is usually found in books of medical advice. *We will neither advocate the internationally recommended schedule of vaccinations, nor will we focus exclusively on the advantages of immunization, which are based on isolated statistical studies that deserve more discussion. We hope our approach will help parents make decisions that take into account both their child's individual situation and the long-term good of society.* We assume, however, that parents who avoid indiscriminate vaccination will be able to provide their children with the necessary rest, treatment, and convalescence if the illnesses in question do appear. This includes avoiding travelling with a sick child and allowing adequate time for recovery, for example.

Why are vaccinations recommended or mandated by law?

- Because humankind feels threatened by epidemics of infectious diseases;
- To protect individuals from the dangers of certain infectious diseases.

What do vaccinations do?

The purpose of vaccinations is to prevent specific infectious diseases. Vaccines (administered orally, by injection, or by scratching them into the skin) stimulate the body to produce protective substances identical or similar to the "antibodies" that develop when the body overcomes an infectious disease. The resulting immunity confers varying degrees of protection from the illness for periods of time that may also vary among individuals. In this book, we use the term "vaccination" to refer to both active and passive immunization. *Active immunization* uses either "live" vaccines containing attenuated pathogens (which have been weakened but are still capable of reproduction) or "dead" vaccines produced from killed pathogens or their breakdown or metabolic products. *Passive immunization* involves injecting a person at risk with protective substances taken from other people or animals. Because these foreign antibodies break down rapidly in the body, passive immunization confers effective protection for two months at most. In contrast, active immunization is supposed to confer immunity for years.

Vaccination reduces susceptibility to specific infectious diseases. In contrast to other preventive medical measures such as mountain or ocean cures, vaccination does not improve a person's state of health. Vaccinations make sense when they prevent risks to specific individuals and entire demographic groups, but they are justifiable only when the prevented risks are not outweighed by significant new risks (damage due to vaccination, reduced immunity). Vaccination is valuable when the illness in question is typically dangerous and when immunization is effective and long-lasting. Possible complications of vaccination are dangerous only when the illness itself is very dangerous.

The value of a single vaccination can be assessed by weighing the following factors.

- On the one hand, how dangerous is the illness? Are epidemics typical? How frequent are serious cases involving complications? What is the mortality rate?
- On the other hand, how effective is the vaccine? How long does immunity last? How frequent are complications and what damages and side effects is the vaccine known to cause?

Points of view other than official recommendations may apply to individual decisions of whether or when to vaccinate. Some of these considerations are:

- Vaccination may trigger or exacerbate other illnesses that usually appear in milder forms or even go unnoticed. The risk of this happening is greater in children who have recently experienced a shock, accident, or prior illness.

- Parents often wonder whether the ever-increasing number of components of combined vaccines (together with their inert ingredients, which would otherwise never enter the body in this way) places excessive demands on the immune system. The standard answer (that all recommended or required vaccines are safe and effective) in no way lessens the validity of this question.
- It is difficult to either prove or disprove whether vaccinations change the immune system in ways that favour the development of allergies or autoimmune disorders, and mandatory studies conducted prior to the introduction of vaccines certainly do not address this possibility. One example of a possible questionable effect on the immune system is the as yet unexplained increase in juvenile diabetes in industrialized nations.
- The emotional trauma associated with vaccination is also a factor, especially in children whose family situation is not secure.
- Fear of illness may be inflated in parents who have their children vaccinated according to the officially recommended schedule and who therefore have little experience with their children's self-healing abilities.

Additives and contaminants in vaccines

All *tetanus* and *diphtheria* vaccines as well as the new vaccine against *Haemophilus influenzae B* (Hib, see Section 10.8) are made with germs killed with formaldehyde or similar compounds, of which only trace amounts remain in the vaccine. *Hepatitis B* vaccine, which is produced using genetically altered yeast cells, contains not only these compounds but also still smaller traces of thiocyanate. All of these vaccines are preserved with 0.025 mg of mercury per ampule. Since mercury can provoke hypersensitivity, dermatologists are recommending that it be replaced.

The active ingredients of these vaccines are bound to aluminum hydroxide or aluminum phosphate. These chemicals enhance the efficacy and tolerability of the vaccines through more even distribution. The dosage of aluminum per ampule is between 0.2 and 0.5 mg. Aluminum actually does not belong inside the body at all, especially not if administered in this way. In infrequent cases, the body reacts to the presence of aluminum by forming granulomas, little nodules of tissue that develop around foreign objects.

The manufacturers claim that more suitable substances have not yet been discovered. To date, no connection has been established between aluminum administered in this way and Alzheimer's disease (premature aging associated with aluminum deposits in the brain). Injectable *polio* vaccine, which contains the dead virus, contains traces of antibiotics and formaldehyde.

Production and composition of individual vaccines

Tetanus and *diphtheria* vaccines contain weakened forms (toxoids) of the bacterial toxins that cause the illness. The purpose of these toxoids is to stimulate the body to produce antibodies. The first vaccination is intended as a very weak stimulus, while the second is stronger and is meant to provide protection for one to two years. An existing study, however, proves that infants at the age of two months do not develop antibodies after the first injection but lose much of the remaining immunity conferred by their mothers' antibodies.[23] Antibody formation still remains inadequate after the second vaccination at four months; effective antibody levels generally develop only after the third vaccination at age six months. A third (or fourth) vaccination six months to a year later usually produces antibody formation that persists for several years. If the vaccinee is infected with the germs that cause the illness several weeks after the second or third vaccinations, the disease-causing toxins are usually rendered harmless, either by existing antibodies or through rapid production of many new antibodies. As a rule, the ability to quickly produce new antibodies is generally achieved through the third vaccination or contact with the germs several weeks after the second vaccination.

This is known as the "booster" effect.

Until a few years ago, *whooping cough (pertussis)* vaccines were manufactured using whole, dead germs and thus contained not only the pathogens' toxins but also their other components. The vaccines now used in many countries contain only a few components of the pertussis germ and are therefore better tolerated.

The injectable *measles-mumps-rubella (MMR)* combination vaccine contains attenuated (weakened) viruses that are still capable of reproduction. This vaccine and the *oral polio* vaccine are produced in cell cultures derived from monkey kidneys, chicken embryos, or human tissue. For children with specific allergies to chicken protein or certain antibiotics, the Swiss vaccine Triviraten is safe. Except for traces of an antibiotic, the inert ingredients of this MMR vaccine include only hydrolized gelatin, some human albumin (non-allergenic human protein), and traces of various other substances. Only a single injection of MMR vaccine is needed to develop full immunity (but see the recommendations for measles revaccination in Section 10.13).

All live vaccines can trigger reactions similar to, but supposedly weaker than, the original illnesses. In our descriptions of individual vaccines (see below), we will not go into accounts of rare, disputed, but sometimes serious cases of side effects because we feel that reporting them here would cause uncertainty all out of proportion to the actual risk. They are described in detail in the

10

manufacturer's package inserts. As a general rule, parents can assume that their physician has never seen serious side effects resulting from the vaccines he or she uses and therefore cannot say anything more about them than what is included in the manufacturer's information.

Vaccination should always be postponed if your child has any acute infection, including the beginnings of a cold. Intervals between immunizations, combination vaccines, and counter-indications are best discussed with the physician who will administer the vaccines.[24]

10.5 Government recommended immunizations

Following is an overview of immunization schedules, as they are currently in North America and the UK. These continually change and there are variations between different countries. Parents should find out about the latest recommendations locally. Further discussion on the individual illnesses and their vaccinations follows.

Birth	HepB$_1$ (*USA*)
2 months	Diphtheria, Tetanus, Whooping cough (DTP)$_1$, Hib, Polio, Meningitis C; Pneumococcal$_1$, HepB$_2$ (*USA*); HepB$_1$ (*S Africa*)
3 months	Diphtheria, Tetanus, Whooping cough (DTP)$_2$, Hib, Polio, Meningitis C; Pneumococcal$_2$ (*USA*); HepB$_2$ (*S Africa*)
4 months	Diphtheria, Tetanus, Whooping cough (DTP)$_3$, Hib, Polio, Meningitis C; Pneumococcal$_3$ (*USA*); HepB$_3$ (*S Africa*)
12-18 months	Measles, Mumps, Rubella (MMR)$_1$; HepB$_3$ Varicella (*USA*)
4-5 years	Diphtheria, Tetanus, Polio (DTP) booster, Measles, Mumps, Rubella (MMR)$_2$
13 years	Tuberculin testing and BCG
14 years	Tetanus, Polio and Low Dose Diphtheria

10.6 Tetanus (lockjaw)

The world-wide standard is passive immunization of all patients with dirty puncture wounds who have not been actively immunized. Passive immunization consists of an injection of concentrated antibodies taken from highly immunized human donors.

Active immunization, which stimulates the body to form antibodies of its own, is the more effective prophylactic measure. Two injections at intervals of about one month, followed by a third six months to a year later, are enough to confer immunity for approximately ten years. Booster shots are administered every ten years.

In USA and the UK, the officially recommended schedule of vaccinations includes three tetanus shots administered monthly in combination with diphtheria and whooping cough (pertussis), beginning at the age of two months, and a combined tetanus-diphtheria booster at age four to five. One-time booster shots of vaccine are also administered after injuries occurring more than five years after the last vaccination, or even earlier if the wound is very dirty or if the patient has severe injuries, especially burns. These extra boosters are precautionary measures; whether they are really necessary remains uncertain. More frequent vaccination can cause complications.[25]

This vaccination is one of the most harmless, and the illness in unvaccinated patients is one of the most serious ones we know, with a mortality rate of one-third to one-half of those who contract the disease. Even parents opposed to immunizations on principle generally accept vaccination for a child who has survived a case of tetanus. (Strangely enough, natural cases of tetanus do not produce immunity.) Nonetheless, tetanus (lockjaw) is a rare illness, which is why very many people must be vaccinated multiple times to insure the statistical probability of protecting even one person from the illness. Because the risk of contracting tetanus during the first year of life is extremely low in the developed world, we recommend beginning tetanus vaccinations at one year instead of the usual three months. Broad effects of immunization are very difficult to recognize in infants, and one-year-olds are physically much more stable.

10

10.7 Diphtheria

A diphtheria epidemic in the former Soviet Union in the early 1990s, in which reportedly 80% of those affected were adults, was apparently stopped in its tracks by a massive vaccination campaign. At no point in this epidemic did the number of reported diphtheria cases increase in Germany, although it is quite obvious that few German adults are "adequately" immunized against diphtheria.

Experienced older doctors emphasize repeatedly that passive and active immunizations have made diphtheria a much less dangerous disease than it once was. But because the vaccine used in passive immunization is derived from horses and its use entails some risk of allergic reactions, it cannot be considered a totally safe treatment for diphtheria. In some countries it is no longer been available due to a "lack of suitable imported source material." Active immunization remains the only means of prevention.

In USA and the UK, officially recommended diphtheria immunization, like tetanus immunization, consists of three injections at intervals of one month, starting at the age of two months, followed by a booster at age four to five. Fever is common after the second and third vaccinations, and the injection site may also become inflamed, especially if some of the vaccine flows back out of the muscle and collects under the skin. Complications are very infrequent. The protection conferred by this series of injections is considered adequate for about five years, after which a booster shot is administered. Subsequent boosters every ten years are recommended. After age six, the vaccine is less well tolerated and the dose is reduced to approximately one-tenth of the amount administered to toddlers. For reasons discussed above in the section on tetanus vaccination, we recommend that when diphtheria vaccination is desired, parents should postpone the vaccination until the child is a year old, unless there are concerns about a possible epidemic or when travelling in areas of higher risk.

10.8 Haemophilus influenzae type B bacteria

Haemophilus influenzae type B bacteria (Hib) are involved in cases of acute life-threatening epiglottitis (see page 70), and, before vaccination was possible, often in purulent meningitis, and middle-ear infections in childhood. The germs are also found in approximately five percent of healthy children. Approximately one infant in 250 will experience a serious Hib infection. This means that the other 249 develop immunity with no signs of illness. Immunity is also conferred by several harmless intestinal bacteria (for example, several strains of *E. coli),* which trigger production of the same antibodies needed for protection against Hib. Before the vaccine became available, in Germany it was estimated that approximately 100 children per year died of serious Hib infections in a population of 60 million, with approximately the same number suffering permanent damage. The risk is greater in low-income populations and highest in children with congenital or illness-induced immunodeficiencies. Contrary to popular belief, Hib vaccination does not offer universal protection against meningitis but only against one of several meningitis germs. It also does not protect against *Haemophilus* germs of types A, C, D, E, and F (which are currently even more rare than type B), nor does it protect against the so-called unencapsulated types. Since the introduction of the vaccine, infection rates have declined rapidly, as have the occasional initially reported cases of vaccine failure.

Since children under the age of eighteen months are considered most at risk, vaccination makes sense only very early in life. The current recommendation in USA and the UK is for three vaccinations in the first four months. The vaccine is included in the new multiple-vaccine shots, along with whooping cough, tetanus, diphtheria and polio.

Immunization through contact with wild germs probably offers the best protection, and the average level of immunity may decline in future as the vaccine becomes widely available and the use of antibiotics continues to increase. We advise parents to make the decision for or against Hib vaccination on the basis of their own well-informed stance on artificial immunization in general.

10

10.9 Whooping cough (pertussis)

In the 1920s, a dead vaccine manufactured from whole germs was introduced as a protection against whooping cough. Some years ago, several different "acellular" vaccines containing only two to four antigens were developed. These newer vaccines are used almost exclusively in combination with diphtheria and tetanus vaccines (DPT). The original whole-germ vaccine was suspected of causing serious or even fatal complications in the form of brain damage or seizures. Comprehensive studies were conducted, but depending on the criteria applied in each study, they identified either very infrequent specific brain complications or none at all. On the basis of personal experience, however, some experts still hold this vaccine responsible for causing neurological diseases or increasing their severity.[26]

The recommended vaccination schedule for pertussis — three injections at intervals of four weeks, beginning at the age of two months — is based on experience with the whole-germ pertussis vaccine, which requires three injections to develop temporary immunity because higher doses in any individual injection cause significant side effects. In some countries, the booster shot administered six months to one year later is intended to confer protection that lasts many years. A number of studies from different countries, however, conclude that it remains possible for children who have received three or four of these injections to contract whooping cough at age five.[27]

Premature infants and babies under the age of three to six months are the group most in need of protection. As we explained earlier, however, this group cannot be effectively protected by vaccination. The recommended strategy is aimed at reducing the likelihood that older siblings will infect infants. In fact, however, cases of whooping cough in highly immunized populations are declining significantly, and the recommended strategy is full of holes because (as we discussed earlier) it cannot eliminate whooping cough entirely. The more people are immunized, the more likely it becomes that adults — most of whom experience only a nagging cough that persists for several weeks — will serve as sources of infection for small babies.

To help us see the total picture, it is informative to consider the following contrast. In Great Britain, after years of a comprehensive vaccination program that prevented whooping cough from circulating in the population, vaccination was discontinued because of concerns about damage. A few years later, a major epidemic occurred with many serious cases. In Germany, where the level of immunization was never as high, the increase in confirmed cases was not as significant when pertussis was removed from the list of recommended vaccinations, and mortality rates (almost always less than ten per year in a population of 60 million) did not increase over previous years. Thus the post-World War II decline in mortality (compared to high rates in the 1930s) was due to reasons other than lack of or consistent implementation of vaccination. In our experience, the fact that mothers are now allowed to stay in the hospital with their babies plays a decisive role in improving the outcome. (For the dangers associated with whooping cough in infants, see Section 7.11.)

Vaccination makes sense for patients with certain lung and heart diseases and in certain social situations such as refugee camps or crowded dwellings with large numbers of children.

10.10 Poliomyelitis (infantile paralysis)

More than forty years of vaccination efforts have virtually eliminated epidemic infantile paralysis (polio) in the developed nations of the world, where epidemics had become larger and more dangerous as westernized standards spread and hygiene improved. In the USA, for example, more than twenty-five thousand cases of paralysis were expected in peak years. Nonetheless, these numbers are relatively low in comparison to other epidemic diseases such as dysentery, cholera, or influenza. During the epidemic years, the incidence of forty cases in two years in a city with a population of 600,000 was considered a major epidemic. During those times, a large part of the population developed immunity to polio viruses without experiencing symptoms. Vaccines were developed because of the insidious character of the disease, with its sudden paralyzes and sometimes life-threatening symptoms, not because of its prevalence.

There are two different types of vaccine: the injectable Salk vaccine (IPV) made with dead viruses and the oral Sabin vaccine (OPV). The oral vaccine uses the natural path of infection and has the advantage of being painless to administer. A disadvantage, however, is that its use entails a slight risk of paralysis, which one source lists as one case in every one to four million vaccinations. The oral vaccine can also lead to infection of an unvaccinated close relative.

We used to recommend the oral vaccine. But since almost all recent cases of paralysis in developed countries have been traced to the oral vaccine, public health authorities in a number of countries now recommend the injectable, dead-virus vaccine. It is available combined with tetanus, diphtheria, pertussis, Hib, and sometimes hepatitis B; recommended timing of the first vaccination is at two months. Later boosters are available either as the single vaccine or in combination with tetanus and diphtheria. US recommendations as of 2003 were to vaccinate at 2, 4 and 6–18 months.

10.11 Rubella (German measles)

A live vaccine against German measles has been available since 1969. Its only purpose is preemptive immunization of girls to prevent the damage to unborn children, since various types of deformities often occur when mothers-to-be contract German measles before the twelfth week of pregnancy. For a pregnant woman, having German measles and knowing that she has no antibodies to protect the fetus is a very stressful experience.

Rubella vaccination is now officially recommended at the ages of 12 months and 4–6 years. The first two vaccinations are combined with measles and mumps (MMR). This policy, however, is inappropriate. From the epidemiological perspective, the vaccine should be administered as late as possible to avoid disrupting the acquisition of immunity through natural means. Meanwhile we know from experience that widespread vaccination of women of childbearing age results in lower levels of antibodies in vaccinated women than in unvaccinated people, assuming that the latter have developed immunity through infection or contact with the wild virus. Even if their antibody titres are lower, unvaccinated women are much less likely to contract German measles for the second time during pregnancy than are vaccinated women. Repeated vaccinations are also less effective than being infected with the wild virus. The argument that mass immunizations have significantly reduced the number of children born with virus-related damage is diluted by the fact that an unknown number of fetuses with suspected damage have been aborted.

German measles vaccination, like measles itself, can cause rheumatic joint disorders, which are usually temporary. These symptoms are more frequent in adults and in revaccinated adolescents than in children.

10.12 Mumps

There is a live vaccine against mumps. Its only legitimate purpose is to prevent permanent damage due to mumps. As with whooping cough, arguments in favour of vaccination include statements like, "We must not forget that whooping cough and mumps place a great deal of strain on families due to weeks of losing sleep," and so on. In response to such arguments, we can only question whether manipulating children's bodies to minimize the disruption to their surroundings is a worthy ideal. Nowadays, almost all children recover from mumps meningitis (meningoencephalitis) without lasting damage (see also Section 7.10), and the symptoms are not severe enough to be used as the chief argument in support of vaccination. The only possible remaining motive for vaccination is to prevent permanent damage such as male infertility due to inflammation of the testes or occasional (and fortunately usually one-sided) hearing loss. Mumps vaccination is officially recommended in most developed countries in combination with measles and rubella vaccines (MMR).

Once again, it is quite difficult to assess actual risks of testicular inflammation with or without vaccination. The current state of our knowledge, with the exception of epidemic differences in severity and susceptibility, suggests taking the following approach to mumps vaccination. Let's suppose that parents are wondering whether or not to have their eighteen-month-old son vaccinated. Prior to the introduction of the vaccine, most children contracted mumps before the age of fifteen. 70 to 90% of adults today developed antibodies through either infection or exposure prior to the era of immunization. Assuming that the boy does not grow up to be one of these adults but remains susceptible to mumps into adulthood, the question remains whether he would develop silent immunity or a symptomatic infection as a result of exposure to the wild virus. If he does contract the disease, his chances of developing one-sided testicular inflammation are 10 to 14% and the probability that he will experience one-sided loss of function is approximately one-third as great. At the moment, even physicians cannot provide more precise information. Lay people need to be aware of this state of affairs because the simple statement that "mumps can cause testicular inflammation with permanent infertility" is not a very accurate characterization of the actual risk.

Permanent inner-ear damage is also one-sided in most cases. Because it is often diagnosed only much later, incidence figures are unreliable, but in general we can expect roughly one case of serious hearing loss for every fifteen thousand cases of uncomplicated mumps. In thirty years of practicing pediatrics, we have met only one child with mumps-related hearing loss. But as vaccination becomes more common, we must expect the age of peak susceptibility among unvaccinated individuals to increase, and complications are more frequent in adults.

Mumps encephalitis which can cause lasting damage to the brain or nerves, is a rare complication of mumps. This must not to be confused with mumps meningitis/meningoencephalitis, a common and usually harmless complication of mumps. Sources disagree about its incidence. Mumps encephalitis is reported to cause less severe symptoms than measles encephalitis. We have never seen a patient with mumps encephalitis.

It is not known how long immunity due to vaccination lasts. In the UK the mumps vaccination is combined with measles and rubella at age 12-18 months, with a booster shot recommended at age four to five. The current vaccination strategy will certainly not achieve the high degree of immunity formerly common among adults. We believe that universal vaccination is inappropriate.

10.13 Measles

Since around 1970, an injectable live measles vaccine has been recommended along with the vaccines for mumps and rubella. It is now administered as early as twelve months of age, since the protective effects of maternal antibodies do not last as long as they once did. In countries with high rates of vaccination, serious cases of measles in infants are increasing because vaccinated mothers who never had the illness pass few or no antibodies on to their children. Measles vaccination was first introduced in the form of a one-time injection that was supposed to confer lifelong immunity. In many countries, repeated vaccination or boosters at age four to five and in adolescence are now recommended to catch vaccine failures and cases of missed vaccinations.

Reasons cited for measles vaccination include high mortality rates (especially from pulmonary complications) in the tropics and in countries with low standards of living. In affluent countries in the temperate zones, complications are rare but include lung and heart complications and (rarer still) encephalitis (see Section 7.1, for the frequency of measles encephalitis).[28] The World Health Organization and its regional affiliates are taking steps to eliminate measles worldwide.

It is well-known that in countries heavily committed to freedom (in Switzerland, for example), willingness to accept vaccination actually declines among the general population when pro-vaccination propaganda peaks. Hence health authorities must realize that they will be able to eliminate measles only through measures such as legally required isolation of patients and mandatory vaccination. But where the proportion of unvaccinated to vaccinated individuals is similar to what it is in Germany, for example, failure to isolate cases of infection offers vaccinated individuals repeated opportunities for additional immunity, while preserving freedom of choice with regard to vaccination. *We must emphasize, however, that many measles epidemics do cause a few fatalities.*

There is also an important emotional consequence of vaccination that remains to be considered. Parents who have their children vaccinated against as many contagious diseases as possible, including measles, are as a rule more afraid of these and other illnesses than parents who do not. We have seen instances in which vaccinated kindergarten children were not allowed to ride in the same car with unvaccinated youngsters, in spite of the fact that exposure to the wild virus would have enhanced the limited immunity conferred by vaccination. Even in cases of vaccine failure, an outbreak of measles in vaccinated children is much less dangerous at this age than it is later.

Having said all this, we feel that a parental decision not to vaccinate children against measles is fully justifiable in most cases, and we support this decision. On the other hand, in individual instances including special risk factors, parents are grateful for the possibility of vaccination. If unvaccinated children do not have measles before the age of nine (or at most twelve), the question of vaccination should be revisited because both symptom severity and the risk of complications increase with increasing age. At this age, too, one should consider mumps vaccination for boys and German measles vaccination for girls, if they have not yet developed antibodies in the blood.

10

10.14 Tuberculosis (BCG vaccine)

Recent empirical evidence suggests that tuberculosis vaccination does not offer reliable protection against infection or illness, nor does it (as is repeatedly claimed) lessen the severity of symptoms. Vaccination certainly does not play a large role in limiting the spread of tuberculosis. More important in this regard are:

- diagnosing, treating, and supervising actively tubercular patients
- ensuring that TB patients do not infect small children
- vaccinating cows and pasteurizing milk from farms that cannot be reliably certified as TB-free.

Tuberculin tests yield positive results in both vaccinated and infected individuals, so vaccine failures (infections that occur in spite of vaccination) are more difficult to identify in vaccinated populations. Newborns must be protected from infection by isolating them from suspected actively tubercular patients. In Germany, TB vaccination has not been officially recommended since 1998 due to its inadequate efficacy. In North America, it is recommended only where there is a special risk of infection. In the UK, BCG is administered at age thirteen at the time of tuberculin testing. In South Africa, BCG is administered at birth.

10.15 Hepatitis A

When cases of jaundice appear in schools or kindergartens, vaccination with active hepatitis A vaccine (HAV) is recommended for the children who are not yet ill. Since hepatitis A infections are almost always mild in children, we recommend thorough bathroom hygiene and case-by-case decisions on whether or not to vaccinate. Vaccination is often recommended for children travelling to countries where the risk of infection is high. A booster is recommended after six months.

10.16 Hepatitis B

In North America and South Africa hepatitis B vaccination is universally recommended for infants beginning in the third month and especially for adolescents. The reasons for this recommendation are increases in prevalence of the virus among teenagers and adults and the presence of chronic contagious cases in the general population (see Section 7.13). However, in the UK the vaccination is not routinely administered.

The vaccine, which uses a surface antigen from the hepatitis B virus to stimulate formation of antibodies, does not contain viruses capable of replication. Three vaccinations are considered necessary. According to various sources, approximately 95% of those vaccinated develop effective immunity. A booster shot for school-age children is no longer recommended. Combination vaccines are now being developed. Introductory information does not always mention the possible side effects of vaccination, but they are included in the package inserts that accompany the vaccine.

In a number of countries, the long-term goal of health authorities is to eliminate hepatitis B through expanded vaccination programs. This would require vaccinating more than 90% of the population, however, which is hardly realistic. Side effects of vaccination, although infrequent, are potentially serious and must also be considered. Is still one more vaccination really desirable for very small children at an age when they would normally be developing their immune systems by coming to grips with the germs of the real outer world rather than with substances that suddenly appear in their muscles in the form of injectable vaccines? Furthermore, the risk of infection in infants in the western world is extremely low. Of course we provide passive and active vaccination when needed to protect an infant whose mother has contagious hepatitis B. In general, we restrict our use of the vaccine in infants and older children to cases of special risk.

10

10.17 Flu (influenza)

Serious flu epidemics, usually originating in China, seem to appear every ten to twenty years. The most serious epidemic occurred in 1918, the most recent major one in 1977. These epidemics are triggered by a highly variable group of viruses. Hence vaccines (made of isolated antigen) must be reformulated each year according to which type of virus appears. There is always a degree of uncertainty as to whether the new vaccine contains the appropriate antigens. We recommend flu shots only for high-risk patients and for age groups or professional groups that face exceptional risks.

10.18 Tick-borne encephalitis

Spring-summer meningoencephalitis (also called tick-borne or Central European encephalitis) is an infection carried by ticks. It occurs in a broad band from Central Europe to East Asia, which can be seen on special maps that are published by health authorities and are available in local health centers.

Active vaccination is recommended for agricultural and forestry workers and for people travelling or taking part in recreational sports in areas of known risk. Effective protection requires an initial vaccination followed by two others (two weeks to three months later, and nine to twelve months later), or, on an accelerated schedule, an initial vaccination followed by second and third shots seven and twenty-one days later with a booster one year later. Boosters are recommended every three years for those who spend long periods of time in areas of risk and no later than eight years after the last injection for travelers. High fevers are not uncommon after vaccination; they prompted the recall of one vaccine shortly after it was introduced for use in children.

Children seldom experience severe symptoms or lasting damage from tick-born encephalitis (but see Section 7.14 Lyme disease). In Germany, the risk of infection in one high-risk area in 1999 was estimated at one case for every one to two thousand tick bites. Passive vaccination is no longer used preventively in children bitten by ticks because it has been known to cause more serious cases of spring-summer meningoencephalitis.

Tick bites can be largely prevented by wearing clothing that covers the entire body and by applying natural insect repellents (such as carnation oil/Aetheroleum caryophylli). In South Africa, Tick Safe is an available product.

10.19 Vaccinations recommended on a case-by-case or emergency basis

Parent's freedom of choice with regard to vaccinations varies from country to country. Wherever vaccination is a matter of individual decision, parents bear the responsibility for the consequences of their choices. Parents must also realize that vaccination as a preventive measure is not the same as a physician's therapeutic activity in cases of actual illness: *in no case can a physician state with certainty that either vaccination or the illness it prevents would damage or not damage your child.* Moreover, vaccination policies are based on a view of health and illness that merits debate but not unconditional acceptance. Your doctor's job is to support your child in sickness and in health and to help you as parents arrive at mutually acceptable solutions and responsible choices that will support your child's development as an individual.

Parents who want to minimize vaccinations generally seek advice from homeopathic or anthroposophical physicians or from naturopaths. We subscribe to the following approach, which is based on the recommendations of the pediatric departments of several holistically oriented German hospitals.

In conversations with parents, holistic physicians explore the parents' level of knowledge, attempt to eliminate misconceptions, and mention aspects that might broaden their perspective, while avoiding any moral pressure. These discussions provide the basis for making individualized decisions about specific vaccinations.

- When parents ask us for help in making decisions, we recommend vaccination against **tetanus** and **diphtheria** at age one, or sometimes as early as nine months. In most cases, polio vaccination is also recommended.

- With regard to **whooping cough (pertussis)** vaccination, we make it clear that vaccination offers no protection during the first three months of life, when whooping cough is most dangerous. We administer the vaccine if parents request it.

- *Hib* vaccines are also administered on request, after discussing the risk of serious infections.
- *German measles* vaccination is recommended for all girls in puberty unless they test positive for rubella antibodies.
- Parents increasingly request *measles* vaccination for their older elementary-school children, and we administer the vaccine or a combined measles-mumps-rubella (MMR) vaccine on request (in some exceptional cases, as early as age one).
- Because *hepatitis A* infections are almost always mild in children, we do not recommend vaccination except in infrequent cases involving foreign travel.

- Passive vaccines against *tetanus* or *chicken pox* are administered in case of unusual risk.
- Newborns whose mothers have *hepatitis B* are immediately given both active and passive vaccines, since in most cases that is the only way to prevent infection. Prophylactic vaccination is recommended in high-risk cases, and we make sure our teenage patients are informed about behaviors that put them at risk, such as frequent infection through unprotected sex.
- In serious cases of congenital or acquired heart or lung disease and certain other syndromes, we make parents aware of what immunizations are important and possible.

11. Meeting Challenging Problems

11.1 Dealing with disabled or chronically ill children

Living with disabilities

The experiential realm of children who are born blind or lose their eyesight through accidents is limited by the absence of the dimension of light and color; only through their sense of touch can they develop mental images of the objects around them. Their other senses compensate for the absence of sight by becoming stronger and more sensitive to details. Hence, hearing and touch become much keener and more precise in visually impaired children than in sighted individuals and are associated with emotional experiences that make these children more receptive to the inner character of a person's tone of voice or any other auditory expression. Moods and subtle soul gestures are often literally "overlooked" by people who can see; blind people, however, are much more attuned to them.

While all deaf-mutes were formerly believed to be mentally handicapped, we now know that their ability to express thoughts and emotions was limited only because they could not learn to think through speaking. Sign language has made it possible for deaf children to develop normal intelligence. The soul world of the deaf is filled with profound silence. For them, objects display their nature and character on the surface, and any internalization is difficult. Because they sense that a more profound and emotional type of perception remains hidden from them, they are in danger of becoming mistrustful, and it is difficult for them to achieve an attitude of trusting devotion.

What about children who are colorblind or cannot smell? What dimension of experience is concealed from them, and what emotional possibilities do they realize most strongly? How does a child experience the world when he or she is confined to a wheelchair, limps, cannot run, or has only a stump with fingers instead of an arm?

We often find that children with impaired mobility have above-average emotional energy, as if all the pent-up will that cannot be transformed into bodily activity becomes available as the capacity for emotion. This phenomenon is also evident in children with cleft palates or harelips. Because of genetic or other predisposition, certain forces needed for shaping the skeleton have not been channeled into shaping the body and instead remain available for soul activity. As a result, raising such children is not always easy. They always seem to be "bursting at the seams" and easily get carried away because they have not yet learned to manage their excess of emotional forces.

Other children have to cope with congenital or acquired damage to internal organs. For example, an eleven-year-old girl is taken to the doctor because she has stopped growing and is always pale and tired. Her physician discovers that her kidneys are only barely functioning and will eventually shut down totally due to a congenital, progressive condition. What is life like on dialysis? What is the significance of having an organ transplant? What is the meaning of this type of illness?

How do we deal with children with heart defects, juvenile diabetes, rheumatic disease, asthma, psoriasis, or cancer? The main premise of this book — that child development and overcoming disease are related processes — can be helpful in coming to grips with these serious questions. Each illness conceals a specific task, a unique opportunity for development, learning, and mastery. Learning to recognize this opportunity is the first step in overcoming the problem. The task, however, cannot be generalized; each individual discovers and experiences it differently. For example, we cannot assume that all blind people have the same problem to solve. At this point, therefore, we would like to present a few basic thoughts that can provide a helpful direction in individual cases.

Practical suggestions

In confronting a child's illness or a disability, we must first learn to deal with our own fear, anxiety, and worry, at least to a certain extent. In the process, it may be helpful to ask ourselves what aspects of the world a chronically ill or handicapped child experiences differently, and perhaps uniquely, as a result of his or her limitations. How can I help my child learn something essential from the experience of disability? If we manage to achieve this attitude, the insights that result are much more likely to be useful in coping with the child's situation.

An important point to consider is that preschool children experience their disability only to the extent that adults allow them to do so. They often become aware of it only through inappropriate overprotection, or when adults discuss their illness in their presence or pamper them with expressions of regret and sympathy. But children with handicaps, if simply given the necessary care with a no-nonsense and matter-of-fact attitude and otherwise treated just like their normal siblings, will experience themselves as "normal." They will identify with their condition and find ways to cope with it without sensing that it "ought" to be different. This attitude lays the foundation for an inner confidence that they will most certainly need at some point. When the shocks start coming — when your child is teased on the street, for example, because she limps or is cross-eyed, or if he notices that people choose not to sit next to him on the bus because they think eczema is contagious — it is especially important for parents to convey to the child that such experiences are quite natural. Two- to four-year-olds can be distracted with a story or an activity or something to look at. To an older child, we can say, "That boy doesn't know you at all. He wouldn't behave like that if he knew what you're really like." Or, "You know, there's always something about everybody that other people can dislike or make fun of. Let's not get upset about it." We can also tell older children the stories of *Bearskin* and *The Ugly Duckling,* which describe how learning to bear the burden of an unsightly and ugly exterior transforms it into something exceptionally beautiful and valuable. We can also tell them how an oyster copes with the pain when a foreign object gets inside its shell — it coats the object with mother-of-pearl to make it harmless, and the end product is a gleaming, pinkish-white pearl!

Depending on their situation and maturity, children of school age may be able to discuss their disabilities openly with their parents. In our daily life together, we can at least make it clear to them — in the case of diabetics, for example — that we respect their ability to obey certain necessary rules and that we value the discipline they have learned in dealing with their illness. In these conversations, the issue of fairness is bound to come up. For example, why do other children have it easier? But then, why does one person enjoy a life of ease and luxury while another lives in dire poverty? Why do external or personal circumstances allow one person to travel to distant countries and have great learning experiences while another is denied a similar opportunity? Such questions are challenging not only for the ill or disabled but also for healthy people. None of us is exempt from the need to come to grips with personal destiny. Chapter 8 on the purpose of childhood illnesses contains more discussion on this issue.

How real is the idea of reincarnation?

This is the unspoken question that every child with a severe handicap poses to us. How are we to understand and affirm a destiny that makes it impossible for someone to have a job or a family or to take their own life in hand in any way? If the answer to these questions were, "Serious handicaps have no meaning or purpose. These children cannot develop in any way, and they actually should never have been born," everything that can be said about the human I and its destiny (seeSection 8.1ff) would be called into question. At this point, we would like to pose a different question, namely, "What perspectives lead us on from here?" Religion speaks of God's unfathomable will and of His grace, which compensates us in the hereafter for what we have been denied in this life. Both of these concepts, however, are made more concrete by the idea that individuals progress through repeated earthly lives (reincarnation). Here are two examples of how children spontaneously express this idea, even if they have never heard adults talk about it:

• A mother knows that her eight-year-old daughter is seriously ill and dying of leukemia. The girl comforts her, saying, "Don't be so sad, I'll come back!"

• A four-year-old girl visits the family of her aunt, whose son died eight months ago at the age of two and a half. Since then, both families have talked a great deal about this terrible misfortune. That afternoon, the aunt hears her niece saying to the two-year-old sister of the dead boy, "How big you are already! When your brother David comes back, he's going to be really glad to see how you've grown!"

Where do children get this idea? The girl in the first example had never had any religious education. Their statements, however, coincide with an experience that many people have when someone close to them dies — they sense that the person is still there on a soul-spiritual level. Mothers whose children are very dissimilar

have a similar experience; the idea of reincarnation offers a very direct explanation of the very different talents and abilities that these children bring with them. Of course all kinds of objections are possible: "It all sounds too simplistic, too much like wishful thinking." "I can't take that seriously without some kind of proof." The question of our own continued existence after death, however, can never be satisfactorily answered by outer evidence or tempting prospects alone. More decisive is our own experience: Does it lead us to see the possible truth in this idea? Do we experience that much in life remains obscure and incomprehensible if we reject the idea of reincarnation? Or, does the thought of repeated earthly lives help us understand and support destinies such as those of people with severe handicaps? If the answer is yes, we have a direct experience of the efficacy and thus also the reality of the concept of reincarnation.

Here are two clarifying examples:

Imagine meeting a child who can neither speak nor walk. Lying in bed or sitting in a wheelchair, she is totally dependent on those around her. She spends an entire lifetime receiving their help; she emits sounds of comfort or discomfort, but she is incapable of "doing" anything.

A sixteen-year-old boy enjoys working under supervision and works tirelessly. His head is very long and narrow, his body heavy set, his speech awkward, his expression kind and open. At his group home, he helps in the garden and does the same things every day in the house. He performs these simple tasks with a pleasure that contrasts starkly with the attitude of many "normal" people, who approach their daily work as if they would rather be doing something completely different.

Approaching these destinies by asking what these people can learn in their present lives and what capacities they are developing for future earthly lives points us in a very productive direction. Teachers, special educators, doctors, and therapists who take this approach enhance their options for supporting handicapped and chronically ill children and their parents. We may realize, for example, that the girl in the first example is experiencing a lifetime of receiving, a whole life in which to learn that we must receive as well as give, that we owe all of our own possibilities to other people and to the world in which we live and act, that the Self becomes evident begins only when we decide what to do with what we have received. After spending an entire life unable to do anything except receive and be dependent on her surroundings, in her next life she will certainly not make the mistake of believing that she does not need other people. She will not have the egotistical tendency to attract whatever is useful to her and reject what she does not need. Ingratitude, superiority, and overestimating her own ability will have no place in her character.

The young man who spends a life-time working gladly and regularly is undergoing an especially intensive training of his will. Nothing strengthens the will more effectively than regular activity performed with complete sympathy. Just as our muscles need daily activity to grow strong, so too our will activity as a whole needs constant practice (see also Sections 9.4 and 20.1). In view of the absence of enthusiasm or strong intentions that we can observe in many people today, it is like a ray of hope to imagine the strength of purpose that can develop through such an exceptional will training.

Thus the concept of reincarnation is anything but an "ideology of retribution." Rather, it offers opportunities for us to resolve to correct our errors and further our own development and that of the world. The educator Michael Bauer once formulated this future-oriented aspect of the concept of reincarnation like this: "The idea of reincarnation is a postulate of love. Those who truly want to help will not grow tired in a single earthly life." This view of reincarnation emphasizes not its fateful aspect but the free will that allows us to take the situation that is given to us and make it meaningful for ourselves and for the world around us.

Reincarnation and Grace

Religious people often object that such thoughts are incompatible with the Christian concept of redemption and even less compatible with the essence of Christian grace. In view of this objection, we would like to ask, what could be stronger proof of the

11

reality of grace than being given repeated opportunities to lift ourselves up out of failure and powerlessness and take our own development in hand again? Isn't the most humane view of "divine judgment" the idea that after death, in the spiritual world, our past life is assessed in all its details, and everything we could not see or do correctly from our subjective earthly perspective is judged and put right? Could anything but grace transform the lessons from this judgment into strong impulses for learning in our next earthly life, incentives for new discoveries and free deeds? If the Gospel according to John is right in saying "you will behold the truth, and the truth will make you free," this prophecy about human evolution and development must apply to each individual, not just to a very talented few. But if this prophecy applies to all of us, a great deal of time (that is, repeated earthly lives) will be needed for us all to reach this goal through God's grace, the help of others, and our own efforts.

As part of this same line of thought, we must apply questions of destiny not only to illnesses and handicaps but also to talents and genius. We often accept our own gifts and abilities as matters of course. But do we know how we achieved them? Could it be that the things we are so proud of in ourselves or admire in others can be traced back to handicaps or illnesses in earlier lives?[29]

As a rule, sick people grasp such issues more easily than healthy people do. Parents and physicians experience repeatedly that people affected by chronic illness or disability deal with these questions very differently from the sympathetic people around them. They often sense that their suffering belongs to them and is part of the current manifestation of their personality. At times this goes so far that they themselves comfort those who grieve for them. This "victory" over illness is a sign of instinctive, subconscious understanding of the necessities of personal destiny. On the other hand, it is only natural for people with chronic illnesses or disabilities to experience anger and denial and to refuse to accept their illness. This attitude is difficult to transform or overcome if disabled people's education and life experience constantly confront them with the view that illness and suffering are meaningless coincidences in life. We see it as one of the essential tasks of education to foster an attitude toward life that unites all of life's many different elements into a single meaningful field of experience and approaches even the problematic elements from the perspective of what can be learned from them.

11.2 Sudden Infant Death Syndrome (SIDS)

Possible Causes

For how to treat an infant who suddenly appears lifeless, see First Aid Section, page 42. Sudden infant death syndrome, otherwise known as "cot death" syndrome, is listed as the cause of one-third of all fatalities between the end of the first month and the end of the first year of life. In the majority of cases, the children are discovered lifeless in their beds.

Recent studies in many different countries reveal a series of statistical factors that increase the risk of sudden infant death:

- cramped living quarters
- adults who smoke during pregnancy and after delivery
- formula feeding rather than breast-feeding
- allowing the baby to sleep on her stomach or side
- allowing the baby to sleep in her parents' bed (especially if they smoke)
- putting the baby to bed in an overheated room or under over-insulating covers, or dressing her in a warm cap or bonnet for sleeping
- covers that a baby can slide under
- excessive cooling.

Simply educating the public about the risk of allowing babies to sleep on their stomachs has lead to an almost 50% reduction of SIDS cases in some areas. The low rate of SIDS in the Netherlands is attributed to the Dutch practice of putting babies to bed on their backs in sleeping bags that extend up to the armpits. For practical details about putting your baby to bed on her back, see page 197.

Other statistical studies, which found pertussis germs in some autopsied infants, conclude that early, undiagnosed stages of whooping cough contribute to some cases of sudden infant death (see Section 7.11).

"Acute life-threatening event" (ALTE) is the term applied to a case where the infant survives, either through resuscitation or because she begins breathing again on her own.

Early Recognition and Prevention

On the assumption that certain infants are predisposed to SIDS as a result of seizure disorders or disturbances in respiratory regulation, specialized laboratory equipment has been developed to simultaneously monitor heart rhythm, respiration rate, brain waves, blood gas levels, and other factors on a 24 hour basis (so-called polysomnography). When excessively long pauses in respiration are suspected in an infant, electronic monitoring of respiration in the hospital for several days can help to assess risk of SIDS. Today these tests are performed on all infants who are either medically at

11

risk or who have survived an acute life-threatening event.

It is important to realize, however, that only 10–25% of SIDS cases occur in children considered medically at risk. This means that there is little overlap between tested children and those truly at risk. Cases of SIDS have been known to occur even when polysomnograms (with or without subsequent consistent monitoring) revealed no cause for alarm.

11.3 Thoughts on dealing with sudden death

One mother whose infant son survived an acute life-threatening event wrote us this letter:

The survival of our two-month-old son raised many questions in us, as parents, about his destiny and path in life. There is no satisfactory medical explanation for this phenomenon; we must look for answers in other domains. It has become increasingly clear to us that our son's near-death experience and return to his body will probably influence his entire life. He has changed in positive ways since this event. The alertness, clarity, and radiance of his facial expression give the impression of someone who has been born a second time. Our concern about this child has disappeared gradually, replaced by a sense of security provided by electronic monitoring.

This boy's mother found him lying lifeless in bed and was unable to resuscitate him herself, but he was revived in the ambulance on the way to the hospital and released after two weeks in intensive care and in the pediatric ward. His condition has been monitored electronically since the event.

Parents who lose a child to SIDS face questions that can only be explored on a spiritual level. Why did their child leave his body?

A riddle confronts anyone familiar with the will to live displayed by infants and premature babies, and the difficulties they have to overcome. Some mothers who lose a child to SIDS and soon become pregnant again have the strong impression that it is the same child, while others do not. We are still extremely ignorant about life before birth (see also Section 11.5). Are SIDS children trying to alert us to the threshold to the spiritual worlds, where birth and death hold out their hands to each other? These children leave behind questions directed to us, to the earthly world, and especially to the world where the dead and the not-yet-born meet. As we work on these questions, our life is deepened and enriched — another reason for being grateful for the gift of the short time these children spend with us.

11.4 Ethical Issues

11

It is clear from our discussions thus far that there is no such thing as a meaningless illness or a life not worth living. Our conceptions, personal desires, and capacity for understanding, however, may prevent us from properly asking or answering the question of the meaning of illness or disability.

Almost no question leads us so deeply into connections of destiny as the issue of good deeds. The Greek-derived word "ethics" means a doctrine of good behavior and good actions. Here, too, scientific discussion, especially in the field of medicine, has faced increasing difficulties in recent decades. After World War II — especially in Germany, where experiences under the Nazi regime were fresh in people's minds — legislation prohibited euthanasia in any form. The situation looks different now, and not only in Germany. Throughout the world, people are invoking scientific, legal, and economic reasons for questioning whether incurable illnesses and disabilities and long-term geriatric dementia have any meaning or purpose. At the same time, however, some important questions relating to destiny are also being asked. For example, what does terminating a pregnancy mean for the unborn child, the mother, and the physician who performs the abortion? What does brain death or donating or receiving an organ transplant mean for the human body, soul, and spirit? How do the circumstances surrounding a person's death affect life after death? What does senile dementia mean if not seen from exclusively materialistic perspectives?

As soon as our perspectives on human life expand to consider the human body, soul, and spirit as extending beyond birth and death, ethical questions are transformed into questions of individual responsibility for one's own destiny and the destiny of others. One's motive for action then takes center stage. After all, motive is what determines the quality of an act. What are the real reasons for or against a particular immunization, a specific therapy, physician-assisted death, or terminating a pregnancy? What personal, professional, or health-related motives are at work? Any system of ethics that takes the human soul and spirit seriously never asks about the act itself without also asking about the motives that lead to it and about the perpetrator's relationship to its consequences. In addition to insight and understanding, profound fears, concerns, anger, love, trust, and hope shape ethical reality and influence the quality of an action. The consequences of such actions, however, constitute the destiny of children and adults.

For example, parents who allow their child to be vaccinated against measles out of fear of encephalitis need to know that encephalitis can also be triggered by other infections.[30] The pre-eminent issue in this case is *how* to support the child with our own best forces, *how* we develop confidence in his destiny and attempt to help him find his way into his body and into his own life. We surround our decision with thoughts and feelings that strengthen the child's experience of existence and his constitutional state of health. Each decision, however, may have both positive and negative consequences. There is virtually no such thing as a decision that is "all good." For example, if my hope in having my child vaccinated against measles is to prevent possible damage, of course my motivation sounds good.

On the other hand, by having her immunized I also deprive her of an opportunity to exert herself in coming to grips with this illness, an opportunity that would result in more permanent immunity and a better match between her body and her incarnating soul and spirit (see Section 8.1). In each decision, a great deal depends on how we live with its consequences. To what extent can we stand behind the positive consequences of our actions and counteract any negative consequences?

From this perspective, it is becoming increasingly impossible for ethics to take direction from existing values and norms. It is in the process of being transformed from normative ethics into individual ethics. Regardless of the legalities that apply, each action must always be judged individually, and an individual must take responsibility for it. Even if, as in the Netherlands, euthanasia is permitted by law under certain circumstances, the physicians, patients, and relatives involved must live with the consequences of their actions and take personal responsibility for them, for they are the ones who perform the act. The same is true of legislative regulation of organ transplants. Even when brain death is the legal criterion for organ removal, the donor, the receiver, and the doctors performing the operation are linked in relationships of destiny that the participants should enter into deliberately and responsibly.

For example, we have vivid recollections of one of our patients, an eleven-year-old girl with polycystic kidneys who received a transplanted kidney from her identical twin sister. Without the transplant, she would have survived for only a few more weeks or months. Of course, for a living donor to contribute an organ is a more transparent situation than receiving an organ from a dying person. In the latter case, however, it is all the more necessary for all of us as potential donors or receivers to make conscious efforts to understand the processes and circumstances surrounding both the donor's death and the recipient's extended life. Anyone who has carefully weighed up the reasons for becoming a donor or a recipient as aspects of personal destiny will live with the consequences of their decision very differently from situations where doctors or legislators decide the issue. In individual ethics, the decisive criterion for judging the ethical validity of any action is always whether the action promotes or hinders human values and human development. This judgment must always be left to the individuals who will personally experience and take responsibility for the action and its consequences.

Questions for human genetics

Today we are aware of a number of hereditary illnesses and congenital malformations that can be predicted with the help of chromosomal analysis during pregnancy. For example, amniocentesis (extraction and analysis of amniotic fluid), which is usually performed in weeks 16 to 18 of pregnancy, can identify serious hereditary illnesses of the fetus in time to permit legal termination of the pregnancy. The arguments in favour of *in utero* diagnosis are self-evident. Its proponents emphasize that the possibility of early diagnosis may encourage more parents to risk pregnancy and that the number of children identified as seriously handicapped (and thus the number of subsequent abortions) is at most 3%, so that ultimately the availability of this procedure benefits children. Furthermore, the risk of miscarrying or damaging a healthy child due to amniocentesis is only around 1%. Further mention is made of national economic considerations, which carry increasing weight in view of the explosive increase in the cost of health care.

In response to these arguments, we feel obliged to question whether statistics and considerations of this sort do justice to the individual destinies of human beings. Very few people die exactly when their actuarial life expectancy is up. Each human life and destiny can be assessed and understood on the basis of its own unique circumstances. If we could perceive and trace the destinies of the unborn healthy children concealed behind the 1% statistical "damage rate," we would certainly speak in different terms. And if *in utero* diagnostics is recommended to prevent malformed, congenitally ill, or otherwise seriously handicapped children from being born, the underlying assumption is that such lives are not worthy of human beings.

11

On the other hand, if we acknowledge that human beings exist before birth and that even a life of severe handicap or disability has meaning and purpose, the decision will be less easy. It is not the purpose of this book to lay down guidelines as to what is "generally" ethical or responsible (or still or no longer acceptable) in this context. Our intention in joining the ethical debate is rather to offer perspectives that take life before birth, life after death, and questions of destiny into account. In reality, all ethical questions are questions of destiny.

We have also known mothers who — thanks to *in utero* diagnostics — have consciously prepared themselves for the birth of their handicapped child. From the perspective of individual destiny, the often despairing question, "Why me? Why is my child handicapped or malformed?" leads to other questions. "Why do you need me in particular?" "What connects me to you?" "What can I do to further your destiny?" "What do my own experiences and insights owe to you and your suffering?"

We are living now in a time when our knowledge and capabilities have far outstripped our capacity for responsible action and ethical sensitivity. This, however, is not simply a problem for experts. We are all affected by it. Even if it is more comfortable to leave decisions for and against *in utero* diagnostics, artificial insemination, and genetic manipulation, or experimental cloning to experts, the church, or the government, every adult citizen needs to work on these questions. This is the only way to develop a sense of responsibility based on personal insight , which is the foundation of a new morality, a new "ethical individualism," as Steiner called it.[31]

11.5 Born too late? The reality of life before birth

Children bring their own destinies with them into this world. After the birth of a baby, parents frequently experience that they develop relationships with neighbours who were almost strangers before. Children get to know their age peers in the neighbourhood and develop a variety of friendships as well as problematic connections. This process continues in school, resulting in different constellations within each class — lonely or excluded individuals and the cliques, friendships, and enmities that shape the character of children's daily lives. But do we ever stop to consider that practicing family planning may mean that our next child is born three or even five years later than he or she originally intended? Especially in childhood and adolescence, isn't it important to be part of a particular peer group in order to come into closer contact with other specific individuals? Could it be that a lonely child who feels somehow lost and unaccepted in her class or social context was simply *born too late?* That her comrades in destiny from earlier lives are too old for her or have already left school?

The choices made available by contraceptives, abortion reform, in vitro fertilization, treatment of sterility, and early diagnosis of congenital malformations have not only vastly increased women's freedom of choice but have also focused awareness on a single question — "When and how do I want and plan to have a child?" — when it comes to family planning. Unborn children are now much less concretely involved in the actions and decisions that result in a family. Parents' desire — or emphatic lack of desire — for a child may conflict with an unborn child's affinity for a specific parent or parents. Many women clearly sense whether a child wants to come to them or not. This book brings these inklings to the surface of consciousness. Often, a woman will report that she has felt for years that a child is waiting in the wings for her. When the feeling disappears, it may leave behind either a sense of sadness or the happy feeling that the child has found a different solution and will now leave her in peace.

Rudolf Steiner's research makes it clear that an unborn person's approach to a new incarnation can be very difficult and complicated:

For example, a soul intending to incarnate knows that it needs to experience a certain type of upbringing and absorb a certain kind of knowledge during childhood in its next earthly life. The soul also knows which parents will be able to insure that these experiences will indeed occur. This set of parents may not be able to provide a happy life in other respects, but if this soul were to choose different parents, it would be unable to achieve its most important goals with regard to this particular incarnation.

We must not imagine that life in the spiritual world is always so very different from life on Earth. An unborn soul may experience tremendous internal conflicts because it knows, for example, that it can expect to be mistreated as a child by the abusive parents it feels obliged to choose. Many souls approaching rebirth experience terrible inner struggles, and these struggles are visible all around them in the spiritual world. In other words, these struggles are not exclusively internal, private conflicts but are projected outward for all to see. In very graphic imaginations, we perceive the internal conflicts of souls approaching their next incarnations.[32]

When we apply the realities of spiritual life and the spiritual world to everyday earthly life, many aspects of family planning that we now take for granted become open to question again, and thoughts about the unborn begin to influence how we think about our own life. We begin to listen to intuitive ideas and the voice of conscience. Our perspective on our own life situation — what we ourselves and our partners need or feel is right — undergoes a shift when we consider the unborn, whose presence becomes more tangible when we think about them and listen for them.

The use of hormonal or barrier contraceptives may initially force an unborn child to wait in the surroundings of the couple selected as parents. After a certain time, however, if that soul has reasons for wanting to belong to a specific generation or peer group, it is forced to seek out a similar couple or a couple in the immediate area, who will enable it to absorb the specific impressions it needs and to meet the people who were its first choice as parents.

The Foundations of
Healthy Development

*All education is self-education; as teachers and educators, we merely
provide the environment for children who are educating themselves. We must
deliver the best possible environment so that through us, these children can
educate themselves as their inner destinies require.*
                                                                    Rudolf Steiner

12. The First Months of Life

12.1 Preparing for birth

Where will you give birth if your baby arrives prematurely?

Early in your pregnancy, it makes sense to inquire how your local birthing center or maternity unit deals with a sudden premature birth and where special neonatal care facilities are available in your area.

Modern obstetric units adopt minimally traumatic handling procedures with premature infants, in terms of transport, movement, noise and disturbance. Where possible, even babies with very low birth weights are allowed to spend many hours a day in the "kangaroo position," resting on the ribcage of their half-reclining mother or father in skin-to-skin contact. In this protected position, where they can hear and feel their parent's heartbeat and respiratory rhythms, premature babies sleep more soundly and their oxygen needs are often measurably lower. Hospitals experienced in the care of premature infants encourage these babies to nurse much earlier; they sometimes learn to drink from the breast at weights well under 2000 g /

4.5 lb and can often leave the hospital earlier, too.

Giving birth in hospital

If you give birth in hospital, normally you will be allowed to keep the baby with you in your room at all times (see Figures 18 and 19). The first few days after birth are especially critical for mother-child bonding. Hospitals nowadays routinely involve the father by showing him how to support his wife during delivery and allowing him to help receive the infant. If the father cannot be present, a female friend or relative should be allowed to take his place.

Immediately after birth, it is best to place the newborn where she came from — that is, on the mother's belly (covered with warmed towels, of course). This "kangaroo position" is not always possible when infants require intensive care, but new procedures allow even many of these babies to spend hours at a time lying between their mother's breasts.

Babies also usually suck much more

forcefully right after birth than if they are forced to wait for hours before nursing — an empirical observation that had been forgotten for many years.

The vernix caseosa — the white creamy substance that covers the new-born baby's skin at birth — is a natural protection absorbed by the skin after a few hours. Bathing is unnecessary; traces of blood can usually be dabbed off with a cloth.

In some local areas, efforts have gone into making hospital births as comfortable and intimate as traditional home birthing, with technological devices being kept in the background to avoid a cold and impersonal atmosphere. The birthing team accompanies the event discreetly, with a surgical team and a pediatrician standing by in case of emergency.

Giving birth at home

Home delivery may be an option where the mother does not fall into a category considered to be at risk. Your doctor or gynecologist will advise you as to the normal procedures for your area.

Giving birth at home allows for an intimate, natural birth process which is better for both mother and baby, and increasing numbers of parents request this where possible. In spite of all the modern technologies used to monitor delivery, it should be remembered that giving birth is *not* an illness. Ideally, it is an active, co-operative process that involves both parents as well as an obstetrician and/or midwife. Each birth, like each child, is unique.

12.2 First impressions

When a mother is allowed to keep her newborn baby with her at all times, her happy, questioning glances often meet his own searching gaze. Physically small and inexperienced, he seems large and expansive on the soul level. In the first few days after birth, his every movement will be noted with pleasure — each sucking gesture as he sleeps, each yawn, and each little movement of his fingers. His breathing, sometimes barely aud-

ible, is occasionally interrupted by a series of somewhat deeper breaths or a little grunt as he stretches. When his mother bends over him, he responds happily to her presence with a few deeper or faster breaths. If the baby sleeps in his mother's room, she can sometimes observe his eyeballs "swimming" under closed lids (a phenomenon that is apparent in premature babies even when their eyes are open). The transition between sleeping and waking is still fluid at this point.

The baby's gaze does not yet focus or rest on objects, but it does suggest that his soul experiences are now becoming associated with visual perceptions for the first time. We adults instinctively look for expressions of the baby's personality, but they are different from what they will become later. When his eyes are open, they seem to be searching for something in the area around his mother, where they linger for a few moments before he exhausted, they close again. But soon his eyes open once more and attempt to find that something. This rhythmical alternation of seeing and not seeing is an essential part of the baby's initial experience of self. Through repeated sense impressions, he experiences the certainty of his earthly existence. Over the months that follow, he discovers himself with increasing clarity through his efforts to associate perceptions with each other. Later, between the ages of two and three years, he will summarize

this experience of his own activity in the word "I."

This desire to experience himself through sensory impressions of the outer world underlies all of the newborn's movements. He enjoys drinking his fill, searches greedily for the breast when he is hungry, and is a master at sucking. When not sound asleep, he takes in the light, sounds, warmth, and cold around him. His soul experience is totally given over to this alternation between receptivity and self-containment, desire and satisfaction, which shapes time for him long before he has any awareness of days, hours, or minutes.

Parents recalling their first child's first day of life often say they knew that everything would be different from then on. No amount of preparation for the birth of a child can even approximate the experience of how profoundly this little being, in all his helplessness, moves and shapes the feelings, thoughts, and actions of those around him.

12

12.3 Routine checkups (well-baby visits)

Mothers are not always aware that their baby's vital functions are checked immediately after birth. In the UK, this is a legal responsibility for the midwife or pediatrician.

Once you are back home, your local doctor or health visitor will be responsible for following up your baby's progress and giving help and advice with handling and feeding. In some areas, you will be provided with a schedule of routine checkups ("well-baby visits") for your infant and pre-schooler. Parents may also be given a record chart or booklet to be kept of the baby's growth and development. This is completed at each checkup and also records the child's immunizations.

The purpose of routine checkups is to discover, treat, and monitor any disturbances or developmental delays, whether physical or psychological, in a timely way. These examinations are a good opportunity for your family doctor to keep track of your child's healthy development, since you would otherwise consult a physician only when the child is ill. The main areas covered in these checkups are: *early recognition of heart defects and congenital hip problems; disorders of development, sensory perception, nutrition, and metabolism; prophylactic options including vaccinations and the prevention of rickets and dental caries; communication disorders and their causes,* and *questions related to child-rearing.* Premature infants require specific checks because of the added risks of cerebral palsy or visual problems. Such checkups and the opportunities they offer for talking with your doctor can help you gain confidence in how your child's development is progressing. The recommended program for checkups marks important stages in child development when progress and abilities become apparent or their absence points to disorders or illness. Because this schedule also coincides with the timing of required or recommended vaccinations, we recommend giving some thought in advance to which optional vaccinations you want your child to receive and which not (see also Section 10.4). Laboratory testing is indicated when a checkup reveals a possible pathological deviation. Later checkups include urine analysis. At age four (or before the child enters kindergarten), a tuberculin test may also be performed.

12.4 Cultivating early sense impressions

Sounds and tones

Even if she makes no sound, our behavior changes instinctively and immediately when we enter an newborn baby's room. Even lively and rumbustious children quietly approach the cradle on tiptoe. Conversely, everyone around her comes running when she screams. Her parents' words and expressions of pleasure and loving attention interact subtly with every sound she utters that attracts their attention.

Even before birth, a baby's sense of hearing is fully functional and her body is profoundly affected by voices and noises in her parents' surroundings. We recommend exposing unborn and newborn babies to as little recorded music and mechanical noise as possible. Everything we do with children in their first few years of life has profound effects on their development and contributes to habits that may persist for the rest of their lives.

Initially, any mechanical noise — whether from construction equipment outside or vacuum cleaners and dishwashers inside — is foreign and disturbing. Sleeping babies often react to this type of noise with a change in breathing or a faster pulse. We adults need to consider whether the sounds in a baby's environment are age-appropriate. Our auditory experience occupies a spectrum ranging from absolute silence through a multitude of human, instrumental, and mechanical sounds. The more sensitive and careful you are about your baby's auditory environment, the more subtle the sounds she will later be able to distinguish.

As pediatricians, we often have to ask mothers who phone us about their feverish infants to turn off the radio blaring in the background. Before children learn to speak and think, they have no way of preserving any distance between themselves and the impressions — especially noises — that their surroundings impose on them. The ability to distance oneself from perceptions develops only gradually, as a result of naming things and thinking about them. *Especially in the first year of life, a child is totally incapable of shutting out the external world; her entire body is highly sensitive and is forced to participate in all the impressions that affect it.* Subtle or not-so-subtle changes in respiratory and circulatory rhythms are a sensitive indicator of these impacts. Of course this does not mean that we need to refrain from all enjoyment of music when there is a baby in the house, but it does mean that we should attempt to keep it at some distance from the baby and to adapt our selections to her sensitivity. *As much as possible, babies should be spared mechanical noises and "acoustic bombardment" with media such as radio, television, videos, and recorded music.*

The powerful effects of sounds and tones on infants are evident when we watch them play. If you put a plastic rattle in your baby's hand or suspend a noise-producing mobile over her cradle, the effect is clear from the baby's movements. It is as if her kicking gestures are directed inward, shaking her body. The effect of playing with a simple wooden clapper with its sliding part is totally different. Her movements adapt to the sounds she perceives and become noticeably more deliberate and regular. In both cases, the baby seems happy and excited by the noise, but in the latter instance, she seems more composed, self-contained, and able to process the sense impression.

Still different is the impact of a simple series of notes sung or hummed by the baby's parent. She pauses in amazement, her movements become more relaxed, and if she is tired, she soon falls asleep. In opening herself up to these tones, she becomes more able to surrender her soul to sleep.

Fresh air and humidity

Everyone agrees that infants need fresh air, but when we open a window in a big city, we have to take what we get. Exposing your baby to cool air is fine, but do avoid drafts — another practical reason for a veil over the child's bed (see below, Section 12.7). Whether or not and for how long to open the window depends not only on the outdoor temperature and noise but also on indoor dryness. A good solution is to open the window wide several times a day when the baby is in another room. Avoid exposing him constantly to cooking odours or cigarette smoke, however.

With regard to moisture in the air, most modern heating systems dry out the air and are unsuitable for children. Water containers suspended from the radiators help but do not evaporate enough water (several litres/quarts a day) to totally replace lost moisture. This level of humidification can be achieved only with electrical devices, which you may not want to use for other reasons (noise, bacterial risks, and so on). If you must purchase a humidifier for health reasons such as frequent colds in the family, make sure to get one that operates without a motor, uses ordinary tap water, and does not require a filter. This type of humidifier brings water to the boiling point between two electrode plates. If you do not have a humidifier, the best alternative is to air the baby's room briefly but frequently. Alternatively, you can keep water steaming on a small electric hotplate (out of children's reach!) set on low. When your baby has a respiratory infection, adding a few drops of pure eucalyptus oil to this water (not directly on to the heater) enhances the quality of the humidified air and reduces the effects of irritants such as ozone and nitrogen oxide.

Sunlight

In semi-darkness, newborn babies open their eyes and seem to be looking for something, but if you let light fall directly into the cradle, their eyes close again immediately. After a few weeks, however, they begin to look around in different directions even when the room is brighter. Now is the time to let your baby sleep by an open window or outside, protected from wind and direct sun. It is important to expose his face to the blue sky (see "rickets prevention," Section 10.2). Begin with fifteen minutes to half an hour a day, depending on the weather, and gradually increase to two hours or longer. Of course you'll need to check on him occasionally, even if he's sleeping. The mere thought of putting a three or four-week-old infant to bed outside under a clear blue sky is abhorrent to some people, even if the baby is warmly covered and wearing a cap, but in temperate latitudes this is one of the best steps you can take to insure your baby's healthy physical development. Next to mother's milk, light from a clear blue sky is the most effective way to stimulate healthy bone growth.* *An infant whose forehead is exposed to blue sky for two hours a day will not develop rickets.* In cloudy climates or industrial areas where blue sky may not be seen for months on end, other steps must be

* The ultraviolet radiation wavelengths that prevent rickets are transmitted much better through blue sky overhead than through the paler sky near the horizon. We believe that the polarization of sunlight is also important. It enables bees to orient themselves in space, and with a little practice humans can also perceive Haidinger's brushes (a fleeting pale yellow image like a stack of hay). The structure of the sky as a whole in relationship to the sun certainly has very different effects from a plain blue, radiant surface.

taken to prevent rickets, but they are usually not necessary in areas with more sun. We urgently advise you not to expose your child to too much light early in life (no sunbathing that exposes all or most of his skin, for example). *Too much light causes premature hardening throughout the body and overtaxes the nervous system.* To confirm this statement, simply consider the state of your own skin and mental acuity after excessive sunbathing. Here, too, moderation is in order.

Heat and cold

A newborn baby's thermoregulatory system is immature and easily disrupted (see the section on rhythms, Section 9.4). Infants delivered in cold surroundings tend to have subnormal body temperatures for hours afterwards, even if they are wrapped warmly right after birth. Doctors and parents are still learning how important it is to keep babies consistently warm during the first few days and weeks of life. Formerly, premature babies were placed naked on cotton cloth in incubators heated with fans, and they still lost too much body heat. Today they are given clothes or at least placed on a sheepskin.

Whatever the situation, make sure that your baby does not get chilled. For example, fan-air heating in the bathroom is not as good as a radiant heater, but the radiant heater should also not be located directly over the baby's head. Marbled skin coloration or a red, hot head will let you know

12

you've made a mistake. Outdoors, cool cheeks and cool exposed hands are normal in warmly dressed babies. Under a blanket, however, hands and feet should always be comfortably warm. A baby's uncovered head radiates a lot of heat and should therefore be covered with a thick woolen bonnet outside and a light one, perhaps of silk, inside (see Figure 48). Hot days and hot climates are exceptions to this rule, but in these situations your baby should wear a sunhat (see Figures 57 and 59).

In the first few weeks of your baby's life, you may need to place a hot water bottle in her bed for extra warmth. Be careful not to make it too hot, though! Even 40°C/104°F can "burn" a baby's sensitive skin after a while. If your baby's room is cool or if you prefer not to use a featherbed, cover her with a woolen sleeping bag or a blanket of similar weight.

If your baby often has cool hands for no apparent reason, it usually helps to dress her in a long-sleeved woolen undershirt. Leave it on when you change her, even if it gets a bit damp around the lower edge. Try to find a brand of wool underwear that is soft enough for your baby, but if you can't find wool of this quality, use a thin cotton undershirt under woolen clothing. We also recommend woolen nappy (diaper) covers and rompers because wool has the unique ability to absorb up to 30% of its own weight in water without feeling damp and to evaporate moisture without cooling the skin. Wool also draws away perspiration better than any synthetic fiber and is less likely to trap heat next to the skin. This is why desert Bedouin wear clothing made of wool or sheepskins. Some people object to wool because it feels scratchy against their skin. Even soft wool becomes scratchy if it mats or felts, so wash your baby's wool garments carefully in lukewarm water and a suitable detergent. Undershirts and bonnets of raw silk are good for babies with very sensitive skin. This fabric regulates warmth nearly as well as wool and is extremely comfortable to wear. Pure cotton underwear by itself is practical only when the weather is very warm and temperatures do not fluctuate much. Synthetics are never good, because they trap body heat and do not absorb moisture.

We have discussed wool clothing in such detail because as pediatricians we all too frequently see infants who are not dressed warmly enough. We only rarely see the other extreme — a baby dressed in layer upon layer of wool, with a wool cap coming right down to her eyebrows so that even her forehead is not allowed to be cool. Seeing these two extremes of excessive cooling and excessive warmth makes it easy to understand the need for moderation — everything at the right time and in the right place. Too much warmth overprotects the body and prevents it from developing effective internal thermoregulation. And at this stage of life, too little warmth — or worse still, deliberate exposure to cold — establishes reflexes that bear no relationship to normal circumstances and therefore trigger excessive reactions. In either case, the baby cannot learn to respond flexibly and moderately to changes in temperature.

Gravity and your infant's lying position

From carrying newborn babies, we know that they cannot yet hold their heads and torsos upright against the force of gravity. Only when lying on their stomachs are they able to hold their heads up briefly (see Figures 27 and 28). Less obvious is the fact that gravity can actively deform a baby's body during the first months of life. A baby who always holds her head turned to the same side (towards the light or towards approaching people, for example) develops a flat area on her skull on that side. This deformation may extend all the way down the torso to the pelvis. If recognized only after the third month, this position-inflicted damage cannot be fully corrected. To prevent this deformity, alternate sides with regard to the position of the baby's head when you put her down. If a head deformity has already developed, your physician may advise you to turn her head consistently toward the neglected side for a while.

If your baby can already turn her head by herself and prefers the lit side, for example, you will have to turn her (or her bed) around so that her feet are where her head used to be and the light falls on her from the other side.

Other possible reasons for prefer-

ring one side over the other include *broken collarbone* at birth, *muscular torticollis* (wryneck, see Section 1.8), or a swelling on the baby's head.* When either wryneck or a swelling on the head is the cause of her preference for one side, these cases need to be discussed with your doctor.

Sleeping positions: back, side, or stomach?

According to more recent studies, the stomach position that American experts used to advocate for infants in the sixties contributed significantly to the increase in sudden infant death (SIDS, see Section 11.2). At present, the general recommendation is to put infants to sleep on their backs, not on their sides or stomachs. No pillow. If the baby has a soft skull or begins to develop a flat spot on the back of her head, a homemade pillow, 20 by 20 cm (8 by 8 in.) and loosely filled with millet, can be used to distribute the weight of her skull over a larger area.

When awake, the baby lies either on her back, looking at faces and objects and playing with her hands, or on her stomach, which gives her opportunities to hold up her head (and later her shoulders, arms, and hands). If your baby has a definite preference for lying on her back, place her on her stomach several times a day while you

* A *caput succedaneum* (a swelling that forms on the presenting part of the fetus during delivery) disappears after a day or two, but a hematoma (a mass of clotted blood resulting from a broken vessel) recedes only after several weeks or months. It is better not to lay an infant on that side until the hematoma has resolved.

12

play and talk with her. If she has a hard time falling asleep on her back, try giving her plenty of body contact during the day by carrying her in a sling, and place a rolled up sweater or other garment belonging to her mother in the bed at night.

Always make sure that blankets, etc. are placed and secured so that the baby's head cannot possibly slide under them.

12.5 Observing a newborn baby's excretions and other bodily functions

Burping the baby after drinking

All infants swallow a certain amount of air while drinking, especially if they are bottle-fed. To minimize spitting up and to allow your baby to sleep as comfortably as possible, the resulting air bubble in the stomach needs to be released upward. This is done by holding the baby with his chin resting on your shoulder, which you should cover with a cloth to catch any spitting up. Unfortunately, many parents then proceed to clap the baby quickly and repeatedly on his back. It is much more comfortable and pleasant for the baby if you sit down with him leaning against you and stroke his head in the area of the fontanelle — the soft depression at the peak of the head — applying gentle pressure with the flat part of your fingers.

Hiccups

Hiccups are caused by spasmodic, rhythmical contractions of the diaphragm. In infants, hiccups are easily triggered by a cold draft on the stomach, by putting the baby down or turning him over too quickly, or by a strong burp. Often, however, they occur for no apparent reason. In newborns, hiccups mean that parents will wait in vain for a burp but can be sure that the baby will not spit up, simply because the diaphragm's contractions temporarily keep the entrance to the stomach closed. Placing a warm cloth on the baby's abdomen can help to prevent hiccups.

Consistency and frequency of stools

After discharge of the black or dark green meconium, which accumulates in the bowel of the fetus in the last few weeks of pregnancy, a breastfed infant's stools are yellow or light green with a typical aromatic odour. Occasionally they may be very fluid, dark yellow, and contain only lentil-shaped solid particles of a cheesy consistency. Frequency generally varies between two and six times a day, but in breastfed babies bowel movements as frequent as ten times a day or as infrequent as once every ten days are no cause for alarm as long as the baby has no other symptoms and seems to be thriving. The stools usually change when other foods are introduced. The smell becomes less pleasant, the color yellow or brownish, the consistency mushy or paste-like, the frequency generally two to four times a day but at least every other day. At this point, a yeasty smell is a possible sign of a fungal infection *(Candida albicans),* while a green color and loose stools indicate a mild digestive disturbance (dyspepsia). Consult your doctor immediately if your infant's stools contain traces of blood, including threads of haematin blackened by contact with stomach acid (not to be confused with banana fibers, which look similar!) or if they are bleached, grayish-white, and accompanied by obvious jaundice.

Urination

In the first few months of life, an infant's urine is almost colorless; it becomes somewhat more yellow only in cases of pronounced jaundice. Urine left in the diapers for some time develops a biting odour of ammonia, especially if the baby is fed formula. Ammonia promotes nappy rash, so if you notice this odour, change your baby's nappies more frequently and pay special attention to skin care and cleaning (with water only). If the weather is hot and your baby has not been drinking much, her urine can easily develop a brickdust color due to precipitation of harmless phosphate salts. Painful urination is often due to a urinary tract infection; in such cases the urine usually smells bad or at least markedly different than usual. Urinary tract infections should be diagnosed and treated by a physician. If two meals pass without a wet nappy, the baby may be feverish or thirsty; other symptoms will determine whether professional advice is needed.

Perspiration

Perspiration is unusual in the first few months of life, but it can occur if the baby is overheated, drinks a great deal, or has a fever. It may also be due to vegetative disorders that usually cannot be pinned down. Increased perspiration for no apparent reason when your baby is around six weeks old may be a sign of early-stage rickets; consult with your doctor about rickets prevention.

12.6 Diaper (nappy) changing and related questions

Diaper techniques and their consequences

Increasingly, parents are avoiding disposable diapers or nappies for newborn babies because cloth nappies keep babies warmer and save on waste disposal. Newborn babies can wear gauze nappies covered with wool soakers or the like (see Appendix, page 437f). After changing, wrap your baby in a large brushed cotton or flannel cloth (wool is also very practical for this purpose) instead of rompers or leggings. Depending on the season, you may need to add a loosely knitted wool blanket over everything. Babies born in the breech position often have immature hip joints and need wide nappies from the very beginning to hold their legs apart. An extra cotton cloth folded into a broad strip and placed between the legs usually does the trick. When your baby begins to kick his way out of this swaddling (usually after a few weeks), "onesies" or "babygrows" with snaps between the legs are a practical solution. At this point, you will probably find that it works well to combine two gauze diapers — a triangular one for wrapping and a rectangular one placed between the baby's legs. A little later, you may want to add a nappy liner for easier cleanup. Soakers made of unbleached wool hold everything in place. Add wool rompers for daytime wear. At night, cotton rompers may be more practical; on top, wrap your baby in the knitted wool blanket mentioned above so that he is not always kicking freely.

We do not recommend allowing your baby complete freedom of movement all the time from a very early age. If you observe your baby's many involuntary and reflexive movements during the first few months of life, you will notice that they interfere with his ability to look around him. The need to support the activity of quiet looking is evident when you realize that the calmer and more alert a baby's gaze, the more readily he learns to use his hands. Hence it is important to choose a nappy technique that puts the brakes on extensive kicking gestures and limits your baby's movements.

Do not diaper your baby so tightly, however, that his hip joints have no freedom of movement at all. Too tight nappies can have negative effects on the development of the hip joint sockets, a special consideration in cases of so-called *hip dysplasia* (underdeveloped hip sockets) or weak ligaments that cause loose hip joints. In these cases, the hip may eventually dislocate. It is important to recognize and treat hip problems as early as possible. Today the diagnosis will be confirmed through ultrasound imaging. If hip dysplasia or congenital dislocation of the hip are overlooked and are noticed only because of the baby's wobbly gait when he learns to walk, surgical correction (usually involving several operations) becomes necessary.

If you carry your baby in a sling (see Figure 23) from the very beginning, first lay him diagonally on a wool blanket, turning the lower corner up over his legs and wrapping the side corners around him so that his whole body, including his feet, is already warmly inclosed when you put him into the sling.

Washing, bathing, and skin care

An infant's skin, like that of adults, has a fine layer of natural oils whose quality cannot be duplicated. It makes no sense to wash these oils off every day and replace them with other fats. In most cases, one bath a week is enough for infants (see Figure 20). Between baths, wash your baby's face, diaper area, and the folds of her skin daily with a soft washcloth and comfortably warm water (no soap). Cleaning with plain water without soap is usually enough even for areas soiled by urine, stools, or spitting up. Stuck remnants of stools or diaper rash ointments are fat-soluble and can be removed with sunflower seed oil, which is more economical for cleaning than skin care oils.

The best baby oils for skin care contain calendula or chamomile oil. Apply a thin layer of one of these oils to the folds of skin on your baby's neck, under her arms, behind her ears, and in the diaper area. Do not use powder on these areas because it can combine with moisture and become crumbly, causing irritation. Powder is indicated only for mild skin irritation such as heat rash on the baby's back or ribcage. In any case, clouds of powder can make your baby cough and are dangerous for her lungs.

Fun on the changing table

In early infancy, a considerable part of a baby's contact with his parents takes place on the changing table. At changing time, infants are generally well fed, in a good mood, and ready to enjoy movement and contact. The minutes during and after cleaning, washing, and oiling your baby's skin can serve both necessary and playful purposes. Hum, sing, and talk with your child and play with his hands and feet. After a few weeks, you can expect to hear his first contact-seeking sounds in response (see Section 15.3). As the months go by, playtime on the changing table becomes increasingly lively as the baby begins to ask to be picked up and learns to turn over and then to crawl. At that point, you may have to keep your wits about you to make sure that your baby has something interesting in his hands to keep him occupied so he won't fall off the table. If he's really lively, it may be safer to change the little fellow on the floor.

With the exception of medically prescribed massage, we advise against regular, systematic massages for infants, although they are currently very popular and recommended with enthusiasm. For infants,

12

physical attention should arise spontaneously out of natural needs and should not be programmed. Your infant's need for deep pressure sensations (which make him feel comfortable in his surroundings) is naturally met by being carried on your arm or in a sling (see also Section 13.8). His own desire to move and explore will provide all the other tactile sensations he needs. This process of discovery is two-sided. Every time he looks at or touches something, pulls himself upright or crawls, he is learning to "grasp" both his surroundings and himself.

Everything adults do with infants includes an additional factor — the attitude with which the action is performed. Anxious holding back, effusive exaggeration, consciously or unconsciously applied educational principles, fear of spoiling the baby, the desire to insure that your baby is physically fit — all of these shadowy aspects need to be eliminated so that you can respond appropriately to your baby's advances. Patience and a cheerful, loving attitude, not anxieties and specific ideas about what to do, will help you provide imaginative, spontaneous, and helpful stimuli.

12.7 Why a veil over the cradle?

For your baby's bed, we recommend a basket or cradle completely lined with a single-color fabric and covered with a pale pink-violet veil. The veil keeps out irritating drafts and admits a pleasantly dimmed light conducive to peaceful sleep. If the cradle is located near an open window, the veil prevents sun from falling directly on to the baby. (Of course it also blocks ultraviolet light, a consideration when light is needed to prevent rickets. In this case, pull the veil back so that direct sunlight is still mainly blocked but the baby's head is exposed to blue sky.) It doesn't matter whether you use a laundry basket on a home-made frame with

rockers or four wheels, an antique cradle, or any other type of movable baby bed or cradle, but it must fit beside your own bed. Parents often don't think of this, and as a result Mum has to get out of bed countless times each night. The best mattress for a baby's bed is a one-piece, flat mattress that is well filled, preferably with natural materials such as horse hair, kapok, or sea grass. The baby should have either no pillow at all or a flat pad filled with millet or rice, which you can make yourself (see page 197). The grain adapts to the curvature of the baby's head and cannot block her airways like a fluffy feather pillow.

12.8 Appropriate transportation

A sling (see Figure 23) is initially the best way to carry your baby, as long as it is tied correctly and the baby is dressed warmly enough in winter. Slings, like other carrying devices you may use later (see Figure 24), allow parents to take their babies with them wherever they go from a very early age. This allows greater mobility for the mother in particular and lets the baby experience more of her daily activity. Remember, however, to avoid noisy environments, extreme weather conditions and other sensory impressions that are not appropriate for very young babies (see also Section 12.4).

A baby carried by a walking adult experiences rhythmical movement and pressure in his muscles and skin. These sensations not only enhance his sense of self and his feeling of comfort but also provide models to imitate in his own later walking, whereas being pushed in a pram is more likely to prepare him for driving a car!

When you can no longer avoid using a pram, choose one with a high base and sturdy springs. Large wheels also give a smoother ride. The height protects your baby from car exhaust fumes which are concentrated near the ground. If at all possible obtain a pram or stroller in which the baby faces you and can keep eye-contact with you. Unfortunately most modern strollers make the baby face away from the person pushing him. Once the child is older, the eye-contact is longer needed.

12

12.9 Swimming for infants

With few exceptions, we do not recommend swimming or outdoor bathing for infants. These activities are usually associated with temperature fluctuations, chlorine or pollutants in the water, and other children's yelling, all of which can overtax a baby's highly sensitive system. We also believe that infants should learn to deal with gravity (through standing upright and walking) before experiencing the buoyancy of water.

Your infant's motor development will be quite adequately stimulated by spontaneous movement, the joy of repetition, and little games with adults who take pride in each new movement she masters. It is important, however, to find time for such games and activities on a daily basis. Sitting in front of the television with the baby in your arms does not count!

13. From Infant to Toddler

13.1 Daily routines

The transition from infant to toddler happens when your baby learns to walk and is able to approach objects on his own. Abandoning crawling in favour of uprightness means that his hands are now free to grasp, tug, and examine anything within reach. Being independently mobile puts a totally different face on his daily routine. He can wander off on his own, follow you from room to room, and take his place at the family dinner table. This new situation presents challenges for other members of the family, who must allow the youngest member to participate in age-appropriate ways without making him the constant center of attention. How and whether this is accomplished establishes a pattern for family interactions at a later age. *The child benefits greatly when he experiences that his real needs are recognized and respected, his moods are handled with humour and patience, and limits are calmly set when his behavior is chaotic and demanding.*

His sleeping habits also change at this age. In their first year of life, babies nap both in the morning and in the afternoon and have no trouble sleeping outside or near an open window. After age one, children generally nap only in the afternoon and find it difficult to sleep outdoors or near the window. Give some thought to the timing of your toddler's afternoon nap so he can be outside either before or afterward and doesn't spend the nicest part of the day sleeping. Obviously, it will be easier for him to fall asleep at night if his afternoon nap is earlier rather than later. The more routine and predictable you can make his times for eating and sleeping, the less likely he is to be moody, cranky, or at loose ends. *Little children like nothing better than fixed habits.* Experiencing a regular routine gives your child a feeling of security and trust that is reflected in his sense of self (see also Section 13.6) and is the best possible foundation for developing his will (see Section 20.1).

13.2 Elimination and toilet training

In the second year of life, your child's digestive system is challenged to the utmost because she still chews poorly but wants to try everything edible. The intervals between bowel movements may vary tremendously and her stools, which may make a mess up to her shoulder blades several times a day, look undigested and usually smell sour. If she seems otherwise well and does not lose weight, your pediatrician will simply call this condition "irritable bowel." Regular mealtimes and restricting bloating or laxative foods such as coarse oat flakes, whole or coarsely ground grains, and raw foods will help her digestion somewhat. Urination becomes less frequent; the quantity of urine increases and it develops a stronger odour (see also Section 12.5).

For convenience, most parents switch to disposable diapers when their babies become independently mobile, but some experienced mothers (imagining the resulting mountain of rubbish) continue to have success with cloth diapers, wool soakers, and "babygrows." This combination keeps the stools adequately contained, the smell signals when a diaper change is due, and the baby's skin stays fresh. Because toddlers urinate less frequently but in larger quanti-ties, they soon begin to indicate when they need changing, so they are less likely to stay wet for long periods and problems of evaporative cooling and skin irritation recede into the background. At this stage, too, you are more likely to recognize the critical times in advance and change your child's diapers promptly.

Systematic attempts at toilet training should not yet play a role in the second year. The process is least complicated if you can find a combination high chair/potty chair, preferably with a detachable potty seat that can be used on the floor between meals. With this type of chair, it is a simple matter to remove your child's diapers quickly after meals and spend the next ten minutes in pleasant "table conversation" with her and the rest of the family. With a little luck, this approach will work, and your child will develop regular times for bowel movements that will later carry over to the potty chair or toilet. The more unself-consciously and routinely this process is managed, the better — regardless of when your child ultimately becomes toilet trained. The less emphasis you place on toilet training as such, the more likely it is that your child will learn to use the toilet as a matter of course.

13.3 Your baby's clothing and first shoes

Toddlers are very attracted to shoes and love putting them on and taking them off. Later, they identify shoes with the people who wear them and enjoy trying on other people's shoes (and roles). Of course Daddy is supposed to know that Mummy or Big Sister is coming into the room!

Initially, however, putting on shoes is difficult. Toddlers tend to curl their toes instead of sticking them straight into the shoe, so it helps to loosen the laces of "beginner" shoes as much as possible before putting them on your child's feet.

Shoes make feet passive and spoiled. They are *not* an aid to learning to walk. For this purpose, going barefoot or wearing socks or soft-soled slippers is better, since feet develop best when covered only enough to keep them warm. Outside, lawn grass provides a good surface for your child's first steps; indoors, a natural-fiber carpet provides tactile sensations.

Flat feet are normal in childhood, since foot arches develop only as a result of coming to grips with gravity and usually only after age four. Children who do not learn to walk also do not develop arches. Orthopedists now agree that truly flat feet, which develop only later, require orthopedic shoe inserts only in extreme cases that threaten to affect overall posture. In other cases, stimulating independent activity and walking on tiptoes work best. Making a game out of this activity and setting it to a little song or poem works better than conscious demands. Your child is less likely to lose interest if you simply "fly like a bird" or "dance on tiptoe like an elf" and, as you go through the house, she will imitate and follow you on tiptoe.

The best material for children's shoes is unlined leather. Flat heels are best. Because synthetic or sheepskin fleece linings usually cover only the uppers, not the soles, they are not nearly as effective at keeping feet warm as wool socks, which surround the feet on all sides. Synthetics do not absorb moisture and increase the likelihood of perspiration and athlete's foot. Of course you need to buy shoes large enough to accommodate thick wool socks in winter. Sales staff in shoe stores can help you determine your child's size.

The purpose of shoes is to increase our mobility on rough ground and in bad weather. In puddles or snow and on muddy or gravelly ground, heavy soles with good tread are best. Soft soles are comfortable on pavement. Children's shoes are available in many styles to meet these different needs. *In summary, the function of shoes is to protect feet from adverse environmental conditions. The healthy shape and function of feet develop through use and activity, not through wearing shoes.*

13

With regard to *clothing,* take advantage of your experience during the first few months and years of your child's life. If you have already recognized the advantages of wool, you will continue to avoid synthetics and won't begrudge your preschooler her wooly undershirt. For night-time wear for ages one to four (or sometimes even six), a knitted sleeping bag of natural unbleached wool will keep your child evenly warm yet allow her to change position freely. At this age, children are still likely to kick their covers off at night and may not yet be able to cover themselves up again. Your choice of day wear for your child should be based on practicality — that is, freedom of movement, durability, warmth, and absorbability. Beyond that, your child's affinity for a special item of clothing can help create the right Sunday or holiday mood.

And what about the color of clothing? According to Rudolf Steiner, the after-images of colors are what affect us psychologically.[33] When we look at a red surface, a green afterimage develops inside us. For an overactive child who tends to "bang her head against the wall," clothing on the red end of the spectrum can have a harmonizing effect by constantly creating an after-image of soothing green. Conversely, dressing a more lethargic or reclusive child predominantly in shades of blue, which create after-images of active yellow and orange, can help stimulate to greater activity. Due to the especially close connection between physical and emotional life in early childhood, your toddler experiences after-images of color much more intensely than an adult does, and they affect a child's bodily constitution as strongly as any other influences at this age.

13.4 Playpens and cribs: Are they prisons?

For your infant, a playpen is an activity area midway between the intimate, familiar surroundings of the child's little bed and the whole room, which is still too big (see Figure 25). Of course the playpen should be well made, with wooden bars and a solid base raised 10 cm/4 inches above the floor. If your playpen does not have a raised base, attach a narrow band of fabric to the bottom of the bars to block drafts that run along the floor. Wrap tape or cloth around any joints in the upper rail so your baby won't pinch her fingers. Choose a location for the playpen that allows your baby to see the places where you spend the most time working or resting. A six-month-old can go into the playpen after each diaper change and stay there as long as she is awake, playing and watching you as you go about your work or sit close by doing smaller projects. This arrangement avoids the unfortunate situation of having to go to the baby's room every time she whimpers or gets cranky, and it makes the baby a participant in your life rather than the other way around. Because you are always doing something and know what comes next, your baby has plenty of opportunities to exercise her urge to imitate. She can begin to imitate your uprightness by pulling herself into a standing position for the first time hanging on to the bars of the playpen.

Most babies are content to stay in the playpen during the morning whenever they are awake. If your baby grows tired, you can either cover her in the playpen or put her to bed. Because her need for visual contact has been satisfied, she is more likely to go to bed without protest. In the afternoons, on the other hand, most children enjoy being outside, so this is the obvious time for walks and similar activities.

Once your child is independently mobile, she will inevitably begin to experience the playpen as confining. At this point, your own attitude is inci-

sive. There is a neat distinction between using the playpen as punishment — in which case it does become a prison — and using it as a safe place for your baby to stay while you get on with work you couldn't to do if she were crawling around loose. In this case, the playpen is simply a limit imposed by real-life necessities. Of course your baby would have more freedom of movement without the playpen, but you would have to interrupt your work repeatedly to take things away from her and make sure she's safe as she crawls around on the floor.

If you still have reservations about a playpen, we urge you to at least invest in a crib on wheels, preferably one with a solid headboard and footboard and sides high enough to prevent a toddler from climbing out. This type of portable crib is invaluable when your child is sick or has trouble sleeping, because it can be moved close to your own bed at night. Even during the day, it is unrealistic to expect your baby to stay happily in bed in her own room while you are bustling around the rest of the house or apartment (see Figure 26). A portable crib gives her at least some freedom of movement without exposing her to drafts and dirt on the floor. In the crib, she can lie down by herself if she gets tired.

13

13.5 Furnishing and decorating your baby's room

If you have enough space for a separate nursery, you will be able to plan for future needs as you arrange your baby's room. Because an entire modern industry is devoted to furnishing children's rooms, we would like to offer two examples here. Clearly, we prefer the second.

A room with a white ceiling, practical vinyl flooring, an equally practical synthetic carpet, and colorful wallpaper with repeated motives of balls, sailboats, and jumping jacks. The colors of the curtains are bright and contrasting, and a calendar from a baby-food company hangs on the wall. The furniture is made of orange washable plastic. You can tell simply by looking at the room that it cost a pretty penny to furnish.

The walls and ceiling are painted a warm pastel color, and one corner and the sloping ceiling are covered with inexpensive wood paneling. On the linoleum floor is a jute carpet, which in turn is partly covered by a rag rug and a sheepskin. The furnishings consist of a refurbished wardrobe; a small, unfinished wooden table with a couple of child-sized chairs; a simple bunk bed; a wooden shelf for toys; and a few boxes to use for climbing, sitting, or building. Mom's favourite picture hangs on the wall, and over the baby's bed is a Renaissance angel. (Looking at the angel picture just before falling

asleep can become a favourite habit.) The curtains have been chosen to provide cozy darkness for an afternoon nap, and their color does not contrast starkly with the walls. The colors of the room as a whole make visitors feel comfortable. It is important not to use drawers and baskets to hide a chaotic jumble of toys. If you set an example during your child's first few years by cheerfully picking up his toys once a day and returning them to their places on the shelf without making him participate, the sheer force of imitation will guarantee that he will later enjoy tidying up by himself.

Spending his first few years in appropriate spaces is important for your child's later development. But how can you be sure about your choices of colors and furniture? Simply ask yourself whether each item is the same on the inside as it is on the outside. The grain, construction, and proportions of an unfinished wooden table and the thickness of its top and legs correspond exactly to its inner quality and outer purpose. In contrast, a veneered table top conceals the poor quality of its chipboard base; its surface gives an illusion of quality that its underpinnings do not possess.

And what about wallpaper? Typical patterns for children are meant to be cute and kid-friendly, but what do we see if we take them at face value? In reality, where do we ever find infinitely repeated identical motifs and untrue images? Where on earth do we see countless kittens, balls, and Red Riding Hoods floating in space? Not to mention that they are so often drawn as grimacing caricatures. (Contrast this with the face of the doll described in Section 13.7 and illustrated in Figures 55 and 56.) Walls painted in a single color make the room feel like a uniform whole, but patterned wallpaper imposes a foreign and totally unrelated element on the walls. Loud color combinations dull our sensitivity to the quality of individual shades of color. If you have difficulty understanding this statement, simply compare your impressions of a motorway services stop to the many subtle shades and mixtures of green, violet, and brown encountered during a walk in the woods. In the first instance, the colors impose impressions on us, but in the second they lure our souls outward to become actively engaged in the process of perceiving. *At this age, when sensory impressions still have a very strong effect on organ development, it makes a big difference whether a child is constantly exposed to caricatures, bold colors, and smooth surfaces or is allowed to experience delicate, harmonious shades of color that leave him room to breathe.*

Another important factor is whether you yourself enjoy spending time in your baby's room, because he will use it only for sleeping if you are always doing interesting things in other parts of the house and never bring your sewing or other projects into the nursery. Small children want and must be allowed to play where their mothers are.

13.6 Where to go on vacation?

New parents often want to return to their old vacation habits as quickly as possible, but now the baby has arrived and her needs are very different from theirs. For a small child, every change of locale not only removes her forcibly from her familiar living space but also triggers a crisis in self-awareness. A child's sense of identity is based on perceiving familiar faces and objects. For a small child, seeing something for the second time is the same as an adult's recollection of a previous thought. Our adult sense of identity is based on an unbroken sequence of mental images stored in memory. For young children who have not yet developed the ability to think and reason abstractly, sensory experiences serve the same purpose. This means that if you enjoy frequent changes of scenery for health reasons or because the climate where you live is unpleasant, it's best to return repeatedly to the same holiday spot as long as your child is small. If you go on holiday to the same place year after year and your child is already familiar with the house and the lifestyle you encounter there, she will acclimatize much faster and will look forward to recognizing and reliving her familiar vacation world. Such experiences strengthen your child's self-awareness and sense of identity.

If their mother or both parents are forced to travel for business or health reasons, children should be either taken along on the trip or left at home in the care of someone they know well. Being separated from their caregiver and their familiar surroundings at the same time is a trauma that small children should not be subjected to except in dire emergencies (see also Section 15.4 and Section 16).

Sunglasses
While we're on the subject of holidays and travel, a word about sunglasses:

Unless medical conditions such as eye infections or pigmentation disorders make them necessary, we do not recommend sunglasses for toddlers and preschoolers. In any case, there are legitimate health reasons for not overexposing children in this age group to sunlight. Good protective headgear (a hat with a brim or visor) provides enough protection for playing and moving around outside. Do choose a shady spot, however, if you are going to sit for extended periods. Eyes learn to function best if they are allowed to develop in free interaction with the natural colors of the environment. Young children's eyes already adapt very well to different degrees of brightness, ranging from the low light of early morning and evening to the bright sun of midday. For school-age children, we do recommend sunglasses, especially under holiday circumstances such as prolonged walks, hikes in the mountains, or hours of playing on the beach. In such cases, choose wraparound sunglasses that also filter light coming from the sides.

13.7 Age-appropriate toys

The variety of toys available today is a problem in itself. Children are overwhelmed with commercial products that represent the toy industry's definition of "age-appropriate," but any- one who has every observed young children absorbed in play knows how little their activity has to do with what such toys have to offer (Figure 71). Play is a child's natural tendency to become active in his environment. He does whatever he sees others do. A two-year-old will enthusiastically "stir soup" with a stick on the floor. He wants to turn the knobs on the stove like Mummy, go "click" when Daddy takes a photo, and investigate the plates that come clattering out of the cabinet before supper. What satisfies him most is *activity,* not looking at a perfect plastic doll or a caricature of an animal. But if a doll has no face, or only three dots that suggest a face, his imagination creates the rest (see Figures 54–56). He can make the doll laugh or cry or be angry or tired. Eternally smiling doll faces — or worse still, dolls that "talk" — create false after-images that fixate a child's imagination.

What makes a toy age-appropriate? In your baby's first year of life, for example, an appropriate toy is a simply made doll consisting of a small piece of silk with the center filled with wool and tied off to form the head, while the knotted corners become hands. Later, your child can have a wooden doll to stand up and lay down, later still a soft homemade flannel doll. Any object that encourages imaginative activity and is unspecific enough to be used in many different ways is a suitable toy. A toy can be a finger: see how it moves, see everything it can do. It can be the corner of a pillow, to bend and poke inside out. It can be a jar to open and close, to put things into and take them out again. It can be a piece of wood to bang on the table and discover what kind of noise it makes. Later, it may be a water

faucet or tap, or a bottle cap to scoop up water and fill a pond. A pot and a spoon for drumming are also interesting. So is a colorful knitted ball stuffed with wool, for rolling, throwing, and pushing, or small pieces of colorful cloth for covering and uncovering all sorts of things.

It is very important for fathers, mothers, uncles, and aunts to give children good toys. Our perfect, rationally conceived modern toys leave no room for a child's imagination, and their materials, colors, and shapes usually offend both our sense of reality and our sense of esthetics. The fascinating, sophisticated movements and optical effects of technological toys turn children into observers instead of active participants. The purpose of play is to provide opportunities for healthy physical development through independent activity and creative imagination. In his essay *The Education of the Child,* Rudolf Steiner says:

Children learn not by being taught but by imitating. Their physical organs take shape under the influence of their physical surroundings. Healthy vision develops when we insure that the right colors and lighting are present in the child's surroundings. Similarly, the physical basis of a healthy moral sense develops in the brain and circulatory system when children see morality at work around them. If a child experiences only the foolish actions of others in the first seven years of her life, her brain will assume forms that make it suited only for foolishness later in life. If we were able to see into the human brain as it develops, we would surely provide our children only with toys that stimulate the brain's formative activity. All toys that consist only of dead mathematical forms have deadening and hardening effects on a child's formative forces, but anything that stimulates mental images of life has the opposite, desirable effect.

Developmental perspectives of this sort often conflict with economic interests intent on developing new markets among juvenile consumers.

But if families understand what harms and what strengthens children, far-reaching negative impacts such as inner emptiness, apathy, and lack of imagination and creativity can be avoided. Many parents today are already beginning to suspect that one important factor in the pervasiveness of drug dependency is the fact that we are taught from a very early age to rely for "entertainment" on devices that leave no room in our lives for satisfying independent activity and involvement with our surroundings. (Suggestions for stimulating independent activity can be found in the publications of Waldorf kindergarten groups, see the Bibliography aat the end).

13.8 The senses, sensory experience, and self-awareness

Especially during the first three years of life, the way a child uses his senses influences his developing self-awareness and his experience of his own body, which in turn form the basis of how he instinctively uses his body.

In recent years, the recognition that both our self-awareness and certain intellectual accomplishments depend heavily on our senses' harmonious interaction has resulted in increased emphasis on sensory education. New therapeutic measures such as sensory-motor integration therapy have been

developed to provide intensive training that attempts to compensate for inadequate development and education of sensory functions. To these perspectives on the significance of sensory education, especially in early childhood, we would like to add another view, which we owe to Rudolf Steiner's research: While it is true that the development of sensory organs depends on how well children learn to use them based on the models and stimuli they are given, this is only part of the picture. In addition, *a child's body responds as a whole to everything that happens to it, and it bases its response on the sensory impressions it receives. Children see, hear, smell, or taste with their entire bodies.* Jumping for joy at a positive experience is a whole-body response. In other words, the body as a whole receives the most important sensory stimuli. Hence sensory education is of constitutional — or constitution-shaping — importance in the truest sense of the word, both for a child's emotional and mental development and for the development of his or her entire body. Sensory experiences in early childhood, supported by associated body functions, form the basis of our sense of self and self-awareness. At this point, therefore, we would like to summarize our experience with a few important perspectives on sensory education based on Rudolf Steiner's research on the human senses. In addition to the conventionally recognized senses, Steiner describes the additional senses of life, word, thought, and the "I." (See Figures 63–80).

Steiner's indications help us understand that our self-awareness, our experience of who we really are, is based on twelve types of sensory experience. By perceiving light and colors, we experience our own being as light-filled and endowed with the empirical qualities of color. Through outer warmth, we awaken to our own inner warmth; that is, to the fact that we ourselves are warm and possess warmth. The twelve qualities conveyed by our senses are the source of healthy self-awareness.

13

The sense of touch
conveys
the experience of the body's limits (through touching);
the security that comes from bodily contact; trust in our own existence.

suggestions for sensory education:

— *Being able to put your baby down is as important as picking her up. She should experience a balanced alternation between feeling protected and relying on her own resources, between gentle physical contact and being alone.*

harmful influences to avoid:

— *lack of emotional involvement on the part of the caregiver*
— *too much security or too much solitude*
— *touching that has more to do with the caregiver's pleasure than with love for the child*

The sense of life
conveys
comfort and the perception that events are in harmony with each other.

suggestions for sensory education: harmful influences to avoid:

— *rhythmical daily routine*   — *conflict, violence, anxiety*
— *an attitude of confidence in life*   — *hurry, fear*
— *moderation and appropriate*   — *dissatisfaction*
  timing; that is, harmonious   — *lack of moderation*
  practical arrangements   — *nervousness*
— *happy mealtimes*   — *disjointed sequences of unrelated*
                                                          events

---

The sense of self-movement (kinesthesia)
conveys
perceptions of one's own movement; the experience of freedom and
self-control as a result of mastering movement

suggestions for sensory education: harmful influences to avoid:

— *allow your child to do things for*   — *overly restrictive rules*
  himself   — *inadequate stimulation due to*
— *make his room safe for*   *parental passivity or inadequate*
  unsupervised play; he should be   *modeling of active behavior*
  able to touch everything in it   — *sitting immobilized in front of the*
— *meaningful sequences of*   *television*
  movements   — *automated toys that turn children*
                                                          into observers

---

The sense of balance
conveys
experiences of equilibrium and compensation;
places of rest; self-confidence.

suggestions for sensory education: harmful influences to avoid:

— *movement games: seesaws,*   — *lack of movement*
  walking on stilts, jumping, etc.   — *restlessness*
— *calmness and certainty when*   — *inner conflict or unrest*
  dealing with your child   — *depression or resignation*
— *parental efforts toward inner*
  balance

The sense of smell
conveys
information about aromatic substances.

suggestions for sensory education:

— *seek out differentiated
experiences of smell (plants,
foods, in city and country)*

harmful influences to avoid:

— *poorly ventilated rooms*
— *overly strong odors*
— *nauseating sense impressions
and behaviors*

The sense of taste
conveys
*sweet, sour, salty and bitter tastes;
complex, differentiated tastes in conjunction with the sense of smell.*

suggestions for sensory education:

— *food preparation techniques
should allow the food's own taste
to come through*
— *"tasteful" assessment of people
and things*
— *esthetically satisfying
surroundings*

harmful influences to avoid:

— *uniform, one-sided sensations of
taste (e.g., "ketchup abuse")*
— *tasteless or tactless comments*
— *unesthetic surroundings*

13

The sense of sight
conveys
sensations of light and color.

suggestions for sensory education:

— *draw your child's attention to
subtle color distinctions in nature
by expressing your own interest
in them*
— *harmonious color combinations
in clothing and interior
decorating*

harmful influences to avoid:

— *fixating on silly or destructive
images*
— *loud, strongly contrasting colors*
— *television abuse*
— *pessimistic attitudes*
— *lack of interest*
— *sad, colorless surrounding*

The sense of warmth
*conveys
sensations of heat and cold.*

suggestions for sensory education:

— *fostering the development of
your child's warmth system by
selecting age-appropriate
clothing*
— *an atmosphere of emotional and
spiritual warmth*

harmful influences to avoid:

— *exaggerated toughening
measures*
— *overheated rooms*
— *not dressing your child warmly
enough*
— *cold, impersonal atmosphere*
— *exaggerated or insincere
cordiality*

The sense of hearing
*conveys
sounds and tones;
opens up one's inner, emotional space.*

suggestions for sensory education:

— *when telling stories or reading
aloud, adapt the pace of your
speaking to your child's ability to
follow*
— *singing and playing musical
instruments*

harmful influences to avoid:

— *excessive auditory stimulation,
especially through electronic
media (too loud, too fast,
impersonal)*
— *superficial or insincere talk*
— *inhuman tone of voice*

The sense of word
*conveys
perceptions of form and physiognomy,
up to and including the sound structure of a word*

suggestions for sensory education:

— *warm, cordial tone of voice,
gestures, and body language*
— *sensitivity to individual
differences in self-expression*

harmful influences to avoid:

— *negative gestures*
— *cool, neutral behavior (your child
never really knows whether you
are happy or sad, distant or
paying attention*
— *any form of lying or false
impressions (discrepancies
between what you say and what
you think or feel)*

The sense of thought
conveys
the meaning of a train of thought

suggestions for sensory education:

— *cultivating accuracy and*
  truthfulness
— *relating things and events to*
  each other
— *experiencing meaningful*
  connections in your surroundings

harmful influences to avoid:

— *meaningless actions*
— *confused, uncoordinated thinking*
— *distorting meaningful*
  connections
— *meaningless associations*

The sense of "I" and "Other"
conveys
impressions of another being; direct experience
of another person's characteristic configuration.

suggestions for sensory education:

— *early physical and emotional*
  contact with a loving caregiver
— *adults' love for each other and*
  for the child
— *a family culture that encourages*
  visiting and social gatherings
— *truly perceiving the other person*
  (Martin Buber's "thou")[34]

harmful influences to avoid:

— *manifestations of love*
— *media consumption and virtual*
  realities that do not involve
  experiencing real beings
— *a materialistic view of human*
  beings
— *sexual abuse*
— *absence of interest, respect, or*
  other

13

Having said that healthy self-awareness awakens these twelve areas of sensory experience, we must emphasize that our senses do not *produce* self-awareness but simply provide information about the self. There is an old Greek proverb, "If I were king and didn't know it, I would not be king." The spiritual human being — the "I" — is immortal, but it "knows" only as much about itself as it becomes aware of through living in an individual body on earth.

This spiritual being, this "I am I," is bright, warm, capable of sympathy and antipathy, and endowed with inner calm and the capacity for freedom, harmony, and trust. These qualities allow it to become conscious through sensory impressions and to experience itself as a unique and self-contained being within a body. The degree of self-awareness we acquired in and through the body is an essential part of our experience on earth, and we take with us into the spiritual world at death. Here we touch on the meaning of "embodiment" or life on earth. We do not simply dissolve into the spiritual world at death, because the self-awareness we have developed on earth is preserved when we enter the spiritual world.

14. Nutrition for Infants and Children

Although nutrition issues remain relevant throughout childhood, they are most acute in infancy. In recent decades, a growing number of mothers have once again discovered the advantages of breastfeeding for their babies' health and social development, and new insights have emerged with regard to weaning babies and introducing supplemental foods as part of the transition to family meals.

The first two sections in this chapter are devoted to these subjects. The third part is aimed at mothers who cannot breastfeed (or choose not to, for whatever reason) but nonetheless prefer to avoid commercial powdered formulas. This section includes age-specific recipes for bottle foods based on diluted cow's milk, with tips on the special dietary needs of bottle-fed babies.

In the next section, we discuss the pros and cons of individual foods and their importance in nutrition for children.

Nutrition, however, is far more than just a question of providing energy. The health of human beings and of the natural world depends heavily on our attitudes toward eating and digesting and on how we grow our foods. The end of this chapter includes some thoughts on the digestive process itself, the industrialization of food production, the development of genetically altered foods, and the relationship between nutrition and consciousness.

14.1 Breastfeeding

Up to the 1970s, for a number of cultural reasons breastfeeding had become quite unusual and even discouraged by modern attitudes. Much has changed in the intervening years. A new culture of breastfeeding has developed, and comprehensive advice is widely available through midwives and La Lèche leaders, who have a wealth of collective experience and literature to answer any detailed questions you may have. Nonetheless, especially among socially disadvantaged populations in many countries, too few mothers today breastfeed their infants. Since the 1990s, in most western countries the health care services, midwives and breastfeeding counselors (see page 453) have been providing recommendations for breastfeeding to every new mother.

Here is a list of reasons for breastfeeding to help mothers everywhere educate themselves and their neighbours about its advantages.

- breastfeeding creates an intimate bond between a mother and her child and is a very direct way for both to experience that we humans need each other and are there for each other.
- Mother's milk is always available, sanitary, and pre-warmed.
- The composition of mother's milk is ideally adapted to the needs of a growing baby.
- breastfeeding is simple and economical and saves time.
- breastfeeding stimulates contractions to help shrink the uterus back to its original size after delivery.
- breastfed babies have fewer and milder infections.
- breastfeeding largely protects babies against dangerous inflammatory digestive disorders, septicemia, and encephalitis.
- Exclusive breastfeeding for the first six months can prevent the development of allergies in the child.

Practical questions

How do I learn to breastfeed? From your baby! A health visitor, midwife or La Lèche advisor can also give you tips on different nursing positions, and so on.

Frequency of feedings

If possible, a mother and her newborn baby should remain together at all times in the first few days after birth. While they are still in the delivery room, the baby should be placed on her mother's breast. She should be allowed to nurse as often as she wants, even during the night. This means she gets all of the highly nourishing colostrum, and there is no delay in getting the milk flowing. Her mother should accept offers of competent help and try to relax and get enough sleep between feedings. breastfeeding at two-hour intervals makes the most sense at this stage, since milk flow may be inadequate if the baby is allowed to nurse only every four hours and only on one side for fear of causing nipple fissures. The right concept for this stage of life is that a baby belongs at her warm mother's breast, hearing her familiar heartbeat. This is especially true of premature infants, who do much better in the "kangaroo position" than in isolation. Meanwhile we also know that the heartbeats of a mother and her infant tend to become synchronized.

As the baby begins to drink more, the interval between feedings can be increased. Only at this stage can each feeding really be considered a distinct "meal." It is important to learn how to interpret your baby's behavior. Not every little stretch or sign of discomfort means "I need to be fed," but if you consistently respond by allowing her to nurse, your baby will make a habit of it and you will not be able to establish a rhythm. This is why we recommend beginning with a two-hour break between feedings, gradually stretching it to three or four hours depending on your baby's needs. After about six weeks a longer break of up to eight hours should be possible at night.

How long should each feeding last?

As long as you and your baby want. After a few weeks, a baby who is a strong sucker will nurse for about seven to ten minutes on each side, for a total of fifteen to twenty minutes. Each feeding should totally empty one breast and at least relieve the pressure on the other.

What if I don't have enough milk yet?

Mothers who begin breastfeeding promptly and get enough help with housework seldom have problems with too little milk. Make sure to drink enough, eat well, get enough rest, and keep your upper body and arms (including elbows) warm. It's best to consult a midwife or lactation specialist before resorting to lactagogue teas or special diets. If you really do not have enough milk for your baby, see the recommended alternatives in Section 14.3.

It's a mistake to give your baby dairy-based formula in the first few days of his life if you intend to breastfeed him exclusively later. An allergy-prone baby may become sensitized to cow's milk and develop severe allergic symptoms (up to and including anaphylactic shock) when he is started on cow's milk for the second time after a long interval of exclusive breastfeeding.

Vitamin K prophylaxis

Your midwife or obstetrician will alert you to the need for this type of supplementation. See Section 10.3, for our discussion of this issue.

In case of jaundice

Most newborns, especially breastfed infants, look a bit yellow for several days or weeks after delivery. This condition is generally harmless. For severe jaundice, see Section 5.2.

What if my baby doesn't gain weight?

The experienced eye of a health professional is actually just as good as a pair of scales, but if you suspect your baby is not gaining weight rapidly enough, weigh her naked once before a feeding. A second weighing several days later will tell whether she is actually gaining enough weight. It's not in the baby's best interest to wait for weeks before turning to your pediatrician with concerns about inadequate weight gain. If you need to determine your baby's daily milk consumption, weigh her (in a diaper) before and after each meal for twenty-four hours — that is, from her first feeding in the morning to the last one at night. The sum of the differences between weighings is the amount she drank that day. By itself, the statement "I still have milk in my breast when she's done" does not necessarily mean that your baby isn't getting enough to eat.

14

How long should I breastfeed?

The official recommendation for exclusive breastfeeding is six months. Between the ages of six and twelve months, most babies gradually wean themselves. Weaning problems are unusual in babies who have had enough physical contact in their first months of life.

Toxins in breast milk

Not all toxins in mother's milk come from the foods you are eating and the air you are breathing now. Since they are stored in body fat, they accumulate over a life time, and it is impossible to avoid passing many of them on to the developing fetus. In recent years, concentrations of toxins in breast milk in Central Europe have declined significantly, and there is no longer any official recommendation against extended breastfeeding.

All the evidence suggests that it is important to consume foods with as few toxins as possible from an early age so that mother's milk can once again become what nature intended it to be.

Reasons for not breastfeeding

Mothers with active tuberculosis, advanced HIV (see Section 10.14 and Section 8.2), or (in some cases) an advanced milk gland abscess should not breastfeed.

Continue breastfeeding if either you or your baby has an infection or digestive disturbance, with or without fever. Your milk will soon contain the appropriate antibodies. Unfortunately, gas and abdominal pain are no longer infrequent in breastfed babies (see Section 1.7).

How often should I expect my fully breastfed baby to have a bowel movement? Anywhere from once every ten days to ten times a day. The well-being of breast-fed babies is usually totally unrelated to the frequency or consistency of their stools. Occasional green coloring also means nothing.

What should a nursing mother eat and drink? Any normal, healthy foods (preferably organically or biodynamically grown) that are not constipating and do not cause excessive gas. Acceptable beverages include herb teas, low-sodium brands of mineral water, a 7% dilution of almond butter, milk, buttermilk, or mild natural yoghurt. Avoid dairy products only if you yourself have eczema related to milk allergy. If you have symptoms of low blood pressure, drink more fluids and treat yourself to an occasional cup of weak coffee. Lactagogue teas (usually mixtures of anise, fennel, and caraway seeds) are fine even if you have enough milk, since they also help prevent gas. Drink about three cups a day. Fruits and pressed juices are also acceptable, but don't drink too much at once to begin with. If your baby seems to develop gas or diaper rash when you drink juice, try another kind. After several weeks, try smaller amounts of the kind that caused the problem.

The first months of life

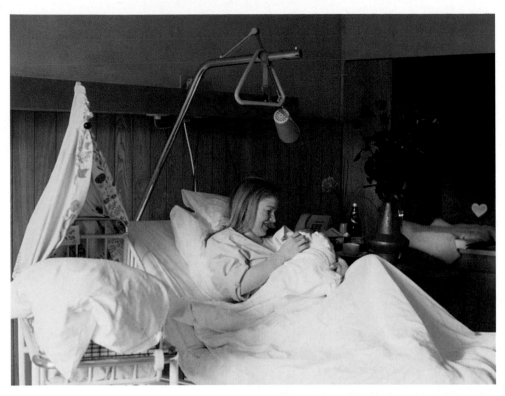

Figures 18 & 19. After delivery.
Mother and baby should stay together.

Figure 20. How to hold your baby's head securely. Grasp the baby's left upper arm with your left hand.

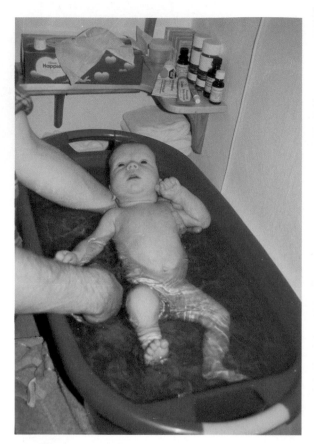

Figure 21. The carriage's collapsible canopy protects your baby from too much sun.

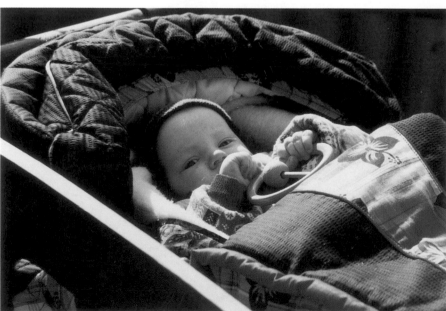

Transporting your baby

Figures 22 & 23. Carrying your baby in a sling. Younger ones should be carried in front, but older babies can go on the back.

Figure 24. A backpack is comfortable for vacations and everyday use.

Figure 25. The playpen as activity area.

Figure 26. A portable cot.

Dietary changes in the first year of life

	number of meals per day
12–6 ▲▲ 6 ▲▲ 5 ▲▲ 4	
ca. 100 (4) ▲▲ 160 (6) ▲▲ 200–250 (7–9)	ml (fl oz) per meal

morning

breast milk

vegetables with cereal

fruit with cereal

cereal made with 67% cow's milk

evening

| 4W | 8W | 12W | 4M | 5M | 6M | 7M | 8M | 9M | 10M | 11M | 12M |

W = age in weeks
M = age in months

Table 1: Dietary plan for a fully breast-fed infant. The baby's ages increases from left to right. Read the times of day from top to bottom (night feedings decrease as the baby gets older). Horizontal divisions indicate the most common number of meals. The baby's daily intake gradually increases to 800–1000 ml (28–35 fl oz). Between the ages of six and ten months, fruit and vegetable meals (mixed with cereals) are introduced. Cereals made with cow's milk are introduced whenever the amount of breast milk becomes inadequate. Most babies begin weaning themselves around the age of nine months. Bottle feedings are not necessary in this example (see Table on page 440).

14

Dietary changes in the first year of life

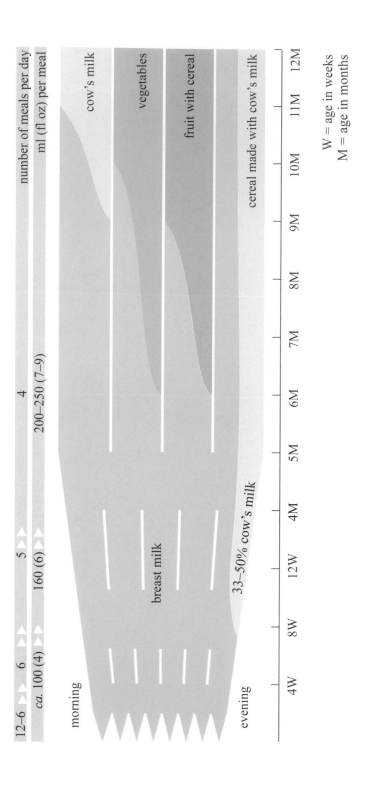

12–6	6	5	4	number of meals per day			
ca. 100 (4)		160 (6)	200–250 (7–9)	ml (fl oz) per meal			

cow's milk

vegetables

fruit with cereal

cereal made with cow's milk

morning

breast milk

33–50% cow's milk

evening

4W   8W   12W   4M   5M   6M   7M   8M   9M   10M   11M   12M

W = age in weeks
M = age in months

Table 2: If supplies of breast milk remain inadequate in spite of lactation counseling, supplemental feeding with diluted cow's milk is recommended. Evening supplemental feedings are best because they have the least impact on breast milk supplies and the rhythm of breast-feeding.

Dietary changes in the first year of life

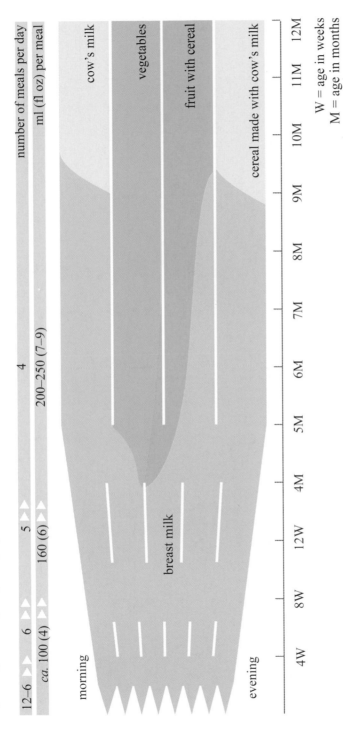

Table 3: Dietary plan for an infant whose mother begins working half-time again when the baby is five months old. At four months, this mother begins offering her baby spoonfuls of pureed carrots alternating with applesauce mixed with rice cream and a little oil. At five months, the baby's second meal of the day can be entrusted to the day-care provider or the mother's partner. In this case, the mother's breast milk is no longer adequate for the third meal, so she introduces cereal with fruit in the afternoon. This baby weans herself quite rapidly at nine months, but such quick weaning is neither necessary nor typical. Between the ages of six and nine months, the calcium content of this baby's diet is relatively low. Adding a total of about 100 ml/ half a cup of natural yogurt or cow's milk to her cereal-fruit or cereal-vegetable meals would make up the difference.

14

Dietary changes in the first year of life

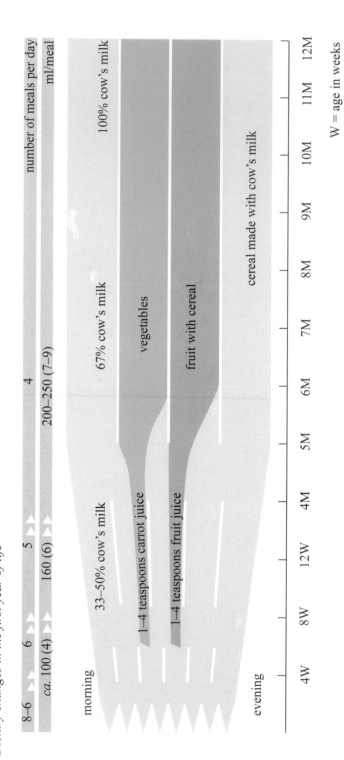

| | 8–6 | 6 | 5 | 4 | number of meals per day |
| | *ca.* 100 (4) | 160 (6) | 200–250 (7–9) | ml/meal |

morning

33–50% cow's milk   67% cow's milk   100% cow's milk

1–4 teaspoons carrot juice   vegetables

1–4 teaspoons fruit juice   fruit with cereal

cereal made with cow's milk

evening

4W   8W   12W   4M   5M   6M   7M   8M   9M   10M   11M   12M

W = age in weeks
M = age in months

Table 4: Dietary plan for a baby who is not breast-fed. For the first one to two weeks, mare's milk (enriched with 2 g sunflower seed oil for each 100 ml) should be used instead of diluted cow's milk. This plan is based on the recipes in this book and approximates the nutrient content of commercial formula. No vitamin D is added, however, so you will need to consult your pediatrician about measures to prevent rickets.

Smoking during pregnancy significantly reduces birth weight in babies, and smoking while nursing also causes damage because nicotine is excreted in breast milk, not to mention the dangers of exposure to second-hand smoke. Smoking also increases the risk of sudden infant death (SIDS, see Section 11.2).

Alcohol, if consumed in large quantities during pregnancies, causes physical deformities and delays in mental development. Alcohol consumption while breastfeeding may cause dependency in the baby that persists even after weaning. We recommend complete abstinence from alcohol and nicotine during pregnancy and lactation.

Nipple fissures can usually be prevented by correct nursing positions, which an experienced midwife or lactation consultant can demonstrate. As preventive skin care for your nipples, allow a little milk to dry on them or apply a small amount of St John's wort *(Hypericum)* oil. Ointments and nipple protectors should be reserved for acute situations.

Milk retention, even if accompanied by a slight fever, can be treated with hot, moist (not wet!) compresses or by placing a hot water bottle on the affected breast twenty minutes before you begin breastfeeding. Massage the breast while your baby is nursing to help press the milk out. Afterward, apply your choice of another hot compress or a cool Quark poultice. For deep-seated blockages, eucalyptus past warmed in a water bath is usually effective. Apply the paste to your breast with a swab.

In cases of mastitis, even if accompanied by high fever, it is often possible to continue breastfeeding, but treatment by a physician is necessary.

After dental work involving local anesthesia, pump out your milk once or twice and throw it away. If you have plenty of milk, you can pump beforehand and store it in anticipation of this time when you should not breastfeed.

Medication: Whenever your physician prescribes a medication for you, ask whether it might harm your nursing infant and (if possible) choose a medication that is not excreted in breast milk.

Every healthy woman who has more than enough milk should try to give it to a baby who needs it. Many premature and critically ill infants owe their lives to this kind of help. Today, because of the danger of AIDS, many mothers hesitate to accept a stranger's milk for their babies, but there is a way around this new problem. The parents on the receiving end get to know the donor, who must be willing to be tested for HIV. How to get the milk to the needy baby depends on individual circumstances, but it is generally picked up twice a day by the baby's parents. Good advice on hygiene is indispensable so that the milk is not contaminated before it reaches the baby.

Still not enough milk? What about supplemental feeding?

If counseling does not produce the desired results, or if you are forced to offer your baby feed supplements for other reasons and want to avoid commercial powdered milk formulas, use Recipe 1 on page 233. We also hope that you will be able to find a physician, midwife, or breastfeeding consultant who has experience with natural, dairy-based supplemental for-mulas. The less milk you have yourself, the more your baby's diet approximates that of a non-breastfed infant.

To find a breastfeeding consultant

La Lèche League International, 1400 N. Meacham Road, Schaumburg, IL 60173–4808, USA Tel. (847) 519–7730 www.lalecheleague.org.

This is the world headquarters. The website has many links to national affiliates.

14.2 Supplemental foods for breastfed babies

Today's mothers are breastfeeding longer. Based on their experience, we have updated our recommendations on the timing and order of introducing supplemental foods. Nutrition physiologists and allergists now recommend this basic approach:

- Breast milk is the optimal exclusive food for babies under six months.
- If possible delay introducing cow's milk and other dairy products. Instead,
- beginning at six months, gradually introduce a variety of supplemental foods including vegetables, fruit, and grains.

According to these guidelines, fully breastfed babies are given no supplemental foods at all, not even teaspoons of orange juice or carrot juice, as was previously recommended. After the age of six months, gradually increasing amounts of vegetables, fruit, or cereals can be offered after a milk meal. Introduce no more than one new food per week. Try giving your baby apples (either cooked or raw and grated); cooked pears, peaches, plums, or cherries; or pureed berries (either straight or added to cereals). As soon as your baby tolerates a steamed fruit or vegetable, you can also give her a raw piece to gnaw on, which provides new opportunities for touching, biting, tasting, and swallowing. These experiences encourage your child's initiative and independence with regard to foods. Vegetables should be steamed and enriched with a teaspoon of good-quality vegetable oil. Nitrate-rich vegetables (see pages 244f) should not be a frequent choice. Use them as fresh as possible, and do not reheat vegetables of this type for your baby's use. The gluten-free grains (rice, buckwheat, corn, and millet) are best for babies of this age. Pour boiling water over them and drain before cooking. One-year-olds can also be given quinoa, which is washed and then rinsed in boiling water to remove a somewhat bitter taste. In infrequent cases (ca. 1:1000), glutinous grains (wheat, spelt, oats, and barley, as well as rye, which is introduced later) can cause an intolerance syndrome known as celiac disease (see page 231). For breastfed babies, all grains are usually cooked in water only, without adding salt or sugar. Vary their natural taste by adding fruits or vegetables. A bit of fruit juice mixed with barley cereal is said to improve absorbability of the iron it contains. Wherever possible, we recommend biodynamically grown food (see Section 14.4 and the Bibliography) for your baby. Substitute organic foods if biodynamic products are not available.

Vitamin deficiencies are highly unlikely if your baby's diet includes a variety of fruits, vegetables, and grains, even if you resort to commercial baby foods from time to time. European Union regulations require vitamin enrichment of all foods produced specifically for children between the ages of five months and three years. For example, all grains and flour products aimed at this age group (cream of rice, spelt cereal, teething biscuits, etc.) are enriched with vitamin B_1. Fortifying foods with artificial vitamins has long been customary in the USA and certain other countries, but its purpose is to prevent vitamin deficiencies due to very one-sided diets. In Europe, where a wide variety of foods is readily available, this requirement makes no sense and causes problems for producers committed to providing natural foods. If you want to avoid feeding your baby or toddler foods that contain added vitamins, you can make these items yourself from untreated ingredients or choose brands not intended specifically for small children.

When your baby shows increasing interest in the foods you give her to sample, you can begin offering them at the beginning of the meal and save breastfeeding for "dessert," or the other way around. By the age of eight months, she will become familiar with a whole new palette of foods, and you will know what she likes to eat and can digest without problems. By this time, your breast milk will begin to decrease and you can start introducing dairy products. Begin by mixing a little mild, natural yoghurt with cereal. If your baby tolerates it well, try whole milk. When your own milk is reduced to about half of its original amount, about 200 ml (one cup) per day of cow's milk is needed to prevent protein or calcium deficiency. As breastfeeding draws to a close, 400 ml ($1^2/_3$ cups) is enough.

14

A baby who sits in her high chair watching her parents at mealtimes has ample opportunities to gnaw on pieces of apple, carrots and other vegetables, and bread. Her front teeth are adequate for dealing with these foods, but dishes made with unground grains, whether soaked or cooked, should be avoided until her molars appear. Meanwhile, cracked grains are better.

For children who are truly at risk for allergies, the official recommendation is to avoid cow's milk, eggs, fish, and nuts in the first year of life. "At risk for allergies," however, is often too broadly interpreted. With the exception of children with a family history of allergies, we recommend introducing cow's milk as described above.

The longer period of breastfeeding, as currently recommended, is good for the development of your baby's jaw and prevents lazy eating habits, since nursing from the breast takes much more effort than drinking from a bottle. Most fully breastfed babies never use a bottle but simply learn to drink from a cup at the table.

Potential nutritional problems

In our experience, arguments such as "my baby will develop an iron deficiency without meat" (or a protein deficiency without cow's milk) seldom apply to babies fed a varied diet. *A real bottleneck can occur in your baby's calcium intake, however, if your breast milk begins to run out while you are still avoiding giving her calcium-rich cow's milk.* Under certain circumstances, this problem can be exacerbated either by the phytin in glutinous grains (especially oats), which binds the calcium in foods and makes it insoluble, or by a dark winter, which can trigger rickets (see Section 10.2). Caution is always advised in these cases. A great deal of responsibility for preemptive education falls on your lactation advisor, since mothers of children in this age group are less likely to take advantage of consultations and many families are reluctant to approach a doctor with questions about nutrition.

14.3 Nutrition for bottle-fed babies

Any infant food other than mother's milk must be considered "artificial." All substitutions are compromises, and under primitive living conditions they may even be dangerous. Commercial formulas have become entrenched worldwide because they are easy to handle and most babies digest them well. Unfortunately, the fact that their use has been accompanied by significant increases in infant mortality in economically disadvantaged countries has done little to reduce their popularity.

A quick look at the composition of formulas reveals very careful attempts to adjust their ingredients to correspond to the nutritional value of breast milk. In addition to adequate amounts of all imaginable trace elements, minerals, and vitamins, every formula includes a few chemicals that make the product economically competitive by improving its appearance, shelf life, and taste. It is quite obvious, however, that all these ingredients do not add up to a living, whole food. For many parents, wanting to see and understand what goes into their baby's food is reason enough to make their own "natural" formula. We would like to support such efforts because modern formulas, like their forerunners, may one day be shown to be inadequate or even harmful. The fact that most food allergies appeared only after the invention of formula is also food for thought.

In recent years, researchers and manufacturers have addressed the problem of intolerance reactions to their formulas by breaking down the protein components of their products still further (protein hydrolysis). Some of these "hypoallergenic" formulas are in fact more digestible, but unfortunately their taste suffers. (For alternatives, see page 231.)

Natural alternatives to formula

After the baby's first two or three weeks, cow's milk still forms the basis of most bottle feedings, except for children with an obvious family history of allergies. Whenever possible, however, cow's milk should be introduced only after six months of breastfeeding. Due to its high protein content, cow's milk *must* be diluted for children under the age of nine months, and lactose and fat must be added to get closer to the composition of breast milk. Cow's milk contains almost four times as many minerals as breast milk and is relatively high in calcium and phosphorus.

Mare's milk, with its high lactose content and little casein, is closest to human milk, but oil must be added at the rate of approximately 2.5 g per 100 ml if mare's milk is used as your baby's sole food for any length of time. Mare's milk is hard to find and is available frozen from only a few specialized dairies. Because it is very expensive, it is not a realistic option for long-term use, but it may help bridge the gap for preemies, infants with eczema, and mothers who do not have enough breast milk.

Milk quality

If possible, buy fresh, untreated milk from a biodynamic farm or other farm that treats animals responsibly. If not, buy the freshest possible full-fat or pasteurized commercial milk. We do not recommend sterilized or ultra-high temperature pasteurized milk. For infants, milk not previously pasteurized must be heated as soon as possible to 80°C/175°F and then cooled. Especially in summer, this heating is necessary to prevent bacterial activity.

14

Composition of different types of milk

Nutrients

Average values g/100 ml	human milk	cow's milk	mare's milk	goat's milk
lactose	7.0	4.8	6.2	4.2
fat	4.0	3.7	1.5	3.9
protein (total)	1.0	3.3	2.2	3.7
casein	0.25	2.7	1.2	2.9
minerals	0.21	0.74	0.36	0.8

Cow's milk stands out for its high protein and mineral content, but if it is diluted, its lactose content is too low. Mare's milk with its low mineral content is more similar to human milk, but it needs added fat. Goat's milk is quite similar to cow's milk.

Immunoglobulins *(Ig, average values)*

mg/100 ml	newborn	colostrum	human milk	cow's milk
Ig A	2	620	100	3
Ig G	1030	30	11	60
Ig M	11	38	4	3

Clearly, mother's milk contains the specific immunoglobulins that the newborn still lacks.

Milk reactions (as shown by increases in neurodermatitis) are no longer rare, but are often a temporary problem that disappears after about two years. If your baby does not tolerate cow's milk, try goat's milk, mare's milk, or (if all else fails) hypoallergenic formula (see page 229). It is essential to consult your physician if your baby has multiple allergies. Bottle feedings based on mare's milk may help.

Added fat

Almond butter works well because the fat in it is already emulsified. Look for brands that are certified free of bitter almonds and tested for toxins. Vegetable oils may be substituted, but it is difficult to emulsify them without producing a lot of foam, and they tend to cling to the sides of the bottle.

Added cereals

The finely ground baby cereals once recommended as starter foods are now considered inappropriate for children under the age of four months, but after that you can begin adding cream of rice. Other grains should be introduced gradually only after your baby is six months old.

Pros and cons of different grains

Cream of rice is very easily digested. It makes the stools somewhat firmer and should be the only cereal you give your baby when he has diarrhea. Finely ground oats produce somewhat softer stools. Barley is easily digested. Whole wheat flour is usually not used for baby cereal; sift it if you use it, or choose semolina, preferably not a vanilla-flavoured brand. Millet flakes, recommended because of their iron content, are sometimes introduced as early as four months. Again, we recommend biodynamic products wherever possible (see Section 14.4, for an explanation of biodynamic farming, and Bibliography). Instant products have increasingly taken the place of home-made baby cereals, but both their taste and their texture are inferior.

Gluten intolerance (celiac disease)

Before the age of one year, approximately one child in one thousand develops symptoms of celiac disease after eating grains that contain gluten (wheat, barley, oats, spelt, and rye). This syndrome is characterized by failure to gain weight, a distended abdomen, massive stools (more than a large cupful per day), anemia, and crankiness. Because mothers today breastfeed longer and delay introducing grains, the onset of symptoms may be less pronounced, but the disease can still be diagnosed through antibody tests and a biopsy of the mucous membrane of the small intestine. Children with celiac disease are sensitive to the gluten component of grains, which attacks their intestinal lining. If you suspect your child has celiac disease, consult your pediatrician, because careful testing is required to confirm the diagnosis.

How much to feed your baby

During your baby's first few weeks of life, gradually increase the amount of the bottle food you have chosen. After that, give him as much as he wants (up

14

to a daily total of one-seventh to one-sixth of his current body weight) until he weighs 6000 g/ *c.* 13 lb. After that, his daily total should remain approximately the same (between 800 and 1000 g / 3½ to 4½ cups) until he is one year old. No more than half of this amount is cow's milk (400–500 ml; see color charts before page 225 and recipes on pages 233ff). Other beverages are usually not necessary, but if your baby wants them, offer them at meal times rather than between meals.

Supplemental foods
As you can see from Tables 1–4 (page 225), fruit and vegetable juices should be introduced earlier if you are not breastfeeding. Begin with one to four teaspoons a day, gradually increasing to ten. You should also begin building toward a full meal of vegetables or fruits earlier than you would if you were breastfeeding.

Cleaning bottles and nipples (teats)
For the first few months, boil used bottles and nipples once a day. Place them on a clean dish towel to dry.

After every use, clean the bottle with a bottle brush and hot running water. Clean the bottle brush under hot running water, too, and hang it in some place where it can dry quickly. Between sterilizations, the nipple can be cleaned with table salt. We do not recommend disinfectants.

What you need to know about milk
Bacterial growth: Decay-causing bacteria are active at temperatures over 5°C/40°F. It is important to precool filled baby bottles in a water bath so they do not remain lukewarm for long periods of time in the refrigerator. Refrigerate them at temperatures only slightly above freezing. Be aware that adding large amounts of unchilled foods to the refrigerator may keep it above the desired temperature for hours.

Pasteurization or boiling kills most pathogens, including tuberculosis bacteria. Pasteurization destroys some of milk's nutritional value but is important (especially in summer) to prevent infectious diarrhea. Rapid heating and cooling minimizes nutritional losses in untreated milk, where available. For use at home, heating untreated milk to only 75°C/170°F is enough.

Sterilization or ultra-high temperature pasteurization: Ultra-high temperature (UHT) pasteurization involves heating milk briefly to 140°C/285°F; milk is sterilized by holding it at 100°C/212°F or above for a longer period. Both techniques guarantee sterility, and the resulting products will keep for a long time. We do not recommend them, however, because they are totally lifeless "foods." Furthermore, repeated tests have shown that they contain large numbers of dead bacteria.

Homogenization breaks milk fat into smaller droplets so the cream no longer rises to the top. This is an advantage for milk packing plants but not necessarily for consumers. (One theory, which has been difficult to prove, points to homogenization as a factor in the development of arteriosclerosis.)

Milk-based formulas

The recipes for infant foods in this chapter are based on twenty years of positive experiences. Their protein, fat, and carbohydrate contents correspond to commercial formulas but without added vitamins and minerals. If you use these recipes, which may,

depending on the milk used, contain inadequate amounts of vitamin D, consult your pediatrician about additional measures to prevent rickets.* Because all infant foods based on cow's milk are poor sources of vitamin C, begin giving your baby small amounts of fruit juices at age five weeks (see page 236).

* The necessary intake of vitamin D is around 300 IU per day (1 µg = 40 IU). In the USA commercially sold milk contains added Vitamin D.

Recipe 1: One third milk with almond butter and lactose (milk sugar).

Volume:	600 ml (20 fl oz)	750 ml (25 fl oz)	900 ml (30 fl oz)
Makes bottles:	4–6	4–5	4–5
1 part cow's milk	200 ml (7 fl oz)	250 ml (8 fl oz)	300 ml (10 fl oz)
2 parts water	400 ml (13 fl oz)	500 ml (17 fl oz)	600 ml (20 fl oz)
4% almond butter	24 g ($^3/_4$ oz)†	30 g (1 oz)	36 g ($1^1/_4$ oz)
6% lactose*	36 g ($1^1/_4$ oz)†	45 g ($1^1/_2$ oz)	54 g (2 oz)

* Corresponds to the amount of lactose in breast milk; do not substitute other sugars. Some health food stores carry lactose from whey, which still contains vitamin B$_2$.

† Measure this amount once using a gram scale and then measure the weighed quantity in level teaspoons.

Directions: mix the almond butter with a little warm water. Add milk, lactose, and the rest of the water and heat briefly to at least 80°C/175°F. Strain into bottles and cap tightly. Filled bottles that will not be used immediately should be pre-cooled in a water bath before putting them in the refrigerator. If refrigeration is not available, each meal must be prepared individually just before use. Each bottle should contain only enough for one meal. Divide the daily total (not more than one seventh to one sixth of your baby's body weight) by the number of meals to find the amount per bottle.

Look for brands of almond butter that are guaranteed not to contain bitter almonds and toxins.

14

Recipe 2: Half milk with almond butter, lactose and cereal-flour.*

	Total daily quantity: metric (imperial) (depending on body weight)	
Volume:	600 ml (20 fl oz)	800 ml (28 fl oz)
No. of bottles:	4 (later 3)	5 (later 4)
1 part cow's milk	300 ml (10 fl oz)	400 ml (14 fl oz)
1 part water	300 ml (10 fl oz)†	400 ml (14 fl oz)
2% cereal	12 g (¹/₂ oz)‡	16 g (¹/₂ oz)‡
3% almond butter	18 g (²/₃ oz)‡	24 g (³/₄ oz)‡
4% lactose	24 g (³/₄ oz)‡	32 g (1 oz)‡

* Or use an instant rice cereal powder that does not contain powdered milk

† At the end of cooking, measure carefully and replace evaporated water (ca. 10%).

‡ See note about measuring under Recipe 1, page 233.

Directions: Combine the cream of rice powder (e.g., Holle baby cereal) with the water and cook briefly or according to directions on package. Then add the milk, almond butter, and lactose as described under Recipe 1, page 233, and heat again briefly to 80°C/175°F.

Recipe 1: For infants up to 3 months
33% milk with almond butter and lactose
This recipe is suitable for infants up to the age of about three months.

Variation: *50% milk with almond butter and lactose*
You can use this variation on Recipe 1 when your baby is three or four months old. Increase the proportion of milk to 50% (that is, one part milk to one part water) and reduce the almond butter to 3%.

Recipe 2: *50% milk with almond butter, lactose, and cereal powder*
Switch to this recipe when your baby is still hungry after eating the recommended amount of Recipe 1. The official recommendation is to postpone adding cereals until your baby is four months old, although younger babies still tolerate rice cream just as well as they always did.

Recipe 3: Two thirds milk with cereal powder* and sugar, optional almond butter

	Total daily quantity: metric (imperial) (depending on body weight)		
Volume:	750 ml (25 fl oz)	500 ml (18 fl oz)	250 ml (9 fl oz)
No. of bottles:	4 (later 3)	3 (later 2)	1
2 parts cow's milk	500 ml (17 fl oz)	330 ml (12 fl oz)	165 ml (6 fl oz)
1 part water	250 ml (8 fl oz)†	170 ml (6 fl oz)	85 ml (3 fl oz)
2.5% cereal	19 g ($^2/_3$ oz)‡	12 g ($^1/_2$ oz)	6 g ($^1/_4$ oz)
3% sugar	22 g ($^3/_4$ oz)‡	15 g ($^1/_2$ oz)	7.5 g ($^1/_4$ oz)
(1% almond butter)	(7.5 g)	(5 g)	(2.5 g)

* Or use an instant rice cereal powder that does not contain powdered milk

† At the end of cooking, measure carefully and replace evaporated water (ca. 10%).

‡ See note about measuring under Recipe 1, page 233.

14

Directions: See Recipe 2.

The amount of cereal powder can be increased to 2.5% if desired. If you use a non-instant cereal powder or grind your own, cook it for 3–5 minutes before removing from heat. Additional standing time may be needed for the cereal to absorb the water. The almond butter can be omitted at this point. The sugar in this recipe may be either evaporated cane juice (see page 236) or, for older infants, malt extract or honey.

The first column (750 ml, 25 fl oz) of Recipe 3 contains 500 ml of cow's milk which somewhat exceed your baby's minimum protein requirements (the amount in 400 ml of cow's milk) during the first year of life. If you feed your baby only 500 ml of this recipe per day (center column), the amount of protein falls a bit short. Make up the difference by giving him 70 ml ($2^1/_2$ fl oz) of cow's milk in addition to his bottle meals, or add a little cottage cheese to a meal of mashed fruit. The right column shows the quantities for a single bottle (usually given in the morning).

Recipe 3: *67% milk with cereal powder and sugar, optional almond butter*

Switch to this recipe when your baby is five or six months old, or a little earlier if she is not gaining weight adequately or is still hungry after a meal. Use this recipe until she is about nine months old, and then replace it with whole milk (no need to add rice cream and sugar). At age one at the latest, replace the bottle with milk from a cup and bits of bread.

If this recipe makes your baby *constipated,* try replacing part of the sugar with lactose or malt extract. A little orange juice may also help, but probably the best approach is to replace part of the cow's milk with mild home-made or commercial yogurt made with pasteurized milk.

Some general points

In case of *loose stools,* replace the lactose in any of these recipes with 3% table sugar or evaporated cane juice, and *temporarily* reduce the amount of almond butter.

Gas (wind) and *spitting up* are often due to factors other than sensitivity to foods (see Sections 1.7 and 4.1). If excessive fermentation of lactose causes gas, replace the lactose in any of these recipes with 3–5% table sugar or evaporated cane juice. If you suspect your baby is sensitive to almond butter, replace it with the same volume of sunflower seed oil and stir or shake thoroughly just before feeding. For sensitivity to *cow's milk* or *grains,* see Section 5.5, and page 231. In general, consult an experienced physician before making changes to your baby's diet.

Introducing vegetables, fruit, and cereals

If you are bottle-feeding your baby but do not use commercial formulas, introduce fruit and vegetable juices by the teaspoon beginning at the age of about five weeks. Suggested daily amounts are generally one to three teaspoons of pure blackcurrant or other fresh berry juice either added to the bottle feed, or diluted with herb tea or carrot juice; otherwise three to four teaspoons of orange juice (up to ten teaspoons if it does not cause diaper

rash) plus one to four teaspoons of carrot juice. (You can make small amounts of carrot juice yourself by grating carrots and pressing them in a strainer. A pinch of sugar helps get the juice flowing.) Continue these amounts at least until your baby begins eating vegetable or fruit meals.

Unsprayed oranges and biodynamic carrots (see Section 14.4) are preferable for making your baby's juice. Fruit syrups such as sandthorn *(Hippophae rhamnoides)* and sloe *(Prunus spinosa)* usually contain a great deal of sugar and not much vitamin C, at least in the amounts your baby will consume. If you know their sugar content, you can use them for sweetening, but do not consider them substitutes for juice. If your baby gets diaper rash when you introduce fruit juices, stop for a few days before trying again with smaller amounts. If your baby is exclusively breastfed, delay introducing juices until he is six months old (see Table I).

Preparing vegetable meals for your baby

Cook the vegetables until soft and purée them. For babies six months old or older, steam and mash the vegetables. Begin with carrots, then introduce winter squash, zucchini, small kohlrabi, cauliflower, fennel, spinach, or salad greens (no more than one new introduction per week). The last three types of vegetables listed are nitrate accumulators; do not serve them to your baby too frequently and never reheat them. In the beginning, carrots will have to be cooked for a long time, which does no harm. For other vegetables, though, brief steaming is better as soon as your baby tolerates vegetables that are not extremely well cooked. If your baby is bottle-fed, give her vegetables by the spoonful before a milk meal (either straight or mixed with a bit of whatever she gets in the bottle) or add them to the bottle. If you are breastfeeding, offer your baby vegetables when she is done nursing. Children are ready for spoon-feeding only at six months. Sometimes you may need to add a little banana, agave syrup, or sugar for a while to help your baby adjust to the new taste. Gradually increase the amount of vegetables (prepared without salt but with a little butter or sunflower seed oil) until your baby is eating an entire meal of vegetables. After the age of six months, all children who already have teeth can be given raw sticks of familiar vegetables to gnaw on. We do not recommend meat or any other supplemental foods (see also page 248). Biodynamic products are preferable. Baby food in jars is definitely a compromise; the best of these are made with biodynamic squash, carrots, or other single vegetables.

Preparing fruit meals

Moisten a slice or two of rusk in boiled water or mild yoghurt and add washed, peeled, cored, and finely grated apple (all preferably a Demeter or biodynamic produce). You may add a small amount of sugar or honey. Depending on the season, raspberries, currants (pressed through a strainer),

peaches, bananas, strawberries, or fruit juices may be used. For older infants who need to gain weight, add a few spoonfuls of full-fat cottage cheese. Always begin by offering small amounts and increase gradually to a full meal. Gnawing on slices of suitable fruits is also recommended for babies six months and older.

Cereals cooked in milk

Bottle-fed five-month-olds can have an evening meal of cereal cooked in milk instead of a bottle, and the same meal is fine for weaned breastfed infants who have never used a bottle. Use the same proportions of milk to water that you would use for a bottle. Cook your choice of semolina, thin oat flakes, barley cream, or (later) millet (do not use bran) in the water portion before adding the milk and some fresh fruit. Don't forget to include the milk used in making cereal in your baby's total daily quantity.

Apple and cereal

Some parents begin adding a little stewed or grated apple to a cereal pap by the fourth month. This is a good solution if your baby has a big appetite and is gaining weight too rapidly.

What about other beverages?

If adults consumed as much liquid in proportion to solid food as a six-month-old baby, their total daily fluid intake would be ten litres/quarts. In other words, infants get relatively large amounts of liquids in their diets in comparison to adults. Again and again, we are advised to give children

— and infants in particular — plenty to drink because their needs are higher, but the amounts recommended are usually excessive and may result in inappropriate drinking habits. Of course your baby does need extra fluids during hot, dry weather, when she has a fever, or during bouts of diarrhea or vomiting (see also Sections 4.1 and 14.5).

The transition to a toddler's diet

When your baby nears his first birthday, the transition from infant foods to a toddler's diet begins. At first, the change means nothing more than continuing with familiar foods while your baby sits in a high chair to eat with the rest of the family. You will soon notice that your baby's eating is no longer motivated exclusively by hunger. He now wants to eat whatever you are eating, and you can begin giving him bits of bread. At a certain point, he will also want to hold the spoon, and the messy process of learning to eat by himself begins. When this happens, be careful not to let him make the transition to the full variety of adult foods too quickly.

14.4 Questions of food quality

"Quality" always refers to *how* a food is produced — in other words, to its specific and unique place in the context of nature as a whole. It has nothing to do with quantitative analysis, which tells us *how much* protein, fat, carbohydrates, vitamins, and trace elements are present in whole wheat flour, for example. "Quality" has more to do with the unique ways these components appear in wheat, potatoes, rice, and legumes. The question of *how* also raises issues of cultivation, storage, and preparation. Differences in the quality of starches in grains and potatoes, for example, result not only from the different circumstances surrounding their growth but also from differences in post-harvest processing. The overall quality of our diet is the every-changing interplay of the qualities of the individual foods we eat. Thus it makes sense to combine foods derived from different parts of plants (root, stem, leaf, flower, fruit). Each of these parts interacts differently with environmental forces as the plant grows and develops. Earth, water, air, light, and warmth interact differently in roots, leaves, and flowers. Qualitatively speaking, it makes a big difference whether starches are deposited in a plant's root, leaf, or flower, even if quantitative analysis cannot tell the difference. A substance that develops above ground, surrounded by air, light, and warmth, supplies the human body with very different forces than a similar substance that develops below ground, in the roots. We immediately summon up the different types of energy we need to digest foods — that is, to destroy their unique qualities. The more varied our diet, the greater the variety of forces we need to apply to the digestive process. All of the body's functions (from motor functions through instinctive, conceptual, and imaginative functions and related sympathies and antipathies) are stimulated accordingly.

Rudolf Steiner's observations, which compare human beings and plants and describe the polar relationships of their organ systems, supply a conceptual model for the stimuli provided by different foods. Human neurosensory processes correspond to the activity of a plant's roots, which sense the presence of salts and other compounds and absorb them from the soil. Human metabolic and reproductive processes, on the other hand, correspond to the upper part of the plant where flowers and fruits develop. In humans, these polar opposites are mediated by rhythmical functions (circulation and respiration), which correspond to the respiratory organs of a plant's leaves. These relationships make it clear why, for example, consuming root vegetables or juices and teas made from roots tends to support the activity of the human neurosensory system. In contrast, teas made from flowers and from apples and other fruits have been used since ancient times to stimulate metabolic functions. Clearly, it is important to avoid one-sided diets that may lead in the long term to deficiencies and functional weaknesses in understimulated organ systems.

Another qualitative issue is the question of what circumstances allow a plant or an animal to thrive. When a pig, for example, is allowed to live a species-appropriate life and is not stimulated with medications or raised under conditions that artificially restrict its movement, it contributes different forces to pork chops or sausage than a pig that is fed a one-sided diet under conditions that disregard its other natural needs. The same is true of plants. Radishes or lettuce grown with artificial nitrogen fertilizers have a higher water content and less flavour than their unfertilized counterparts. They also keep less well. Stimulation with synthetic nitrogen fertilizers produces spinach with higher nitrate levels and radishes with atypical root shapes. This type of fertilization also produces plants that tend to bloom and fruit either late or not at all, so potassium and phosphorus salts must also be added to the soil to guarantee timely, adequate bloom.

For this reason, we recommend eating food from plants and animals raised in ways that support the health of soils, plants, and animals alike. Farming methods that increasingly impoverish the soil, require yearly applications of inorganic fertilizers, and further exploit the soil through

14

one-sided crop rotations are not exactly forward-looking, nor are cultivation methods that focus exclusively on quantitative aspects and maximizing economic gain. In the long term, such approaches to nature will inevitably prove harmful for all concerned. Biodynamic farming methods are the most consistent in their efforts to keep soils, plants, animals, and humans healthy by taking interactions among living systems into account. The literature listed in the bibliography biodynamic methods of fertilization (some of them radically new) and the results of years of experience in optimizing crop rotations, combating pests, and breeding plants and animals. These truly forward-looking methods can be used even on poor or heavily exploited soils. After several years of biodynamic management, soils show increasing signs of regeneration and are recolonized by helpful soil bacteria and other microorganisms. Biodynamic experiments in plant breeding also offer wholesome alternatives to genetically manipulated seeds (see also Section 14.7).

14.5 Individual foods

Teas suitable for infants and toddlers

Fennel and chamomile teas are generally recommended for infants and toddlers as well as for older people with digestive disturbances. *Fennel seeds* yield more tea if they are crushed before steeping. Allow this tea to steep only briefly and strain it when its color is still pale yellow. For *chamomile tea,* use home-grown or purchased whole flowers rather than teabags. Less common but also very well tolerated are apple-peel and rosehip teas. The latter is made with rosehip kernels with the hairs removed. Boil the kernels for about ten minutes or soak them overnight and then cook them for only three to five minutes. Rosehip mixtures in teabags usually contain hibiscus flowers, which produce a red, sour tea. Pure rosehips, however, produce a pleasantly mild, refreshing beverage.

Children also enjoy *peppermint* and *lemon balm* teas. (The former is not recommended for children who have been vomiting, however). *Lime blossom tea* has a sweetish taste that is not universally liked, but most children enjoy it with a few drops of lemon and a little honey. It is especially good to induce perspiration and is useful when your child has a cold or a rising fever. A good substitute for cough syrups is a tea made of $^1/_3$ each *coltsfoot flowers, narrow-leaved plantain, and sage,* flavored with honey and lemon. Many books on medicinal herbs are available and offer other useful tips.

For preschoolers and older children, set out a big pitcher of unsweetened tea on warm summer mornings. (You may want to improve the taste with a little fruit juice). Whenever they are thirsty, your children can drink this tea (which should replace all sodas and chilled drinks) without ruining their appetites for meals. Except in summer, it is better to restrict drinking to mealtimes. Some years ago, beverage manufacturers managed to convince numbers of parents that children should be allowed to drink as much as they want because they "need more fluids." The result was permanent damage to countless sets of teeth. The sugar was eventually removed from many soft drinks, but they continue to disrupt the rhythm of meals and produce mild dependencies that are later transferred from soda to other stimulants. Children who learn at an early age to satisfy their hunger and thirst at regular intervals in the company of adults are more interested in what they eat and more intensely involved in other activities between meals. If we see our internal organs as a wisdom-filled system for regulating the life processes that take place in body fluids, we are more inclined to support their rhythmical functions with regular meals (see also page 338).

Milk

Cow's milk has become one of the most important foods in our culture. However, in recent years, we have seen cases of serious *calcium deficiency* (sometimes accompanied by bone deformities and tetany, see Section 10.2) in children under the age of two. The common factor in all of these cases was that the parents, whether out of fear of allergies or radioactivity or simply as the result of personal conviction or misinformation, had totally withheld cow's milk from their children.

An infant's daily intake of whole milk should gradually increase to about 400 ml / $1^3/_4$ cups, diluted as described in previous sections. In some cases you may need to temporarily increase your baby's intake to 500 ml / $2^1/_4$ cups, but this should be considered the maximum. No minimum applies once your baby's diet has expanded to include other dairy products such as yoghurt and kefir and, later, cheese. In addition to spoiling your baby's appetite for other foods, too much milk encourages infections.

Beginning in the third year of life, it is not uncommon for heavy milk consumption to cause *digestive disturbances due to acquired lactose deficiency.* People who don't like cow's milk are often deficient in this enzyme.

Occasionally, a diet too high in milk protein (for instance, too much cottage cheese) may cause constipation with gray, pasty stools.

Milk bottles or cartons figure

14

prominently in how we think about milk, but this image obscures the fact that milk actually remains hidden under natural conditions. In suckling calves or nursing infants, we actually see only the secondary signs of milk's qualities — the young creatures' intense activity, their bonding with their mothers, their contentment, and the fact that they grow and thrive. Steiner called the give-and-take of milk consumption as nature intended it, "an education for the body," because a baby's growing body comes to grips with the forces that grow and shape the human body by digesting warm, living breast milk. As a stimulus for vital activity that shapes the body for a lifetime, milk cannot be replaced by any other food in the world. If at all possible, no child should be deprived of it.

To be suitable for human consumption, cow's milk needs to be expertly and lovingly prepared and supplemented with other foods. Nonetheless, it is still a much more suitable option than either consuming large amounts of soy and grains or introducing meat and eggs too early. (For more about so-called hypoallergenic formulas based on hydrolyzed components of cow's milk, see page 229.)

Mare's milk is more similar to human milk, but it is available only from specialized dairies and is very expensive (see page 230).

Goat's milk, a more readily available substitute for cow's milk, is an option for some eczema-prone families. Use goat's milk only if you know that the animals are appropriately fed and not permanently confined to stalls. Safe processing is the same as for cow's milk (see page 232). Because goat's milk is low in folic acid, long-term exclusive use may cause anemia.

Fats

Oils are an important addition to vegetable meals for infants and toddlers because they are very satisfying and improve absorption of fat-soluble vitamins. Cold-pressed seed oils are preferable; sunflower seed and olive oil are the best types.

The most common fat in children's diets is butter. In infrequent cases, health considerations may force a switch to special diet margarines. Avoid artificially hardened fats because they contain no metabolically active unsaturated fatty acids. Artificially saturated fats are found in many sweets and candies — one more reason to avoid them whenever possible!

Grains

The first grains were developed from grasses through careful selection during the ancient Persian culture around 5000 BC Since that time, these Indo-European grains (along with rice in the Far East and corn in the Americas) have served as the backbone of agriculture, allowing later civilizations to develop under conditions totally different from those that supported hunter-gatherer cultures. The transition to agriculture and animal husbandry, which created new staple foods and new living conditions, was humankind's first major, active intervention in the history of the natural world.

Qualitatively, grain species are characterized by intense and direct exposure to the effects of the sun. Water, air, and especially fire are also involved in transforming grain into bread. Baking, which helps make the nutrients in grain more available, can also be seen as a digestive process. Human work that enhances natural processes also contributes to making bread a food of exceptional quality. In this context, it is interesting to note the great respect accorded to bread in the cultures that introduced it. The consecration of bread in the Christian rite of Holy Communion is a case in point.

In recent times, *grain consumption* has been significantly reduced due to increased fat and protein consumption on the one hand and potato consumption on the other. The 1960s saw the beginning of a countertrend that reintroduced home-made bread and an assortment of grain dishes into our menus. Extensive experiments have been conducted in mixing grains, using sourdoughs, and testing other fermentation methods such as the honey-salt method. A new culture of home baking and natural ingredients has developed with no lobbying whatsoever.

It is a misconception that whole-grain breads have to be coarse, heavy, and hard to digest. Even very finely ground flours can contain all the nutrients of whole grains, which are unlocked by the baking process to produce an easily digestible whole-grain bread. Coarse breads are diet foods for adults who suffer from chronic constipation.

We believe it is important to give grains a larger place in our choice of foods. Unlike the roots, leaves, and flowers we eat, grains support the harmonious interaction of different body functions instead of stimulating the human body in one-sided ways (see also page 239).

Potatoes

Potatoes are native to western South America, where they have been cultivated in the Andean highlands for more than two thousand years. They were introduced to Europe by way of Italy around the seventeenth century. The advantages of growing potatoes were soon recognized. With the exception of crop failures to fungus infestations, potatoes proved much more resistant to weather than grains.

From a quality perspective, it is important to note that potatoes belong to the nightshade family. Most nightshades are poisonous, and even potatoes contain small amounts of solanin, a toxin whose concentration can be increased by bacterial infestations or by greening of the tubers through exposure to light. As a result, occasional cases of poisoning have been known to result from eating potatoes.

Comparing potatoes to grains, we find that they exhibit opposite tendencies. While the edible parts of grain plants are totally exposed to the

14

influences of light and air, potatoes are stem tubers that develop underground. As we discussed in the section on qualitative aspects of nutrition (see Section 14.4), it makes a difference whether a plant organ develops in the ground or in the domain of air and light. Potatoes are especially interesting in this respect. When a seed potato sprouts, the main shoot grows upward, but the sprouts that emerge from the cotyledon axils bend down and grow into the soil. Roots and other subterranean storage organs correspond to the human neurosensory system, while seeds and fruits tend to stimulate the metabolic system. Potatoes, unlike true roots and root tubers, develop underground as the result of a partial reversal of the principle governing the development of stems. In combination with their toxic potential, this phenomenon makes potatoes an obvious exception among subterranean plant organs that serve as food. As stem tubers, potatoes have a one-sided effect on the organs of the human nervous system. Rudolf Steiner comments that excessive potato consumption weakens meditative, inward-directed thinking in favour of rational reflection, thus promoting conceptual activity that is limited to considering materialistic aspects of life. From this perspective, it is not surprising that the emergence of our modern materialistic way of thinking, which depends totally on superficial sense perceptions, coincided with the spread of potatoes as a staple food. (Obviously, we do not mean to suggest that eating potatoes is the only cause of materialism! Our point is simply that potato consumption may have supported this shift in consciousness.)

What conclusions can we draw from these observations? We can attempt to gradually limit our potato consumption in favour of grains, roots, and other vegetables. When we use potatoes we can try more varied forms — in salads, dumplings, puffs, or home-made French fries. We can get the full benefit of the potato's advantages as a food (high protein and vitamin content) and avoid additional disadvantages by purchasing organic potatoes. Within a month or two after making these dietary changes, you will notice an increase your alertness and in the freshness and flexibility of your thoughts. *We recommend avoiding potatoes during pregnancy and in the first year of life, when the cerebrum is still making major steps toward maturity.* Similarly, potatoes should be avoided by patients with neurological diseases and malignancies.[35]

Vegetables and salads

Every adult knows (and tells children) that vegetables and salads are good for you. As we saw earlier (Section 14.4), their value lies not only in the nutrients they contain but also in their relationship to a great variety of forces in living nature. In emergency situations or nutritionally unbalanced diets, the trace elements and vitamins of vegetables become very important. A few details are important with regard to infant nutrition.

Until the 1970s, it was assumed that formula-fed infants could safely be fed raw carrot juice beginning at five weeks and well-cooked pureed carrots at three months. (Earlier introduction of carrots often caused gas.) More recently, however, instances of intolerance and allergies have increased, making carrots one of the most allergenic vegetables. This phenomenon can only be related to cultivation methods and/or to a general decline in digestive functions. As a result, however, carrots should be introduced into the diets of infants with neurodermatitis only after the age of six months and only on a trial basis. In any case, breastfed babies do not need carrot juice any earlier than six months. Some of the harmless yellow pigment in carrots is deposited in the body (see Section 5.2), while the rest is transformed into vitamin A. Because cooked carrots produce firm stools, they are good insurance against diarrhea. Grated raw carrots, however, should be added to your baby's diet only when she is one or two years old and never when she has diarrhea.

During the second six months of her life, give your baby a wide variety of vegetables to try, but do not expect her to make an entire meal of vegetables. To support their curiosity about foods and their interest in chewing, all infants six months old or older should be allowed to try out their teeth on chunks of raw vegetables.

It is important to know the difference between nitrate-poor vegetables (such as cauliflower, kohlrabi, zucchini, eggplant, and winter squash) and the nitrate-rich varieties such as spinach, fennel, beets, and salad greens. Nitrate-rich vegetables should not be served too frequently, should not be stored for too long, and should never be served reheated, as under certain conditions nitrates can be transformed into toxic nitrites. Contrary to earlier assumptions, spinach is not especially rich in iron, and its oxalic acid content renders dietary calcium insoluble. For this reason, it should not be served together with dairy products.

Almost all vegetables can be transformed into interesting and tasty raw salads. Try dressing them with yoghurt or a sweet-and-sour lemon dressing or add raisins or pieces of tangerine. Well-grown raw vegetables have more flavour, encourage more chewing, and are more satisfying and nutritious when eaten in smaller quantities than cooked vegetables.

Fruit

Most babies like to eat fruit, but if your baby is an exception, you can disguise grated fruits or freshly squeezed juices in cottage cheese or cereals. Your baby does not need large amounts of fruit. Half an apple and a little lemon juice is enough for a baby who really prefers other foods.

Whenever possible, children should be given unsprayed, unwaxed fruits so they can eat them skin and all. We really need to sit up and take notice when we hear children asking, "Is it all right to eat this apple with the skin on, or has it been sprayed?" What kind

14

of impression of life do our children get when we ourselves see foods as dangerous or poisoned and have to check the labels before deciding whether we can trust fresh produce? Adults should always model well-considered, trustful handling of foods — along with gratitude that we do not have to go hungry.

Although all children like bananas, make sure your baby doesn't eat too many. Bananas contain valuable nutrients but few enlivening forces. They are very filling but may cause constipation and tend to make babies a bit lethargic. Furthermore, the process of ripening bananas, which are picked green, is not totally unproblematic. Citrus fruits, which keep well even when fully ripe, are a very different matter; eating citrus is refreshing and enlivening. Again, large amounts are not necessary. For babies, we recommend untreated citrus fruits and berries (a few sections or a few teaspoons per day).

Sugar, honey, and other sweeteners

Sugar is unique among foods in that it crystallizes readily but is not a salt. It is closer to a dead mineral than any of the foods we have already discussed. Commercial sugar keeps indefinitely. As a carrier of energy, sugar is synthesized in the green parts of plants and stored in the roots, leaves, stems, flowers, or fruits in the form of starches or fructose. For humans, sugar offers a ready supply of energy that requires little or no digestion.

Hence sugar does not stimulate the vital activity of organs the way fresh plants do. Instead, it replaces a substance that a healthy body makes for itself in adequate quantities. When the body is ill, tired, or exhausted, however, sugar consumption supplies needed energy and replaces the work of digestion. This is especially evident in the case of a limp, weak, premature infant who weighs only 800 g / 1 lb 12 oz and may not survive. While the baby is lying in the incubator, sugar-water is dripped onto her lips. As soon as she tastes its sweetness, she appears enlivened and "moved" down to the tips of her toes and stretches out her lips for more. The drops of sugar-water become the coveted water of life.

As adults for whom tasting is no longer an activity that engages the entire body, we nonetheless remain directly and sympathetically affected by sweet tastes. Sour, salty, and bitter qualities are more awakening and aggressive, but sweetness comforts, surrounds, calms, and supports us. It also directly strengthens our sense of self; we feel better and stronger in the body. This effect encourages repeated sugar consumption. We enjoy the temporary boost and do not notice the letdown that follows, which we attempt to compensate for with increasing amounts of sugar. "Sugar-addicted" children are typically restless, unfocused, and unconcentrated. Since the introduction of sugar into post-Napoleonic Europe, increasingly excessive sugar consumption has correlated with the spread of diseases of civilization such as dental caries (see Section 10.1) and diabetes.

It is also interesting to discover that many adult diabetics experienced excessive emotional or intellectual challenges during childhood and adolescence. Heredity also plays a role in this illness. Everything that weakens the physical and emotional activity of the human I and prevents it from becoming master in its own house fosters derailment of our sugar metabolism. Because blood sugar is an expression of the I's activity in the blood, consuming sugar supports the I when we are exhausted or need to increase our productivity to the utmost. Too frequent sugar consumption, however, accustoms the I to not producing its own sugar by digesting starch. In combination with other I-weakening environmental and hereditary factors, excessive sugar intake increases the likelihood of diabetes and other forms of metabolic weakness, and especially of addictive behaviors later in life. This certainly does *not* mean, however, that the appropriate conclusion is to eliminate sugar entirely from infant foods. We have seen many thin, pale infants on sugar-free diets transformed within a few weeks into healthy, rosy babies simply by adding a three-percent sugar solution to their formula. Sugar is an extremely active substance that must be carefully handled, but moderate use may be just the right thing, depending on your baby's temperament and constitution. Every family needs to discover the right types and amounts of sugar for themselves.

What type of sugar is best for infants? *White sugar* should be used sparingly. Although bleach is no longer used in its production, repeated crystallization eliminates all impurities, so white sugar lacks all the minerals and vitamins present in unrefined cane or beet juice. As a rule, natural unrefined products contain all the substances that animals and humans need for the product's digestion. The sugars in pressed cane, beet, or fruit juices contain enough trace elements to support their processing in the body. *Evaporated cane or beet juice products* are available in natural food stores. Ordinary brown sugar is not suitable for infants because it eliminates only the last few refining stages and contains traces of additives from the entire process.

Lactose, which is only weakly sweet, is suitable only for infants. Fructose generally offers no particular advantages. Because it requires no digestion, *glucose* raises blood sugar rapidly, which is usually undesirable but may be very important when blood sugar is very low — due to vomiting, for example.

If natural evaporated cane juice products are not available, you can make do with white sugar in combination with other healthy foods. Popular sugar substitutes include *agave syrup* and *maple syrup,* which is expensive. *Dried fruits* such as dark apricots, dates, figs, and raisins can also help satisfy a desire.

Honey should not be used simply as a substitute for sugar. It is the result of a complicated process that begins with

14

nectar in flowers and ends with the processing activity of bees. As a consequence, honey is not as neutral as sugar in its effect on the human physical body. It is a highly active substance that stimulates human metabolism. As such, it can easily provoke diarrhea in infants. Rudolf Steiner recommended honey for aging, sclerotic people and (in small quantities) to prevent and treat rickets and allergies. We recommend giving your baby honey only after she is nine months old. Even then, give her no more than one teaspoon a day, dissolved in foods.

We do not recommend *artificial sweeteners*. On the one hand, their effects on the human body are not totally unproblematic, and on the other, it makes no sense to encourage a taste for sweets for its own sake without triggering the associated work of digestion.

Eggs, meat, and fish

A great deal of attention has been devoted to protein intake since the discovery that protein deficiencies can develop when specific amino acids, the building blocks of proteins, are absent from the diet. It is true that the human body cannot synthesize all of these building blocks but is dependent on getting the so-called essential amino acids from foods. These particular amino acids are abundant in meat products, and milk also contains complete proteins. To a lesser extent, the limiting amino acids are also present in legumes such as soybeans and in almonds and other nuts. Thus it is not

absolutely necessary to eat meat, fish, or eggs. Dietary habits have developed differently in different parts of the world. People in the Orient tend to prefer vegetarian diets, while the people of the Americas, especially South America, consume the most meat. The dietary needs and preferences of Europeans fall somewhere in between.

The following perspective may help you decide when to begin feeding your baby eggs and meat:

Breast milk, with its low protein content (about half that of cow's milk), is unquestionably the best food for babies during the first months of life. During this period and throughout the first two years, the brain continues to mature until it is able to serve as the foundation for thinking. (In contrast to this process, the adolescent growth spurt, which occurs long after the development of the nervous system and sensory organs has been completed, serves primarily to develop muscle mass and physical strength.) It seems logical, therefore, to follow the example nature provides in breast milk and to feed your baby a so-called lacto-vegetarian diet (dairy products, grains, vegetables, and fruits) until he is three years old. When self-awareness awakens and your child begins to call himself "I," his individual instinctive preferences for certain types of food become stronger than before. At this age, it is already apparent whether a child will become a vegetarian or not. Some children reject meat and eggs whenever they are served, while for others they instantly become favourite foods.

This was the situation in one family with five children: Beginning with his third birthday, the first child enjoyed moderate amounts of meat and eggs whenever they were served. The second developed an inexplicable hunger for animal products, begging bits of meat off of other people's plates and leaving everything else aside in favour of sausage, fish, or egg. Following the example of this older sister, the third child asked for fish for his third birthday meal and was greatly disappointed to discover that he didn't like it. Meat and eggs also did not appeal to him especially, although he ate them occasionally. The fourth child was definitely a vegetarian — no birthday meal of fish for him! — while the fifth was more like the first. This example shows that individual instincts rather than imitation are the decisive factor in developing food preferences.

Another reason for avoiding eggs and meat during the first few years is that they encourage accelerated physical growth and weight gain. Human development, unlike that of animals, however, is characterized by extremely protracted physical maturation to allow time for emotional and intellectual development.

In summary, we recommend a lacto-vegetarian diet for infants and toddlers. For older children, offer a varied diet of high-quality foods adapted to their individual needs, but do not overemphasize proteins. If your child's appetite is one-sided, persist — through subterfuge, if necessary — in your efforts to get her to eat a wider variety of foods.

Salt and mineral water

Infant foods should never be salted. Toddlers should also not eat a lot of salty foods; they get enough salt in bread and milk. For the occasional child who develops a pronounced taste for it, salt does no harm, although this preference may be an important constitutional sign for your holistic physician.

We are sometimes asked which brands of mineral water are suitable for preparing infant and toddler foods while traveling or for use when a baby has diarrhea. As a rule, mineral waters with low sodium content are suitable. French parents commonly use Evian water which is available in other counries. Many brands of mineral water are so high in minerals that children of this age cannot process them properly, and they may eventually cause fever and oedema if used for mixing formula.

14

14.6 Nutrition and thinking

The issue of food quality, which we have already discussed from several perspectives, is a prerequisite to understanding the connection between nutrition and thinking. The human etheric body, which we described as the body encompassing the laws of life, is the vehicle not only of vital activity in the form of growth, regeneration, and reproduction but also of our conscious thought life — that is, the activity of thinking itself (see also Section 15.4).

In a conversation with the chemist Ehrenfried Pfeiffer, Rudolf Steiner made a groundbreaking response to the question of how human thinking can lead us back to true perception of the spiritual world: "That is a problem of nutrition." How are we meant to understand this connection? In Section 14.4, we said that the human body needs to exert energy in order to process the foods it ingests. The more natural — that is, the more "alive" and (in the case of animal products) "ensouled" — these foods are as a result of how they are grown and processed, the more energy the body has to apply in order to break them down and transform them into human substance. On the one hand, it is possible to overburden the body with too many raw foods; on the other hand, it is also possible to expect too little of it by feeding it denatured foods that are "dead" in the truest sense of the word. In this case, the body itself has too

little to do in the process of "denaturing" and digesting foods. This is the trend in all modern methods of food preparation, from fast foods to processed foods of all sorts. Although individuals vary greatly and each person must discover the right balance for him or herself, onesided raw food diets run the risk of engaging the etheric body too strongly in the digestion process and leaving too little energy left over for the activity of thinking. Conversely, consuming heavily denatured foods full of additives and chemical "enrichments" places too few demands on the ether body. It becomes lazy, and this laziness manifests in the form of "weak minded" materialistic thinking that is capable of reflecting only what the senses convey. This type of thinking has difficulty becoming conscious of the enlivening etheric force of its own spiritual nature.

Meditative thinking, which frees itself from sensory perceptions and delves into the etheric, spiritual nature of thinking as the inherent, living context of the cosmos, is supported by an etheric body activated by working on digestion. This does not mean that it is impossible for people raised on denatured foods to achieve spiritual activity; it simply means that achieving it costs them significantly more effort and (as we can see from Western culture as a whole) becomes substantially more difficult and not the general rule.

From this perspective, nutrition in childhood is highly significant, because the digestive organs (and with them, the higher members of the human constitution — ether body, astral body, and I-organization) learn to do their work only gradually as a child grows and develops. If they are "well educated" in the early years of life — that is, stimulated and strengthened by appropriate foods — and if this process is accompanied by a corresponding education of the child's emotional and spiritual forces, the child's thinking will also learn to actively "digest" and "process" the contents of consciousness. Stimulating physical digestion in healthy ways supports a child's actively developing thought life. In adulthood, it becomes clear that food is not the only factor in preserving the health of the body; active spiritual work and meditative "digestion" of important universal connections become increasingly important. For adults in particular, it is quite true that we cannot live "on bread alone." The pleasant and healing habit of singing or praying before meals enables even very small children to experience this connection between nutrition and consciousness (see Chapter 24 on religious education).

The diagrams below offer a graphic summary of this relationship.

The etheric body in childhood
The metamorphosis of growth forces into thought forces is still in its beginnings.

Preponderance of etheric forces that insure growth and regeneration

conscious thought activity

unconscious bodily activity

The etheric body of an old person
Preponderance of etheric forces available for body-free thought activity

No growth; declining regenerative ability

conscious thought activity

unconscious bodily activity

14.7 Genetically modified foods

This is not the place to attempt to do full justice to organic agriculture and biodynamic methods in particular. Nonetheless, we do want to point to the invaluable work of the agricultural pioneers around the world who are opposing and supplementing modern agrochemistry and agrotechnology — which are increasingly remote from nature — with natural agricultural methods focused on healing and regenerating the soil. Although scientists repeatedly maintain that genetically and chemically manipulated monocultures are essential to solving the problem of feeding the world's population, we must point out that although this propaganda has been repeated for decades, three-quarters of the world's total population are still undernourished and that this situation has not really improved in the last hundred years. Furthermore, the result of agricultural aid to developing nations is often either to remove land from the hands of small farmers and turn it over to agrobusinesses or to encourage the cultivation of more profitable crops at the expense of staple foods that meet the needs of local populations. On the other hand, the automation of agriculture is also responsible for the fact that increasing numbers of people are free to choose occupations other than growing food. This trend is one of many factors in modern efforts toward individual liberty and is unlikely to be reversed in any foreseeable future.

Our concern here is to point out that children need foods grown using ecologically beneficial methods, foods that contain etheric forces and (in the case of species-appropriate animal husbandry) protein of a quality that has served an animal living in harmony with nature. Adults with well-developed metabolisms can afford to feel that they can digest anything and that they are largely independent of what they eat. For children, however, whose bodies are still developing and whose digestive functions are being shaped and educated by what they eat, the utmost care in selecting and preparing foods is appropriate, even if it involves choices that are costly in terms of both time and money. The payback comes in the quality of the child's health (and consciousness!) later in life (see also Section 14.6).

In this context, we must also deal with the question of genetically altered foods, which began entering cultivation in the late 1970s. In addition to dairy products and fermented foods produced using genetically manipulated microorganisms, these altered foods include strains of soybeans, corn, rice, and other grains. It is highly unlikely that quantitative considerations alone will lead to satisfactory conclusions on the pros and cons of genetically altered foods, which can be manipulated to contain higher concentrations of aromatic substances or proteins than are possible in crops bred and raised using natural methods. But because a plant's genetic material is the vehicle of its etheric body, we must apply non-quantitative standards when we consider the significance of gene manipulation. An obvious attribute of all genetically altered life forms is that their reproductive capacity (and thus also their etheric stability) is reduced. Genetically altered organisms cannot reproduce over multiple generations and will be able to survive only if they are constantly recreated from healthy, naturally occurring forms. It is to be hoped that this type of food will not cause noticeable harm in healthy adults, who will be able to digest it just as they digest everything else. For reasons we discussed above, however, children should not be given *any* genetically manipulated foods.

As debates about species-appropriate cultivation of foods becomes more intense, increasing support is developing for agricultural and soil-enhancement methods that are future-oriented and healing — both for human beings *and* for the natural world. This applies not only to plant-derived foods but also especially to animal products. Here, too, consumers will have the last word. We can only hope that the aftermath of the mad-cow disease crisis will force a reversal of agricultural policies.

14

15. Child Development and Related Social Issues

15.1 Learning to see

In an earlier section (12.2), we described a newborn baby's unfocused gaze, which barely maintains its direction although the baby appears to be looking for something. Over the next few weeks, the baby's eyes remain open for longer and longer periods. During and after nursing, she usually looks in the direction of her mother's head. Her eyes may also turn repeatedly in a direction where there is nothing in particular to see — perhaps an unremarkable piece of wall or cloth some distance away. If you turn her head, her eyes will continue to look in the same direction for as long as possible. This inborn reflex, known as the "doll's eye phenomenon," is the next stage in learning directional vision; it serves as a transition between the floating, random eyeball movements of a sleeping or premature infant and the stage when the baby's visual axes actually connect with objects in her surroundings. At first, when your come into your baby's line of sight, she seems to look through you, unaffected by your material presence. Later, she becomes aware of you and responds by breathing faster and moving her eyes and limbs. Her eyes begin to rest on your head and follow it when you move away. If you remain still, however (as a mother tends to do when she senses that her baby's eyes are "drinking in" her appearance) you can see your reflection in the lower part of your baby's pupils, which means that she is looking slightly above or to one side of your head rather than directly at your eyes, nose, or mouth.

The astonishing thing about this stage of visual development is that a baby participates emotionally in what she sees. When she sees her mother, her response is calm, happy, and attentive, but if an uncertain, exhausted, or harried person enters her line of sight, she becomes restless, or perhaps her mouth twitches in a fleeting expression of displeasure or anxiety. Although she does not yet perceive clearly and specifically, she certainly "sees" something, namely, the emotional state of the adults around her. This type of perception is also evident when you approach the cradle where your baby lies sleeping — you may notice a fleeting, subtle, usually one-sided smile. It is difficult to avoid the impression that the baby is perceiving something, even though she is asleep with her eyes closed.

Directional vision and *perceiving emotional states* appear at the same time, before true object perception becomes possible. We may wonder whether babies are able to perceive purely soul-spiritual qualities that are hidden from the completely object-oriented vision of adults. This thought explains why medieval painters still painted halos around the heads of angels, madonnas, and saints to represent the nobler aspects of the human being. During a visit to the doctor, one mother asked us, "Why does he always look over my head instead of at my eyes?" The answer both surprised and satisfied her: "At this stage, he's interested in what your halo looks like." In this connection, it makes sense that babies of this age are especially attracted to shiny, sparkling, or red objects, which supply sense impressions similar to what they perceive in a person with a light-filled attitude.

At age four or five weeks, your baby's first long-awaited, radiant, deliberate smile appears when her eyes meet yours. Her gaze has shifted from the periphery to your centrally located pupils. In other words, she has found the material, sense-perceptible location where soul-spiritual qualities manifest directly in earthly life. Onlookers invariably feel a sense of joy at the soul meeting expressed in this meeting of the eyes. "You're here, I'm here, we're here" more or less expresses this moment in words. One of the essential prerequisites of being human — seeking and perceiving another human being — has taken hold. Your baby's smile lights up when she perceives her mother or father, and from then on she always attempts to meet their gaze. In later years, she still feels discontented if she does not feel a parent's loving, understanding gaze resting on her at least once a day. In school, too, her progress is impeded if she doesn't meet a teacher who looks at her with true interest.

As personal interactions develop, your baby also begins to pay attention to other things. "Something light" passes through her field of vision when you carry her past the window. As she alternates between excited movement and holding still, "something moving" appears and disappears and is joined by "something else moving"; tactile sensations are triggered as her own little hands touch. At this stage, your baby's visual perception acquires a distinctly tactile character as she begins to structure the random interplay of her own hands. Touching herself reinforces her perception of self, as do the tactile sensations around her mouth as she nurses. Your loving touch also awakens her experience of self.

Infant development

Figures 27 & 28. At the age of six weeks, a baby's limbs are still slightly bent, as they are in newborns. From the very beginning, babies lying on their stomachs raise their heads.

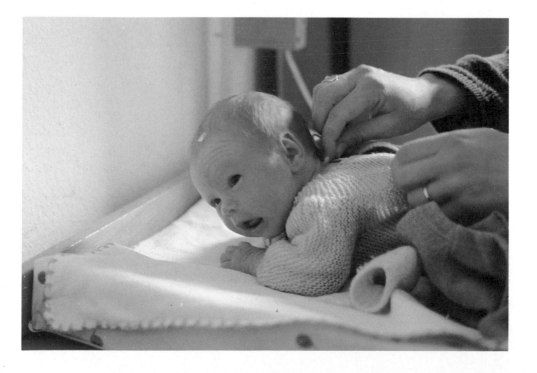

Figures 29 & 30. At the age of eight weeks the baby begins to initiate movements such as making a fist, sucking, and lifting his head.

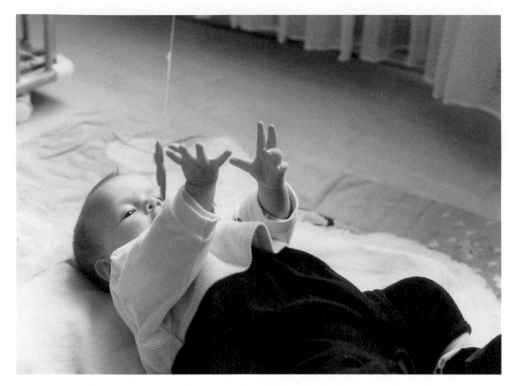

Figure 31. When your baby is three months old, his hands appear in his field of vision when he lies on his back.

Figure 32. When lying on his stomach, he can raise his head and shoulders slightly.

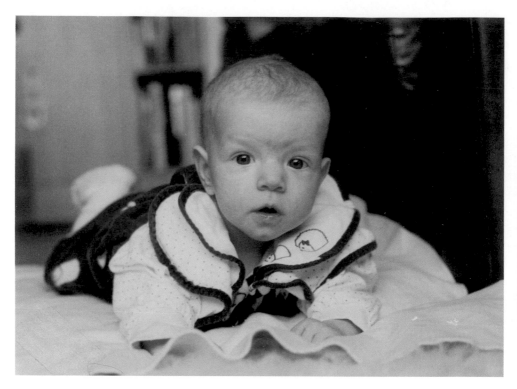

Figure 33. At four months he lifts his head higher, using first his forearms and then his closed hands as supports. His gaze can lift to the horizontal.

Figure 34. At five to six months, he can free one hand to grasp objects.

Figure 35. Supported on his elbows, the first attempts at turning and moving are made.

Figure 36. At six months, he can look up supporting himself on his hands.

Figures 37 & 38. Baby has discovered a first means of locomotion (ten to twelve months).

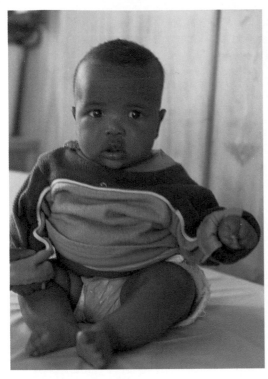

Figures 39–41. At about ten months, babies learn to sit upright on a firm surface.

*Figure 42. Pulling himself upright by holding
onto furniture or the bars of his playpen.*

Figure 43. The first steps. An act of balance.

What your baby sees becomes important at this stage, and it makes a difference whether the contents of her perceptions agree or clash. A stuffed cloth sphere with a moon face on it, for example, bears no relationship to the music box it conceals, and the material a plastic rattle is made of has nothing to do with the pictures on it or the sounds it makes. In contrast, a stick of wood always remains the same, even if it is used to make noise. The everyday objects your baby enjoys expose her to either truthfulness or untruthfulness, and if adults do not make this distinction for her at this stage of life, she will have difficulty making it for herself later on. Exposure to misleading or inauthentic sense impressions lays the groundwork for doubting the reliability of sensory perceptions, which are demoted to the level of inessential or deceptive images. Do not underestimate the importance of surrounding your infant with authenticity. At this age, all sense impressions still sink deep into the unconscious.

At about five months, your baby begins to distinguish between familiar and unfamiliar faces and to associate eyeglasses and hairstyles with specific voices. She identifies with familiar faces but not with those of strangers, and she begins to be afraid of people she doesn't know. Anyone unfamiliar to the baby can easily observe an interesting and important aspect of young children's fear of strangers: the degree to which your baby rejects a stranger (as evidenced by sullenness, clinging to you, or an outbreak of crying) depends on how far she is from you and from the stranger. In your arms, she may tolerate the stranger's presence at a distance of one metre but not any nearer. If she is farther away from you — on the changing table, for example — her tolerance limits contract, only to expand again when the stranger sits down or when you hold her on your lap. Activity breeds trust, so an unfamiliar person will be able to get closer if he distracts the baby and begins playing with her.

On the other hand, telling your one-year-old, "You don't have to be afraid of this person," may alert her to the fact that the person is indeed a stranger, and she will pull back. At this stage, you may be able to stretch your baby's comfort zone simply by picking her up — that is, by allowing her to slip back into an earlier stage of development (regression).

For our purposes, it is important to recognize that a baby's visual field is a coherent but ever-changing entity that expands or contracts with her sympathy or antipathy and is heavily dependent on her mother's example. Its boundaries may expand when the baby is alert and contract when she is tired. They also expand when she receives strong, isolated impressions of color or other stimuli. For example, your baby may recognize her father immediately when he returns home alone but fail to recognize him in a group of people until he extricates himself from the group and walks toward her. This example demonstrates that single, coherent events catch your baby's interest

15

and attention better than multiple impressions.

Until now, we have been considering how your baby makes eye contact. At a certain stage, however, she will begin to deliberately avert her eyes. The transition to this stage is marked by the peek-a-boo phase, when small children truly believe that the other person disappears when they close or cover their own eyes. Your baby may also be unable to meet your eyes when she is overcome with pleasure at seeing you again. Inevitably, however, a day comes when she averts her eyes out of shame. At this stage, the appearance of an adult may signify a warning that she is misbehaving. Averting her gaze becomes an expression of shame; she feels that she has cut herself off from you. Shame is a powerful feeling that needs to be handled with care. The "I" itself is what feels ashamed of the consequences of its actions and wants to correct the mistake. Later in life, blushing with shame remains a sign that the "I" would rather not be seen in its present condition and wants to hide from the other person's gaze. Anyone who deals with children knows much damage adults can do in this connection. We can err in one of two directions. At one extreme, we attempt to eliminate all difficulties and obligations from the child's life and taking the pedagogical stance that children should never have to experience shame at all. At the opposite extreme, the child's personality is ground between the millstones of the dogmatic moral concepts of judgmental parents.

The visual field and "comfort zone" we have sketched here are the parts of your child's emotional space where she already experiences herself consciously. Whether this soul space expands or contracts depends on her momentary mood and degree of alertness.

15.2 Motor development and learning to walk

A baby in the womb is already constantly moving. Even conception itself is characterized by movement — the slow movement of an egg and the rapid motion of the sperm cell that penetrates it and unites with it. Subsequent development is also full of movement: flowing, rotating, turning, involuting, separating, uniting, differentiating, growing together or apart, or even dissolving in favour of wholly new organ structures. Before birth, we speak of the fetal movements of growth and development, but these movements continue after birth as the baby continues to grow. As the weeks go by, however, the play of outer gestures is increasingly emancipated from inborn, wholly organically determined movements (see Figures 27–43).

During a routine checkup, your pediatrician may check various postures and reflexive movements:

- A newborn in a relaxed position keeps all joints slightly bent (Figure 27) and still looks slightly curled up. His arms and legs are bent, his fingers lightly closed.
- If you touch one of his cheeks, his head turns in that direction and he attempts to suck.
- If you turn his head to one side as he lies on his back, he can stretch the arm on that side out along the surface he is resting on and bend the opposite arm at head height, but he cannot lift his arms off the surface.
- If you pick him up and hold him face down, his head often still hangs below the horizontal line of his back.
- If you hold him in mid air and turn him on his side, his upper leg bends more than the lower one.
- If you hold him so that the soles of his feet touch a flat surface, he pushes his front leg away from him and moves the other leg forward and then repeats the gesture on the other side, giving the impression of taking a step.
- If you lay him on his stomach, he frees his nose by raising his head and turning it sideways (Figure 28).
- If you hold him in a lying position and allow his head to fall backward

slightly, his arms move abruptly apart and then together again.
- Lying on his back on a firm surface, he moves his arms outward when you tap the surface close to his head.
- If you pick him up in semi-darkness, his eyes open. If you place your finger in his hand, his fist closes around it and cannot let go.
- If you leave him lying naked on his back in a warm place and watch closely, you can see the rudiments of four-legged walking in the spreading and coming together of his arms and the kicking of alternate feet.

It takes about two and a half months before most of these inborn reflexes yield to voluntary movements. At this age, your baby begins to initiate movements such as making a fist, sucking, and lifting his head (Figures 29 and 30). He stops making automatic stepping motions when his feet touch a surface, and although he continues to kick with alternating feet, the associated arm gestures disappear. If we compare human and animal development, we realize that the losing of inborn abilities is a significant step. Animals take advantage of the stepping reflex to learn to walk shortly after birth. Two hours after birth, a foal can already keep up with the herd. A human infant, however, is still engaged in building up his brain and the rest of his body, and it takes him a full year of effort to learn to stand upright and walk. When he does, he "stands on his own two feet" and

15

makes decisions about where he wants to go. Unlike an animal, he is not forced to blindly obey organ-bound instinctive tendencies. If we compare the development of different animal species, it soon becomes evident that the faster an animal develops, the more organ-dependent and less "learned" all of its capabilities remain. The more slowly it develops, the more time it has to expand its abilities through learning.

Because we must learn everything that makes us human, we can apply our abilities freely, and our options for doing so expand with each new skill we learn. This is why our development, which takes sixteen to twenty years, is uniquely retarded in comparison to animal maturation. Lifelong learning and the development of freedom become possible for us. In human infants, therefore, persistence of inborn reflex patterns indicates a developmental disturbance that should be diagnosed by a physician as soon as possible.

At three months, your baby can already control his head and hold it upright. When lying on his stomach, he can raise his head and shoulders slightly (Figures 31 and 32). From month to month, he lifts his head higher, using first his forearms and then his closed hands as supports (Figure 32). At five to six months, his fists open and he supports his head and upper body on his outstretched arms. (As adults, we can still experience remnants of the arms' support function if we play blind man's buff or feel our way around a dark room with our arms outstretched.)

When your baby is three months old, his hands appear in his field of vision when he lies on his back. In the course of the next three months, he learns to grasp objects (Figure 34). Anything movable finds its way to his mouth. His grip slowly matures from a simple closed fist to the pincher grip to grasping with the tips of the rounded forefinger and thumb. Meanwhile your baby conquers the space around him. His gestures of resistance show the extent to which he has taken possession of his body. A three-month-old no longer likes to have his head touched; a six-month old will push you away if you touch his ribcage. Acquiring uprightness also proceeds from the head downward (Figures 35 and 36). This progression becomes obvious if you think about how a mother holds her child at different ages. She supports her newborn baby's head but her three-month-old's shoulders, and when she carries her six-month-old, her second hand supports only the middle of the baby's back. When her baby is eight months old, she supports only his pelvis and legs, and when he is eleven to thirteen months old, she carries him in a sitting position using one arm only, and her other hand is free to do something else. At about ten months, babies learn to sit upright on a firm surface (Figures 39, 40 and 42). A younger baby sits bent forward with his head centered over the triangular base of support formed by his feet and pelvis.

At five or six months, the bent or curled-up position typical of younger infants gives way to increasing pleasure in stretching out. At this age, babies like to lie on their backs with arms and legs outstretched, kicking with both feet at the same time. Don't confuse this stretching tendency, which allows your baby to become receptive to his surroundings, with the development of uprightness. At this stage, the force of uprightness has descended only as far as his hands and middle and lower back, but the stretching tendency has taken over his entire body, including his legs. For example, he stretches his legs out against a blanket that covers them. He may also bend his legs and bounce when held upright, but he shows no other signs of being ready to stand. When you pull your baby into an upright position, his head remains straight and no longer turns to the side as before.

Neither the infant's early gestures of bending and stooping nor his stretching and opening, are true precursors of human locomotion. Upright walking is more closely related to a third movement, which first becomes recognizable in the third month of life and is associated with the downward thrust of the force of uprightness. This movement is rotation of the torso, the first step in learning to turn over.

At approximately ten months, your baby's hands become fully available for grasping objects when he is in a sitting position. Simple grasping predominates at first, but it later alternates with deliberately letting go of objects and — later still — throwing them away. Your baby has not yet fully taken possession of his feet, the only remaining parts of his body that he will still always allow you to touch with impunity. Kneeling on one leg is soon followed by pulling himself upright by holding on to furniture or the bars of his playpen (Figure 41). Expect a few miserable moments when your baby has learned to pull himself into a standing position but has not yet learned how to sit down again.

By this age, your baby has discovered a first provisional means of locomotion. He may roll, pull or push himself over the floor, either on his stomach or in a sitting position, or crawl on all fours (Figures 37 and 38). He will probably stick with whatever form of locomotion came first for him, which also depends somewhat on the type of surface he learns on. Artificial aids to locomotion — rolling walkers, bouncing swings, and the like — disrupt the highly individual process of learning to walk. We do not recommend using them because they allow your baby to engage in activities that he has not yet mastered on his own, and his independent initiative suffers as a result.

Some children lean to crawl on all fours only after they learn to walk; others never use their arms to pull themselves over the floor; still others walk as well at ten months as others do at a year and a half. Parents often ask us what is "better" or "normal," but this question can't be answered in general terms because the development of each human being, unlike that of individual animals, is unique and individualized, always alternating

15

both physically and on the soul-spiritual level between "too early" and "too late." Doing the right thing at the right time is the real art of life; either consciously or unconsciously, each individual moves toward this goal. Early maturation is often coupled with a lack of inner freedom. Early bloomers are more strongly influenced by their own endowed talents and may put them to use without acquiring many new ones. Late-bloomers, who have to acquire their abilities through patience and effort, have more freedom in how to apply them and are often more understanding of other people's problems. In any case, learning to walk anywhere between the ages of ten and eighteen months is considered "normal" (Figure 43).

After learning to walk, your toddler has a series of other tasks to master — climbing stairs, hopping, jumping, and many more. Walking itself still undergoes many changes before a toddler's broad, foot-smacking gait is transformed into the narrow-based, springy step of a nine-year-old. Like upright walking, other forms of movement are also learned through imitation; none of these voluntary movements are inborn abilities. Thus the best way to support your child's motor development is to provide a good example. You can be sure that your child will imitate all of your own hectic or sluggish movements and how hard or softly your feet hit the floor. By absorbing the soul-gestures expressed in the movements of the adults around him, he also learns to express the stirrings of his own soul through movements.

15.3 Learning to talk

Even in the noises and cries that a newborn baby makes, we can detect indications of hunger, pain, tiredness, weakness, or of feeling neglected. At eight or ten weeks, soon after her first deliberate smiles, your baby begins to play with the throaty, palatal sounds produced when breathing out encounters saliva. Hearing her own utterances, she attempts to repeat them. (These subtle sounds appear only when babies are in a good mood — that is, usually after feeding and changing. Children who grow up in institutions never make such sounds.) Charmed by the sounds your baby makes, you instinctively imitate them. Your astounded baby responds with attempts to copy you, and a "dialogue" develops that is repeated daily with minor variations. After the age of three months, this type of sound formation stops. Often, the baby spends the next few months simply listening.

Around the age of six months, the baby begins to produce different sounds — forceful, trumpeted vocalizations such as "da–ba–la," which now include labial sounds, accompany her rhythmical, two-legged kicking. These sounds are pure, joyous self-expression. In and of themselves, they do not lead to speech. For that, your baby has to hear the speech of others around her. Over the course of the next few months, she copies their examples and thus gradually learns to talk. From the very beginning, it is quite obvious that her single-word utterances are "whole sentences" that include meanings and contexts beyond mere naming. "Mama" may mean "Mama, come here," "Mama, where are you?" or "Mama, pick me up," to list just a few possibilities. Similarly, "car" and "bow-wow" signify whole sentences and entire events. As your baby learns more words, she gradually begins to describe activities and attributes in two and three-word sentences: "Dada car," "soup hot," "Mama go home."

Here's an example: A mother tells her eighteen-month-old, who wants to go along on a shopping trip, "No, you can't come. It's too noisy downtown. There are lots of people there and lots of stinky cars puffing out smoke." Her older sister, who looks after her that afternoon, later reports that she said "Mama town tar pouf moke!" several times. The nicknames and shortened words of baby talk show that children always express whole concepts when they imitate speech.

Copying these early attempts and conversing with your child in baby talk deprives her of linguistic models to imitate, and she may get stuck for a while at the single-syllable stage. Using normal adult speech around your child is preferable because it gives her plenty of opportunities to experience all the nuances of her native language. Most children speak their first word soon after age one. It is interesting to note that children whose parents are teachers or academics often learn to speak relatively late, probably because it takes them longer come to grips with their parents' extensive vocabularies. After a few months, however, they catch up and get a head start in terms of vocabulary and expressive ability that lasts for the rest of their lives. Children whose parents have limited vocabularies cannot learn words that they do not hear modelled. These children often begin to talk earlier, but their initial vocabulary is limited. They catch up only when they enter school and are exposed to more varied verbal stimuli.

More difficult to correct is the situation that develops when children are exposed to adult speech that is affected, pretentious, brash, exaggerated, euphemistic, emotionally uninvolved, or "untrue" in any other way. The perception that adults use words and voices to convey impressions not supported by their inner experience destroys a child's subtle feeling for the truth or falsehood of verbal expression. Adult speech also conveys

15

moods and emotions that children process along with the meaning of what they hear. Children understand the emotions expressed in an adult's tone of voice before they understand the meaning of individual words. They experience and imitate the pleasure, severity, coldness, sharpness, or gentleness conveyed by the words even before they are able to grasp the all details of their meaning.

Normally, learning to speak does not require conscious practice. It's best to avoid correcting your child when she mispronounces words. Talking is a very direct means of expression, and if you interrupt the flow to make corrections, you disrupt the immediacy of your child's attempt to communicate. The only thing children learn from this adult behavior is to interrupt their parents. Why shouldn't a child say "uptairs" or "vakoom keener" for a few years? If you simply continue to pronounce the problematic words and sounds especially clearly and beautifully yourself, you can be certain your child will eventually learn to do the same.

Almost all children show signs of stuttering from time to time, because their urge to communicate overwhelms their ability to express themselves. Patience and disregarding the stuttering will help overcome any temporary problem. If your child develops obvious, lasting speech problems such as lisping or stuttering, it is especially important to avoid narrowly focussed exercises or speech therapy before the fifth birthday. Making the process of speaking too

conscious too early disrupts the natural process of imitation. At this stage, the best corrective measure is to always speak well and clearly — and most importantly, *slowly* enough — whenever your child can hear you. Children's songs, nursery rhymes, and reading (or better yet, telling) fairy tales will encourage your child to have fun with speech sounds and her own ability to express herself.

It is a very prevalent misconception that speech therapy is the only way to correct speech disorders. We have already seen that motor development precedes learning to talk, and speech can be seen as a metamorphosis of body movements. The smaller movements of the larynx reflect the larger movements of the body as a whole. This is why speech disorders are always accompanied by more or less obvious disturbances in gross or fine motor development. Catching up with motor skills through games such as ball throwing, walking on stilts, balancing, stringing beads, and so forth can be surprisingly effective in improving articulation of troublesome sounds. Age-appropriate eurythmy is especially helpful for toddlers (see Section 22.4).

If a child's speech problems have not improved by age four to five, it is recommended to see a child speech therapist. Most children develop an interest in working on any remaining speech problems when they reach school age, when there is no longer any reason not to address the problems with specific exercises and training programs.

In conclusion, we would still like to address the issue of bilingual upbringing. In Argentina, for example, there are many children with one Spanish-speaking and one German-speaking parent who grow up hearing two languages from the very beginning. Such children start to talk a bit later and initially use words from both languages interchangeably, but they are surprisingly quick to learn to separate the languages and express themselves in both. Later, they often learn additional languages with enviable ease. But when we ask bilingual adults if they would raise their own children in the same way, they often say, "No, I want my kids to start with one language and learn the second one later, after they've become really fluent in the local language." One bilingual man who had observed his own situation especially closely added something like this: "I don't feel totally at home in either language. I dream in Spanish, for example, but I think in German, and I speak whatever the situation demands."

In the next section, we will show that thinking takes its lead from language to a very considerable extent. For this reason, we recommend raising children in one language only at least until they are old enough to say "I' to themselves. Each language has its own unique logic, which is inherent in its grammar. This logical structure influences both how we think and how secure we feel in our thinking. Being able to identify completely with one such structure is a support in learning to think and helps strengthen a child's personality.

In real life, it may not be easy to raise your child to speak only one language if other members of the family habitually use two. Here are a few tips. It is important to always speak to your baby in the same language. If older siblings or friends often speak the second language among themselves, ask them to make sure that they always use the local language when addressing the baby directly. Simply hearing the other language is less likely to affect her as she learns to talk. The same is true if you want her to learn the language you speak at home instead of the one you use on the street or with visitors. In this case, fortunately, your native language is the one your baby will identify with and take as a model. The situation is different, however, if the baby's primary caregiver is a domestic helper who speaks only the local language. In this case, the parents should also speak the local language, even if they are not completely fluent in it, whenever they spend time with the baby.

15

15.4 Learning to think

What is thinking? It is the ability that allows us to recognize the context, meaning, and structure of all our experiences. The distinctions we make between "sensory" and "non-sensory," or "supersensory," perception is based on the experience that we can understand both things we can see and things we can't see — such as mathematical relationships — which we understand only through concepts. Our thought life consists of a nexus of relationships that we use to understand everything we encounter. It allows us to feel included in and related to the world around us. When we transform our thoughts into realities, we experience ourselves as co-creators in our own and others' lives, and we incorporate our activity into a larger context. We experience something of the outer world's lawfulness in ourselves and learn to move ever more freely and independently within it. The next few sections describe characteristic stages in learning to think as adults can observe them in children.

"Body-bound" intelligence

Your baby knows what to do with the object in his hand long before he knows that it is a wooden block. For him, the ability to create meaningful connections has not yet become an abstract thought process but is still a matter of direct sensory experience. He touches, observes, tastes, and listens to that wooden block. He experiences its weight and the fact that it can be picked up and falls when dropped. He finds out whether it will roll and learns that it always remains the same. You can watch him repeatedly removes the block from his field of vision, never tiring of "finding" it again. Through this manual and sensory activity, he enjoys experiencing the permanency of things, or so-called object constancy. When we adults attempt form a concept of a little wooden block, we describe it in terms of its position, shape, permanence, relationships to its surroundings and to ourselves, and so on. We use *thoughts* to understand what a baby experiences through his *senses*. Adults can separate sense perceptions from concepts and relate them to each other. For us, the world is separated into "I" and "you," "mine" and "yours" — distinctions that the baby cannot make, since he always experiences himself as an active and intrinsic part of the process. For him, sense perceptions and concepts are not yet separated. This is the key to understanding a small child's mental processes: For him, the activities of abstract thinking and sensory perception, which we adults have learned to engage in separately, are still a single, unified experience. This is why perceptions of sound, small, and taste are so incomparably much stronger and "saturated with reality" for children than they are for adults. Our childhood memories also retain this character and are therefore more vivid than our later recollections. The unique strength of young children's ability to imitate also makes sense in terms of this body-oriented unity of sensory perception and thinking. A small child's whole body adapts to every subtlety of what he perceives; his whole body applies the greatest possible innate intelligence to sensory experiences. He also remembers what he perceives. For example, long after his mother has stopped stirring the soup in the pot, he can repeat her gesture in his play. One mother told us that his fifteen-month-old son, sitting in his playpen, suddenly interrupted what he was doing to fold his hands in prayer as he did every evening with his parents. He remained in this position for a few moments until something else caught his attention.

Thus children's ability to imitate can be understood as the result of three interacting factors: With the help of *perceptions,* a child grasps an event as such. *Thinking,* which is still active in and inseparable from sensory perception, is the ability to directly grasp the meaning of individual perceptions and the relationship between them. Thinking is what makes the body capable of "practicing" understanding in association with perception until we learn to dissociate the process of understanding from perception and can carry it out independently. In other words, a child's newly acquired skill persists as a *"body memory."* The high degree of correspondence between a child's imitation and the modelled behavior is due to the thought that is common to both. Any imperfect examples of imitation are due to one-sided perceptions and the limitations of an inexperienced bodily instrument. It is misleading to speak exclusively of "motor intelligence" in the context of imitation. There is only *one* intelligence, namely, the universal lawfulness present in all things. During the first year of life, however, this intelligence works exclusively through the body. Through the baby's active participation in the process, intelligence guides the growth and development of his body and its sensory organs.

Thus the first step in the development of thinking is your baby's direct perception of intelligence or meaning in objects and events in his surroundings.

We act according to the inherent logic of the situation when we put a lid on a pot, open the door when someone wants to go out, put things back where they belong, shut the window if it starts to rain, clean up if we've made a mess, and so on. Unlike adults, who can distance themselves from events and judge them objectively, a baby perceives actively and always feels directly involved in the process and can therefore imitate the meaning of his surroundings in his own active play. To the extent that the activity of thinking separates from motor activity and becomes "abstract" and internalized, the capacity for imitation recedes. Before that happens, however, the greatest accomplishments of

15

our life are already behind us, namely, learning to walk, talk, and think. What would happen if children were born already able to think? What if they critically confronted every necessary step of learning and adaptation with the question, do I really want to learn that? If they had to deliberately and consciously adapt their bodies to walking and speaking, they certainly would not be able to master these skills to the extent that the innate, intuitive intelligence of infants allows. On the other hand, the intensity with which children perceive the meaning or meaninglessness of actions, objects, and events means that active adults bear a great deal of responsibility for how intelligence unfolds in young children.

How speaking influences thinking

A new step in the development of thinking occurs when babies start to learn to talk. Here, too, children creatively imitate adult speech before they have any direct understanding of the thought contents of sounds and words. Talking as an active experience and thinking as a purely inner activity are slow to separate, as this example shows: A little boy picking up sticks on a wet path in the park stops suddenly when he sees a "stick" moving on the ground. Mulling it over, he decides, "Not stick." Names and distinctions emerge from perception, from real life. At this stage, the little boy can already try to search for the right word in the beginnings of his purely soul-spiritual "inner life." He experiences the earthworm as such without knowing what to call it.

In the development of thinking, the initial period of direct sensory experience through perception is followed by a phase of naming (with single words and sentences) that prefigures the later emergence of understanding through pure thinking. In this interim phase, everything in a child's environment suddenly begins to "speak." The ball that rolls away, the stick that bangs, the door that creaks on its hinges and slams when the wind rushes through the house, the water that gurgles down the drain and simply disappears — everything seems to have a life of its own and something to say. For the next few years, this personified mode of perception persists in the imaginative activity typical of childhood: Grandpa's big laced boots look like the tall, grim-faced man who walks around the neighbourhood, the oven door makes threatening gestures in the dark, apples laugh and pears make funny faces, a slice of bread transforms itself into a mouse or a house, and the green semicircular block in the toy chest becomes anything from a watering can to a car to a church tower with ringing bells. Whispering makes everything even more mysterious. If you whisper, it is easier to hear what things are trying to tell you. Even fingers can talk and tell each other stories.

At this age, words can still work magic. When the little ones linger at the table after supper trying to put off bedtime for just another five minutes, it may take nothing more than whispering, "Come on, let's play taxi" to get one of them on your shoulders, steering around tables and chairs on the way to the bathroom. Meanwhile, the next candidate for a bath is itching for his turn as taxi driver.

At this stage, direct understanding through sensory perception is supplemented with and increasingly supplanted by the use of naming to express meaning. This completes the second step in the development of thinking.

The first signs of pure thought activity

As the preceding section clearly indicated, the phases in the development of thinking are not clearly separated, with distinct beginnings and endings. Rather, they are successive accents or emphases that continue to make themselves felt in subsequent years, even after a new element appears and lessens the impact of the last one. The birth of the ability to remember is one of the first signs of pure (abstract) thinking. During the second year of life, toddlers still identify strongly with their surroundings, calling themselves "Annie" or "Fred" or whatever they hear their mothers call them. A child of this age who bumps his head on the edge of a table experiences the pain most strongly where it is incurred and may even hit back. If you take him into the next room, where the offending table is nowhere to be seen, his tears will probably stop quickly, but if he sees that "naughty table" again soon,

he may begin to cry again. His memory is still tied to actual perception of the object because his thinking remains concretely linked to sensory perceptions, as we described earlier. He is not yet aware of thinking as an independent activity. At this age, therefore, all memory is "local memory." With the first glimmer of I-consciousness, however, memory begins to separate from sensory perception and become an independent soul factor. Many children experience this moment as both pleasurable and frightening. It often occurs in connection with a sudden feeling of being alone, an especially strong sense impression, or a sense of rejection that intensifies their feeling of being different from their surroundings. For example, Chris comes into the kitchen at age two-and-a-quarter and sees his mother cooking. There's an empty basket standing by the stove, and he grabs it with both hands and starts to carry it away. His mother says, "Leave that there; Daddy's going to need it." Chris puts the basket down, stands up straight and says, "No, I do it! Take it to Daddy!" This first I-experience is also characteristic of the moment when a child begins to distinguish between himself and his surroundings. He is no longer content with perceiving and naming things but wants to complement what he sees with thought activity that he creates within himself. The passionate "Why?" questions typical of this age support this process.

We saw that children learn to internalize the experience of sensory relationships in three steps. First they

15

understand these relationships through direct action and spontaneous imitation. Next they grasp the meaning of words that name objects and create connections between them. And finally the capacity for immediate, internalized insight emerges when children directly experience the idea of their own selfhood and call themselves I instead of using the names others apply to them. That this is a consequence of independent thought activity is evident from the fact that memory as a purely internal mental experience begins the first time someone says "I." It is also interesting to note that baby talk — the strings of words that serve as sentences during the second and third years of a child's life — begins to disappear within a few weeks of the child's first "I" statement as he or she rapidly masters the logical grammatical structures of language. From this point onward, the structure of a child's interconnected thoughts continues to expand from year to year, undergoing further transformations at the change of teeth (see Section 15.9) and at puberty, until ultimately adult abstract conceptualization emerges (see also Chapter 17).

We owe the differentiation and development of our inner thought structures to our ether body's life forces (see Section 8.1), which gradually become available as they are no longer needed for building up the physical body. For education and medicine, the discovery of this connection is one of the most significant insights of Rudolf Steiner's research. In the book *Fundamentals of Therapy*

co-authored with physician Ita Wegman, Steiner writes:

> It is of the utmost importance to know that the human being's ordinary forces of thinking are refined form and growth forces. A spiritual element reveals itself in the form and growth of the human organism. For this spiritual element then appears during the course of later life as the spiritual power of thought.

In other words, we think with the same forces that we use for growth and regeneration. This fact has far-reaching educational and medical consequences, and we will return to it again and again. It also explains why we "come of age" with regard to thinking and become fully responsible for managing our own thoughts only when growth ceases. Furthermore, it explains why the mental life of people who have learned to think creatively can become increasingly lively and alert until very late in life. An aging body continues to free up forces no longer needed for regeneration (see also Sections 14.6 and 18.1). At death, when the remaining life forces separate from the body in the form of thought forces, all of the past life's conscious and "forgotten" memories are revealed to the individual in question in the form of uniquely clear and complete images. This graphic survey of a lifetime, which occurs when the physical body relaxes its hold on the life (or thought) body, is also described by people who have undergone near-death experiences. (See Bibliography for descriptions by Kübler-Ross, Moody, Ritchie, and Steiner.)

The younger the child, the more closely his thinking is still bound up with his body's growth forces. For children, therefore, thinking is not the abstract experience it becomes later. It is much more "alive," more creative and imaginative, than adult thinking. For this reason, the best way to cultivate and encourage children's thinking is by telling them fairy tales. (Dry, abstract language and thinking games, on the other hand, are not suitable.) Fairy tales — especially those by the Brothers Grimm — depict not only individuals striving toward the ideals of human evolution as a whole but also all of life's major relationships and interconnected ideas. In fairy tales, we discover the good in its struggle against evil; processes of development and transformation unfold. Fairy-tale images speak for themselves, require no explanation, and continue to work in children's hearts and souls. People who hear many fairy tales as children find it easier to grasp the idea of inner development and self-education as adults. The goal of inner development is union with one's own higher being. In fairy-tale images, the search for this being is depicted as the adventures of the king's son as he searches for the princess whom he ultimately marries.

Anyone who tells the same fairy tales repeatedly gradually becomes aware of the truths they conceal. In many cases, we adults find their contents "cruel" or "violent" only because we misread their symbolic character. Little children have fewer inhibitions in this respect and simply accept the fight with the dragon as a test to be passed on the way to finding the good. Fairy tales scare children only when they are presented in overly dramatic ways. Evil and the overcoming of evil play major roles in the realities of human soul life, and matter-of-fact storytelling allows children to feel emotionally "at home" in fairy-tale depictions of the negative side of life. Neither denying nor overemphasizing the existence of evil is helpful for children's development, but fairy tales help them learn to come to grips with this aspect of life. For this reason, we reject the argument that children should not be exposed to fairy tales because of the violence they contain, although we do recommend only those stories in which the good emerges victorious. Because understanding the tragic outcome of a developmental crisis requires a certain degree of emotional maturity, many of Andersen's fairy tales are not suitable for children.

Comic books, unlike fairy tales, corrupt rather than enhance children's ability to think. For more on this subject, see Section 27.3.

15

15.5 Learning to walk, talk and think: Developmental steps in childhood and adulthood

What do we adults see when we trace a child's development through the stages of learning to walk, talk, and think?

- The child pulls herself upright, stands on her own feet, and gradually begins to determine where she goes. She learns to master her movements and use them to express her own intentions.
- She begins to talk. Until she begins to say "I" to herself, which indicates the beginning of self-aware thinking, she is incapable of lying. Initially, learning to talk means telling only the truth.
- She begins to think for herself. Initially, she experiences making distinctions by speaking the names of people and objects. In saying "I" to herself, she becomes aware for the first time that she is a person. (The joy that this discovery sparks is evident in the eyes of every two-and-a-half to four-year-old.) From this point onward, the capacity for memory runs like a red thread through her subsequent biography; her independent inner life of thoughts has begun.

These facts prompt many questions: Later in life, what becomes of this pattern of human development? Do we ever again say "I" to ourselves with such radiance? Are we ever again as certain of who we are as small children seem to be? Now that we have achieved consciousness, is our inner life truly self-aware? Don't we often simply reflect outer circumstances? Aren't we simply glad to have our life somewhat under control.

What happens to our sense of truth? How many falsehoods do our polite, conventional phrases conceal? Do we really want to know how or what the other person is feeling when we ask, "How are you?"

Do we really stand on our own two feet as adults? Have any of us not felt manipulated by others or out of step with our destiny? Are we truly able to determine where we are going?

The Gospel according to John contains the words, "I am the way, the truth, and the life" (John 14:6). The stages of a small child's development up to the point of saying "I am" allow us to experience the reality of these words.

As soon as self-awareness is kindled, however, the eventual existential crisis of later life begins to build: I don't know where I am going; I don't know what I really want. My social surroundings are full of untruths and compromises. I know what I am not, but who am I really?

Anyone who emerges victorious from this existential crisis looks back on it as the actual birth of his or his I, and in literature this experience is often described as a second birth. It is also the subject of the nocturnal conversation between Christ and Nicodemus (John 3:1–21). This inner victory or second birth forges a conscious connection to the being of Christ. During childhood, Christ's strength is at work unconsciously, granting children the ability to stand on their own feet and walk and to learn to tell the truth and have an inner, spiritual life. Walking, talking, and thinking are the basis of all personal and universally human expressions of one's being. If we consciously connect later in life with these forces that worked unconsciously in our own childhood, we discover three goals for our inner development:

- To affirm our destiny as our life's unique path and to learn everything we can from it in the service of our own development.
- To look for truth in our interpersonal, social life and make no inner compromises. This is all the more important because our outer life very often demands adaptability and willingness to compromise.
- To cultivate and take co-responsibility for our inner life, our inner development of soul and spirit.

As Rudolf Steiner repeatedly emphasized in his lectures, even the wisest adult can learn from children. This statement is confirmed whenever we consider child development, which presents a natural image of the highest ideals of human development for all to see. What children do and experience on an unconscious and bodily level is transformed into the highest possible moral force when adults learn to apply it consciously.

15.6 Is a playgroup right for my child?

Mothers of only children often wonder how to overcome their own isolation and help their toddlers learn to hold their own in a group. Cooperative play groups for infants and toddlers can offer real help by providing the children with playmates and their mothers with opportunities for socializing, mutual support, and free time.

Playgroup meetings create a stimulating, sociable atmosphere for young children if their parents work on group projects such as baking, weaving, singing, or playing musical instruments. It's less stimulating for the little folks if the adults just talk, knit, or drink coffee as they supervise in the background.

Developing social skills, however, requires other circumstances not provided by playgroups. Learning to enter into and cultivate interpersonal relationships requires models that other babies and toddlers cannot supply, since the ability to establish consistent I-you relationships develops only around age three, when children begin to say "I" to themselves. Before this point in their development, daily life with a few consistent, familiar caregivers (or only one) is the best way to support children's ability to make appropriate social connections. In this respect, consistent housemates can accomplish more than a play-group.

An additional problem is that the need for parental guidance and/or child care is snowballing because increasing numbers of couples or single parents face the task of raising a toddler with a sense of helplessness or even estrangement. In view of the rapidly declining birth rates and aging populations of many developed nations and the fact that many children grow up with few relationships, there is great cause for concern about how children will continue to develop the social skills that they need later in life. With this problem in mind, many Waldorf kindergartens now sponsor parent-child programs to provide parents with suggestions and guidance about how to meet their toddlers' developmental needs. Young children need an educational approach that allows them to experience loving interest, stimulating activities, and dependable interpersonal relationships to the greatest possible extent. Perhaps the task of children who might otherwise be marginalized is to break down family barriers by soliciting the attention of other loving adults who can provide the conditions necessary for later mutual understanding and respect.

15.7 Kindergarten, day care, and early childhood education

Many countries either provide or encourage preschool programs for children over the age of three, and many parents need day care for even younger children. Committing children under the age of three to the care of strangers is always a compromise at best, although it is often unavoidable because parents need to work or for other reasons. Time-tested alternatives include parents taking turns to go to work, a group of mothers caring in a rota for each other's children, and hiring a nanny/housekeeper. Other possibilities for informal day care include families who have the space, time, and energy to include another child during the day or a woman who cares for one or more children in her home. When such solutions are not available — and often they are not — a day care center becomes the toddler's transition to kindergarten. A good kindergarten experience can help reverse some of the damages due to inadequate stimulation in large-scale day care centers. It is laudable that researchers are now working on many models for infant stimulation and early intervention and that many resources are available for children with special needs.

When it is possible for mothers to spend the entire day at home, the question becomes, *why* should my child go to kindergarten at all, and *when* should he start? These questions must be answered on a case-by-case basis. Under favourable circumstances, when one parent can stay at home and there are playmates in the neighbourhood, attending kindergarten is certainly not a necessity. Whether it is advisable depends on the daily routine at home, the parents' ability to provide suitable early educational experiences, the philosophy of the kindergarten in question, and last but not least the personality of the kindergarten teacher. For a child from a high-tech home, it may be helpful to attend a kindergarten that emphasizes baking, cooking, and washing up. Conversely, a kindergarten that emphasizes electronic media, cartoons, or early intellectual training programs is a good reason to keep your child at home. We recommend sending children to kindergarten when our conversations with their parents suggest that the atmosphere at home is tense and there is no rhythmical daily routine at home. In such cases, having conversations with the kindergarten teacher often provide the input parents need to learn how to make their home more child-friendly.

There is no reason to avoid kindergarten for a child who has a chronic illness or handicap or is not yet toilet trained. In such cases, of course, make sure to discuss your child's situation in depth with the kindergarten teacher and, if needed, with your pediatrician. From a social perspective, it is extremely important to integrate children who are handicapped or ill into a kindergarten class — not only for their own sake but also for the healthy children, who learn to accommodate and respect people of differing abilities.

15

15.8 When is my child ready for kindergarten?

Your child is ready if she can go on short errands or walks by herself — for example, if she has ever wandered or run away from home and found her way back by herself, or if she decides to come home from a playmate's house without waiting for you to come and get her. She is not ready if she's still "clinging to your apron strings," but if she is, you may need to ask yourself if your behavior is preventing her from developing the necessary independence.

A second sign of kindergarten readiness is that your child can listen to fairy tales and stories from beginning to end. This shows that her mental processes respond to the guidance of the spoken word and that she is therefore ready for the challenges of being in a group.

In our experience, these two signs of kindergarten readiness usually appear around the age of three-and-a-half. If they are not yet evident in your four-year-old, we recommend discussing the situation with your doctor. (See Section 17.2, for what a day in kindergarten may be like.)

15.9 What are the signs that my child is ready for school?

In most countries, the mandatory school-entry age falls somewhere between five and seven years. Certain signs of maturity, however, suggest that it is best to send children to school only at age seven whenever possible.

Change of physique

The physique of a toddler is very different from that of a school-age child. A toddler's head is very large in proportion to his torso and limbs. His entire figure is rounded, his limbs are short, and until age two he may be physiologically bow-legged. His fingers are short and well padded with fat deposits. His torso has no waist, the angle of his ribs above the stomach is broad, and his belly sticks out as if there were no room for it in his torso yet. A school-age child looks completely different. His arms and legs have elongated, and he can reach over the top of his head and touch his ear with the fingers of the opposite hand. He has a definite waist between his ribs and his pelvis, and his ribs form an acute angle above his stomach, which is now flat. His head, torso, and limbs are on their way to achieving the adult proportions that will appear at the next major change of physique in adolescence.

Beginning of the second dentition

The emergence of the first permanent molar or incisor indicates that the enamel of the permanent teeth — the hardest substance in the body — is fully formed and that the organism's tooth-forming activity is drawing to a close. Educators generally pay little attention to this phenomenon. We have already discussed the anthroposophical spiritual-scientific concept of what happens to organ-forming activities after the respective organ or substance in the body completes its development. Some of these forces are still used for regeneration and organ maintenance, but the rest become available to shape our thoughts (see also Section 15.4) This is not exactly what happens with tooth enamel, however, because it does not regenerate (as we all know from painful visits to the dentist). *All* of the formative forces that originally served the development of dental enamel become available to the I for the purposes of thinking. And because these formative forces are not responsible for regeneration, they are totally liberated from the physical body and available for "abstract" (from the Latin "to draw off") activity. Thus pure abstraction (the basis of the concepts and clearly defined mental images that children learn to manipu-

late in school) becomes possible only once the teeth are fully developed.

School-age thinking

In the section on learning to think (Section 15.4), we saw that a small child depends heavily on repetitious language and habitual activities to support his *local memory*. This type of memory serves as the foundation for developing fully internalized memory, which allows the child to activate the process of remembering without outside prompting. Because it is freed from the constraints of sense-perceptible reality, this later type of memory indicates that the child is beginning to be able to think abstractly. The eagerness to learn that is typical of this age shows that these forces have only recently become available. The child is now able to call up memories in response to direct questioning, independent of concrete situations. As a result, he is able to repeat a story he heard in kindergarten several days ago.

Typically, a child's ability to imitate, which used to indicate that he was best able to "understand" an event by repeating its actions, begins to recede at this age. Let's consider young children's imitation in somewhat greater detail. It is a complex process that becomes fully understandable only when we see thinking as a metamorphosis of the activity of growth. The more a child's forces of growth are still involved in differentiating and shaping the organs of the body, the better he can imitate,

15

because the body's ability to grasp a process directly (through sensory perception) and immediately reproduce it is an accomplishment of intelligence that is still acting through the body. Having to imitate many events that are senseless or chaotic or experiencing frequently interrupted or unrelated actions has consequences for a child's bodily development (see Section 15.5), because each organ develops and matures properly only if appropriate demands are placed on it. This extremely impressionable and malleable phase comes to an end when the capacity for imitation declines as the child becomes ready for school. The beginning of the change of teeth indicates a significant step in the transformation of growth forces into thought forces. The learning that formerly occurred unconsciously, through imitation, must now make the transition to conscious processes.

Social readiness

A child who is ready to take his place in the relatively large community of a school class is socially ready to go to school. This type of readiness involves learning to align his own interests with those of others (with the teacher's help) and to be "all ears," that is, to deliberately suppress the activity of his arms and legs. At this stage, listening to what the teacher says must supplant the urge to imitate as the primary stimulus for independent activity. In other words, the child's intentions are increasingly receptive to being guided by the spoken words

of adults as instinctive imitative activity recedes. In general, social readiness appears later than intellectual readiness and is usually fully acquired only around age 7–8.

Dexterity and verbal expression

Often these skills are not adequately developed, either because of differences in individual developmental timelines or because they have not been sufficiently stimulated by early education. As a general rule, however, children of school age can sing, pronounce all of the speech sounds, retell stories in complete sentences, and express what they want to say in conversation in a variety of different ways.

With regard to physical dexterity, school-age children are often able to throw a ball into the air with one hand and catch it with two. They can stand on one leg and hop sideways, forward, and backward. They can stand and walk on tiptoe, Their fine-motor skills are sufficiently developed for stringing beads, or finger knitting. They have mastered the most important household chores such as setting the table, washing and drying dishes, and the like. They can also dress and undress themselves, tie their shoes, and button a shirt.

The decision to delay sending a child to school is certainly never based on the absence of any single sign of readiness. In case of doubt, parents should discuss their child's overall state of mind and body with a physician or school psychologist and arrive at a decision together. Social perspectives should also be considered; the experiences of the youngest and oldest children in any class are very different. If at all possible, children with handicapping conditions or developmental delays in specific areas should enter school with children of the same age.

We advise parents never to coach their children before school-readiness interviews. Children who have been coached often develop total mental blocks when they meet with the teacher or physician who is supposed to determine whether they are ready for school. School readiness should also never depend totally on the results of so-called IQ tests, which reveal only a portion of the full spectrum of abilities that truly expresses the child and his possibilities. It is the school's job to continue to develop all these abilities and to identify and address special needs in a timely manner.

15

16. Becoming a Family: Child-Mother-Father Connections

The words "mother," "father," and "child" have always had two meanings, a biological one and an ideal one. Through the processes of conception, pregnancy, and birth, a baby makes a woman a mother and a man a father. For the woman, becoming a mother is primarily a physical process; the baby takes possession of her body and develops within her. The man, on the other hand, although he sets the physical process in motion, experiences fatherhood primarily on the emotional level. His role is to observe and support pregnancy and birth. Beyond the first few weeks or months after delivery, this support is extended to providing the material foundations for the growing family's life. Meeting these needs strikes an instinctive chord in the father, who gladly does what he can to insure that mother and child are safe, secure, and provided for. He is offended if these efforts are thwarted or belittled. To be there both physically and emotionally for the mother and child and to acknowledge them and keep them in his consciousness are uniquely fatherly capacities. Mother and child feel emotionally secure in the deep sense of belonging that arises from his support.

The emotional space opened up by the father's interest allows the mother's specific abilities to develop most effectively. Her contribution is to perform the many repeated tasks of the early child-rearing stage lovingly, willingly, and patiently. Relieved of as many material concerns as possible, she can be fully available until her child shows spontaneous interest in regularly spending several hours a day outside the home — in other words, until he is ready for kindergarten. By this time (assuming that the three-way relationship remains intact), the child has been profoundly influenced by his relationship with two fundamentally different adults and by their relationship to each other, which makes his own human development possible.

The basic gesture of this idealized triangle remains the same even if the parents more or less exchange roles. The child remains in the middle, asking and receiving as a matter of course and supported on both sides by parents who accompany his development, take pleasure in his progress, and receive the gift of his love and confidence in return. In this idealized picture of motherhood and fatherhood, the child feels completely secure in his life and in his relationship to his parents. Mother and father, however, are representatives of the divine father and mother principles that all religions know and honor along with the offspring, the principle of eternal becoming. These principles achieve their highest expression in the Christian Trinity.

Anyone who experiences unqualified, loving affirmation of his being in childhood — that is, being loved and accepted exactly as he is — along with his parents' striving for the true, the good, and the purely human will look back on his childhood with pleasure even if it was marked by material poverty and dire circumstances. In his biography *And There Was Light,* Jacques Lusseyran describes his parents' love for him, their blind child, as a "magical armour" that protected him for his entire life.

It is no secret that most of us parents seldom even approximate the ideal, but what conclusions do these idealized reflections allow us to draw about the problems of daily life? In the next sections, we will discuss some of the questions, problems, and situations that health professionals repeatedly encounter in children's routine checkups.

Role reversal

Role reversal poses no problems if both parents agree to it. It is no more difficult for men to learn to fill maternal functions than for women to work outside the home. When the mother is the family's breadwinner, it is beautiful to see how both parents attempt to optimize and harmonize both their natural and their newly acquired abilities. The situation is more difficult if it is forced on the family because the father loses his job. In this case, a great deal of effort is required to avoid succumbing to resignation, especially if the mother also doesn't find work. Even in this case, however, the parents' efforts to maintain a positive attitude, take advantage of the opportunity to cultivate contacts with friends and neighbours, and find ways of being useful to others provide very positive models for the children.

Single parenting

In our experience, a self-confident single mother seldom has problems that end up at the doctor. She represents mother and father in one, and the social network she creates for herself allows her child to find whatever role models he needs. Single motherhood becomes difficult, however, if the mother has unrealistic expectations of her child or applies inappropriate child-rearing principles in the absence of a partner who might counteract them. In such cases, it is often in the child's best interest for separated parents to cultivate friendly contact with

each other if they have no other committed relationships that can help balance the situation.

More frequently, however, we see a
very different scenario, namely, a
mother and child or children who have
been abandoned by the father. This is
almost always an unwished-for situation; surely mothers hope and expect
to raise their children in intact families. In such cases, it generally takes at
least two years before the outer circumstances settle down and the inner
wounds heal somewhat. At the end of
this very trying period, however, the
mothers often become more independent and self-sufficient than they were
before, which in turn has positive
effects on their children.

When a mother wants to work

During a one-year-old's checkup, her
mother suddenly asked in desperation
whether it was more important for a
young child to have a single reliable
carer or a happy, contented mother.
The doctor did not immediately get
the connection. The mother explained
that she interrupted her studies when
the baby was on the way, and now she
simply can't stand it any more. She
wanted to do the right thing and be
fully available for the baby, but now
she notices that she's getting
depressed. She simply cannot accept
the fact that her husband's life simply
continues as before while she feels
pressured to abandon all efforts to pursue her own education and blamed for
attempting to avoid her maternal
responsibilities.

This example is one of the many
maternal destinies that must be considered and overcome on an individual basis, even though they all present
the same question, namely: how can I
do justice to being a mother if I can't
take full responsibility for it? In part,
the tragedy of many young mothers
today is that they initially embrace
motherhood gladly but later discover
that they cannot cope with the limitations of daily life at home with a child.
In most instances, the baby's father is
already heavily involved in his career
and their relatives live too far away to
help out. Another contributing factor
is the superficiality of our career-
focused modern education systems,
which fail to promote or even
acknowledge the beauty and value of
inner development, deepening relationships, and cultural activity.

In young mothers who feel trapped
at home, fundamental questions may
surface: I know that I'm not satisfied
with my situation in life, but what is
the real reason? Is it simply because I
didn't choose it freely and deliberately? Can I still make this choice
after the fact? Both for herself and for
her children, it is a great relief if a
mother who feels that she is stagnating
in her role can replace resignation
with an active approach to the problem. Friends and relatives are the most
important resources. When parents
cannot or do not want to exchange
roles, the way out of this situation is to
look for help as described above in the
section on playgroups (see Section
15.6). One woman discovered that
once she relinquished her fears that

other people would see and judge the imperfections in her own household, she found it very helpful to be able to open up her family to neighbours, friends, grandparents, and other older people who could serve as surrogate grandparents. Such efforts, if successful, can give a mother time to pursue interests such as mastering a foreign language or practicing the guitar, even if only for fifteen minutes a day. It is also very good for children to see their mother totally involved in an activity that has nothing to do with them. Later — at the latest, when all of the children are in school — she will have more opportunities for initiatives outside the house.

Adopted and foster children

A few examples:

A couple with two of their own children applies to adopt a third, saying that they would accept a child with a disability. When they learn of a young mother who is about to give birth to a baby she will not be able to care for, they volunteer to adopt him even before he is born. In the first two years of his life, the little boy needs several major operations simply to survive. His adoptive parents matter-of-factly accompany him through all these hospitalizations and other difficulties, although it takes all the energy they have. In spite of his disability, the boy grows up as a happy, fully integrated member of his family and school class.

Another couple with grown children of their own decides to take in foster children from children's homes and socially difficult backgrounds, including several with severe physical handicaps or chronic illnesses. In their care, the children blossom and become trusting and happy; they feel secure even when medical treatments fail.

After years of waiting, a middle-aged couple finally starts a family by taking in a newborn whose mother wants to give her up for adoption. After a while they learn that the baby has a serious congenital metabolic disorder. Although taking care of the little girl as she undergoes repeated hospitalizations has a major impact on her adoptive parents' lifestyle and destiny, in this case it simply serves to deepen the relationship.

Tragic situations also occur. Soon after the only son of well-to-do parents dies in a traffic accident, his parents have the opportunity to adopt a boy of the same age. Their new son, however, cannot fill the gap in their lives, and the relationship becomes so difficult that they have to send him back to the children's home.

When we see foster children or adopted children in our office, the spoken or unspoken question often is: what kind of a destiny is this? How is what is happening here played out against the background of repeated earthly lives? Although there are no direct answers to such questions, observing the family's circumstances provides glimpses of possible interpretations. It is interesting to see that parents' relationships with adopted children are as individually different as they are in families with natural children. Some relationships are uncomplicated; parents and children get along quite naturally and the relationship is full of gratitude and love. Then there is the "black sheep," the child who fails to live up to her parents' expectations from the very beginning, leaves home at an early age, or later says that she always felt like a stranger in her parents' house. Unresolved "baggage" from earlier lives on earth may persist in this life, or it may be transformed and redeemed to a considerable extent through devoted, caring upbringing. The two faces of destiny are especially applicable to adoptive and foster parenting: On the one hand, parent-child relationships may be based on destinies that were already complex and intertwined in earlier lives. On the other hand, this life may be the starting point for future-oriented constellations, a chance to get to know each other in preparation for a common task in a later life.

Temporary foster care

As a general rule, it is important to avoid taking infants and toddlers away from both their mother and their home at the same time. For example, if an eight-month-old is placed in respite care while his mother recovers from an illness, the double impact of a change in surroundings and a change in caregiver is significant. It takes about a week for him to get used to his new "mother" and her home and to feel as safe and happy as he did before. When his own mother reclaims him, he does not accept her immediately, and it also takes a while for him to feel his way back into his old surroundings.

Both our capacity for abstract memory and our sense of personal identity become "red threads" running through all of our thoughts and memories only after we begin to say "I" to ourselves. Babies, who have not yet developed this type of awareness, experience continuity of consciousness through daily encounters with at least one familiar person and with the same household objects. They experience a sense of identity only through contact with the rest of the world — that is, through sensory perceptions. The more permanent and stable his experience of his surroundings, the stronger a baby's sense of self. Moves, changing caregivers, or his mother's lengthy hospitalizations have negative effects on personality development and often lead to existential uncertainty, lack of self-confidence, and lack of trust in the world unless a big-hearted surrogate mother takes the baby into her own family for the duration. The same is true if a small child is frequently hospitalized, unless his mother or a close and familiar relative stays with him in the hospital.

16

How does harmonious family life develop?

The primary factor in family harmony is mutual appreciation, which may remain unspoken if the situation is truly harmonious. The real challenge comes when one partner fails to appreciate the other. It often takes many years for married couples to realize that each partner can change only him or herself, not the other person. Appreciation at home may not be so important for a man who feels acknowledged at work, but it is essential for any woman who devotes herself almost entirely to the family. Often her spouse is not sufficiently aware of the difference in their situations. Appreciation means repeatedly acknowledging the positive, even when personal weaknesses or bad habits force their way into the foreground. Appreciation is the only way to provide a warm, supportive atmosphere that motivates the other person to change.

Motherhood as a legitimate profession

To varying degrees, the countries of the developed world acknowledge the particular developmental needs of small children by providing financial support and maternity and/or paternity leave with job security for the parents. We would like to take this opportunity to emphasize that being a mother — that is, being there for your children both physically and emotionally, around the clock — is a fully legiti-

mate profession in itself. In an ideal world, its validity would be acknowledged in the form of financial remuneration from public funds. Especially during the preschool age, children's physical health and emotional well-being depend on having a real home with a parent who acknowledges them, has time for them, and is not forced to work outside the home for financial reasons. We recommend that mothers take a break from outside employment whenever possible to raise their children. *For children, there is no substitute for experiencing security, trust, and consistent loving relationships during the first three years of life.*

As in any other occupation, mothers should get time off. Many don't want it, but for the sake of personal development and coping with a mother's workload, it is invaluable to have periodic pauses for reflection and times that are not defined by the demands of others. This might mean that a mother has an hour to herself everyday while her husband or someone else takes care of the children and does household chores. It could also mean that she has one evening off each week, or an afternoon or even a whole weekend once a month, or even a two-week vacation from the family once a year. Although the solution that is most workable for each mother depends partly on her spouse's job situation, it should also reflect her own temperament and interests.

The human connection

Are human beings the product of heredity and environment, and does one of these factors have more impact than the other? This question is constantly being reexamined and debated by experts and lay people alike. Research in fields such as genetics, sociology, child psychiatry, and social pediatrics is constantly yielding new information. In a book with the remarkable title *Separate Lives: Why Siblings Are So Different,* behavioral geneticist Robert Plomin and developmental psychologist Judy Dunn summarize their research on this subject. They say that if heredity and environment were the only determining factors, siblings would be much more alike than they actually are. Plomin and Dunn discovered a third factor that has a decisive impact on development, namely, each child's personal connection to the people and objects in his or her surroundings. This highly individual way of relating determines whether and how strongly a person or an event influences a particular child. Two children from the same family may relate very differently, to the extent that one of them later describes their mother as very caring while the other felt unloved and disregarded from the very beginning, although from their mother's perspective they were both treated the same.

When we discussed the classic childhood illnesses in Chapter 7, we attempted to show that children rework their inherited bodies to adapt them to their own purposes. Seen in this new light, hereditary and environmental factors become simply the raw materials that children use to incarnate in ways suited to their own capabilities. From this perspective, selective expression of specific hereditary endowments cannot be seen as mere genetic coincidence. That the first child in a family inherits curly hair, the second straight hair, and the third his grandfather's sparse hair pattern is no "coincidence" but was "planned" by the children before birth. Each human being already exists and is active before birth and chooses specific parents and thus also the hereditary basis on which his or her personality develops (see also Section 11.5).

Something similar is true of how each child deals with environmental factors and influences. One child greedily absorbs everything that furthers his musical ability, which is evident at an early age, while another shows a special interest in anything technical. Here again we touch on the question of reincarnation. Why do children get such very different starts in life? Where did they learn to actively and single-mindedly pursue what they need in one instance and to allow themselves to be more passively shaped by impressions in another? To anyone who keeps these questions in mind while observing how children develop realizes all too clearly that we do not begin our lives as blank slates. Abilities and weaknesses, goals and predisposition to certain illnesses, stick out in this lifetime as the fruits of earlier earthly lives.

16

From the hereditary and environmental possibilities presented to them, children select the ones they relate to naturally and "ignore" or transform others. The purpose of our child-rearing efforts and the way we shape our children's surroundings is to guide this selection process, to protect children from experiencing too much or too little, too early or too late. Another task is to prevent our children from developing exclusively according to their predispositions. What we gain from each earthly life is not limited to implementing specific "inborn" talents but also includes enhancing, expanding, and continuing to develop one's personality. Both a boundless ability and the possibility of getting stuck are inherent in each person's being. Children need the encouraging, helpful influence of their social surroundings to develop independent activity. Unfavourable circumstances can paralyze their will and jeopardize their progress toward their life's goal. Alarming as it may be to realize how easily we can either hinder or help our children's development, it is simply a fact. Nature does not produce finished human beings. Children are dependent on, and further influenced by, the conscious help of adults. This developmental receptivity and vulnerability is related to the spiritual nature of the human being, which is what makes each of us a self-determining and independent being. Freedom is inconceivable without weakness, uncertainty, and opportunities to choose and to make mistakes. Encouraging rather than misusing this freedom is the great task of all child-rearing, education, and self-education.

Housing cooperatives

In some big cities, more than fifty percent of all people raising children are single parents. This is all the more reason to welcome the trend toward housing cooperatives — some of them publicly supported — that are modelled on the extended families of earlier times. The people who get involved in such projects are united by the desire to combine a familiar, supportive neighbourhood and shared responsibilities with the possibility for privacy and determining their own lifestyles. People young and old — single women, young families, housemates, people with handicaps — get together and administer their living spaces in common. In many cases, they even build together. Housing cooperatives often include people who might have difficulty living independently or finding appropriate housing on the open market. For children, they offer a wealth of social experience while preserving parent-child relationships, because each person determines his or her own balance between community life and private life.

Exploring the world through play.

Figures 44 & 45. Nothing is safe any more. Now the art of education begins, to encourage his curiosity, but averting dangers through distractions.

Figure 46. The whole body follows the activity.

Figure 47. Courage grows with trust.

16

Figure 48.

Figure 49.

Figure 50.

Figure 51.

Figure 52.

Figure 53.

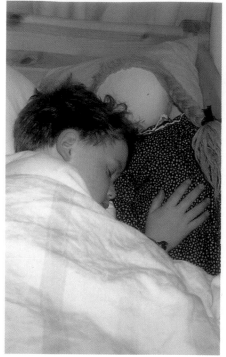

Figure 54.

Figure 55.

Figure 56.

Figure 57.

Figure 58.

Figure 59.

Figure 60.

Figure 61.   *Figure 62.*

Health through Education

Love does not rule;
More importantly, it shapes.

Goethe, in his Parable

17. Health through Education

Children expect adults to educate them. They imitate us, ask incessant questions, and want to do whatever we're doing. They are grateful for secure and happy surroundings and for a clearly defined daily routine. During this time of physical growth and emotional and intellectual development before they come of age, what can we do to maximize and stabilize our children's future health? What concepts should guide us? What steps should we take? Can we constructively apply the universal human ideals of *true* understanding, *loving* relationships, and *free* actions to the practical work of raising children and providing health care? Or have the wars of the twentieth century, our frantic daily life, and cultural pessimism in the face of increasing environmental degradation somehow superceded these ideals, forced them into the background, or called them into question?

Our children themselves provide the answer. Everything they do shows us that they are endowed with these ideals to a very great extent. Even as infants, they look at us radiantly and full of confidence. The younger they are, the more they forgive all our failures and aberrant behaviors and approach us full of expectation. And aren't they also the ones who are always open and honest with us, ready to love and full of hope?

Above all else, *raising a child to be free* means taking appropriate timing into account. Anything we introduce too early catches a child unprepared, unready, and unable to handle the new element independently. In this case, we "train" the child instead of empowering her. Conversely, any skill or subject that we introduce too late no longer catches her interest; as a result, she cannot fully appreciate its value. The consequences are dependency in the first instance and indifference in the second — two different ways of being "un-free" in one's independent activity. Hence age-appropriate education is the basic prerequisite of *healthy development.*

Raising a child to be loving is based on cultivating a rich interpersonal life — relationships to other people, to surroundings, to objects and events. In this process, learning to cope with yes and no, with being allowed to do some things and forbidden to do others, plays a decisive role, because the ability to love also involves respect for other people's life situations and hence the ability to see the positive meaning of a "no." How many relationships in later life suffer from the fact that we never really learned to deal with yes and no, with sympathy and antipathy, or to accept failures and errors as part of life? For example, a request such as "Please leave me alone just now" usually does not signal a real withdrawal of love but simply indicates that the best way for me to show my love for the other person is to leave him or her in peace at the moment. An upbringing oriented toward human understanding and tolerance is the basic prerequisite of a *healthy emotional life.*

Raising a child to be truthful is helped by our own efforts to harmonize our thoughts and feelings with our actions. The point is not that we should appear as good as possible and make the best possible impression on others but that we should really be what we appear to be. Encouraging your child to be attentive to how things are, cultivating her sensory functions, and stimulating her independent reflection are important aids to developing the prerequisites for *spiritual and mental health.*

17.1 Education and physical health

In everything we do with our children and teenagers, from infancy through the entire growth period, we ought to ask ourselves, what impact will this activity have on their physical development? Will it promote or hinder the age-appropriate developmental processes? The diagram below shows the most important maturation phases of different organ systems: the nervous system and sensory organs, the circulatory and respiratory systems (rhythmic system), and the metabolic and motor systems, including the reproductive organs. It takes the nervous system and sensory organs eight to ten years to become fully functional, although of course the finer networks of the central nervous system maintain a certain degree of plasticity throughout life. Rhythmic functions mature during the next developmental stage, which lasts until about age thirteen to fifteen, while full maturity of the metabolic and skeletal systems is achieved only in adulthood, at nineteen to twenty-one years of age. If we hope to raise and educate children in ways that promote their physical development, we must always ask ourselves how we can support these successive physical maturation processes.

Buildup and breakdown processes in the human body and the corresponding stages in the maturation of thinking

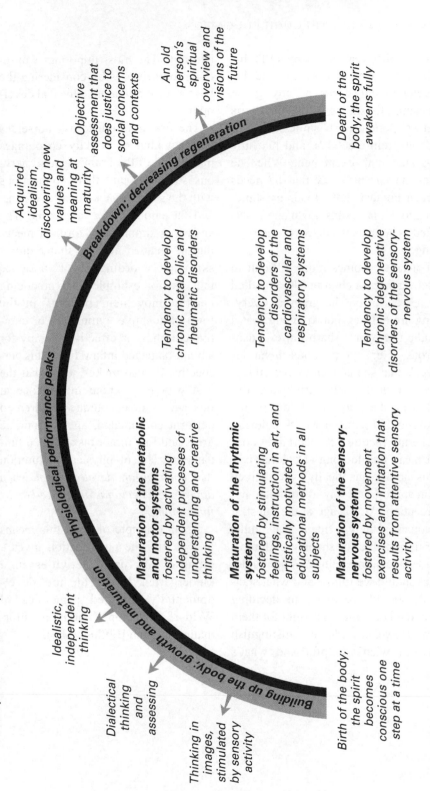

Physiological performance peaks

Breakdown; decreasing regeneration

Building up the body; growth and maturation

Acquired idealism, discovering new values and meaning at maturity

Objective assessment that does justice to social concerns and contexts

An old person's spiritual overview and visions of the future

Idealistic, independent thinking

Dialectical thinking and assessing

Thinking in images, stimulated by sensory activity

Maturation of the metabolic and motor systems
fostered by activating independent processes of understanding and creative thinking

Maturation of the rhythmic system
fostered by stimulating feelings, instruction in art, and artistically motivated educational methods in all subjects

Maturation of the sensory-nervous system
fostered by movement exercises and imitation that results from attentive sensory activity

Tendency to develop chronic metabolic and rheumatic disorders

Tendency to develop disorders of the cardiovascular and respiratory systems

Tendency to develop chronic degenerative disorders of the sensory-nervous system

Birth of the body; the spirit becomes conscious one step at a time

Death of the body; the spirit awakens fully

The arrows indicate forces that are no longer needed for growth, development, and (in old age) regeneration and become available for thinking. At death the etheric body, the living body of thoughts, is released from the disintegrating physical body.

17

In the first year of a baby's life, his behavior makes it easy to read his developmental needs at any given moment. His smiles warm our hearts and we spontaneously smile back. Our pleasure reinforces his, and his little legs kick with excitement. When he cries, he lets us know that he needs human contact, talk, food, or something to do. He calms down and is satisfied as soon as we discover the right thing.

Later, it becomes more difficult to discover what a child needs. Impelled by her curiosity, she grabs at everything around her, not knowing that a candle flame or a sharp knife is dangerous. Her spontaneous behavior reveals that she is open to everything, ready to learn and participate. But although she may crawl toward the television, fascinated by its colorful, flickering pictures, this certainly does not mean that looking at colored patterns moving chaotically over a screen is an appropriate way to stimulate her perception. At this age at the latest, it becomes acutely evident that adults are responsible for shaping children's immediate surroundings. What guidelines should we follow and what standards should we apply in deciding what (and how much) is right for them now? How can we learn to distinguish between what's helpful and what's harmful? The most important way to orient ourselves is by considering the laws governing human physical development.

The first question to ask ourselves is, what kind of activity encourages maturation of the brain's central nervous structures and their connections with the sense organs, internal organs, and the entire motor apparatus? The answer is simple: any form of meaningful, unaided activity that requires skill and coordination. Experience tells us, for example, that practicing healthy movement patterns in the form of adaptive gymnastics or curative eurythmy is effective therapy for a brain-damaged infant. From this perspective, it also makes sense that the best way to promote intelligence at this age is to encourage children to perform coordinated, age-appropriate gross and fine motor tasks. It is a fundamental law of physical maturation that *each organ develops best when appropriate demands are placed on its functioning.*

As an example of what this means in real life, the next section gives a glimpse into daily activities in a kindergarten based on the developmentally oriented principles of Waldorf education. (For more information, see the Bibliography).

17.2 A day in kindergarten

Within an hour after the kindergarten opens, the children begin arriving. Very young children are brought straight to the teacher by their parents, while older ones run ahead, confidently stepping through the open door alone or in small groups. After taking off their coats and boots, they say hello to the kindergarten teacher, who is usually already involved in some kind of work. The youngest children remain close to her, watching or helping, while the older ones already have very specific games in mind. Together they stack tables and shelves, draping them with cloths to make a playhouse, or perhaps a fire truck, a garbage truck, an ambulance, or even an ocean liner. The four- and five-year-olds enjoy getting out the horses and wagons or building trains to transport stones, pine cones, and other small objects. They also like to dress and feed the baby dolls and take them for walks. Dressed up in veils and pieces of cloth, they become mothers, nurses, or mail carriers.

This first part of the morning is full of the hustle and bustle of varied free play that revolves around the kindergarten teacher as its quiet center. Although busy with some type of work herself, she watches the children's activity with interest. Without needing to intervene, she makes sure that the life of this big "family" is both structured and stimulating. For herself, she selects household chores that are simple, easily comprehensible, and fun for the children to imitate: doing hand laundry, baking bread, making snacks, and so on. From time to time she leaves her work to help celebrate a doll's birthday with one small group, or to take a trip on the ferry (by invitation, of course!), or to give one of the children a comforting word. Conflicts or stereotyped behaviors catch her attention, and she steps in to help the children in question.

As play time draws to a close, the kindergarten teacher begins to tidy up her own work place. Some of the children notice and begin to put their things away, too. Seven to ten minutes elapse before the last children are cheerfully involved in this activity. After the classroom has been swept and the children have been to the bathroom, the whole group gathers for rhythmic play — songs, singing games, and movement games set to verse. The content focuses primarily on the cycle of the year, seasonal farm activities, and events in the natural world. Christian seasonal festivals also take up a great deal of time and are high points in the daily life of the kindergarten. Because the same games and songs are repeated every day for a longer period of time, the children gradually acquire an extensive repertoire of verses and songs without even trying. In some kindergartens, the large-group session of rhythmic play is preceded by a morning circle —

17

reciting a verse or prayer in unison and singing a morning song. The snack that follows the large-group activity consists of bread, muesli or other little dish, fruit or carrots, and herb tea.

Snack time is followed by either another period of free play (usually in the playground or the sandbox) or — if possible — a trip to the park or a short walk. At the end of the morning, the children come together again in a loose circle to hear fairy tales. The little ones love (and need) to be allowed to sit close to the teacher. Her storytelling style is a simple narrative, not dramatic or emotional but loving and matter-of-fact. This style allows the children to absorb the often highly dramatic scenes as images instead of as threatening or irresistibly compelling plots. They sense her love for each word and sentence that she speaks. She does not allow herself any variation in the telling; the children would notice it immediately and correct her, because they hear the same familiar tale every day for a number of weeks. Most of the stories are taken from the Brothers Grimm, whose style, structure, and contents are especially suited to stimulating and enriching fantasy and feeling in children's souls (see page 271).

Thus the course of the day is divided into two large blocks of time when the children can engage in age-appropriate activities suggested both by the rich selection of materials available and by the example of the teacher, who goes about a variety of useful household activities just like a mother at home. Cooking, baking bread, and doing laundry are all part of the morning's work, as are mending and ironing clothes, fixing toys, and artistic activities with watercolors and other media. This extensive selection of activities means that at the right time and in the right way, each child finds what he or she needs to imitate at this particular stage of development. The children themselves are allowed to decide what, how, and whether to imitate. Two shorter periods are devoted to large-group activities (rhythmic play/snack and listening to fairy tales). The alternation between free play and common activity is like a great, repeated inbreathing and outbreathing.

This type of daily structure in the kindergarten requires close cooperation with parents, who often have reservations about fairy tales, for example, which they may experience as overly violent or moralistic. A parents' meeting is a welcome opportunity for the teacher to introduce the parents to the world of fairy tales, allowing them to experience the warm and loving tone of her quiet yet epic style of narration. Most fairy tales — especially Grimm's — are full of images that clearly differentiate between human strengths and human weaknesses. Evil appears only in order to help the good triumph and to contribute to the development of more profound human qualities such as modesty, friendliness, persistence, honesty, bravery, and loyalty.

Children who watch a great deal of television at home and have little opportunity for independent, creative activity are often conspicuous during periods of free play because they do not know how to participate appropriately, preferring either to watch or to stir up chaos, depending on their temperament. It often takes six months before they are fully integrated into group activities and stop bothering the others with "bang, bang" or other mannerisms they have learned from television. Parents who entrust their child to a Waldorf-oriented kindergarten always notice that they come home strengthened, often bringing ideas that introduce changes into their family's daily routine. For example, some children want to say grace before meals at home, too, while others want their siblings or parents to do the singing games they've learned in kindergarten or tell the fairy tales they have heard.

The Waldorf approach to early childhood education is adapted to the developmental needs of preschoolers. In the mornings, the first thing children want to do is to take possession of their surroundings. Repetitive events and familiar objects allow them to recall what happened the previous day or week, and they enjoy deepening their grasp of these events by repeating them in play. *Children of this age are never content with one-time experiences. They always want to unite with events by continuing and repeating them.* This natural imitation strengthens their will, their ability to act, just as daily exercise strengthens muscles. The entire daily schedule of a Waldorf kindergarten focuses on educating the children's will. Our will, however, needs repeated stimulation outside. Children's need to imitate reflects their dependency on this kind of repetition. The more a kindergarten teacher identifies with her work, the more the children love to imitate it. Her efforts are all directed at shaping the course of the day in a way that allows the children to learn to use all of their senses and engage in all possible activities.

It is important to realize, however, that all of this takes place in a joyful hustle and bustle; the children are free to structure their play as they wish, and any organizing on the part of the kindergarten teacher never puts the damper on their activity or interrupts it forcefully. If a child is enthusiastically immersed in his play when it is time for a snack, the teacher needs to find a way to help him make the transition from his "work" to the shared meal. Of course this is a very tricky moment. Everyone is familiar with the whining and complaining of a child dragged away from play to do something more "important" or necessary. Children are most content when they can decide for themselves what to do. This transition will be easier for the teacher if she can already count on the group's well-established habits. For some children, seeing her begin to tidy up or hearing the clatter of cups is enough to signal that something else is about to happen. Imposing necessary changes on a single child at home is much more difficult, so it is all the more important to give preliminary signals a few minutes before it is time

17

to stop playing. For example, "What a nice castle you've built! Are the people inside sitting down to eat already? We're also going to eat soon. I'll call you in just a few minutes."

Failing to understand the laws that govern children's activity can cause a great deal of damage. Our experience of freedom in later life is based on how we were allowed to express our urge to be active as children and whether are not we were allowed to use our play space freely. Constantly interrupting or correcting children in their intentions and activity has damaging effects on their will development and the physical maturation that accompanies it. Physiological functions proceed smoothly when children play happily and actively but get "stuck" when they are frustrated. This phenomenon must not be underestimated. Our children will have to spend the rest of their lives with the body functions and organs whose development must now be stimulated by active and appropriate use.

The younger the children and the more immature their bodies (especially their nervous systems), the more susceptible they are to disturbances in their development. *Thus the most significant help and the most severe damage occur in the first three years of life.*[36] For this reason, we also advise you to keep your children at home if at all possible until they are three years old. On the other hand there may be compelling reasons making this impossible. In selecting a caregiver it is important that your child's development and "incarnation" — the active process of learning to use and identify with his or her own body — will be promoted, and that the mother (and father) remain the central suport on the child's life. (Some parents who have not had a harmonious childhood themselves may find that they are now able to experience the nature of childhood through their own children.) Recently Waldorf educators have devoted increasing attention to issues of childrearing during the first few years of life.[37]

When making selections from the many different toys available for preschoolers, we recommend asking yourself whether the toy you've chosen encourages independent, imaginative activity. Overly detailed, mechanically perfect toys have pronounced negative effects on a young child's unprotected, instinctively imitating body, deadening fantasy and creativity. Building with Lego blocks does a ten-year-old no harm, but handling the standardized pieces that can be assembled only in certain ways severely restricts a five-year-old's imagination. The falsehood inherent in the material is also damaging, because Lego pieces make it possible to build structures that conflict with our sense of equilibrium and thus disrupt its development. Structures made with ordinary building blocks collapse when unbalanced, showing children that they have not yet completely understood the material and the effects of its weight, but Lego pieces stay together because of friction and thus present falsified sense impressions.

If we watch children closely as they

play with computer games or remote-controlled cars and trains, it is obvious that all they can do with them is watch in fascination or at most take them apart and put them back together again — functions that foster development only at a later stage. If introduced too early, when children's bodies are very activity-oriented and are still being shaped by activity, such toys have crippling effects on independent, creative activity and will development.

Summary

The most important ways to support children's development at the preschool stage are:

- Stimulating initiative and independent, creative play by engaging in activities for the children to imitate.
- Cultivating their perceptual ability by providing a variety of age-appropriate sensory activities (see also Section 13.8)
- Laying the foundation for good habits through regularly repeated activities and little rituals in the morning, at meals, and at night before going to sleep.

- Observing and celebrating daily, weekly, monthly, and seasonal rhythms (see also Section 9.4).
- Establishing regular times when your child has your undivided attention, for example when getting up and going to bed and now and then during the day.
- A primarily nonverbal approach to childrearing. To put it differently, actions speak louder than words in meeting children's need to imitate.
- Simple toys that leave plenty of room for imagination and can be used and combined in many different ways.
- Opportunities for contact with the natural world.
- Avoiding electronic media and technical toys.
- Carrying your child in your consciousness, even if your day is filled with all sorts of other responsibilities. This is especially important for the parent who spends less time at home, because reestablishing contact when you come home is easier if you've kept your child in mind during your absence.

17

17.3 School age prior to puberty

During this period of school age prior to puberty, as we mentioned earlier, physical maturation concentrates on the respiratory and cardiovascular systems, which achieve adult capacity around age fifteen. Once again we must ask which activities and learning processes support the development and functioning of the relevant organs. Here, too, meaningful physical activity certainly helps, but it no longer addresses the body's age-specific needs. At this stage, *the rhythm and quality of respiration and circulation are much more directly and specifically modified by all aspects of a child's emotional life.* Relief, pleasure, and excited expectation have mild stimulating effects: the child's heart beats steadily and he breathes easily and rather fast. Boredom, lack of enthusiasm, hopelessness, shock, and depression slow his breathing and heartbeat. In contrast, fear and restlessness make his heart beat faster, and his breathing becomes irregular.

It is interesting to note that the natural talent for unselfconscious imitation typical of toddlers and preschoolers declines rapidly at this age. Increasingly, children do only what they feel like doing; how they feel about an activity becomes their primary motivation. Unless they've already established good habits, their only motivation for doing "boring stuff" like tidying up or clearing the table is their desire to do the adult a particular favor. Their assessments of everything around them are based on their personal likes and dislikes, sympathy and antipathy — in other words, on feelings.

In the previous developmental stage, our educational efforts drew on young children's natural talent for movement and willingness to imitate. In this next stage, it is still important for parents and teachers to take advantage of age-specific talents — in this case, the ability and inclination to judge everything on the basis of feeling, esthetics, and personal taste. All sorts of artistic activity — artistic applications of movement and speech, vocal and instrumental music, clay modeling, and crafts — are especially important tools. These activities allow the children's feeling life to express itself in the tension between beautiful and ugly or successful and unsuccessful artistic efforts. When children of this age lack artistic opportunities, their natural tendency to make judgments based on sympathy and antipathy shifts to the intellectual level and is applied to other people's actions, and the result is criticism, grumbling, and an unpleasant degree of resistance to adult requests.

Art's stimulating effect on children's emotions works in two ways, through passive perception and through active creativity. When a child puts all her attention on practicing a piece of music or working with colors to produce a picture, her perception and her actions interact harmoniously and enhance each other.

To illustrate what we've just described (and, we hope, to encourage the application of these developmental educational principles at home or in other types of schools), let's take a quick look at elementary instruction in a Waldorf school. This example from a third-grade (age eight to nine) arithmetic lesson shows how the principle of artistic instruction can also be applied to scientific and intellectual subjects, not just to art classes.. The topic of the day is primary numbers. The teacher could simply define the concept, telling the class, "A prime number is a number that is divisible only by itself and by 1." Or he could say, "Prime numbers are the lonely beggars of the number world, the poorest of the poor. They are all alone in the world. They are divisible only by themselves because they have no number friends to share things with. Prime numbers are 'beggar numbers'.."

The saying "only with the heart do we see truly" indicates the right approach to this age group. This means, however, that elementary school teachers cannot depend exclusively on standard textbooks. They must add questions of their own and draw parallels to the immediate experiences of the specific children sitting in front of them. They must also be able always to summon up new enthusiasm for their subject matter. Any teacher who works like this is quite naturally accepted by the class as a "beloved authority" who serves as fixed point of reference for the children's developing emotional life with its fluctuating sympathies and antipathies. Being able to look up to at least one teacher with respect based on love also helps children develop healthy self-esteem. This is especially important when the lack of strong family relationships impacts on a child's emotional life and developing self-esteem. A stable sense of self-worth can develop only being recognized and acknowledged as a person in the context of sustainable, trust-based relationships.

Seen against this background, there is nothing more problematic for this age group than a boring lesson, which is simply an opportunity to practice alienation. When children are bored, their emotional life searches for nourishment but comes up empty handed. Their rational minds retain an approximation of what is discussed, but their hearts remain uninvolved. And when feelings and thoughts go their separate ways, a cleft begins to develop in the children's soul life.

In concluding this section, we would like to point to another specific turning point in child development in the tenth year of life. Rudolf Steiner calls this point the "Rubicon of child development." For Caesar, crossing the Rubicon made it impossible for him to return. Similarly, at some point between their ninth and tenth birthdays, children leave their early childhood behind and can never go back. Parents are often able to pinpoint this moment, and anyone who visits a third or fourth-grade class sees the change in the students immediately. All of a sudden, a child's open and unselfconscious gaze becomes serious and withdrawn, as if gently testing the teacher. The child is overwhelmed by the feeling that her place in the world and her secure sense of belonging to her parents can no longer be taken for granted. The loneliness of a destiny only she can fulfil dawns on her for the first time. At this age, a child may question where she comes from. These questions are not a request for sex education. She simply wants to know the exact circumstances of her birth because she wonders whether she may have been a foundling or adopted or confused with someone else's child in the hospital. Her questioning reflects the awakening of her emotional experience of selfhood, which now supplements to the sense of personal identity that dawned on her when she first said "I" to herself between the ages of two and three. She experiences herself as unique and different from her father and mother, which makes her feel profoundly lonely. At this age, children become much more selective about whom to trust and whose guidance to accept. They experience injustices more acutely than before and are less ready to forgive. Their conscience awakens in the form of the distance needed to judge what is good or evil, beautiful or ugly.

Summary

The most important ways to support a school-age child's development are:
- cultivating a "culture of conversa-

tion" — allowing your child to participate in interesting adult conversations.
- always keeping these questions in mind:
— When was our last conversation?
— When did I have time and interest available for my child?
— Did I notice the most important things? Have I praised my child enough, or is it easier for me to express dissatisfaction than praise?
— Do I allow her to make mistakes, and how?
- structuring lessons artistically and relating content to the children's experience
- providing clear guidance on basic issues throughout the day, while taking the children's wishes into account.
- encouraging artistic activity, especially learning to play musical instruments
- allowing TV and other media as little as possible and only by prior agreement. Watch programs together and discuss what you saw.

17.4 School after puberty

If you have ever watched "the light go on" for adolescents who truly understood something through their own efforts, you can see how this experience literally makes them "straighten up." This is a daily experience for anyone who sits in on high school classes. When good questions are asked, the students who are involved in the discussion sit upright or at least in alert, somewhat tensed postures, even if they lean back or support their heads with their hands. Those who remain uninvolved, however, are more likely to sit in a relaxed position with their arms and legs extended or to rest their heads on the desk or on their arms.

It is not true that the work of thinking activates only the nervous system. It is also accompanied by tension and activity in the entire metabolic and motor system. Thus it is all the more depressing when the postures and movements of teenagers on the street reveal the absence of any thought that might provide direction or any ideal worthy of enthusiasm that might help overcome the body's heaviness. Drug addicts can be recognized at a distance by how they walk. So can idealistic, motivated teenagers. We can see from how they move, how they look at things, and how they hold their bodies whether they have a sense of purpose in life and enjoy tackling challenges or whether they haven't been able to develop an active relationship to the world during childhood and adolescence. Our body posture corresponds to our attitude toward life. *We are held upright by inner factors* as well as by muscle tone. Not everyone who has learned to stand upright, however, really stands on his or her own two feet in the spiritual sense.

Lessons that include good questioning and dialog foster scientific ability, encourage experimentation, and help teens acquire the autonomy they need. Good ideas increasingly take the place of role models and authority figures. For teens, the important adults are those who understand them. Adolescents become increasingly interested in anything that supports and stimulates their own deliberations. They are now capable of learning from people they do not like; they learn to separate the personal element from objective fact. They also consciously resist much of what they used to trust as they attempt to go their own ways.

The independent thinking that develops at this age helps them distance and protect themselves from unpleasant events. They are no longer as vulnerable to them, nor do they need to imitate them. They can now debate and philosophize for hours and busy themselves with interesting and satisfying thoughts of their own if a class gets boring. In fact, boring classes produce astonishing numbers of good ideas, poems, and drawings that are completely different from the uninspired graffiti younger children scrawl on their desks.

The educator Michael Bauer once formulated the goal of adolescent education as follows: "Educators can neither force nor create anything that is not there; they can simply challenge teens to stay alert, utter words of encouragement, and ask stimulating questions. Many educational methods do nothing but overcome obstacles and shed light on the path, but educators cannot be content to do only that. They can rest on their laurels only when an independent educator emerges within each student and makes their efforts unnecessary."[38]

Summary:

- Foster a culture of asking questions
- Be a friend and companion
- Respect your teenagers' growing awareness of their freedom and self-reliance
- Hold "family councils." Make decisions in common, review their good or bad consequences, and consult about what to do next
- Learn to enjoy personal differences
- Risk having confidence in your teenagers; let them know that you support them and are eager to see what their lives will bring.

18. Child-rearing and Education as Preventive Medicine

18.1 Life processes and thinking

In several different contexts in the first and second parts of this book, we mentioned Rudolf Steiner's spiritual-scientific discovery that the mysterious activity we call thinking has the same origin as the body's life processes, which include regeneration and healing (see Section 15.4).

The typical steps in the development of thinking through childhood and adolescence to maturity coincide with steps in the maturation of the body's processes of growth and development. For example, the imaginative thinking of young children, which is directly tied to sensory impressions, coincides with the maturation of the nervous system and sensory organs. Similarly, the opinion-based thinking of the next stage coincides with the maturation of rhythmic body functions, since forming an opinion is nothing more than a rhythmical weighing and moving of thoughts and questions. And finally, independent, discriminatory thinking, along with

creative thinking, emerges during the years when the metabolic and skeletal systems are reaching full maturity.

In the last third of life, however, the body's regenerative capacity declines, and new possibilities of spiritual development appear in people who are aging healthily. As the performance of the metabolic and limb systems declines, the resulting "savings" in regenerative forces can appear in the form of new, creative possibilities of thinking. The same is true of forces liberated from the aging rhythmic and sensory-nervous systems. The wisdom of old age emerges as a new idealism, mature judgment, and a lively, pictorial inner life.

Considering this connection between physical and spiritual processes of growth and development leads to a new view of education as preventive medicine. The more children and adolescents are stimulated in ways that support the healthy growth of their organ systems, the more effectively premature aging and avoidable illnesses are prevented. This is the goal of all of the educational recommendations in this book.

When we consider the physiological stimulation of organ functions through age-appropriate education, the obvious question is, what happens when such stimulation is neglected? Don't inappropriate demands on the sensory-nervous, rhythmic, and metabolic-motor systems predispose people to illnesses in the second half of life? This hypothesis is supported by evidence that the three main forms of age-related chronic illness (see diagram on page 293) respond well to types of therapy that are directly related to the educational approaches recommended during the corresponding period of physical development. For example, biography work or psychotherapy (if it explores the purpose and meaning of life, the ideals one still possesses, or completely new possibilities for reacquiring idealism on the basis of experience to date) is very effective in treating rheumatic disorders and symptoms of menopause. Consciously making the transition to aging, posing new questions for this last stage of life, and working out new motives for living significantly improve the prognosis in these particular metabolic and motor disorders. Older people who again learn to ask independent questions fare significantly better than those who rely on medication and otherwise simply continue as before. In other words, the same approach that helps adolescents develop and "take possession" of

these organ functions also helps older adults regenerate and maintain them.

The same is true of complementary treatments for functional disorders of the rhythmic system. For postcoronary patients or those with cardiac arrhythmia, recommended lifestyle changes included learning to relax and finding times to rest during the day. Dealing with one's emotional life again becomes a primary task. Especially effective are artistic therapies (painting, music, speech, eurythmy). Many patients, sensing the beneficial effects on the rhythmic system and associated emotional activity, make a lifelong habit of specific artistic exercises that support their ability to relax and behave more flexibly.

For the third complex of chronic age-related diseases, looking up to great models, as during the preschool age, is again helpful. Of course these models or heroes are no longer the mother and father that help preschoolers orient themselves in life. Instead, they are myths and fairy tales, the great religious and artistic truths, and exalted images of creation and human evolution. Whether discovered for the first time or newly called to mind again, they can help stimulate, calm, and consolidate an old person's soul-spiritual life so that he or she preserves the self-confidence needed to live and work with declining mental capacities for longer than would otherwise be possible.

But the connections between educational influences and a person's state of health in later life go beyond these basic relationships. What happens, for example, when a growing child experiences repeated, startling outbursts of violent temper from a parent or teacher? At each outburst, the child's peripheral circulation shuts down and he or she turns pale. But what does it mean when this happens repeatedly and is inadequately counteracted by experiences of loving acceptance and help, exhalation and relaxation, and being allowed to make mistakes? A circulatory system "educated" in this particular one-sided way remains subtly predisposed to inadequate arterial perfusion. As physicians, we often see examples of how an adult's soul functions are transformed into bodily functions in their children. Adult emotional problems reappear in their children in the form of predisposition to physical illnesses. For example, children who stutter often have a parent who speaks too fast and somewhat breathlessly but has never developed an actual stutter. Such examples make it obvious that illness is related to issues of destiny and development and that the capacity for self-education and personal growth is the foundation for adult educational behavior that promotes health in children. The ideas presented in this section aim to awaken understanding of this insight and to strengthen parents' and teachers' motivation for self-development. Although many of our reflections may seem farfetched, we hope they will encourage you to think about the possible connections and to adjust your parenting or teaching style accordingly — just in case! In his educational lectures, Rudolf Steiner pointed to many more ways in which a child's upbringing and education may relate to physical predispositions later in life. Here are a few examples:

Educational influences	Effects later in life
Experience of pleasure, happiness, love, and attention	*The physical body remains flexible longer; easy to establish relationships to other people and to one's surroundings*
Admiration and awe	*Loving the world*
The belief that life is beautiful; an accepting attitude based on love for an authority figure	*Fundamental satisfaction with life*
Absorbing religious images and moods	*Tolerance of religious and personal differences*
Learning to pray in childhood	*Being able to bestow blessings in old age*
How a person learns to play as a child	*An adult's approach to life and the situations it presents*

18

Educational influences	Effects later in life
Knowing and loving the world of plants	Vital, flexible concepts
Knowing and loving the world of animals	Strengthened will
Being attracted to the world's riddles; having many questions	Healthy relationship to eroticism and the problem of power
Being brought up to take an interest in the world	Increasing interest in people
Learning from life	Security in life
Materialistic upbringing	Loss of interest in the world
Absorbing mathematical laws without emotional involvement	Predisposition to materialism
Education that encourages a critical or skeptical approach to life (lack of idealism)	Predisposition to emotional exhaustion
Abstract instruction in grammar	Predisposition to gastrointestinal diseases
Elementary education that places excessive demands on intellect and memory	Sclerotic tendencies and premature degeneration of the nervous system
Learning to judge and criticize too early	Tendency to judge severely and without love
Inartistic, narrowly intellectual instruction	Predisposition to disorders of the rhythmic system, especially over-inhalation; disrupted respiratory rhythm with a predisposition to feelings of oppression and asthmatic symptoms
Quick, superficial understanding	Premature emotional aging due to having nothing left to process in depth
Absence of a primary relationship to a beloved authority	Not finding the strength to help oneself
Undisturbed imitation	Receptive interaction with one's surroundings; open-mindedness
Independent search for truth	Courage and initiative

18.2 Children and technology

Our multimedia, technological culture attracts and fascinates both adults and children. Developmentally friendly use of technology *is* possible if you follow these guidelines.

Understand the significance of technology in human history

The Industrial Revolution in England in the middle of the eighteenth century saw the beginning of the switch from manual work to mechanized production. The invention of the steam engine and subsequent generations of internal combustion engines provided the basis for this revolution in production. Smaller, more manageable machines and a wealth of measuring devices were developed as large-scale technical use of electricity and the electrification of homes became common. After the electric light bulb was invented by Heinrich Göbel in 1854 and made commercially viable by Thomas Edison in 1879, the use of electricity spread around the globe with almost unimaginable rapidity. The film camera and the carbon dust microphone were invented during the same period, ushering in a revolution in communication and media. After World War II, the third great technological revolution began as computers and information technology were developed — machines that could take over the functions of intelligence.

The mechanization of manual labor, communication, and data management (physical, psychological, and intellectual functions, respectively) significantly reduced human work loads but also created mass unemployment and — in addition to poverty — almost epidemic symptoms of alienation, resignation, and depression. Millions of people no longer experience their activity as meaningful to society.

Through the development of technology the results and products no longer relate directly to our capabilities and will. Normally our own work involves the development of skills and an associated experience of purpose. Hence the golden rule for dealing with technology in education is, *as much as possible, to experience doing the work yourself before handing it over to machines*. The historical transition from human work to mechanized work took place in successive stages. Similarly, it is important for growing children and adolescents to become familiar with and master the skills involved in various types of work before relinquishing them to machines. Expecting great things of machines and little of ourselves simply fosters demanding and ungrateful attitudes if we have no basis for appreciating how much personal work machines spare us.

18

Allow children to relive the technological revolution through their upbringing and education

Show them by example that hot running water and infinite light or power at the flick of a switch cannot be taken for granted. Arrange your vacations to include stays at an isolated farm or a primitive campsite where you will have to wash clothes by hand and heat water over a fire or portable gas stove, so your children can learn to truly appreciate the blessings of modern technology.

Allow children to learn to do as much as possible for themselves before relinquishing the work to mechanical devices. Make sure that they learn to sing, paint, do clay modeling, dance, and act in plays before audiovisual media overwhelm them with images, colors, and sounds that threaten to paralyze their own creative abilities.

Consult with teachers about delaying the use of calculators until the class has developed some facility with basic number operations, especially mental arithmetic. Why should calculators and computers become constant companions in school before the children understand how these labor-saving devices work and before they have learned to perform the work for themselves and to appreciate it?

Your own use of energy and technology should set an example for your children and should allow them to experience that resources are not limitless and that technology should be used only when really necessary and appropriate.

Avoid confusing nature, human beings, and social interaction with machines

Perfection and optimization make sense in the context of technology. We repair defects in our machines and discard irreparably damaged or outdated models. Extending this behavior to human beings and the natural world, however, causes problems that are simply intensified when children and adults spend much of their free time in intimate association with computers or video games. Attitudes that we so often lack in our interactions with other people — full attentiveness and interest in their reactions, questions, needs, and concerns — are applied with dismaying matter-of-factness to computers. The more we cultivate this type of psychological interaction with machines (which either respond in predictable ways or require predictable corrective measures), the more we practice behaviors that are inadequate for dealing with other people and especially with the natural world. People and nature do not respond predictably; they react on the basis of their own unique development and life circumstances.

To live with other people, we must learn to accept mistakes and misbehavior and to live with them when they cannot be corrected quickly. We must be open to learning new and unexpected things. Our psychologically limiting interactions with technology unconsciously encourage us to distance ourselves from our surroundings, so it is not surprising that our interactions with other people become increasingly "dysfunctional."

In his books *Silicon Snake Oil* and *High Tech Heretic,* astronomer and computer security specialist Clifford Stoll comes out *in favour of* appropriate PC use for teens and adults and *against* their use in kindergartens and elementary schools and at home — that is, an age when the highest priority is developing and cultivating human relationships. At home, it is important to experience peace and quiet, reflection and warmth — not qualities that immediately come to mind when we think of home computers.

18

19. Learning Effective Parenting

These three scenes, which all took place during office hours in our pediatric practice, illustrate three fundamentally different approaches to bringing up children. (In each case, "mother" stands for the parent or guardian accompanying the child.)

"Sit down right here and be quiet!" The boy's mother attempts to talk with the physician. Her four-year-old romps around the room, playing with items on the instrument table and trying to use the telephone. His mother reacts as if she had a butterfly net in her hand and sometimes jumps even before the little boy moves. "Stay there. Don't touch that! That belongs to the doctor. Leave that light alone! Do I have to take you on my lap? Are you asking for a smack?"

During the conversation, a little girl attempts to get her mother's attention with all kinds of questions. She's interested in a picture on the wall that shows the archangel Michael fighting with the dragon.
Child: *Mommy, who's that in the picture?*
Mother: *A man who's killing an animal.*
Child: *Why is there fire coming out of its mouth?*
Mother: *It is meant to be a dragon.*
Child: *Mommy, what's that thing around his head?*
Mother: *The painter wanted to show people that the man is nice, so he painted that yellow circle around his head. [Pause.]*
Mother: *Doctor, she simply can't stay in bed at night.*
Child: *Mommy, why does the man have wings? He's not a biiiiird!*
Mother: *That's supposed to be an angel.*
Child: *But there isn't any devil, is there, Mommy?*
Mother: *No, you know there isn't. Will you let me talk to the doctor now?*
Child: *Mommy, I want a drink. [Her mother gives her a bottle.]*
Mother: *She doesn't want to eat anything at lunchtime, and I don't force her.*
Child: *But Mommy, you said I always like to eat chips. I want a biscuit, Mommy. [Her mother gives her the whole box.]*

Mother: *But we only have them once a week. And she doesn't touch anything else.*

Doctor: *She must be eating something. What else do you like to eat?*

Child: *Jam.*

Mother: *Yes, she eats it by the spoonful, right out of the jar. Half a jar at a time.*

Doctor: *And you just let her?*

Mother: *Yes. Is it all right to stop her? I thought children were supposed to know what they need.*

At first, the third child settles down and plays by himself. After a little while, he begins to explore the room. Sensing that the adults' attention is not on him, he approaches his mother and quietly asks her a pressing question to confirm that he is still "in the picture." His mother either answers right away or takes him on her lap briefly until she is able to whisper him the answer. The interruption is almost unnoticeable. Satisfied, he goes back to playing quietly by himself for a while. He drifts in and out of the conversation from time to time, sometimes even addressing the doctor, to assure himself that he is still included in the "soul space" that develops between the doctor and his mother.

What does each example tell us about the "soul space" of the parent-child relationship?

The first example illustrates a disciplinary approach that attempts to teach good behavior through warnings and corrections. In contrast, the parent in the second example is unassertive

and indecisive and gives in to whatever the child wants. The children's will cannot thrive in either case — in the first instance because the little boy is not allowed to experience anything for himself, and in the second because the little girl does not experience the necessary resistance from her parent.

These two attitudes — the authoritarian principle (usually the one that persists unconsciously in parents from their own childhood) and the anti-authoritarian or *laissez faire* approach — are diametrically opposed, but each one shapes the "soul space" of the parent-child relationship in a very distinctive way. In the first example, the mother hangs over her son, overwhelming him with corrections as soon as he shows any initiative. If this approach is taken to the extreme, the child is left with no options except to adapt passively or to resort to aggression. In the second example, the mother overwhelms her daughter with sympathy, leaving the little girl to search in vain for resistance. The ultimate consequence of this boundless permissiveness is to make the child restless, uncertain, disoriented, cranky, and demanding — all signs that she is searching for appropriate behavior to imitate.

As for the third situation, this little boy decides for himself where to settle down while the adults talk. In this instance, there is a real give-and-take between the little boy and his parent. Words like "don't do that," "leave me alone," or "you're not allowed" are not necessary, nor are lengthy explanations. It is obvious that this mother means what she says and that her son trusts her. She did not have to do anything in particular to "prepare" him for the visit to the doctor.

Of course each of these three examples has a history. How were these children brought up during their first few years? The mother in the last example must have had a real feeling for her child's psychological needs when he was one and two. She was accessible, paid attention to him, and resisted his demands when necessary. When he was one year old and starting to get into everything, instead of wasting a lot of her working time chasing after him saying "no" and "don't touch," she handed him some interesting object and put him in the playpen. She sensed when he was hungry or tired and whether he needed attention or something to do by himself. When she had to tell him not to do something, she probably said it only once or twice. If he still didn't "get it," he found himself gently moved to another spot where he could watch her equally well but couldn't reach that tempting electrical outlet. His mother's words served only to accompany her actions, which were all based on necessary decisions and the logic of the immediate situation. Her child grew up feeling he was a part of what was going on and included in his mother's soul space and that adults' words were consistent with their actions. As he became increasingly independent, he was allowed to shape his own space, which still more or less overlapped with his mother's. When she had to resist his demands, she acted out of the reality of

the situation, not out of emotion. Her son experienced this objective overview as something mysterious, valuable, and available only to adults. He was never expected to make decisions that were better left up to his mother and her better grasp of the situation. She was totally receptive when he needed comfort and company but was able to say "no" when necessary. This alternation between devoted acceptance and an intensified sense of self laid the groundwork for healthy self-confidence.

We can be sure that this mother also often wondered whether she was making the "right" decision, but she never allowed her child to see her uncertainty. Whatever she did, she did as well and with as much certainty as she could muster at the moment.

If you realize you don't have this ability yet and that you've made "wrong" decisions in dealing with your child, what can you do now? What if you don't know what to do or say in a certain situation and are afraid your child will get out of hand? In these situations, it is helpful to remember a few time-tested principles:

- *Mean what you say and do. Consistency is important.* This includes other members of the family, too. If you tell your child that something is forbidden, your decision is binding and no amount of whining and begging will make you reverse it.
- *Take your own work seriously.* Even in the case of seemingly unimportant activities, remember there's a

19

reason for what you're doing, let the child follow and imitate, and don't give in to all kinds of distractions. Do not focus constantly on your child. You also need to be able to do things that are important to you and that *you* enjoy doing. Cultivate your own identity, but at the same time respect your child's identity.

- *Review the day's events each evening.* How was your child today? What did she experience? Was your behavior and that of other caregivers appropriate to her present stage of development? What developmental steps has she accomplished, and which ones still lie ahead? What is she asking of you at this stage?

If you've been able to discuss these recommendations with your spouse, the two of you may decide to set aside specific times for reminding each other of inconsistencies in your words and actions. For example, have you threatened your child with consequences but not carried out the threat? Having parents who agree on disciplinary principles is a great blessing for any child. Conversely, there is nothing more disruptive to bringing up a child than parental disagreements about discipline.

Examples from the daily life of a large family

Quarreling
Usually, it is best to let the children in a large family figure out how to get along with each other without adult intervention. An experienced mother knows that she doesn't need to check up on her children each time she hears minor disagreements. When the kids are still as mice, however, a timely check may prevent the bathtub from overflowing or some other disaster. She also checks when she hears screaming and overturned chairs, which are the children's way of expressing something they don't want to tell her directly, namely, "We need help! We can't get out of this ourselves." So she stands quietly at the door, surveys the mess, and tries to sort out what's going on. Are they tired from playing too long? Are they not getting along because the game isn't appropriate for the younger ones? What can she expect from each of them at this point?

One crying child runs up to her; another says quickly, "I didn't hit her." The oldest yells angrily, "They won't even let me decide what to serve for my own doll's birthday dinner. And now Annie doesn't want to come to the party at all." Crying angrily, she attempts to storm out of the room.

Scolding wouldn't help at all in this situation — they're already so ashamed of themselves. Don't ask questions about the argument either; they'd just cry harder. But questions like, "How old is your doll? Three? Isn't that old enough for a meal with a couple of courses? What did you want to cook?" help them calm down and show them how everyone's wishes could be accommodated. "You two, come help me make supper. The rest of you get this room picked up so we can all read a nice story together afterward. And make sure those dolls play together quietly so they won't be too tired to listen." This strategy breaks up the cockfight, brings the game to a close, and gives the children something else to do and something to look forward to. If one of the girls is still smouldering at bedtime, it helps to ask, "Are you friends again?" If that's obviously not the case, it is usually enough to whisper in her ear, "You know we don't go to bed angry. May I tell Annie that you really do love her, deep down inside?" Even if she isn't sure about that, her mother is, and she whispers it in Annie's ear.

Envy and jealousy

When it is time for pudding, ten-year-old Sarah quickly helps herself to the biggest apple in the bowl — yet again. Thirteen-year-old Thomas glowers and says nothing, but twelve-year-old Kathryn complains, "She *always* takes the biggest one, and you let her get away with it. It is so unfair!" Father asks, "Who do you think should get it?" Silence. Kathryn: "You, maybe, or Mom, or maybe we should take turns." Father: "Sometimes the smaller apples are the ones that taste best. But you know what? Yesterday Sarah *did* wash that huge pile of dishes all by herself without complaining. Do you think you could let her have the biggest apple this time?"

This incident illustrates only one aspect of the multi-layered problem of envy and jealousy, which can strike especially hard when the people involved really do love each other.

In deciding what to do in such cases, it helps to realize that we feel envious when we think that we (or someone else) are more deserving than the person in question. We don't like to admit that we're jealous or begrudge someone something, so instead we justify our feelings in terms of fairness or unfairness. We hide our jealousy and disapproval behind seemingly justified criticism and some kind of moral-sounding excuse. If we understand what's really going on, we can avoid or defuse a great deal of argument and negative criticism.

This approach helps children learn that there are no universal moral principles in life but only individual situations that require ever new decisions about the right way to behave. In this little scene at the dinner table, for example, the solution might look like this: next time, the "greedy" child is allowed to choose the nicest apple and give it to the person she thinks is most deserving. Or she is allowed to serve dessert for a while. Her feelings will be hurt, however, if she simply feels morally reprimanded and gets the impression that her pleasure in finding the biggest, nicest apple is seen as unjustified. In the long run, revealing a child's weaknesses without giving her a chance for corrective action undermines her self-confidence. But such incidents can strengthen her character if you take advantage of them to encourage a new level of consideration or other positive quality.

Tidying up

It is easy for a mother to feel over-whelmed if she spends her whole day tidying up after other people. There's only one solution: from the very beginning, do the tidying up and house-cleaning together, and show your children how nice it is when every-thing is back in place. If you allow them to participate at an early age and gradually transfer the responsibility for specific tasks to them as they grow older, they will be proud of being able to do what needs doing — especially if the adults always notice and acknowl-edge their efforts, even when the job is not done as perfectly as it might be.

A few little rules can help support the process of transferring respons-ibility:

- It is not time to eat until your child's backpack of school supplies is sit-ting by his desk instead of on the floor in a corner by the door;
- ... and his jacket is hung up in the closet;
- ... and his hands have been washed.
- Allow your children to decide for themselves who will do which little job in the house. Rotate tasks on a weekly or monthly basis.
- Don't forget that learning to tidy up, like any other attempts at self-improvement, is best rewarded with acknowledgment and loving recog-nition.
- Avoid too frequent questions like, "Have you already done..." and "Didn't you want to do...." It is especially important to time these questions so that they don't sound like "punishment" or add insult to injury when your child has just done something else out of line. Save them for when he's in a good mood.
- Now and then, make a point of doing these jobs yourself if that's what it takes to avoid constantly reminding, scolding, or correcting your child. Or do it just to give him a pleasant surprise.
- When your children reach school age, tidying up together after supper can become a good habit. It goes quickly when everybody simply does whatever is still left to do.
- Most importantly, don't imagine that keeping the house neat and clean is an issue that can ever be resolved once and for all. It is very important to accept whatever degree of tidiness your family can realistically achieve. After all, tidi-ness supports life, not the other way around!

20. Developing your Child's Will

In this chapter, we will touch on a few basic issues of will development and then address the big topic of rewards and punishments.

20.1 General perspectives

With human beings, nothing happens by itself

Human behavior is learned as we develop; our natural physical abilities do not "automatically" make us behave with intelligence and dignity. All our behaviors must be acquired through imitation, insight, experience, and action. Compared to animals, we have fewer instincts, which is why our eating and sleeping habits have to be learned, practiced, and consciously cultivated throughout our life. To develop our will, we need to experience either external or internal demands as well as resistance and limits that test our strength and spark the acquisition of new abilities.

Conscious repetition strengthens will

This is the succinct summary of the basic principles of will development in one of Rudolf Steiner's educational lectures. Repetition, which quickly becomes boring to our intellect, is the basis of stability in our will. Good pianists know that every repetition brings improvement and that their playing as a whole suffers if they forget to do specific fingering exercises for just a few days. Developing a habit or a behavior is not a one-time effort but depends on faithfully practising the many little steps that lead to the desired ability. There is no point in making all kinds of resolutions if you soon abandon them. In this case, less is more. It is better to practice a few things consistently for years than to allow yourself to drift for a long time and then attempt to change your ways in a couple of weeks. Nothing weakens our will more than resolving to do something but never getting around to it or doing it for a short period and then dropping it. People who do this repeatedly begin to doubt their own ability and eventually no longer trust themselves to even attempt certain things. It is very important for children to feel that they can learn to do whatever they want to do: they have already learned many skills and the current challenge is simply one more thing to learn.

Decisiveness and concentration

Many people have difficulty making decisions. In this area, too, children will develop problems if they lack models worth imitating. The only thing that helps in overcoming indecision is to realize that any decision is better than none. In other words, we try out a possible solution to the problem and then see whether we've made the right decision or whether we need to modify the decision to make it right. A truly wrong decision is simply another opportunity to take action. Being able to recognize mistakes and learn from them is also well worth imitating. It is very good for children to be around adults who tackle decision-making with confidence. It is not good, however, for children to have to make decisions at too early an age, before they are aware of the possible consequences. But if you take your six-year-old grocery shopping and she puts a jar of chocolate spread into the cart, saying, "Don't make a fuss, Mum!" you know she's fully aware of the consequences!

For children, observing something carefully with an adult or watching adults concentrating on their work provides the best possible example for their own developing ability to concentrate.

Also important is allowing enough time for unwrapping and looking at gifts so that each one can be truly "received" rather than merely superficially registered. When a child receives many gifts at once (for birthdays or Christmas), it is a good practice to open only as many as he can digest at one time, saving the rest for later in the day or even the next day.

Quiet and reflection

If you watch people preparing for major physical or artistic efforts, you can see how they "pull themselves together" and become quiet and focused. The greater their concentration and quiet before they start, the greater their chances of applying all their strength and skill to their performance. It is very good for children to grow up surrounded by people who radiate peace and quiet a certain times or simply sit still and concentrate while reading or observing. Sometimes this stillness makes such an impression on a child that he doesn't dare speak to the silent adult in question but finds something to do nearby in the hope of being noticed. No one who is always rushing from one thing to the next and never finishes anything calmly can possibly set an example of peace and concentration. We must balance tension with relaxation and being busy with taking a break. And how nice it is in such moments of stillness to look at a sunset or watch a bird with your child.

Figure 64.

Figure 65.

Figure 66.

Figures 63–80. All the senses develop together. The child is completely open, like one big differentiated sense-organ. While these pictures show one or the other sense predominating, other senses are also activated (sensory-motor integration).

20

Figure 67.
Figure 68.

Figure 69.

Figure 70.

Figure 72.

Figure 73.

Figure 74.

Figure 75.

Figure 76.

Figure 77.

Figure 78.

20

Figure 79.

Figure 80.

Aggressive behavior

In preschool through the early elementary grades, children naturally tend to move and be active, which often leads to physical confrontations — pushing, shoving, pinching, grabbing toys, and so on. This so-called aggressive behavior is nothing more than will that has not been completely mastered on the bodily level and has not yet been adequately directed toward specific actions. Initiative and the potential for aggression are identical. Because aggression is simply initiative without the appropriate guidance, it is especially important to make sure that children who tend to be restless and aggressive are physically active often enough and long enough. This is much more difficult today, in our sprawling cities, than it was when many children still lived in rural areas. Today this issue must be addressed deliberately, and it may need the cooperation of several sets of parents to help these children get enough opportunity for physical activity in the house, in the garden, or in other types of manual work. And don't forget plain old walking. Not long ago, children had plenty of opportunities to strengthen both their will and their ability to concentrate simply because they had to walk for half an hour or so every day to get to school. On the way, they saw the same things every day and experienced seasonal changes along their route. They passed many people, sometimes the same faces and sometimes new ones. This daily activity was not only a will exercise — an exercise in repetition, in seeing the same things in different ways — but also physical activity of the healthiest sort. Now that children are driven to school in cars or buses, few walk on a regular basis, much to the detriment of their physical stability and will development.

A second important element in raising especially aggressive children is to place enough emphasis on clear, cultivated speech, whether in conversation, telling stories, or reading aloud. Verbal disagreements (quarreling and reconciling) are the best way to defuse pent-up aggression .

Replace rewards and punishments with love for the activity itself

Rewards and punishment elicit conditioned responses, because we naturally attempt to repeat pleasant experiences and avoid unpleasant ones. By responding to rewards and punishments, however, we make ourselves dependent on other people's positive or negative judgments. If you're trying to raise your child to be a free individual, a different approach is needed. Take a good look at your child's activity with freedom of action in mind. Does your child have enough opportunity for actions, no matter how small, that are motivated from within and based on meaningful connections that she experiences for herself? Do you set an example for her by performing necessary activities that she enjoys imitating?

Rudolf Steiner often emphasized that the only truly free and voluntary actions are those performed out of

20

love. Actions performed out of fear or expectation of reward are acts of dependency. Freedom of action develops only when children learn to take personal initiative and above all to enjoy what they do.[39]

Stages in will development

A quick look at the stages of child development reveals a small-scale recapitulation of a process that also took place in the history of the human race. In ancient times, most people still felt that they were guided by outside authorities. The subsequent transformation in how individuals saw themselves is clearly evident in the transition from the Old Testament's "thou shalt" Commandments to voluntary obedience to a single commandment (John 13:34). This transition is graphically portrayed in the parable of the woman accused of adultery (John 8:1–11). A group of men haul the adulteress into court and present her to Jesus, asking him whether or not she should be stoned to death for her transgression, as Mosaic law prescribes. Jesus challenges her accusers to enforce the outer law only if they themselves obey it inwardly: "The one among you who is without sin shall cast the first stone." The remark hits home; one by one, her accusers leave. When Jesus is alone with the woman, he sends her away with a friendly challenge to seize the opportunity for self-improvement.

Personal development parallels historical development in that the will of preschool children is still largely stimulated and guided from outside, through example and imitation. During the elementary school years, sympathy or antipathy for the adult in question is the decisive factor in whether or not a child does what she is supposed to do or learns what she is expected to learn. At this age, children are most easily motivated to act out of love, hate, and fear. Feelings rather than examples become their primary motives. Only in adolescence do young people become so independent of their surroundings that they can be guided by their own inner thoughts and insights, determining for themselves what they do and do not do and why. As long as children's ability to act still depends on other people's examples or their own feelings, they have not come of age; their will is not yet mature. During this time, they really do need help (preferably loving help) from outside.

Feeling and thinking must first achieve a certain degree of maturity before they can motivate and guide independent activity. If we keep this fact in mind, the approach parents and educators must take becomes clear: their role is to stand in (temporarily) for the child's own personality. The adult's needing to dominate, requiring absolute obedience, and making threats like "just wait until I get you" are as inappropriate as allowing children to tyrannize you for fear of alienating them. As children's personalities mature through the different stages of childhood, the measures we implement to educate their will must change accordingly. But what constitutes appropriate "punishment" or "reward"? How can we encourage independent initiative and encourage children to love what they do instead of "training" them by praising and scolding them?

20.2 The area of conflict between punishment and reward

A small child's will rebels when it comes up against limits established by his parents, and his experience of selfhood becomes painfully acute as he opposes adults and feels out of harmony with them. In contrast, if his parents simply watch as his urge to be active plays itself out, or if they allow him to do something that is ordinarily forbidden, his will unfolds freely and he is happy because he "gets his own way." Giving in, providing resistance, making promises, asking for cooperation, distracting or threatening the child — there are so many ways adults can attempt to influence children's behavior in the spectrum that ranges from punishments to rewards.

As parents and teachers, how can we learn to function within this spectrum in the way that is best for our children? A few of the questions and examples we have heard from parents may help clarify this issue:

- My son is stealing from me (age four).
- He's so aggressive, my hand has already slipped a couple of times and I've smacked him. Will he be damaged emotionally if I do that? (age two-and-a-half).
- My five-year-old says "I didn't do it" just as convincingly as his older brother, but in this case I'm sure he's lying. What should I do?
- I think children should be praised or rewarded at least once a day to strengthen their self-esteem.
- My fourteen-year-old plays his CDs at full volume; he's totally inconsiderate about it.
- Why won't she help around the house a bit? She leaves everything lying all over the place. What have I done wrong? (age thirteen)
- He's become so lazy and unenthusiastic. What can I do about it? (age fifteen)
- He was angry, so he kicked a window and broke it. (age eight)
- I told him not to touch my favourite vase, but he grabbed it anyway and broke it. (age three)
- Twice already I've called the kids to come in for supper, and one of them still hasn't come.
- There's enough dessert for everybody, but they still argue about it.

20

These are the kinds of disciplinary issues pediatricians hear about from parents who wonder about how to respond appropriately in each situation.

Conflicting intentions are inevitable, whether among children or adults. Who is allowed to say what to whom? Who has to obey whom? Who has the power? This is one of the most sensitive questions of modern life. In this age of equality and participation, we are becoming increasingly aware of the need for individual freedom and self-determination.[73] And yet life is still full of limits, tasks, and necessities. Individuals function within social contexts — whether in a family, on the job, at play, or during free time — and must learn to manage their intentions and actions in socially acceptable ways.

Examples of punishment

For preschoolers

When Mom's favourite vase gets broken as a result of his carelessness, the best way for a three-year-old to experience the consequences of his actions is to see her sadness and watch her pick up the pieces and get rid of the mess. Because imitation is so strong at this age, he will also feel her sorrow. His mother, however, needs to realize that commands like "You're not allowed to touch that; you might break it" are not appropriate at this age. Precious vases should not be left where a toddler can reach them. At this age, if his mother values something and enjoys handling it, he wants to have it, too, but if the precious vase is out of reach, his imagination will find a substitute for it.

For preschoolers, nonverbal discipline is best. What you do is much more effective than what you say. Putting the vase in a location where nothing can happen to it tells your toddler, "You're not allowed to touch." He needs the logic of reality, not logical explanations. The more unambiguous and certain your actions are (without a lot of talking and endless repetition), the less argumentative and provocative your preschooler will be. By imitating appropriate and meaningful actions, he learns how to act carefully and appropriately himself. This is also the best way to handle other problematic issues at this age.

A four-year-old who takes money out of the drawer usually does it because he's watched his mother do it so many times. This is imitation, not stealing. The same is true of "stealing" toys. At this age, he has not yet learned that the whole world doesn't belong to him. If your child tends to make off with other children's toys, an adult needs to be present when it is time for him to leave and help him put his friend's toys back where they belong.

What should you do when your children make a mess during the meal and climb giggling over the table and chairs even though you tell them to "behave"? In this case, the problem is that they already know that you probably won't enforce what you say. In the past, you probably gave in to them — either laughing or with threats —

when they misbehaved. Or perhaps your spouse said, "Oh, let them do it." The only way to regain control in this situation is to recognize the inconsistency in your own behavior and draw the appropriate conclusions.

What about a five-year-old who lies? He knows exactly what he did. In this case, you should tell him clearly that you know he was involved. But your reaction should also show him that you realize that he says he didn't do it because he really doesn't *want* to be the one who did it. For the sake of his further development, he needs you to trust in his regret *and* let him know that you saw through his lie.

Parents who "let their hands slip" need to realize that when they lose control, they're behaving just like the wild child who is provoking them. In this case, it is important to act emphatically but calmly to set the limits your child needs. It is equally important to avoid exposing him to your own uncontrolled emotions. He is defenseless against them and they will inevitably have negative effects on his development. At this age, any shock works right down into how his organs function. Furthermore, if you hit him, you set a very bad example because your response bears absolutely no relationship to the situation that provoked it. You can be sure that when the opportunity arises, he will imitate you and hit a smaller, weaker child, simply passing along the injustice that was done to him. Later, as an adult, he may wonder why he tends to lash out at others.

For school-age children

At this age, children are ready to be involved in deciding how to make up for damage they have caused. Appealing to their conscience, however, makes sense only when their inner life has developed enough for them to hear their own personal "voice of conscience," which seldom happens before age nine (see also Section 17.3, page 301). Furthermore, developing a conscience depends on processing experiences of good and bad luck, damages and benefits — in other words, on real-life situations, not moralizing sermons.

The eight-year-old who kicks in a window, should watch as the damage is temporarily repaired (by inserting a piece of cardboard or covering the frame with a curtain) so he realizes that it is no longer possible to look out that window. If possible, the new pane of glass should be set in place when the child is present so he can experience how much work and effort is involved in repairing the damage. Here again, his mother should consider the circumstances surrounding the accident and see if she could have done anything differently.

Now let's look at a much more frequent incident: Dinner is ready, and one child is still missing. Hot from running, he arrives fifteen minutes late and reports breathlessly that he hated to drop out of the ball game just before the end. This is not at all the same as habitual lateness and disregarding his mother's calls because her words don't carry much weight with him. He's well aware that he actually should have been home in time for dinner, but he really wanted to finish the game, which is quite understandable. In this case, it is enough for his mother to say, "I'm glad you made it. I thought we were going to have to eat without you." But if adult inconsistency has led to habitual lateness on the children's part, the family will have to start over again to develop good habits together. If someone comes late even after all have agreed to come on time, an appropriate reaction might be, "Please go and eat in the kitchen; the rest of us are nearly done already. We'll try again tomorrow." Another option is to welcome the late child to the table with as few words as possible, meanwhile carrying on a highly interesting conversation about something else.

For adolescents

At this age, "punishment" or "making amends" increasingly becomes something that teenagers should impose on themselves, with adults simply advising or helping them as they make the decision. Teenagers need to practice adapting their actions to the requirements of their surroundings. They need to set their own goals and monitor their own progress. Your fourteen-year-old know that everyone in the family had agreed to keep the volume low, so when your fourteen-year-old plays his CDs at full volume, it is either a deliberate provocation or just carelessness. The appropriate approach is to gently point out that it is too loud. If he doesn't agree and continues to provoke you, tell him that

you'll have to discuss it again and leave it at that for the moment. When the problem comes up in your "family council," it is important for him to take an active part in working out the new agreement. If the overall situation has already deteriorated to such an extent that it is almost impossible for all of you to agree on anything and stick to it, working out the immediate problem will be possible only with the help of a neutral third party or a family therapist.

The thirteen-year-old who leaves her things lying around should be allowed to do so in her own room but not in the rest of the house. Here, too, it is important to reach clear agreements that are revisited and either renewed or adjusted from time to time. At this age, "punishment" consists of the personal insight needed to make up for one's behavior, while the "reward" is the joy and gratitude of others when it works. Adolescents, even more than younger children, need praise and recognition, even it it is just a smile or a little sign that you've noticed their efforts and don't take them for granted.

If your teenager hurts someone, you should consider together what he can do that would help or please the injured person. If he steals or damages something, returning, repairing, or replacing the item is in order. Such incidents, however, are always signals that your teenager is either missing out on conversations or close contact with you or carrying around disappointments that he cannot overcome. It may be necessary to find someone else who can talk with him, because parents may no longer be the right people to do that at this age.

Examples of "rewards"

"When we get to the top, we'll all have some juice!" When you're on a long hike, this incentive lends speed and strength to your family's tired limbs. In this case, the reward actually does have something to do with the effort you've expended and helps you celebrate reaching your goal.

"If you get to bed quickly, I'll read you another story." This is also a legitimate reward, because if your child doesn't hurry, it will be too late for reading aloud.

"If you run to the corner store and get some bread for me, you can buy yourself an ice cream while you're there." In this case, there is no connection between the action and the reward. The situation is somewhat different if Marian, after having a visibly hard time tearing herself away from her doll, experiences how grateful her mother is for her help when she returns. She might even find a nice new red bow in her doll's hair.

What about praise? Acknowledgment and praise strengthen a child's self-esteem. By experiencing your pleasure at his accomplishments, she learns something about the effects of what she does. If your praise is emphatic and exaggerated, however, she will be slightly surprised to learn that some-thing she did as a matter of course is so praiseworthy, and she may realize that she could in fact have done some-thing different (and less desirable). Although she was totally immersed in her action, hearing it praised as some-thing special sets her apart from it. This type of distancing is not good, especially for preschoolers.

When your child has an urgent desire for something, it should always be taken seriously. In some cases, the item is an immediate necessity — for example, a hinge for the playhouse door — and should be purchased soon. In other cases, it may need to wait for Christmas or the next birthday because "maybe we can manage it then." In a third instance, it may be desirable to try to shift your child's burning desire to something else. How about a new ball or a dart board instead of that toy pistol? Granting or not granting a specific wish, however, should not be used as a reward or punishment.

Is money ever an appropriate reward? If we pay children for doing dishes, cleaning up, running errands, and so on, we teach them — as unpopular as it may sound — an erroneous social attitude, namely, that the primary purpose of work is personal material gain rather than helping or pleasing others. When children are paid for routine chores, they usually spend the money on things that they assume their parents would not take seriously or would not let them have. As a result, they unconsciously begin to believe that we have to look out for ourselves when it comes to fulfilling

20

personal desires, since we can't expect much from others in this regard. Conversely, if your child senses that you recognize her needs and desires and that her work is useful to others, this lays the groundwork for a very different view of society, namely, that we serve others through our work, and these others in turn take care of our needs. If we encourage this attitude in our children, we might gradually be able to transform our modern attitude toward life, which is based almost exclusively on manifestations of egotism, into a brotherly or sisterly approach to society's economic aspects.

The situation is different, of course, when your child needs to save up for some larger item. In this case, it is appropriate for him to help make the purchase possible. Beginning around age nine or ten, it is important for your child to become aware that money has to be earned to make it possible to buy things. At this point, children can be paid for doing work they formerly did simply to please others or because they enjoyed it. We all must learn to live with the important paradox that work that we do out of our own free will can nonetheless be paid for. Accepting this paradox is the only way we adults can avoid selling our labor as if it were a material product. Viewing our work as both voluntary and paid also allows us to separate our sense of self-worth from our monetary income and makes it easier for us to find meaningful activity if we become unemployed.

Inappropriate rewards unrelated to the offence lead to a self-centred attitude towards life — that is, to doing things primarily for recognition, honor, or financial gain instead of for their own sake.

Inappropriate punishment leads to the attitude that misbehaving and making mistakes are inherently bad or "evil" and that being "nice" and not making mistakes are the normal state of affairs. If we do not realize that learning and becoming human are not possible without mistakes, failures, and errors, we attempt to construct a facade or semblance of infallibility and moral perfection around ourselves. Learning from experience, working to correct our mistakes and imperfections, and being *privileged* to make mistakes, however, are specifically and universally human attributes.

21. Sleep Disorders and Other Problems at Home

In this chapter, we will discuss frequently asked questions about the strange behavior or physical disturbances parents notice in their children. Pinning down the exact causes of these problems may involve extensive conversations with your family doctor or pediatrician, and in some cases referral to a child/adolescent psychiatrist is also indicated. Often, however, some help in understanding the child and some tips on discipline are all that's needed.

21.1 Sleep disorders

Not sleeping through the night

Here are a few examples to show how greatly children's sleeping problems vary:

A nine-month-old infant wakes up every night between 11 pm and 1 am and cries inconsolably as long as he remains in his own bed. Against their principles, his parents eventually give in and take him to his mother's bed, where he sleeps soundly. One night they realize, quite by chance, that nothing separates him from the uninsulated outer wall of the house except

the bars of his crib. As soon as they hang a veil over the head of the crib, he sleeps through the night. Cold air sinking down along the wall past his head had been waking him.

A two or three-month-old infant wakes up each night at exactly 11:12 and is sound asleep again thirty seconds later. It takes a while before her parents discover the cause — the faint drone of a jetliner passing by high overhead.

A toddler is finally able to sleep with her door shut, and her parents are greatly pleased at this accomplishment. But one night a sudden gust of wind blowing across the top of the chimney produces a dull sound like the foghorn of an ocean liner. She wakes up screaming, and from then on she is reluctant to sleep in the dark and shutting her door is out of the question.

An infant who sleeps in his parents' room cries every night. Even in his mother's bed, he is so restless that no one gets any sleep. They go through hour-long rituals with bottles, singing, games, and so on, but the effect never lasts long before the whole show starts over again. When the situation assumes emergency proportions, the baby is put back in his older brother's room, where he had originally slept. His parents had taken him into their own room as a preventive measure because the older boy always got up and came over to his parents whenever the baby woke up. Strangely enough, the house is quiet from that night onward. Both children sleep through the night without waking up.

We mentioned earlier that babies sometimes smile briefly in their sleep as if sensing a parent's presence. Similarly, some infants and toddlers open their eyes whenever their father or mother tiptoes into the room, no matter how quietly, but sleep soundly when a sibling is crying loudly right next to them. Sometimes a screaming toddler will calm down if you simply allow him some space and are not anxious about the situation. Conversely,

his restlessness increases if you yourself don't know what to do and your thoughts are going around in circles.

Possible causes

The causes of children's sleeping problems are as varied as their manifestations. Below is a list of possibilities to check in each individual case. This information is also important if you need to consult a doctor about the problem.

- How was the child feeling that day and that evening? Was she outside a lot and did she have enough exercise? Did you notice any physical or emotional symptoms — stomach wind, constipation, sweating, chills, jealousy, discontentedness?
- How were you feeling? Were you overtired, unhappy, discontented, working outside the home? Did you feel unappreciated, overstressed, or unable to enjoy life? Did you have problems with your in-laws, housemates, or neighbors? Were you anxious or worried about the future?
- What about the child's surroundings — the bed, the apartment, noise, radio and television, toys? (See the relevant chapters.)
- Has your child ever woken during the night for a legitimate but temporary reason that may have become a tyrannical habit? (For example, did you let her sleep in your bed when she was ill?)

Some other possibilities are:
- an evening meal that included high-fiber, wind-producing foods

- wearing a wool cap during warm weather
- a younger sibling who just learned to walk (feelings of jealousy typically appear at this time)
- constant scolding and prohibitions during the day. (For example, do you often have to tell your child to be quiet during the day because you will be threatened with eviction if she makes too much noise in the apartment?)

After considering these different perspectives and coming to a conclusion about why your child can't sleep through the night, the next question is what to do about it. Here are a few recommendations:

The most important but least expected rule for parents is: *A mother's sleep is sacred.* As a mother, you (and, if need be, your partner) must make sure that you get enough sleep. Without it, you can't possibly put in sixteen to eighteen hour days and remain patient and interested. The baby is the last person to worry about, since it is usually easy for him to make up for lack of sleep.

Do not get up at night more often than absolutely necessary. You may be able to place the baby's crib next to your bed and reach a hand between the bars when she gets restless. Most children fall asleep again as soon as they know that Mommy's right there. If there's no room for the crib beside your bed and you can't rearrange your bedroom furniture to accommodate it, sleep on a comfortable mattress in the baby's room. If you're dealing with a toddler, she should sleep in a crib; an open bed is impractical because it is much easier for her to tyrannize you if she can get out easily. Reaching one hand into her bed works well until your baby is about a year old. After that, a better strategy is to let her see you lying there quietly in the dim light from the street. Outwardly, you are totally quiet and relaxed (inwardly, too, as best you can manage). Say only once, "Sleep well, Mommy's sleeping too." After that, don't respond to anything your child says or does. After five minutes, she'll put her thumb in her mouth and lie down and go to sleep. Since she's a natural imitator, there's nothing else she can do. The situation is totally different if you jump up every time she makes a peep. Of course you'll find her standing straight up in bed and making all her usual demands.

Take your child into your own bed only as a last resort and only if you yourself are able to sleep under those circumstances. You may want to make an exception to this rule when your child is ill, but in that case it is best for the other parent to sleep somewhere else.

Regardless of what you do when your child wakes up at night, only one parent should respond. The disruption is simply multiplied if two adults have their sleep interrupted and have different ideas about what to do next.

At roughly eighteen months, when they are learning to talk, children develop an intuitive understanding of the measures their parents are implementing. At this age, they quickly

21

learn to recognize limits, which they could not do before. For example, during a serious illness at age fifteen months, one little boy developed the habit of waking up once or twice each night and crying until his mother came to him. By the time the legitimate reasons (discomfort due to illness or thirst due to fever) disappeared, waking up and crying had become a habit.

It is quite normal for children to wake up either fully or partially at some point during the night. This has nothing to do with a real sleep disorder. Some children simply put their thumbs in their mouths and go back to sleep, others just turn over, still others sing themselves to sleep. Some, however, develop the habit of having Mommy pick them up, give them bottles and kisses, sing songs and play other little games. By the time this scenario has been repeated every night for three to five months, Mom is at the end of her tether and takes the problem to her doctor, who advises her to accommodate her child only to the extent of leaving a door open or night light on, or letting him fall asleep in her bed before taking him to his own. You can also sleep on a mattress next to your child's bed, or he can sleep a crib next to yours, but if he wakes you up, issue just one loving but significant warning: "Sleep well, Mommy wants to sleep, too." And then, "Otherwise Mommy will have to put you back in your room" (or shut the door or whatever limit you decided on).

Even if your child doesn't understand the content of your words, he senses the mood that lies behind them. That's why it is essential for you to mean what you say. If you're lucky, it works. If not, you must push his crib back into his room and ignore his deafening screams. We know from daily experience that many mothers' entire philosophy of bringing up children falls apart at this point. After all, they want the best for their children; they want everything to be beautiful and loving. In reality, however, children become increasingly unhappy, disagreeable, and unsatisfied if they never encounter firm limits or sincere intentions. When Mom changes her tactics and inserts rational actions into the mother-child relationship, the child's need for clear limits are satisfied. This is usually impossible without a temporary, therapeutic crisis. It is worth it to persist, however, because the success is soon clearly visible in the child.

The most important rule for implementing any of these measures is to speak with actions, not words. Don't ask, explain, or threaten. Often this approach is so foreign to the adults embroiled in such a situation that a conversation with their pediatrician is needed before they can grasp the purpose and importance of such measures. A talk with your pediatrician is also in order if you spouse does not agree on how to proceed or if one of you can't face the turmoil. In the latter instance, the doctor should advise the parent with the weaker nerves to go away on vacation for two weeks.

Meanwhile, let's assume that your

child's bed is standing in the kitchen to keep the disturbance to a minimum. Now the drama unfolds: You hear her screaming. You *must* ignore it for five minutes, but don't ignore it for more than ten. When this painful waiting period is over, regardless of whether your child is quiet or still screaming, open the door and ask in a friendly tone of voice, "Are you ready to be quiet?" and take her back to her room (or wherever you want her to sleep). But if her screaming intensifies, say "When you're ready, I'll come back" and then shut the door. Repeat the procedure after another five minutes — again, regardless of whether your child is quiet or screaming. Your conciliatory attitude is important. If you have been inconsistent in the past, not doing what you said you would do, the torment will continue for a while, but after a couple of repetitions an eighteen-month-old usually understands that there's nothing to be gained from more crying. You may need to stand beside her bed and put up with her screaming for a bit. The important thing is that your reaction is now calm and deliberate — totally different from how you used to behave. No "calming" flood of words, no despairing "Oh, poor baby," no picking her up, no kiss. Maybe just a little quiet humming or singing. If all of this doesn't work in five minutes, go out and shut the door and start over again. The atmosphere will be crawling with intensity because you want her to get to the point where you can say, "Good, now you're ready."

From the very beginning, your attitude must conciliatory, but you must not abandon the objective, necessary limit you've decided on. The next night, calling out to your child to be quiet (again, in a friendly tone of voice) is usually enough. You should be quite sure, however, that your child isn't coming down with an infection — a legitimate reason for crying — just as you begin to insist on a change of habits. And it makes no sense to shut the door if she can open it. Lock it quietly and deliberately, or keep a broomstick handy to jam the handle.

The bad habit of giving your child a bottle in bed makes the situation more difficult. It helps to simply place the usual bottle of herb tea nearby, without giving it to her. She may sleep through without needing to drink if her "slave" doesn't hand her the bottle. You can achieve the same results by gradually reducing the sugar content of her nighttime bottle to zero. Or tell her cheerfully one day, "You're so big now, you don't need a bottle any more. Instead, this little gnome who will tell you a story if you wake up," or something like that. Knitted woolen gnomes and dwarfs are especially suitable sleeping companions at this age (see Bibliography for instructions). They can also comfort sick children and are sometimes even an acceptable substitute for having Mommy around all the time.

21

Bedtime fusses and children who have trouble falling asleep

Like children who wake up at night, little ones who have trouble falling asleep often fuss simply out of habit. Changing your child's bedtime ritual can be the basis for drawing new, helpful limits. For example:

- Hang a blue cloth with a couple of gold stars on the wall or over his bed to make a "starry sky."

- A new sleeping companion — maybe the above-mentioned gnome — appears to wish him good night.

- By candlelight, sing a song or play a piece on a children's harp, kantele, or recorder. If you've been doing all this, it may be time to abandon these habits and try something new and fun that may even take a bit more time. Being allowed to stay up a little longer and hear a brief story as he sits on the sofa with you will make your child feel grown up and privileged. After the story, though, it is definitely time for bed.

- When your child gets up and comes out of his room for the first time, calmly take him back to bed and tell him that you're going to shut the door if he comes out again. The second time, shut the door — equally calmly, of course. If he can turn the light on by himself, disconnect the fuse as a preemptive measure, but make sure the blinds let in a bit of light from outside. Use the five minute wait as described above. The door stays open only when he stays in bed.

- Children are smart — by the second evening, they accept the new limits. These measures actually fail — which is deeply disappointing to the children — only when parents don't have the courage to carry out the consequences they've decided upon.

- A different type of difficulty in falling asleep is due to nervousness; your child somehow gets the idea that she can't fall asleep. There are any number of different possible causes: being overtired, hot weather, excitement, knowing that you're going away, the start of the holidays. In this case, try singing a song or giving your child something of yours — perhaps a sweater or the blanket from your bed — to keep in bed with her. Tuck her in again and stroke her hair to comfort her. Sometimes the best tactic may be to let her come into the living room for a bit and look at a book by herself. Say something like, "When you're tired, you can just put yourself back to bed." In this case, of course, you avoid carrying on a conversation with her and are visibly involved in activities that have nothing to do with her. Boredom, together with pride in being old enough to know when she's tired, will usually send her back to bed soon.

Nocturnal fears

Sudden screaming at night can have a variety of causes, different in six to eighteen-month-olds than in three-year-olds. The first time this symptom appears, check whether your child is wide awake or screaming in his sleep because of a bad dream. If the latter, cuddle him or wake him up gently. Then check for signs of pain (hard abdomen), fever, or difficulty breathing through his nose. Finally, try to recall whether he had a frightening experience that day. Did you notice any unusual fearfulness? Your own assessment of his symptoms will determine whether you need to consult your pediatrician (see also the relevant chapters in Part 1). Children with "night terrors" scream or moan in their sleep or toss and turn in bed and can neither wake up immediately nor go back to sleeping peacefully. Here, too, be alert for unusual events during the day and foods that might cause gas or wind. Restlessness that reappears at four-week intervals may be related to lunar phases. In most cases, anthroposophical or homeopathic medications are very effective.

Sleepwalking

Sleepwalking, which occurs most frequently at full moon, can be dangerous if the sleepwalker wakes up while wandering around. This symptom also responds to the types of medications mentioned above. As with nocturnal anxiety, psychotropic drugs are not necessary.

21.2 Children who won't eat

A few examples from our pediatric practice:

An alert, cheerful three-year-old is brought into the consultation room. His mother says, "He doesn't eat anything at all."

"But what does he eat?"

Mother: "Nothing. He doesn't touch anything I give him. He could drink milk and eat yogurt all day long, though." On closer questioning, it turns out that he also eats a few sweets between meals. Nonetheless, his mother is right; he really doesn't eat any food she makes for him.

Solution: Withhold dairy products completely for at least a week, then give him a maximum of two cups of milk or yogurt a day. No between-meal snacks and no sweetened drinks. He will soon develop an appetite for other foods.

21

Another mother reports the same thing about her little boy, except he doesn't drink milk. In this case, closer questioning reveals that he does eat cottage cheese, eggs, and meat as well as ice cream, soda, and other snacks at regular intervals. At the dinner table, though, he eats very little.

Solution: No snacks between meals; reserve eating for sit-down meals. At the table, it is important to enjoy your own food and the table conversation as much as possible and to disregard your child's eating habits.

A slight, small-boned little girl with delicate features and slim hands comes into the office. She never eats more than a tidbit of anything and refuses to touch her grandma's nice veal broth. Among other things, the pediatrician asks her mother about her birth weight and what her parents looked like at the same age.

Solution: Try to arrange an active vacation in the country or in the mountains, preferably with other children. It is essential to let go of your expectations during this time. Pay no particular attention to your child's eating habits and let her decide for herself how much she's going to eat. Fresh air and imitation will increase her appetite. Back at home, she may not each much more than before, but at least the atmosphere will be more relaxed.

A mother comes in with a rather stiff and sullen-looking boy. He doesn't do many things that she expects of him, and of course that includes eating.

In this case, the solution will probably be found only after a private few conversations with his mother, who needs to realize that children's purpose in life is not necessarily to realize their parents' favorite expectations. Children do best when they do not have constant questions, reproaches, explanations, and requests imposed on them but are allowed to follow the example of their parents' own behavior.

Another child eats absolutely nothing except red grape juice and one particular brand of cookie.

This situation will not improve until her mother can sit at the table and calmly enjoy everything she has cooked; she must find some way other than fad diets to watch her own weight.

Some eating problems arise because mothers are overworked and underappreciated and their children take all of their time and attention. Being clear-headed enough to prepare meals with love, avoid between-meal snacks, do justice to as many family demands as possible, and always be in a good mood is much easier said than done.

By way of consolation, here's a quick glimpse into the paradise that even pediatricians know only in their dreams: The kids come home thirsty, but until the meal is ready they're content with a glass of the unsweetened herb tea that's ready and waiting for them. The candies that they were given or received in trade on the way home from school go into a nice box; when it is full, they can trade it in for a real leather soccer ball or something else useful. The radio is not on when they arrive, so their mother can welcome them home, hear the news about their day, and notice their moods without being distracted. Everyone sits down to eat at the same time. Before the meal begins, everyone says grace or sings a song together and then joins hands to wish each other *"bon appétit"* or say "may the meal be blessed." The meal is a real family event. Everyone looks forward to the food, asks each other questions, and indulges in some gentle mutual teasing. There is almost no talk about the food as such. Each person eats as much as he or she wants, usually something of everything. Each child has *one* dish that he or she never has to eat; anything else that causes difficulties is mashed up and mixed in with something else. Or everyone agrees to abide by a single rule: we each have to eat three spoonfuls of everything on the table. Usually, the conversation is so interesting that the children stay in their seats until everyone is finished. Then perhaps everyone takes hands to follow the Swedish custom of saying "Thank you for the meal" — *tack för maten.*

21.3 Bedwetting

If bedwetting continues until age four, your child should be examined by a pediatrician. The causes may be either constitutional, physical or psychological.

The measures discussed below are helpful when physical causes have been ruled out. In such cases, bedwetting is a symptom that says to parents, "I want to wear diapers so I can feel little and protected again."

The first step is to look for shocks, reasons for jealousy, after-effects of illness, and the like. Once these issues are clarified, it is usually worth trying to accommodate your child's need for more protection and comfort. Allow him to be "little" and "protected" again for a while by consciously reverting to old habits from his earlier childhood. Meanwhile, try to make the course of the day more regular and consistent and carry him in your consciousness more than you would otherwise. At the preschool age, do not address the bedwetting situation directly, but do look for other ways to solve the problem.

When a younger sibling is born or has just learned to walk — events that could make you pay less attention to your older child — give him an extra big hug to help him share your joy in this event. Show him that you are

21

proud of him for being so big. Instead of giving him a bottle like the baby's, give him a special new drinking cup or special silverware of his own — without commenting on it. If he's used to hearing stories you make up, they can include symbolic representations of bedwetting, such as a flooded brook or overflowing spring that people have to control with a little boy's help. Or tell him about an old man who has to struggle every day with the sluice that controls the water level in a fishpond until a little boy comes along and helps him or takes over the job.

Punishing bedwetting with spankings or trying to scare your child out of it with cold showers simply intensifies your child's need for more attention and makes the condition worse. If your child feels accommodated and appreciated, however, some extra attentiveness on your part will eliminate the problem. For example, if your child regularly wets the bed at 10:30 pm and 6:00 am, accompany on his last trip to the bathroom before bedtime and encourage him to make a "nice, big pee." An hour or two after he goes to bed, watch for signs of restlessness; when you suspect his bladder is full, take him to the bathroom, put him on the toilet, and say a few quiet, encouraging words. Do the same thing at six o'clock in the morning (if it doesn't mean you lose too much sleep). You'll need to wake up before your child does. These efforts on your part mean that you accept part of the responsibility for keeping him dry. Watch for the right time to give this responsibility back to your child. This method

doesn't work for children who wet the bed at unpredictable times during the night or who resist your efforts to wake them. It is also of questionable value if your child sleeps so soundly he doesn't notice he's wet. In that case, you'll need to decide whether to resort to diapers at night or whether a rubber mattress protector is enough.

A consistent daily routine, especially with regard to eating and drinking habits, will help strengthen your child's constitution. If you're not willing to establish a regular rhythm for what goes in, you can't expect regularity in what comes out. Attempting to treat bedwetting makes no sense if your child is a non-stop or "on demand" drinker. In this case, the first step is to restrict drinking to mealtimes, when you can control the quantities.

It is important to dress a bed wetter warmly in wool underwear or tights (heavier or lighter, depending on the season) that cover as much of his torso as possible. If his feet get wet and cold, give him a warm footbath and rub his feet with massage oil afterward. Rubbing his legs with St John's wort oil in the mornings also helps. Finally, make sure that your child sees enough activities that are worth imitating and challenge him to develop further. The feeling of "coasting along in neutral" encourages him to regress to earlier stages of development. Other triggers such as conflict at home, having two working parents, or an impending divorce usually indicate that a talk with a child psychologist or pediatrician is needed.

Assuming that physical causes have

been ruled out, the same measures apply if your child wets during the day as well as at night. You will also need to set an "internal alarm clock" for him during the day, which is exactly what you do with a younger child who is learning to stay dry. Introduce new toilet habits, such as specific times for sitting on the toilet or the potty seat, without talking about the situation.

The cause of "leakage" and damp underwear also needs to be clarified. Often this is simply a sign of inattentiveness. If that's the case, accompany your child to the toilet whenever possible, and encourage him to get out the last drop. Abandon this tactic if your child enjoys this type of attention too much.

Once children are seven or eight years old, a different approach is appropriate. Once they are ready for school, they are also ready and willing to listen to adults they respect and trust, such as teachers, godparents, doctors, and so on. Direct reproaches, however, are still too much for them. A time-tested method is for an adult confidant to tell a little story that mentions wetting directly. For example, "At night, there's a little gnome (or a bird or a fairy, as you like) on your shoulder who stays awake while you sleep and whispers secretly in our ear, 'Wake up, you need to go to the bathroom.' But you just lie there and don't hear anything, even though he's trying so hard to help you. Try paying really close attention at night and see if you can hear him. If you do, you'll wake up and go quietly to the bathroom. You just have to decide to do that before you go to sleep. Your mother will remind you about it when she says good night." The person telling the story then asks you to whisper mysteriously in your child's ear each evening, "Don't forget to listen to the little gnome!" It is usually less effective if a parent tells this story.

This approach works because your child really doesn't want to wet the bed any more. The gnome, bird, or fairy becomes a symbol of his intention to wake up, which is still not strong enough. Allowing this symbolic image to grow in your child's consciousness by reminding him every evening can help strengthen his weak intentions and make it easier for him to wake up.

We feel that children of this age are still too young for direct admonishments. "Appealing to their conscience" is appropriate only after age nine, when it is also more effective for a third party (the child's physician is the best choice) to implement the treatment. Sometimes a temporary change of scenery is helpful because it strengthens your child's self-awareness and forces him to rely more on his own. Depending on your child's constitution and maturity, it may also be possible to train his bladder by deliberately increasing the time between trips to the bathroom. At this stage, it is good for children to determine their own schedule of eating and drinking.

Using a bedwetting alarm may also work, but usually only in combination with a parent who cheerfully supervises the trip to the bathroom.

21

21.4 Soiling

By soiling, we mean that your child deliberately deposits her stools in her pants or in a corner of the room. This is different from the dirty pants of a constipated or forgetful child, which simply need humorous attention on your part and increased efforts to adapt your daily routine to your child's bowel habits. Very few readers of this book will ever encounter true soiling (encopresis). Occasional soiling is usually a consequence of turbulent interpersonal situations and a sign that the child is either looking for a way out, testing her parents, or afraid of an unfamiliar toilet or potty seat. These situations are easy to recognize and correct. Soiling that persists for weeks and months, however, is always a sign of resignation on the part of both the child and her parents, and in most cases success is unlikely without outside help. Anyone with connections to the family should encourage the parents to contact a pediatrician, child psychiatrist, or family counseling center.

21.5 Thumb sucking

When a child is sucking his thumb, he is sealed off from the outer world and feels comfortably self-contained. If you pull a two-year-old thumb-sucker's thumb out of his mouth, it pops right back in as if attached to an invisible spring. If you hold it to prevent it from going back in, the child awakens reluctantly from his dreamy state and acknowledges the intrusion with displeasure. But if he hears you scraping pudding off the bottom of a saucepan or getting the stroller ready for a walk, his thumb will pop out by itself at these tempting sounds, and if you tried to get him to put it back in his mouth, he would resist as vehemently as he does when you try to make him stop sucking it.

Specially shaped pacifiers are often recommended because deep penetration during thumb sucking is known to cause jaw deformation. We advise against pacifiers because they encourage children to suck even when they would not do so spontaneously. And because a pacifier on a string around your child's neck is always available, it can easily be misused to keep him quiet or independently occupied or to deceive him into thinking that food is on the way. A thumb, although also always available, is preferable because it has a self-renewing surface that is less susceptible to fungal contamination, and your child will never keep his thumb in his mouth when he wants to play actively. If you do decide to give your child a pacifier, do not fasten it around his neck, but use a simple cordtied to his pajamas.

Jaw deformation due to thumb sucking often reverses itself spontaneously when the permanent teeth begin to emerge and thumb sucking gradually stops. In any case, a thumb (or other fingers) in the mouth is not the only cause of jaw deformation. We have also seen cases due to pacifier use.

Some of our readers will surely ask whether this means it is best to do nothing at all about thumb sucking. We recommend not trying to stop your child from sucking his thumb before he falls asleep at night. For daytime thumb sucking, patience is often the best approach. Five-year-olds sometimes decide from one day to the next that they are done with thumb sucking forever and actually stick to their deci-sion. One mother even noticed her child's hand jerking away from his mouth as he slept. On the other hand, if your three-year-old develops a callus on his thumb, a bandage may help break the habit earlier. Cover the callus with ointment and gauze, secure the thumb bandage with a gauze strip tied around his wrist, and cover his entire hand with a little cloth sack. Your child will be astonished at the changed appearance of this extremity, and your pleasure will tell him that everything is just fine. Change the bandage daily for a week and then leave it off. By then, your child may have forgotten about sucking his thumb. *Do not* use adhesive bandages, which can be swallowed.

Thumb sucking indicates the persistence of an earlier developmental stage (nursing), so neither forbidding nor encouraging thumb sucking are appropriate responses. If you sense your child needs more of the physical self-perception that nursing once supplied, you can help him by lovingly stroking his head as he falls asleep or by encouraging active interaction with his surroundings.

21

21.6 Nail biting and picking

Contrary to popular opinion, nail biting and nail picking have nothing to do with calcium deficiency. They are two of the many nervous or habitual gestures that can develop as a result of psychological pressure, stress, embarrassment, boredom, or fatigue. Children can break these habits if they themselves want to, but parental scolding is more likely to make the habit worse. The first thing that parents can do to help is to pay attention to whether their own behavior toward the child is overly demanding or stressful and whether they are providing enough opportunities for meaningful activities. A nail biter usually becomes very interested in nail care if she is given a nice big nail file of her own and a beautiful little pair of nail scissors. Show her how to file down all the rough edges and remove hanging bits of dead skin each morning. Complete each session with a moisturizing cream, because the soothing effects of saliva on dry, itching skin is the most common reason for nails to find their way into your child's mouth. Once this irritation is eliminated, the habit either disappears or is brought under conscious control. Of course this method is suitable only for older children.

21.7 Harmless compulsions

At some point, almost every child insists on walking *only* on the kerb or stepping only on the joints in the paving stones or the spaces between them, as the case may be. This type of behavior is not truly compulsive, however, unless the child cannot move without obeying specific rules and disobeying them provokes anxiety. All habits and regularly repeated movements have the potential to become compulsive, but actual compulsions develop only when the gesture or action is separated from any meaningful context and is performed exclusively for its own sake. In this case, it is important to find educational approaches and/or medications that will strengthen your child's I and make it easier for her to control her movements again. If you notice compulsive counting, hand-washing, turning round and round, or counting in your school-age child, for example, it is time to consult your pediatrician or a child psychiatrist.

21.8 Rocking and pillow banging

Many children rock themselves to sleep with regular, rhythmical movements, which may also be repeated compulsively as they wake up. These gestures, like thumb sucking or masturbation, intensify a child's perception of his own body. The self-selected rhythm relaxes the child and sends him into a trance-like state. These symptoms occur in their most pronounced form in mentally handicapped, brain-damaged, or neglected children, but most of the children whose parents consult us about them are neither handicapped nor neglected.

Quiet singing and gently stroking your child's restless head, especially his forehead, before he goes to sleep, can help release accumulated inner tension, but don't count on rapid success. Constitutional factors are always involved when children choose this instead of some other way of reacting to stress. Long-term use of an appropriate anthroposophical or homeopathic constitutional remedy is also helpful in some cases. In most cases, the symptom disappears by itself when the child reaches school age, or perhaps even later.

21.9 Tics and restlessness

To physicians, a tic means an involuntarily repeated rudimentary movement such as blinking, grimacing, throat clearing, head shaking, shoulder shrugging, etc. Affected individuals often experience brief tension that is released by the gesture. This tension is not evident during states of heightened concentration but returns when the person relaxes or feels that she is being observed. It is also increased by excessive demands on the senses and by psychological stress that cannot be processed by the child or those around

her. Tics often disappear by themselves if they are ignored.

Less common and less easily identifiable is a subtle, generalized, tic-like restlessness that pervades all of a child's movements and makes her appear clumsy. Poor handwriting or behavior problems may also draw attention to this condition either at home or in school.

These symptoms sometimes overlap but must not be confused with involuntary movements that develop with an excess of audiovisual media.

21

Here, the grimacing is caricature-like and the children's behavior includes stereotypical postures of defense and attack such as the familiar "stick 'em up." Tongue-clicking and funny grunting sounds are also common. These behaviors are pieces of experiential sequences that have assumed an automatic character. The children's imaginations are filled with fixed images that are then transformed into movement. Parents rarely recognize such behavior as problematic, but without their cooperation nothing can be done when a problem due to TV watching or comic books is diagnosed.

It often takes an experienced physician to differentiate these movement disorders from each other and from hyperactivity syndrome (see Section 22.1), and in fact the transitions among these conditions are fluid, especially in children who started watching television before age three (see also Sectrion 27.1). These children may break delicate objects suddenly, deliberately, forcefully, and without provocation. They inspect unfamiliar objects only for their most primitive attributes — that is, hardness, fragility, and whether they are good for throwing or hammering. In such a case, objects no longer "speak" to the child, who cannot relate to them appropriately with the help of his senses and movements. In extreme cases, a child like this may become isolated and relate to other people either not at all or only on a very superficial level. He may give the impression of carrying on a conversation, but it is limited to a constant stream of questions and he does not wait for the answers. We get the impression that we are not meeting the child's I, the central focus of his being. In such cases, physicians will say that the child, although not actually autistic in the psychiatric sense, has autistic traits. The development of language is also often disturbed in such children.

A physician has observed and examined the child and acquired an overview of the factors involved by talking with the child and his parents will then be able to suggest therapeutic measures. Regardless of the predominantly neurological (physical or organic) or psychological nature of the disorders, the following educational measures have proved helpful in all the cases mentioned above:

A structured daily routine that alternately emphasizes movement and perceptual activity. Regular times for eating, going to sleep, and waking up. Concentration and attention can develop when the child's natural urge to move is allowed to express itself in structured ways such as movement games that involve rhythmic clapping, stamping, and singing. Eurythmy and curative eurythmy are also helpful, especially for tics. After periods of free play and running around, telling stories with clear images that have not yet become fixed in the child's imagination provides a calming element for the child's restless inner life.

Constant reproaches, demands, and comments simply increase a child's restlessness. It is helpful to ask yourself why your child has to be just as he is and why he can't be different. Your own objective overview will lead to solutions.

Eliminate all use of media — radio, cassettes, recorded fairy tales, television, video games— and comics.

Substitute daily structured play, such as the constructive, supervised free play of a Waldorf kindergarten. Hand puppets, marionettes, or shadow puppets (see *Bibliography)* also gradually allow fixed, stereotyped images to recede in favor of images that support and stimulate independent imagination.

21.10 Masturbation

Children's masturbation is simply a symptom like any other and is not a sign of "perversion."

In infants, masturbation may be triggered by the itching of diaper rash as it heals, or it may appear as babies discover their own bodies. It will disappear after a while if you simply turn your baby on his side and place a favorite object in his hand.

When your older infant or toddler is falling asleep, you may notice rhythmical rubbing or rocking of the pelvis and upper legs, either with or without a pillow or a doll between the legs. The child seems absent or already half asleep and may be drenched with sweat when the movement ends. Consult your pediatrician before making any attempts to stop this behavior. In any case, make sure that your child

gets physically tired from spontaneous play during the day, and provide more physical contact by picking him up more often and carrying him on your shoulders once in a while when you go for walks.

Habitual, excessive masturbation in a somewhat older child is usually triggered or increased by the same factors as thumb sucking and rocking): rejection, lack of friends, boredom, psychological pressure, or overly strict discipline. The goal in all these cases is to restore balance to the child's soul life. Encourage him to develop new interests that distract his attention from his own body. Physically strenuous games and hikes, avoiding excessive intellectual demands, and reading aloud to your child at night until he is just about to fall asleep are all helpful.

21

21.11 Mischievousness

We hope this section will give you some tips on helping your mischievous child develop consideration for the people around her. Mischievousness has nothing to do with aggression. Thinking up April Fool's jokes, taking the neighbours' garden gate off its hinges and leaving it a couple of hundred yards away, ringing the doorbells of people they don't know and watching their reactions from a safe distance, or putting sugar in the salt container and vice versa are all signs of intelligence and initiative (in other words, signs that the child's "I" has developed a certain strength) as well as a forerunner of that much appreciated adult quality, a sense of humour. Of course this type of mischief must not be confused with the type of sadistic, harmful and seemingly malicious behavior that can be an expression of desperate family situations.

It is fortunate when children grow up around adults who remember their own mischievous days and are therefore able to relate to childish tricks even if they have to intervene when they really go too far. Playing tricks is an expression of excess energy and intelligence at work and a sign that the child's need for activity has not yet found a suitable outlet. Later, such energy will be transformed into thoughtful actions and initiatives, with an ability to have insight into the upsets — large and small, comical or serious — that will be thrown up in everyday life.

21.12 Obesity

The following examples illustrate the two scenarios involving overweight children that most frequently come to the attention of pediatricians.

A two-year-old who weighs as much as a four to five-year-old enjoys food, has a good appetite, drinks a lot, and has at least one parent of similar build. In this case, the pediatrician is usually the only one who has a problem with the child's weight; no one else shares his concerns about the child's impaired mobility, possible respiratory and cardiovascular symptoms, and future health. In the unlikely event that the child's obesity prompted the visit to the doctor, successful treat-

ment depends on the parents being willing to subject themselves to a weight-loss diet and follow it consistently, which is almost never the case. We would be overjoyed to hear of any examples of lasting success in such cases.

A child (usually a boy) between the ages of ten and thirteen, big for his age and very overweight, is being teased in school. Because of his obesity, participation in sports is possible only to a limited extent, and in any case the boy has little interest in physical activity. He is clearly becoming withdrawn and is spending more and more time alone with his computer. His tension is evident in the surprising rapidity with which he answers questions.

The first question his parents ask is whether some glandular or hormonal balance is involved. In itself, the fact that the boy is somewhat tall for his age already suggests that this is not the case, and the pediatrician can usually dismiss this concern as unfounded. Because such children are often sensitive and easily offended, it is important to look carefully for problems and conflicts at home and in school. Psychotherapy is often indicated.

In medically uncomplicated cases of juvenile obesity, success depends on whether it is possible to activate the child's independent will.

With a juvenile the physician may become a person of trust with whom a "contract" can be made covering one to three goals:

First, decide on giving up one favorite drink or food (something that is particularly hard to do without and that has a lot of calories), like chocolate, Coke, pizza or chips. This change of habit will be an exercise of the will which can concentrate on just one point.

Second, take up some form of movement outside school activities (cycling, rollerblading, rowing, or whatever). Swimming is not so suitable as it tends to increase the appetite too much. Easy gymnastics in a group of similarly motivated youngsters makes more sense, and eurythmy or speech formation, which also help strengthen the child's soul constitution, would be even better. Drama can strengthen the constitution and give more self-confidence.

Third, agree on a (realistic) goal for weight loss over the coming week ($1/2$–1 kg, 1–2 lb), and review it weekly.

21

21.13 Anorexia nervosa

Anorexia is a psychogenic eating disorder characterized by disturbed body image, distorted and fixed ideas about food intake, pathological fear of gaining weight, and failure to recognize the condition as an illness. This disorder appears only in the modern industrial world. Although the number of cases among boys is increasing, the overwhelming majority of anorexics are teenage girls and young women. Excessive weight loss is accompanied by amenorrhea (absence of menstruation) and, in most cases, constipation. Surprisingly, most of these young women are athletic and scholastic high-achievers, and many them enjoy gourmet cooking and feeding others. On the whole, these patients appear compulsive; their thoughts always revolve around food, calories, their weight, and their figures and often around purity and transgression as well. They implement strategies that lead to physical deterioration and disrupt their development; weight loss may be so extreme that it becomes life-threatening.

Experts agree that the self-assertive, defiant phase of early childhood and the successful establishment of self-identity after the so-called Rubicon of the tenth year (see page 301) are absent from these young women's biographies. No general links can be made to family ranking or parent-child relationships. As with other psychological disorders in childhood, there is some correlation with early experiences of physical abuse.

In spite of many psychological and social attempts to define this illness, it always presents new riddles. It manifests as a deep-seated urge to break off the process of developing into a responsible personality. Because of the patients' age, puberty was formerly thought to be a triggering factor, but this interpretation conceals the patients' underlying mistrust in the body as a whole as the "house of the soul." The illness presents a difficult therapeutic challenge in that the goal of therapy is to rebuild the entire basis for the life of the physical body. In addition to special diets and intravenous feeding — if necessary — and anthroposophical and naturopathic medications, external treatments in the form of compresses and ointments (see pages 423) are indicated to stimulate and strengthen the senses of life, touch, and warmth. These initial treatments can soon be followed by artistic therapies such as painting, curative eurythmy, or music therapy. Later, speech formation and Bothmer gymnastics are appropriate. Individual and family psychotherapy sessions foster maturation of the patient's personality and increase her receptivity to her social surroundings.

21.14 Fear and anxiety

Most of us will have been amazed at toddlers who, without the slightest hesitation, will climb up a ladder or stand at the edge of a cliff, but this existential fearlessness can disappear from one moment to the next if they are awakened by a bad dream or a loud crash, experience traumatic pain, or are forced to watch someone being abused. The most common cause, however, is feeling abandoned. Anxiety sets in and becomes their constant companion, posing a question and a challenge to the adults around them.

Some children (and some adults) use such events to become stronger, while others must first feed their fears. People who tend to distance themselves from events and prefer to have everything explained, planned, and thoroughly considered are usually more anxious than hands-on types and enthusiastic experimenters.

Of course how we are as adults, not how we would like to be, is what affects children. Here's an example from our pediatric practice: Pre-emptive assurances like "You don't have to be afraid of the doctor" are more likely to trigger fears than calm them since the child's mother is afraid that he might be afraid of the doctor. In such instances, the pediatrician has no chance to connect with the child or to provide the necessary reassuring explanations as she performs the examination. Visits to the doctor are especially traumatic for children raised in institutions, who usually succumb to existential panic during specialized examinations or when blood has to be drawn. This is a sign of the extent to which lack of human love and attention during the first few years of life disrupts the development of healthy self-confidence.

Treating fears and anxieties is one of the greatest tasks not only of psychiatry, psychotherapy, and medicine as a whole but also of pastoral counseling. Conversation, understanding, the passage of time, and medication are all helpful. In this context, we can only offer a few tips for dealing with fears that you and your child may share.

Fear of thunderstorms: Hold your child while you watch the lightning together and comment on the loudness of the thunderclaps. When he calms down a bit, comment on the lightning flashes, saying either "See how bright that one is!" or (later) "Look, how pretty!" — but only if you yourself can truly appreciate its beauty. Children older than nine can understand the statement, "If you heard the thunder, it means the lightning didn't strike you," which is soothing less because of its logic than because someone is capable of commenting calmly on what you both perceive.

Fear of drawing blood: The best preparation is to hold your child and

21

tell her, "I'll hold you, and the doctor will tell us what he's going to do." This establishes the physician's authority and makes your child feels physically protected.

Imaginary fears: Being afraid of a man in black or a dark cellar is usually based on silly talk or snatches of conversation your child has heard. He may develop similarly unfounded fears if he hears himself described as "afraid of the water," "dizzy," or even just "timid." Thoughts like these tend to mushroom in a child's imagination, but he will proudly disprove these statements (away from the person who makes them) by accompanying a trusted companion into a dark room, into the water, or to the edge of a cliff.

In general, acknowledging and accepting fear is the first step toward overcoming it. Your physical presence, time, and brief objective comments will help your child combat fear, but long speeches will not. Distracting your child's attention from his own anxious thoughts to real, understandable perceptions helps even more. Be open to the fact that the presence of children gives you opportunities to become more courageous yourself. Make it possible for your child to get to know people who are not afraid or who have learned to manage their fear.

22. Problems in School

Learning disabilities and behavior problems in school are stressful, not only for the children but also for their parents and teachers. As a result, children with individual or social problems often find their way to the child psychiatrist or psychologist. How can we understand special difficulties due to physical and psychological conditions? How can we help these children? This chapter addresses some frequent problems and basic therapeutic options.

22.1 Hyperactivity and attention deficit disorder (ADD)

We all know children who appear restless and driven, act impulsively, are difficult to engage in conversation, and react to even mild or imagined disruptions with aggression. They have difficulty making connections between thoughts. Their excessive expressions of sympathy and antipathy and frequently destructive behavior are often not met with understanding. In spite of widely varying symptoms, these children have one thing in common: the inability to pay attention and control their impulses, hence the name "attention deficit disorder." Nonetheless, these are wonderful children. Physically, they are strong, often well-built, almost tireless, and always ready for action. They respond to everything that is happening around them with great interest and almost irrepressible willingness to join in. What they cannot do, however, is to channel their energy into meaningful accomplishments and generally acceptable behavior. This is what they have to learn.

Formerly, these children were simply considered fidgety and were marginalized for their "naughty" behavior. Today, however, we know that they suffer from a constitutional disorder for which neither the they nor their parents can be held morally accountable. Only one thing is important: to understand each child's particular situation and do what we can to help.

Constitutional hyperactivity often runs in families. Among boys, it manifests primarily as excessive physical activity and inappropriate initiative; among girls, it appears in a more internalized form, as chaotic thinking and psychological restlessness.

Hyperactivity is sometimes complicated by the presence of other disorders such as nervous tics. Hyperactive children may also have specific learning disabilities such as dyslexia, isolated writing disorders, or difficulty understanding what they hear or listening when several people are speaking at the same time. Thorough examination and diagnosis by a child psychiatrist or experienced specialist pediatrician is an important first step in dealing with the problem.

From the anthroposophical perspective, this complex of symptoms deals with the mastery of the individual's I over his or her soul life. Attention and concentration, emotional balance and readiness to act, are all inadequately controlled. When developing a treatment plan, therefore, it is important to answer the following questions:

- Who are the adults who have or will acquire the strength and ability to understand, empathize with, and stand by this child?
- Where can we find an experienced remedial education specialist who will provide the needed individual time and attention for the child and support for his teachers and parents? It is important that treatment or self-help begins as early as possible.
- How can we reduce and if possible eliminate the factors in daily life that intensify the child's symptoms?

Will we resort to treating the child with stimulants such as methylphenidate (Ritalin) and others, which has become the standard treatment worldwide? Low doses of these medications have calming and attention-enhancing effects on most hyperactive children; the effects last for several hours. Amphetamines (performance-enhancing stimulants that are also used as appetite suppressants) have similar effects. So does coffee, although its effects are weaker. Reports from enthusiastic children, parents, and teachers indicate that taking medications such as Ritalin produces sudden and dramatic improvement in many children's situations in school and at home. It is said that in the US, ten percent of all boys are treated with methylphenidate; In Mexico City, the figure is thirty percent. Clearly, our modern lifestyles seem to enhance the potential for hyperactivity.

We recommend three means of treating the causes of this syndrome:
- Reducing or, wherever possible, eliminating influences in the child's environment that tend to increase symptoms.
- Early directed remedial education consisiting of individual training to strengthen the control function of the I, has been very succesful.
- Medical treatment with anthroposophical or homeopathic constitutional remedies and/or (temporarily) with Ritalin or similar stimulants.

Imitation

Figures 81-96. Imitation.
Skills are developed through work and play "like Mom and Dad."

Figure 83.

Figure 84.

Figure 85.

Figure 86.

Figure 88.

Figure 87.

Figure 89.

Figure 90.

Figure 91.

Figure 92.

Figure 93.

Figure 94.

Figure 95.

Figure 96. Sometimes imitation can make us feel uncomfortable.

The remainder of this section will deal with aids that may be used in individual cases as needed and as the circumstances permit.

Cooperative conversation among all involved in educating and treating the child — parents, caregivers, and teachers, as well as the child's physician, therapist(s), and other important people in the child's life. In the course of this conversation, each person presents a personal image of the child and his talents and possibilities. The collective image is then filled out by characterizing both the child's learning disabilities and difficulties and his abilities and strengths as exactly as possible. Interim objectives and long-term treatment goals are considered. Tasks are assigned according to the participants' possibilities, any necessary helpers are enlisted, and regular reviews are scheduled. It is essential for the child to participate in developing very concrete strategies to overcome each specific difficulty. These strategies should also be fun and lead to successful experiences, for nothing works without strong motivation.

A rhythmical daily routine. Hyperactive children need firm, reasonable, externally imposed routines for every day of the week. The adults around the child must know the child's exact daily and weekly schedule, be aware of less frequent but regular events, and know who is responsible when. Even the first few minutes after waking up and the last moments before falling asleep need to be specially structured.

Bedtime ritual should become a highlight of your child's day. After hearing a brief story and singing a song, exchange a few words about how the day went. What happened today? What will happen tomorrow? A mood of quiet observation and positivity is best. Complete the ritual with a song, a prayer, or a beautiful verse. This routine helps your child "digest" both food and the day's events. Your morning greeting should also be lighthearted and full of warm humour and should radiate certainty that a successful departure for school is in the offing...

Visual help. As mentioned earlier, these children often have a problem connecting spoken words with meaningful actions. A written daily and weekly plan is helpful. They are better able to connect to a visual statement.

Adequate physical activity. Hyperactive children *need* to walk to school. Only after twenty to thirty minutes of walking are they ready to stay in their seats in school, and almost nothing else they do could please their teachers more. Afternoons at home (or at a neighbor's or a nearby farm) must also include plenty of opportunities for physical activity: gardening, sawing wood, helping with the wheelbarrow, woodwork and other crafts; or going on half-day hikes with the family or school groups.

Absolutely no audiovisual media. Television, videos, walkmans, and CDs should disappear from the child's immediate surroundings. Even in constitutionally healthy children, early and frequent media consumption causes obvious damage that manifests as attention deficits and inability to listen or grasp connections. Media consumption can significantly increase symptoms of hyperactivity and thus make the child's overall situation worse. Once your child is ten or eleven years old, you and he can select a limited number of programs or films to watch, but always watch them together and discuss them afterward.

Arranging your living space: We recommend putting away everything you don't absolutely need. Use heavy ceramic tumblers and mugs that can't tip over easily. Instead of candle holders (which can tip over and get blown out), use lanterns with tea lights. Place a footstool under the table so your child has something solid to rest his feet on. Small rooms with doors that shut are better than large, open, multipurpose areas. When he is helping in the shop or in the kitchen, have your child stand on a low stool; the need for balance and the slight change in perspective will increase his attentiveness.

Nutrition: Phosphates, flavor-enhancers, food coloring, and preservatives as well as a number of possible food allergies have been implicated in symptoms of hyperactivity. We do not advise special low-phosphate diets because some very important foods such as milk and nuts contain phosphates. We do, however, recommend a healthy, grain-based diet (including the less common grains such as spelt, millet, buckwheat, and quinoa) with adequate amounts of salad and fruit. Emphasize vegetarian meals or moderate meat consumption.

Any foods that you suspect of increasing your child's symptoms should be eliminated temporarily and then reintroduced one at a time in small (initially imperceptible) amounts mixed in with other foods. Give your child the newly reintroduced food every other day, and gradually increase the amounts until you notice restlessness. Leave the amount the same while you watch to see if he gets used to it. Your goal is to allow him to eat as great a variety of foods as possible.

No form of testing can be considered an adequate substitute for actually trying out the foods. In the case of sweets, begin with raisins and other dried fruits and then move on to good quality honey, small amounts of evaporated cane juice, and even white sugar in very small quantities for sweetening yogurt and the like. We do not recommend ready-made sweetened products because they all contain far too much sugar. In our experience, chocolate and foods containing cocoa powder are also not good.

If your child becomes unusually restless after eating a homemade dessert, don't break off the experiment immediately. Instead, say "We'll try that again the day after tomorrow." This gives him an opportunity to see if he can control his restlessness. Do not do this kind of challenge testing just before school, however, because it sets your child up for disappointment.

One experienced child psychiatrist recommends giving school-age children a cup of coffee in the morning. Like Ritalin therapy, it has a calming effect. It also has the psychological benefit of showing the children that their parents understand them and take their problems seriously.

Summary: A diet that is as varied and free of chemicals as possible, including beverages consumed throughout the day at regular intervals.

Sensory education: By this we mean education of all twelve sensory functions described in this book (see Section 13.8). Especially important for hyperactive children are the senses of touch, balance, self-movement (kinesthesia), and life, which transmit sensations of one's own body. Rhythmical patterns of sleeping, waking, and eating are especially important. Sensory education is part of all the therapeutic and educational measures discussed below.

The right kindergarten can provide significant respite for parents. Avoid placing your hyperactive child in a large-group setting or understaffed program, however, which can lead to early experiences of failure and marginalization. Already at this age, arranging the above-mentioned comprehensive conversation among all concerned adults and implementing the relevant conclusions can be a great help to your child's further development.

In school, a hyperactive child's problems become much more apparent. Small classes or smaller subgroups in large classes are very helpful. (In defense of teachers, it should be noted that even one or two hyperactive children in a large class can wreck the most carefully prepared lesson.) Here, too, it is important to begin conversations with your child's teacher before problems arise, if possible, to establish mutual trust and lines of communication. For example, if you know that your restless child becomes very quiet and attentive on horseback because of the subconscious effort required to maintain balance, the unconventional step of providing a large gymnastic ball or a bar stool for him to sit on whenever he gets restless in class may be very helpful. If deftly managed, this adaptive measure signals to the class that restlessness is a natural occurrence for this child and not something that merits much attention. To the hyperactive child, it signals that he can be confident in his teacher's desire to help him. This and other such helpful measures work well, however, only if good contact has been established among all involved with the child.

Special therapies and educational measures

Sensory integration therapy and/or physical therapy is always indicated if a child has difficulty integrating his perceptions and actions.

Occupational therapy begins at home with Mom and Dad, painting, using

22

modelling clay, and braiding. On a slightly more difficult level, simple hand weaving or stitching with a blunt darning needle are good. If a workshop is available, your child should learn to hammer, to split wood with a wedge, and especially to saw (with a parent helping to guide the saw). If these opportunities are not available at home, look for a professional occupational therapist who can provide them.

Special education and behavioral therapy. Therapy sessions with a licensed education specialist or behavioral psychologist can be limited to once or twice a week. As long-term treatments, they are very successful if the practitioner is experienced.

Parental training is sometimes offered. This offers parents educational help using elements of behavioral therapy. They learn to cope with typical everyday problems independently and learn to better understand their child and his special nature.

Singing and music therapy. Singing also cultivates forces that fall victim to uncontrolled feelings if left to their own devices. The Nordoff-Robbins improvisational model of music therapy attempts to express in music the movements a child is making a at the moment, thus conveying to him on a semi-conscious level that he is understood and accompanied. Its benefits include stimulating attentiveness and reducing problems at home (for details see Useful Organizations, page 453).

Storytelling and speech. A daily "story hour" adapted to your child's age and understanding can work wonders. Read aloud to him in a calm, natural, not overly dramatic tone of voice (see Section 15.4).

Rhythmical massage as developed by Ita Wegman can help your child feel comfortable in his body and take hold of it better.

Bothmer gymnastics, although still relatively unknown, is excellent for developing good body image. It was introduced in the first Waldorf school; since that time, therapeutic applications have been developed specifically for hyperactive children and teens with eating disorders (for details see Useful Organizations, page 453).

Curative eurythmy: Adapted for use with children, it aids in self-discovery by strengthening the movements of both body and soul as described on Section 22.4.

External applications (compresses, baths, and oil rubs), administered for secondary health problems or as additional stimulating or calming measures, can help hyperactive children in a variety of ways. They are generally prescribed by experienced physicians or therapists.

22.2 Dealing with left-handedness

In recent decades, the standard approach to left-handedness has been to allow lefties to write with their left hands from the very beginning. In some schools (especially Waldorf schools), however, attempts are still made to teach left-handed children to write with their right hands. Formerly, learning to write right-handed was often traumatic for left-handed children and caused psychological problems such as nervousness, restlessness, fear of failure, fear of going to school, escapism, and stuttering. The reason for this is obvious: Left-handed children experienced discrimination and learned to write under pressure of time; success was compulsory. Of course this is not an appropriate educational approach. Patience and loving attention are much more likely to help left-handed children feel proud of learning to write "like everybody else." There is one absolutely necessary prerequisite to such attempts, however: The child herself as well as her parents and teacher must all agree that it is worth the effort. The child must be certain that the adults will acknowledge and respect her efforts. Why we recommend such attempts rather than simply allowing children to decide which hand to use is based on a deper understanding of left-handedness, which is explained in greater detail below.

How does writing relate to the brain's speech center?

It is well known that the nerve pathways coming from the body cross approximately where they enter the skull (the so-called corticospinal tract crossing). This is why an injury to one side of the skull causes paralysis or sensory disorders on the opposite side of the body. New and uncontested methods of investigation have confirmed that the two halves of the brain serve different functions in healthy adults. The left hemisphere supports logical, abstract, analytical thinking, while the right hemisphere tends to support synthesizing, image-based thinking. During the early years of life, a center devoted specifically to speech develops, typically in the left hemisphere. The results of several studies have recently confirmed what has long been suspected — that the speech center develops on the left side of the brain even in most left-handed children. Only twelve to fifteen percent of left-handed people have speech centers located exclusively in the right hemisphere. Approximately fifty percent have speech centers on the left, while speech functions are served in both the right and left halves of the brain in the remaining thirty-five percent. Furthermore, we now know that new and additional speech centers can develop later in life in people who learn other languages.

The results of physiological and

22

psychological studies and statistics from brain surgery indicate that the brain is relatively symmetrical at birth but that one-sided regional foci and centers serving specific functions develop increasingly as time goes on. The location of many of these centers is predetermined — for example, spatial orientation on the right, temporal processes and analytical understanding on the left. With regard to writing, however, there is no predetermined location, and no specific "writing center" develops in the brain as we learn to write. Instead, several different centers are active in this process. From the neurophysiological perspective, therefore, there is no reason not to allow left-handed chidlren to attempt to learn to write with their right hands.

Qualitative differences between right and left

Even ancient cultures recognized that right and left are not simply interchangeable but have unique and different qualities. The Delaware Indians, for example, said that "the left hand is holy and the right unholy" and preferred the left hand for specific activities such as using turkey feathers to sweep an oval path around two fires for their dancers to follow.

Lao-Tse said, "When the wise man is at home, he values his left hand, but when using weapons, he values the right. Weapons are tools of misfortune, not tools of the wise ... For pleasant actions, the left hand is preferred; for painful actions, the right."

In ancient China, the left shoulder was bared during joyful ceremonies and the right in anticipation of punishment. In the gesture of greeting used by boys, the right hand was held below the left, while girls placed the left hand under the right. In Sudan, right and left were differentiated in terms of male and female activities. Actions viewed as feminine were performed with the left hand, masculine activities with the right. Gifts were presented with both hands outstretched and crossed.

There are also obvious qualitative differences in the organs and functions typically located on the left and right sides of the human body. The organs that lie more on the right side, such as the liver and the lungs (with three lobes on the right and only two on the left) serve functions that link the body with the outside — the lungs through air and the liver through the flow of blood that absorbs nutrients from the intestines. On the left side, the heart and the spleen serve the more internal function of circulating blood to all of the organs. From the perspective of the human body's structure, therefore, it makes sense to perform an outward-directed activity such as writing, which eventually becomes almost automatic, with the right hand. Writing is more similar to the physiological activities of the right side of the body than to those of the left. Similarly, it makes sense to learn to finger a violin or cello with the left hand, since this activity is more related to hearing; it is more inward and "touches our hearts."

Regular practice strengthens the will
Every conscious repetition of an action, no matter how small, strengthens our will. Thus writing is a will exercise for any child, but especially for a left-handed child who has to overcome the slight discomfort involved in writing right-handed. Since success is proportional to the effort expended, the effect of learning to write is greater for left-handed children, both in terms of writing itself and as a will-strengthening exercise. To make writing practice easier, it helps to begin by developing letter shapes from pictures, then writing large letters first on big sheets of wrapping paper, then on the blackboard, and then on an entire sheet of writing paper, so that the child's whole body is still involved in the movement. If you accompany a child with understanding, love, and humor as she decreases the size of her writing, she will make a great effort to please her teacher and parents and will enjoy practicing in spite of all the effort it takes. This practice strengthens her will in ways that often leads to improvement in other areas, such as clumsiness or inattentiveness. Her self-control and self-confidence are strengthened by learning to write with her right hand.

Left-handedness as a destiny issue
A left-handed person enters life with different tasks and attributes than a right-handed person. Rudolf Steiner pointed out that left-handedness is the consequence of significant overexertion of body and soul in an earlier earthly life. In the following life, the right side of the body remains underdeveloped compared to the left. From this perspective, left-sided dominance presents an opportunity to develop greater inwardness, sensitivity, and consciousness during this lifetime. In this case, the task of education is to support this developmental potential while providing extra opportunities for strengthening the forces of the body's right side. Furthermore, the left side is best used in ways that correspond to its own inherent qualities — for fingering a violin, for example, but not for writing. Similarly, writing right-handed takes advantage of the right side's inherent potential, which favors down-to-earth, outward-directed, hands-on activity rather than sensitive accompaniment or reflection of events.

Because Waldorf education incorporates the results of Rudolf Steiner's spiritual-scientific research, Waldorf teachers recommend allowing left-handed children to attempt to learn to write right-handed. Other skilled activities such as painting, sewing, and using scissors, which always remain more conscious and less automatic than writing, can be done left-handed if the child prefers. *We want to make it quite clear that we are not advocating exclusive use of the right hand, nor are we attempting to change a left-handed child's dominance. Learning to write right-handed is recommended only when all concerned want it and find it reasonable.* Based on the results of modern research into the brain and laterality, this approach also seems scientifically well-founded.

22

Individual decisions

We recommend keeping an open mind in the search for individual solutions that correspond to each child's possibilities. For example, one first-grade teacher discovered five left-handed children in her class. All were examined individually, the situation was discussed with each set of parents, and all decided to try writing right-handed on an experimental basis. In this case, it was interesting to note that the one boy whose right hand was clearly dominant (that is, both stronger and more skillful than his left) was the only one who remained attached to writing with his left hand and did not want to continue the experiment. The four others never experienced any problems with writing right-handed and were perfectly happy with their situation.

In another example, a nine-year-old boy who had become the class clown had learned to write with his left hand but did not write particularly well. The results were no worse when he attempted to write right-handed. After consultation with his parents, it was decided that he would spend the next summer vacation learning to write right-handed. His attempts were successful, and when school started again in the fall he was no longer marginalized by his classmates.

The next example illustrates the importance of fully including the children in the decision. In a parent-teacher conference before her son started first grade, one mother stated that it was important to her for him to be allowed to write with his left hand. Left-handed herself, she still remembered the traumatic experience of having to learn to write right-handed. In the course of the conversation, it emerged that the boy's father, also left-handed, had experienced no problems in learning to write right-handed; he would have preferred his son to do the same, but he accepted his wife's viewpoint because he didn't want the issue to become a source of conflict. The teacher then asked the parents if she could ask the boy in private how he wanted to learn to write. The parents looked at each other and agreed. And when the teacher asked the little boy, "Do you want to learn to write the way your mother does or the way your father does," he promptly replied, "Like Daddy." The experiment was successful and his mother was completely satisfied once she discovered that teaching a left-handed child to write right-handed did not have to happen the way she herself had been taught.

We have already indicated that if learning to write with the right hand is seen as an exciting experiment and is adapted to the child's work rhythm, it can also smooth out other problems the child may have. Of course everyone should agree on the duration of the experiment and on periodic progress reviews. It should also be understood that only writing (and, in Waldorf schools, form drawing) will be practiced right-handed. In all other activities — painting, for example — the child is free to choose which hand to use.

Practical tips

The following tips will help make the process of learning to write right-handed easier for left-handed children:

- Absolute agreement among parents and teachers is the prerequisite for success because it is the only way the child can be sure that adults will continue to support and motivate her efforts.

- To set an example for the children, a teacher who is actively left-handed should also use his right hand for writing on the board (at least in the children's presence) during the first few years of school when the power of imitation is still strong.

- Allow enough time! If your child attends state school, you will need to make individual arrangements with the teachers to make this possible. In Waldorf schools, where writing and reading are introduced much more slowly, there should be no problem. For children who have trouble with writing, provide large sheets of brown paper for writing individual letters on the floor, both in school and at home. After about three to five months of practice, it should be evident whether the experiment is successful and whether the right hand will become the child's permanent "writing hand."

- If parents and teachers decide to abandon an attempt to teach a left-handed child to write using her right hand, they should stand behind the decision completely and give the child every opportunity to learn to write left-handed at a relaxed pace and according to guidelines worked out for this purpose (see *Bibliography*).

- Watch for changes in your child's behavior and check the causes carefully. Are they related to learning to write or to interpersonal problems (being afraid of the neighbour's children, losing a friend, parents' marital problems, and so on)?

- Form drawing and eurythmy offer valuable support for all children learning to write. For ambidextrous and left-handed children who are especially clumsy, dexterity and attention exercises can be added to challenge them to concentrate on their right sides — for example, visually tracking an amusing object as it moves or crawls down the right arm.

- Do not promise material rewards. The child's true reward is her own pride and adults' pleasure in every sign of progress. Promising material rewards accustoms children to doing things for the sake of rewards rather than for their own sake, out of love for what they are doing. On the other hand, it is all right to give the child a semiprecious stone or a beautiful shell to hold in her left hand while writing so she doesn't forget and switch hands. Here's an example: A left-sided firstgrader was initially unenthusiastic about learning to write with his right hand. His teacher discussed the situation again with his parents, who agreed to stand by their decision.

22

The teacher gave the boy a beautiful stone to hold in his left hand. After one week, the boy gave the stone back, saying, "I think you can have it back now. I don't need it any more."

- If children decide to learn to write right-handed at a later date, it is best to make the switch during summer vacation. For these children, we recommend buying an attractive notebook or blank book to write in every day, either using it as a diary or copying poems and other texts they like.

22.3 Dyslexia

Dyslexia is understood as an isolated learning disorder that affects reading and writing and appears in otherwise normally intelligent children. Approximately three to eight percent of children are affected. Parents and teachers are called upon to find effective help before the disorder causes unreasonable suffering. In this section, we will attempt to present a few perspectives that will aid in understanding and correcting this condition.

To learn to write words, children must be able and willing to extract individual sounds from a word they know only as a whole — that is, to break the word down into parts. Instead of paying attention to its meaning, they are now supposed to focus exclusively on specific, isolated sounds. At the same time, a second abstraction is demanded of them: to believe that an arbitrary symbol is the sound itself. Until now, children have been able to "read" an upside-down picture book quite effortlessly. Try to imagine what it means when they are suddenly confronted with these qualitatively equivalent and meaningless symbols:

**d b
q p**

These abstract characters made up of straight and curved lines acquire meaning only through a very specific spatial relationship to the reader, and they can't even be pronounced without adding a vowel. For children, being asked to recreate words from such imprecise characters is a truly impenetrable art. Why is the vowel in "the" an *e* instead of a *u*? Why do we write *h-e-r-e* or *h-e-a-r* instead of *h-e-r?*

We hope these examples make it clear how easy it is for uncertainty and confusion to arise. Children who still try to interpret letters as pictures will have trouble, as will those who take their teacher's statements too literally and believe it when told to "spell it the way it sounds." Already at this point, it should be obvious that teaching reading and writing in child-friendly ways takes quite a long time. Equally obviously, the teacher must know all the details that can trip dyslexics up and be able to break up the process of learning to write into small, manageable steps based on phonetic research.

Remarkably, some children learn to write and read almost by themselves, and mastering all the exceptions to phonetic rules comes as easily as playing. It is as if they simply had to "remember" how to write. For others, however, their world falls apart. Although they were formerly accustomed to having minimal difficulties, or none at all, with spatial orientation and doing whatever their age peers did, now all of a sudden they are asked to do something that remains totally unfathomable to them. For a while, they write according to laws that dyslexia experts recognize as derived from especially good attempts to listen. Later, however, as they become increasingly resigned to failure, their written words become increasingly distorted. At this point, symptoms such as pallor, susceptibility to infection, fatigue, listlessness, insomnia, stomachaches, wetting, and aggression often appear. The list of complaints that eventually lead unrecognized dyslexics to the doctor's office even

includes serious organic illnesses. Even then, the fact that dyslexia is either causing or contributing to their symptoms is easily overlooked. The appearance of physical and psychological symptoms, however, is a clear sign that the condition needs to be treated as an illness. Obviously, it is not enough to base a diagnosis of dyslexia on the fact that a child confuses *d* with *b* or *p* with *q*. Meanwhile, other deficits have developed, and their causes are more difficult to assess. Thorough diagnosis followed by individual help and support is required. Not only the child's writing errors but also her general spatial orientation, control over her body, perception of forms, and her ability to speak and understand speech must be analyzed in detail before deciding on an individual treatment plan. As soon as she begins to experience some success as a result of therapy and the first signs of progress become visible, her confidence begins to grow and physical symptoms soon disappear.

Adequate time must be allowed for remedial instruction in writing and reading to be fully effective — one to two years if the problem is recognized early and approached holistically, usually longer if it is not. For severe cases, we recommend contacting a program specializing in dyslexia therapy. Sensory-motor integration therapy and/or curative eurythmy also helps increase the chance of success. In all cases, however, close cooperation among therapists, teachers, and parents is necessary.

Effective preventive measures for

22

Examples of symmetry exercises for walking or drawing.

preschoolers are described in Chapters 14 and 16. See in particular the sections on sensory education and movement and language development. Toddlers who seem clumsy, sleepy, or slow to learn to talk can be helped by encouraging their sensory activity and memory. Structuring the course of the day and the year as described in the section on Waldorf kindergartens is an example of how to proceed. Stimulation of this sort supports the necessary metamorphosis of growth forces into thought forces (see Section 15.4). This transformation, which is irregular in cases of dyslexia, is the prerequisite of any kind of thought activity.

In the first few years of school, children who have trouble orienting themselves in space, time, and their own consciousness can benefit from measures implemented during school hours by teachers or therapists:

- Perception exercises: observing and describing the shapes of objects together. Pictures, plants, or stones can be used.
- Walking shapes and their mirror images on the floor.
- Drawing the forms with their feet, holding thick crayons between their toes.
- Drawing the forms in the air with their hands, keeping their eyes closed.
- Repeating the process the next day, then helping the children to visualize it and finally drawing the forms on paper.
- Repeating all of the above steps (with the exception of the symmetry exercises) using letter shapes.
- Exercises in writing what they hear, beginning with the simplest syllables. Playful but systematic transition to multi-syllable words with phonetic spellings and only later to words that require knowing spelling rules.
- Later, writing short texts from dictation. To maximize success, all of the words selected for this purpose should be spelled the way they sound.
- Curative eurythmy treatments, where available.

When dealing with dyslexic children, it is important to convey a happy and optimistic attitude, because their problems are often intensified by a sense of failure and either inadequate moral support or resignation on the part of adults. Children can learn to compensate completely for mild cases of dyslexia. In severe cases, special help and systematic practice can achieve significant improvement in symptoms, making it possible to integrate the children into the processes of reading and writing to a considerable extent.

22.4 Curative eurythmy

The art of eurythmy, pioneered by Rudolf Steiner from 1911 to 1924 and developed further after his death, consists of movements and forms that correspond to specific elements of speech and music. Eurythmy, which is based on an exact understanding of the qualities of individual speech sounds and tones, studies vowels and consonants, pitches and intervals, in relationship to the human form. The gestures corresponding to sounds and tones are the same as the movements that can be observed in the embryo, both in the development of body proportions and in the flowing forms of blood and tissue fluids: growth and holding back, extension and involution, expansion and contraction, enclosure and exclusion, touching and penetration.

Eurythmy's basic gestures encompass all of the human organism's potential movements as well as all movements in the living and unenlivened natural world. We find these gestures repeated in the various growth forms of plants and animals and in the play of movements on surfaces where solids, fluids, and gases meet. For this reason, eurythmy can be described as a visible archetypal language in which nature and human beings express their messages through gestures. All forms can be interpreted as movements come to rest; eurythmy makes their development visible and thus offers possibilities for self-education, a means of feeling our way into the development of visible natural shapes.

In *artistic eurythmy,* poems, stories, dramatic works, and musical compositions for one or more voices (up to and including entire orchestral pieces) are practiced and presented on stage either by individuals or by ensembles.

In *educational eurythmy,* students from kindergarten to twelfth grade learn to move skilfully and orient themselves in space. By practising artistic works, they learn to shape their movements in ways that express a great variety of soul experiences. Doing eurythmy in a group also fosters social skills by allowing youngsters to experience that the success of a major artistic presentation depends

22

entirely on selfless individual contributions.

In *curative eurythmy,* repeated practice of specific speech sounds and tone exercises stimulate formative and regenerative activity in the body and counteract pathological changes. The speed or intensity of individual exercises is adapted to enhance or restrain formative impulses in the body as needed. Other specific exercises have harmonizing, stimulating, concentration-promoting, or calming effects. For isolated learning disabilities, specific exercises in dexterity, spatial orientation, and symmetry are helpful. Curative eurythmy is also helpful in treating movement, hearing, and visual disorders because it helps the child's soul penetrate the body more completely. Specific exercises are prescribed by a physician in consultation with the child's teacher and the curative eurythmist.

23. Recognizing and Fostering Children's Temperaments

23.1 The four temperaments

The word "temperament" comes from the Latin *temperare,* meaning "to mix." The ancient medical theory of the "right mixture" of body fluids and associated soul qualities comes down to us through Hippocrates. The diagnostic and therapeutic significance of this theory was largely lost in more recent times until Rudolf Steiner reintroduced it to education and revealed its importance for a deepened understanding of the body-soul connection.

Since constitutional factors are still somewhat flexible in childhood, the temperaments are a rewarding area for achieving therapeutic effects. Educational techniques can make it easier for children to deal with their temperaments. This humorous poem shows how different temperaments influence our reactions and behavior:

> The four temperaments and the stone in the path
> Nimbly and lightly, the sanguine hops over the stone in the path.
> If he misses and stumbles, it bothers him not in the least.
> The choleric shoves it aside resolutely and forcefully,
> Eyes flashing with joy at his total success.
> The phlegmatic's deliberate footsteps slow down only slightly:
> "If you will not get out of my way, I will simply go round."
> The brooding melancholic, however, stands still in his tracks,
> His face discontented about his eternal bad luck.

HEINRICH PEITMANN

Temperament and constitution

In the human body, the solid, fluid, and gaseous elements work together with the fourth element, heat (see page 130). How these elements interact also has a significant impact on our souls. Our psychological experience tends to be heavy and sad if the qualities of the solid state predominate in our constitution, cheerful and happy if air-related functions sound the dominant note. If the unique qualities of the fluid element prevail, we experience ourselves as calm and balanced, but if the attributes of heat predominate, we enjoy being active and taking initiative.

By introducing the four members of the human constitution into the debate about how body and soul interact, Rudolf Steiner bridged the gap between the old Hippocratic doctrine of elements and fluids, on the one hand, and modern, scientific and spiritual-scientific medicine and educational philosophy, on the other.

The choleric temperament

The choleric, with a body dominated by the activity of heat, always seems slightly compressed and "pressurized." Napoleon is the historic prototype of this temperament: short of stature, with an imposing head, short neck, and relatively short limbs in comparison to the long torso. The choleric's pace is resolute and dynamic; typically, his heels strike the ground hard. Initiative, action motivated by idealism, and persistence are choleric attributes. Typically, cholerics love truth, enthusiasm, and punctuality. They are also easily excitable when things don't go as planned. When they pursue self-serving rather than idealistic goals, however, all of these qualities take a negative turn, and inconsiderate behavior, stubbornness, and need for admiration come to the fore. Since cholerics are very goal-oriented, they are often found in positions of leadership.

Dealing with choleric children is

temperament	element/state of matter	constitutional member
choleric	heat	I-organization
sanguine	air/gas	soul (astral) body
phlegmatic	water/fluid	life (ether) body
melancholic	earth/solid	physical body

strenuous. They draw attention to themselves with outbursts of anger or dramatic, emotional scenes. They are physically active and sometimes become aggressive or literally bang their heads against the wall. On the positive side, they can also serve as examples for other children when it comes to doing specific tasks or making amends for mistakes. They are always stimulating to have in class. They can be counted on to pull their own weight (or more) in discussions, don't like to be late, and are always pleased when the teacher calls on them and allows them to demonstrate something for the class. On the negative side, they are demanding and do not necessarily accept advice gracefully or do what they're told.

The sanguine temperament

Sanguines feel truly comfortable only when surrounded by other people. They are receptive, enjoy human contact, and are interested in everything going on around them. They seldom judge on principle or carry grudges. Sanguine children can be recognized by the fact that they are constantly in motion and easily exhaust themselves. As a result, they often need more sleep at night and may need a midday nap even during the early school years. In school, sanguines enjoy universal popularity because they are full of ideas about fun things to do. Even as adults, they are valued for their stimulating entertainment and the fact that they always remember people's names on first acquaintance. This tempera-

ment becomes dangerous when its happy-go-lucky attitude degrades into lack of responsibility and its superficial, will-o'-the-wisp aspect comes to the fore.

Physically, sanguines are usually slim, small-boned, and have wiry, curly hair. They are excellent mimics and use a lot of gestures. They tend to walk with a skipping gait or on tiptoe.

The phlegmatic temperament

Predominantly phlegmatic people "keep their cool" in difficult situations and can continue to exert a balancing influence long after cholerics would have stormed out slamming the door behind them. No human communities could survive without the patience, loyalty, level-headedness, devotion to detail, and love of habit of phlegmatic individuals. Many phlegmatics make ideal mothers and teachers: they are the still pole that everything else rotates around. There is nothing aggressive about them; they are always concerned about resolving differences and balancing extremes, and they are exceptionally reliable. Phlegmatic children can sometimes be recognized at a very early age by the somewhat astonished gaze with which they observe everything around them. In the midst of chaos, they can sit there perfectly calmly and contentedly, especially if they've discovered something good to eat. They remain completely unflappable even in the face of barked commands intended to get them moving. They can easily drive their teachers to despair because

23

they are still taking the caps off their pens when everyone else has already written five sentences. Obviously, this temperament becomes dangerous when peacefulness slides over into boredom and love of habitual actions degenerates into pedantry and bourgeois conformism.

Physically, phlegmatics are well-proportioned as long as they don't become chubby from overindulging in good food. Their gait is stable and measured, emphasizing neither the heels nor the toes. Colloquially, their negative qualities are described as "thick" or "dense."

The melancholic temperament

Even in childhood, the expressive eyes and usually narrow faces of melancholics stand out. The after-effects of events and encounters are long-lasting in melancholic children, who may still be crying in the evening about something that happened in the morning. As school children and adolescents, they often feel misunderstood and unrecognized. Their attention is drawn to tragic events, and they suffer in surroundings characterized by superficiality and lack of commitment. In adulthood, they develop the positive qualities of profundity, sincerity, and empathy. Their melancholic temperament becomes dangerous if self-centeredness and carping criticism, either of themselves or of others, comes to the fore or if their sense of justice degrades into envious comparisons.

Physically, melancholics are usually tall and slim. Slight, generalized connective tissue weakness often reinforces the impression of slumping or poor posture. Their heads are often especially well formed with deep-seated eyes. Their step may be either firm and measured or heavy and ponderous.

Even this brief characterization makes it obvious that an individual's I-activity determines whether his or her temperament manifests as exceptional talent or unusual weakness. Thus the goal of educational measures must be to strengthen the I-function by giving children opportunities to practice dealing with and mastering their temperaments. "Harmonizing" a one-sided temperament never means "leveling" it; it simply means learning how to deal with it.

Educational measures

Experience shows the futility of attempting to spur a phlegmatic to action or to restrain a choleric by telling him not to be so wild. Attempts to cheer a melancholic up with jokes or to make a sanguine pay attention by scolding her are equally unsuccessful. In most cases, such efforts have the opposite effect: attempts to motivate phlegmatics usually make them sink deeper into lethargy, scolding simply makes cholerics angry and melancholics shut themselves off completely, and sanguines will be just as restless again in a few minutes. In managing children's temperaments, the therapeutic principle of "like cures like" is much more effective. In school, this means seating the children according to shared temperaments. Let the cholerics poke each other and try out their strength on each other; slowly but surely, they will wear the rough edges off each other's temperaments and unconsciously experience the one-sidedness and missing factors in their own makeup. Something similar happens with phlegmatics. When they sit together, they eventually bore each other to tears, and the resulting mild discomfort makes them more active and alert. At this point, they begin to either stimulate each other or take more interest in the other children in the class. Melancholics are happy to feel understood by those around them. In this situation, they feel more at peace with themselves and become correspondingly more receptive to what comes toward them from outside. It is especially helpful for a melancholic to find a particular friend who understands her and to whom she can entrust confidences. The sanguines in the class, however, soon begin to get on each other's nerves, and the resulting discomfort makes them somewhat more self-aware and focused.

Successfully addressing all four temperaments and getting them involved in the lesson fosters the temperamental gifts of all members of the class. In his seminars for teachers, Rudolf Steiner placed great value on teachers educating themselves to act out of all four temperaments to a certain extent. To be able to deal with a choleric effectively, we ourselves must be able to be forceful, while in the next moment we must also be able to adapt to a phlegmatic's rhythm and feelings.

Below are a few temperament-specific ways of helping children manage their temperaments actively and constructively:

The development of *cholerics* is fostered by telling them about the actions of great individuals whose achievements they can learn to respect and value. It is equally important to entrust choleric children with difficult assignments that take all of their strength and energy. Learning to play solo instruments also engages their ambition and need for admiration in ways that produce something beautiful for others to enjoy. The basic principle is clear: Positively engaging the child's existing possibilities without suppressing excess energies. Choleric children simply use their surplus energy to play stupid tricks.

Phlegmatics are much more willing to participate in specific projects out of love for their particular friends (whose help you have already enlisted) than they are if you approach them directly. The piano is an ideal instrument for phlegmatics because the sounds are already potentially present; all it takes is striking the right keys. The range and harmonic possibilities of this instrument also address phlegmatics' need for harmony and completeness. And if you manage to convince phlegmatic children that they're strong enough to make it to the next meal without a snack, you will have accomplished a great deal!

23

The flightiness of *sanguines* cannot be overcome through reproaches, threats, and scolding. They can get quite a lot done, however, when they stick to a task out of love for an adult. Thus these children need exceptional amounts of personal attention, understanding, and interest in their difficulties, which are primarily due to their inability to concentrate. Playing wind instruments in the school orchestra addresses their particular abilities. Because they enjoy many different activities and are quick to gain an overview, they can be entrusted with a variety of different tasks. It is important to watch their diet to make sure they don't eat too many sweets, which make them even more restless.

It is helpful to tell *melancholics* about other people's destinies in ways that arouse their natural empathy and allow them to experience other people's great difficulties in life. For melancholics, the best teachers are people who have gone through a lot in life. Singing — especially solos — is good for melancholics' fundamentally lonely souls because it allows them to express their feelings and expand their emotional reach. Learning to play stringed instruments is also good.

Unlike sanguines, melancholics are helped by making sweets a regular part of their diet to counteract their naturally "sour" or "bitter" approach to life. Avoid giving melancholics too many hard-to-digest foods.

When the subject of managing the temperaments comes up in parents' evenings, parents often ask whether it is still possible for adults to work on their own temperaments. Of course it is, although adults' efforts may not produce as much constitutional change as is possible in children. A choleric apologizing for an outburst of anger can say, "You know I didn't mean it the way it came out. I simply lost control of myself." A phlegmatic who recognizes her own temperament can say, "Take it a bit more slowly, please; I have trouble keeping up." Both examples demonstrate that the person's I is aware of its one-sided manifestation and is beginning to work on it. Here, too, the purpose of self-education is not to deny a choleric or phlegmatic nature or to suppress it consciously. The goal is rather to learn to deal with the qualities of one's own temperament in ways that allow them to have positive effects.

24. Why Children Need Religious Education

24.1 Small children are naturally religious

On coming into this world, children bring with them an unconditional trust comparable in intensity only to the deepest religious devotion. This devotion is evident, for example, during a three-month-old infant's checkup. The baby, who has just woken up from his nap, is relaxed and alert as he lies naked on the table; his mother stands nearby waiting for the pediatrician's assurance that "everything looks fine." As the physician begins the examination, she notices the baby looking at her with a penetrating gaze. Who or what is the object of his search? How can he possibly gaze so steadfastly, so openly, and for so long into the eyes of an adult? (It has been determined that in such moments, babies focus on the observer's pupils — "black holes" where there is actually nothing to see but where the other person's I can be encountered most directly.) Later in life, we meet such a gaze only when we open ourselves completely to another person. An infant, however, does this with anyone and everyone. During the next few years of life, this unselfconscious trust will be evident in the child's devoted receptivity and uninhibited approach to everything around him. Everything he does will reveal a deeply moving "archetypal trust" and the boundless expectation that adults will do whatever is right and necessary. In our early childhood, we all experience this time of unlimited devotion and trust. Later in life, this attitude is transformed into the acquired ability to "devote" ourselves to a task and unite completely with it or to turn in conscious religious devotion to God and the angelic worlds.

Little children expect the world to be unconditionally good, trustworthy, and worth imitating — in other words, godlike. When we mention this expectation to parents, they often object, "Shouldn't we make it clear as soon as possible that it is not true? That the world is less than ideal, and that we

have to protect and defend ourselves?" Looking into children's
expectant eyes answers this question
immediately. Opening children's eyes
to suffering and misfortune makes
sense only when they have grown
strong enough to confront such problems. Disillusioning them too early
causes uncertainty, weakness, and —
later — difficulty in overcoming
doubts about the meaning and purpose
of their own existence. A more appropriate question would be, "What can
we do to preserve children's archetypal trust in the world? What can we
do to let them know that the efforts of
the adults around them are directed
toward ensuring that the world is
(also) 'good'? What can we do to help
them grow strong enough to deal with
life's less than ideal aspects?"

In the "paradise" of early childhood, we have a mother and a father
who do everything for us, take care of
everything we need, and love us simply because we exist. Later, such
unconditional relationships are very
rare, but we secretly long to return to
them. As life continues, the standard
set by this longing can help develop
love that is characterized by giving.

The more impressions and experiences we provide that preserve children's archetypal trust, the more it
becomes an inner goal and source of
soul strength for later in life.

Parents often accept this line of rea-
soning with one reservation, namely,
that it has become very difficult to
have confidence in an existence that is
threatened on every hand by war, violence, fear, social uncertainties, personal failures, and environmental
degradation including radioactive
contamination of large areas. We cannot doubt the reality of such threats,
but we also cannot doubt the different
realities that touch on the question of
our spiritual origin each time a baby
looks at us.

Seen in this light, a universally
human religious attitude is something
that adults can learn from little children. But why is conscious access to
the spiritual world so difficult to
achieve, even today when
humankind's longing for real connection with that world is once again
more clearly articulated and when so
much has been written on esoteric
questions?

24.2 How can we learn to experience and understand the spiritual world again?

Our immediate ability to understand religious traditions and believe that they are true declines as critical, sense-directed thinking begins to prevail. Many people stop praying when they no longer sense who is receiving their prayers — in other words, when they begin to think for themselves instead of accepting what authorities tell them. The decline of religious consciousness in recent times is a consequence of modern ways of thinking and acquiring knowledge. Only by deepening and further developing these same ways of thinking can we begin to awaken a new religious consciousness in ourselves.

One point of departure for developing this new consciousness is related to the process of learning to think (see Section 15.4). Through thinking, we can discover the laws governing the natural world's development and behavior. The fact that our thoughts follow and reflect natural processes depends on the existence of a previously created world. Our "reflections," however, lead us not only to natural laws but also to the question of whose thoughts created the world that our thoughts reflect. Obviously, our reflections are shadowy compared to the thoughts at work directly in the natural, created world. We become aware that for humans, thinking and accomplishing an action are separate processes. In the natural world, however, thoughts work directly, as natural laws. Our ability to separate thinking from acting is based on our capacity for independent decision-making. Even our best ideas do not compel us to act upon them. We can engage in thinking and willing separately; they are not directly linked or united as they are in natural events.

We take it for granted that many of our thoughts reflect the laws and realities of the natural world. We are less aware that *all* thoughts, up to and including our ideals, are reflections of things that exist in the world on some level, be it physical, emotional, or spiritual. Thinking, as we mentioned earlier (see Section 15.4) is a living network of reflections that originates in the human etheric or life body. On the etheric — that is, purely spiritual — level, each of our thoughts touches the corresponding natural or spiritual entity. Each time we attempt to realize a thought or implement an ideal, we also enter into an intimate connection with the being this thought or ideal reflects.

St Paul points to this fact when he says, "Not I, but Christ who lives in me" (Gal. 2:20), as does Jesus when he instructs his disciples, "By this all men will know that you are my disciples, if you have love for one another" (John 13:34); and "where two or three are gathered in my name, there I am in the midst of them" (Matt. 18:20). Of

24

himself, he says, "I and the Father are one" (John 10:30) and "I have come down ... not to do my own will but the will of Him who sent me" (John 6:38), indicating that entities in the spiritual world cannot be separated as they are in the sense-perceptible world. In the spiritual world, one being can live in and reveal itself through another being. In our everyday life, we experience this state only when we begin to love another person and experience the relationship as inner, light-filled, strength-giving warmth that enriches our own being. This experience, however, can be consciously extended to our interactions with the higher spiritual beings that are reflected in our thinking and willing when we identify with the ideals that express their being. Thus we human beings are given the possibility of uniting with another being so that our actions serve or express that being.

Through meditative practice, Rudolf Steiner was able to rediscover the spiritual nature of thinking and to develop it into an organ for perceiving the supersensory world.[40] Steiner provides detailed descriptions of human and earthly evolution and of life between death and rebirth as it relates to the beings of the higher hierarchies and to God. These descriptions make it possible for anyone to find their way into the spiritual world through thinking.[41]

Adults who learn to connect with the supersensory world through their own thinking naturally develop a religious approach to life. They learn to approach their own existence with trust and gratitude and to manage their development in harmony with the laws of the spiritual world. They learn that human beings, like thoughts, are immortal and indestructible.

Today, many people believe that religious education should be avoided because it manipulates children and takes away their freedom of choice. In fact, however, children who are not allowed to experience qualities such as reverence, admiration, and devotion grow up "unfree" with regard to religion. They do not realize that have missed out on essential human forces until later, when they may bitterly regret their own lack of idealism. People who establish undogmatic, independent relationships to the contents of specific religious traditions find in them ever new incentives for inner development. As adults, these people radiate the peace and certainty that children need; they *allow* but do not *force* their children to participate in their own religious life. This approach to religious education leads to individual religious activity accompanied by tolerance and freedom of thought. If widely implemented, it would allow different denominations and religions to learn to understand and respect each other.

24.3 Practical aspects of religious education

Since children are very receptive and "religious" in their relationship to the sense-perceptible world but are not yet capable of seeking religion on any internalized level, they need to experience the realities of the supersensory world in sense-perceptible form. Seasonal festivals and bedtime rituals play an especially important role.

Seasonal festivals

Unlike birthdays and other family holidays, seasonal festivals transcend the merely personal and celebrate something that many people have in common. But how can we adults find points of departure for taking the seasonal festivals seriously and experiencing them as outstanding events in the cycle of the year?

Christmas celebrates the gift of the human possibility of experiencing individual development and the birth of the I. How can we celebrate this festival in ways that allow children to experience this expectation and joy in sense-perceptible form? At *Easter,* we celebrate the possibility of transformation and the path that leads us through many moments of dying and becoming. *Whitsun* is the festival of the brotherhood of all human beings on Earth. *St John's Day,* the festival of purification and conscience, calls on us to "change our ways." Since *Michaelmas* (usually celebrated, if at all, more as an autumn festival of thanksgiving), is a less familiar festival, we will use it as a more detailed illustration of possibilities for celebrating with children. For more suggestions about how to celebrate this and other festivals, see the *Bibliography.*

Michaelmas is celebrated on St Michael's Day, September 29. In the northern hemisphere, autumn is beginning. The leaves are starting to change color and drop, but the buds that will become next year's leaves are already present in the leaf axils. The Revelation to St John (Rev. 12:7) recounts Michael's battle with the dragon. This image, which symbolizes the struggle against evil in the world, appears in many legends. How can we help children experience the inner courage that is so necessary for this struggle against evil? And what image can convey to them the element of hope that is revealed in hidden buds as the old leaves fall?

Here is one of many possibilities. On September 29, the family invites friends and relatives to a "test of courage" in their yard. Children of various ages gather, accompanied by adults and teenagers, and find equipment set up for testing their courage — a tall ladder, a seesaw, a sack to reach into and guess its contents (chives, shells, mud, etc.) by feel. For older children, these tests actually do involve overcoming their own hesitation, but they are more likely to test

24

the courage of the mothers of younger ones, who still imitate everything fearlessly. The legend of St George is presented in a simple puppet show, and songs about autumn and Michaelmas contribute to the festive mood. Each year, the tests of courage are different and unexpected, and as the children grow older, the tasks become more difficult — a tree to climb, or a challenging hike in the woods, following a hidden horn player who goes ahead of them. They may have to discover a hidden trunk containing costumes for St Michael and a dragon. They wear the costumes home to improvise a Michaelmas play, accompanied by singing, for their younger siblings.

The essential point illustrated by this example is that the contents of religious revelation need to be expressed in images that children can associate with experiences and activities.

Children from families who celebrate seasonal festivals appropriately seem stronger, develop more harmoniously, and take their place in world with more confidence than children who experience either no festive traditions or only conventional celebrations unaccompanied by inner conviction.

Instead of simply organizing a celebration for their children, it is essential for adults to take up the theme of the festival on some inner level. Even in its earliest stages, this effort imbues outer events with the mood needed to carry any true festival. The outer context (specific songs, Gospel readings, and festive habits) should remain the same from year to year. Children need and love these customs and traditions, which strengthen their will and their ability to remember (see also Section 20.1).

Bedtime rituals

Another fundamental element in religious education for small children is fostering the transition between waking and sleeping. An evening song or especially a prayer creates a mood of devotion that allows the child's soul to come to rest and to transcend everyday life for a few minutes. Even children too young to understand the content of prayers love these moments, as illustrated by the responses of two little boys whose parents said the following prayer with them each evening:

> From my head to my feet,
> I am the image of God.
> From my heart to my hands,
> I feel God's breath.
> When I speak with my mouth,
> I follow God's will.
> When I see God everywhere,
> In mother and father,
> In all loving people,
> In beast and blossom,
> In tree and stone,
> No fear do I feel;
> Only love can then fill me
> For all that is around me.
>
> RUDOLF STEINER

With each line of this prayer, two-and-a-half-year old Jacob, who had just learned to say "I" to himself, became more and more enthusiastic about speaking it with his parents. Beginning with the line that mentions mother and father, he said "me too" after every line, and was satisfied only when his parents added at the end, "Yes, and in Jacob too."

Two-year-old William loved to repeat the lines as his parents said them slowly, but he always left out the line about fear. Instead, he said each of the next lines twice: "Beast and bossom, beast and bossom, tree and tone, tree and tone..." By the end, he was always so happy that he jumped up in bed and flung himself into the pillows, saying "that's so nice!"

We do not mean to suggest that you should begin to pray with children only when they start to talk. The little book *Prayers for Parents and Children* listed in the Bibliography also includes verses that adults can say for newborns, as well as a number of table graces.

Guardian angels

In many difficult situations in life, it can be a great help to know that each person, and especially each child, is watched over by a guardian angel. This statement often prompts the objection, why don't people's angels protect them from the accidents and tragedies that happen all the time? The only possible response is that countless miracles occur each day to prevent adversities. Our guardian angels shield us from all misfortunes except the ones derived from the wisdom that guides our individual destinies. The misfortunes we cannot avoid are events that we can learn from, events that help us grow. This realization leads to a fundamentally thankful attitude toward life, as expressed in this poem by Christian Morgenstern:

Oh wise and higher I, you've blessed
me with the shelter of your outspread
   wings,
with guidance through what each new
   lifetime brings,
with choices that for me were best.

Assailed by doubt in younger years,
I've learned to trust that you know
   best.
Now strengthened and with gratitude,
   I rest
my gaze on you, who calm my fears.[42]

24

24.4 Coping with death

Questions about the transitory and immortal aspects of our own existence, and hence also a sense of what death means, begin only in pre-adolescence (around age eight or nine, or often even later). The following example illustrates how children of different ages relate to death.

When their grandmother dies, all five siblings listen intently as their father tells about her last moments of life in the hospital. Their reactions clearly depend on their varying degrees of emotional maturity. A short time later, the four-year-old is back in the sandbox absorbed in play. The nine-year-old observes everything attentively and notices that she does not feel sorrow in the same way that older people do. Deep inside, she understands that her grandmother has died and will never come back, but her emotional reaction to this event is still very limited. The twelve-year-old reacts very differently. As she listens to her father's account, she recalls her grandmother's last visit. Grandma had rubbed her back with eau de cologne and kept her company when she was sick in bed. Her eyes fill with tears as she realizes that she will never see Grandma again. For days, an awareness of the inevitability and loftiness of death echoes in her soul, and she feels both apprehension and confidence in the face of this superior power.

Children are realists who take the world and death at face value. Their first encounter with death may or may not be dramatic, depending on how their adult relatives act and express their feelings. For example, if the death of a loved one is celebrated as that person's "birthday in heaven," children learn that each person's essential being passes through visible and invisible forms of existence. They learn that dead people's efforts and qualities can be remembered with pleasure. Celebrating these "birthdays in heaven" on a regular basis teaches children that the spiritual world with all its beings extends into the visible world.

In one family, one of the six children died at a very young age. Each year, the whole family celebrated his "birthday in heaven" by doing something special together. Even their annual visit to his grave was not depressing. After tidying up around his headstone, they said a prayer and sang a song. Over dinner, they told stories about his short life, and no one was unduly upset if his mother was sometimes moved to tears. Experiencing death as a natural part of life, solemn and serious yet also happy and confidence-inspiring, adds an element of true piety to everyday life and makes an essential contribution to children's religious education.

But what can we do to help children who are confronted with the possibility of their own death due to an accident or serious illness? Their reactions vary greatly, depending on their ages. The section on chronic illnesses (see Section 11.1) gives several examples. The more sober and objective adults can be in dealing with a child confronting the reality of death, the better it is for all concerned. Children invariably sense adults' concern, pain, and fear and are upset if they feel that something very important is being concealed from them.

When asked what it means when someone dies at a very early age, Rudolf Steiner said that children who die young bring piety to their families. This is something we can observe repeatedly, independent of the reason for their death. The death of a child jolts the parents and siblings who are left behind into a totally new awareness of questions about the meaning of life, human immortality, and death's significance for life.

24

25. Sex Education

There are certain aspects of adult society that children must learn about in order to stay safe. These aspects include not only individual sexuality but also sexual abuse, prostitution, drugs, violence, criminality, sects, and satanic cults. In addition, the media are full of compelling images of war, poverty, and hunger. Children and teenagers are full of questions about these negative aspects of life. How can such things happen? Why are they still possible? Why doesn't the government intervene, or the church, or all the good citizens in town? How can people just go about their work and act as if nothing had happened? How can we simply accept the increasing gap between rich and poor?

For children and teenagers learning to deal with these difficult issues, the best education is the example of trusted adults. As parents and teachers, how do we deal with these subjects? Do we make it clear that all human beings must come to grips with them and that certain viewpoints can help? Do we share how we ourselves view these issues and how we are learning to contribute to positive change? All of these can help teenagers see more clearly. Today, children and teens increasingly educate themselves about sexuality and difficult social issues through readily available reference works, media coverage, and conversations with friends. More than information, they need standards to apply to what they have read and heard. In other words, they need to experience how respected adults deal with and act on these issues. Often, however, they hesitate to ask questions, sometimes because they lack the specific vocabulary but more often because they hesitate to bring up subjects that adults may consider taboo or uninteresting. Education around sexuality requires not only specific information but also — and more importantly — opportunities for processing it. And where in everyday life in a family or in school is there really the space to address questions of this sort as thoroughly and carefully as they deserve?

Sexuality and other issues that responsible adults must confront can contribute a great deal to creating an honest atmosphere of true partnership and conversation between children and adults. After all, adults continue to be affected by these issues and can never claim to have resolved them once and for all. These are far-reaching existential questions related to the shadow side of human

25

existence, to all those areas where goodness and humanity seemingly falter or fail, forcing to take preventive and protective measures to insure our own safety and to help others at risk. Much as we welcome the fact that our society has fewer and fewer taboos and that the problematic aspects of human existence are discussed and documented with increasing openness, this state of affairs nonetheless conceals grave dangers for children and adolescents in particular. They are no match for the resulting flood of information, which can undermine their confidence in life and raise doubts about life's meaning.

25.1 Freedom and responsibility

If we read the laws on the protection of minors, we can be thankfully reassured by legislative measures to insure that all children grow up in safe circumstances. In reality, however, enforcement is difficult and children's safety depends first and foremost on their domestic situations — in other words, on a sphere of privacy and individual freedom that is largely exempt from regulation and oversight.

This is especially true of alcohol, our society's number one drug, and of access to youth-endangering videos and television programs with their endless cycle of cruelty, horror, violence, and sexual abuse. Children and adolescents are almost inevitably confronted with this type of material before they are mature enough to process it appropriately. And of course there is also the natural attraction exerted by anything that forbidden, deviant, or unusual. For educational reasons, it is important for adults to watch or discuss a "forbidden" subject with adolescents from time to time to deprive the topic of its fascination and insure that exposure sharpens their feeling of responsibility rather than dulling their humane responses.

Freedom and *responsibility* are the two key words in dealing with dangerous and forbidden topics. Goethe dedicated his drama *Faust* to these two concepts. In Part I, awareness of freedom dominates. Faust has studied everything, up to and including theology and philosophy, but all of his studies fail to answer his questions about the meaning of life and who he really is. In the midst of this crisis of self-knowledge, he realizes that he cannot aspire to the most profound truths of life and of his own personal development unless he is willing to acknowledge evil as part of his own existence. The poet presents this insight in artistic form in the scene where Faust consciously sells his soul to the devil by signing his name in his own blood. In other words, Faust acknowledges that the forces of evil, like the potential for good, are present in his own blood and will.

Much as we might wish otherwise, we cannot aspire to freedom, the epitome of human dignity, without consciously coming to grips with evil.

This fact provides the background not only for any discussion of sexuality or other areas of adult responsibility but also for understanding and forgiving the repeated shortcomings of ourselves and others. Ultimately, none of us can tell anyone else what to do or what not to do. We can only take responsibility for our own actions and insights.

25.2 Sexuality as a factor that shapes human relationships

Today we may wonder why religious customs so carefully defined the domain of sexual love in previous centuries and ancient cultures. But when we experience how difficult it is to deal with sexuality in truly humane ways, it no longer seems surprising that strict customs and arranged marriages were needed to insure that this aspect of human relationships was managed in socially acceptable ways. In earlier times, when people's consciousness of themselves as individualities was not as strong as their allegiance to specific families, tribes, or ethnic groups, social regulation of sexual behavior was not seen as an infringement of personal freedom as it would be today but was accepted as a natural part of the prevailing social order of the extended family.

Meanwhile, human love has increasingly extricated itself from the bonds of kinship and family and tribal membership. The historical shift away from polygamy meant that individual sexuality was expressed less and less in the context of a social group and became increasingly focused on a personal relationship to *one* man or *one* woman. Today, only the two people involved can stand personally and socially responsible for what unites them across social, racial, or ideological boundaries. Their relationship is virtually exempt from external standards or judgments, even if it seems to offend against any generally accepted norms and ethical values that still prevail.

In a moral system based on individual freedom, the concept of "sin" is applicable only when two people in a relationship violate very basic

25

precepts of humane interpersonal behavior — that is, when they deal with each other dishonestly or without love or infringe on each other's freedom. Human relationships are permanent. Even when we terminate them, we know very well that the connection between us is not completely dissolved. Even when we break off relationships, we cannot eliminate the image or the impact of our former partners. What we experienced with them belongs to us and will remain with us. Knowing this has far-reaching implications and helps us realize that a relationship always involves more than just sexual contact. A relationship may include sexuality but does not depend on it. Thus there is no behavior that is inherently impossible to accommodate in a marriage or partnership, just as there is nothing that cannot be used as grounds for separation. Ultimately, whether a relationship remains fruitful for both partners depends only on the strength of their interest in each other. Even this basic fact makes it clear that relationships can never be permanently "exclusive," since each person needs *both* the relationship to the other *and* the possibility to grow and change as an individual. Thus the most fruitful and lasting relationships are those that can encompass everything that the partners encounter and must come to grips with. Growing up in the context of an "inclusive" relationship characterized by the partners' loving interest in each other and in the world and its problems is the best foundation for learning to deal with sexuality appropriately.

25.3 Physical and mental productivity

We use many of the same words and expressions to describe both the physical union of the sexes and intellectual productivity. Arousal, stimulation, and conception can be either physical or mental. We say someone is "pregnant with" or "gives birth to" an idea. This overlap of terminology is related to a fact that we have already discussed in various sections of this book, namely, that human vegetative functions and thinking share a common origin, which Rudolf Steiner described as the metamorphosis of the forces of growth and regeneration into forces of thought (see also Section 15.4).

How does this insight affect our understanding of the physical and intellectual differences between men and women? On the physical level, males and females have different genitals and secondary sex characteristics.

It is interesting to learn that male and female fetuses are identical during the first seven weeks of embryonic development. At this stage, the primordial genital organs are hermaphroditic or androgynous — in other words, capable of developing into either male or female organs. Beginning around the seventh week of gestation, however, characteristics typical of the opposite sex begin to recede. It is interesting to note that this occurs at the same time as the appearance of the cerebral vesicles, which provide the basis for the development of the brain as the foundation of thinking. Clearly, in terms of inherent growth forces, both men and women are potentially hermaphroditic. Throughout life, therefore, the physical expression of secondary sex characteristics can be stimulated by administering the appropriate hormones. A women taking high doses of testosterone develops a deeper voice, male patterns of body hair, and increasing muscularity at the expense of typically female fat deposits. Similarly, a man taking estrogen develops female secondary sex characteristics.

It makes sense, therefore, that the etheric, formative forces that develop and maintain one gender's reproductive organs should be available on a nonphysical level to serve the development of thinking in the opposite sex. If this is so, then female thinking should be characterized by the highly variable intensity, frequency, and quantity of semen development and ejaculation and the spurting, outward-directed quality of male reproductive behavior. And in fact, isn't a woman's thinking generally more "ejaculatory" and less constant than a man's, more unpredictable and stimulating? Enjoying the unfamiliar and being receptive to new insights and ready to reopen discussion the next day from a new perspective is characteristic of female thinking. Conversely, typical male thinking more closely resembles the dynamics and functions of the female reproductive organs. Like the maturing of egg cells and the development of the mucosal lining of the uterus that receives the fertilized ovum if needed, the basic gesture of male thinking is constant, regular, rhythmical, and characterized by a certain degree of self-containment and reliability. Male thinking has the potential to proceed consistently and systematically, relatively independent of external influence. Thus it also tends to be more abstract, which is why almost all of the world's great works of philosophy were written by men. Men serve the function of bringing ideas to maturity — "carrying them to term" — and shaping entire edifices or "bodies" of interrelated concepts. Admittedly, this process goes hand in hand with greater isolation and independence in a man's emotional life. Men are not so quick to become emotionally aroused; their reactions are generally slower and more deliberate than women's. Physically and emotionally, therefore, the sexes are polar opposites that can stimulate and complement each other in many ways. In the course of a lifetime, men and women can also learn

25

each other's typical ways of thinking, at least to a certain extent.

From the spiritual perspective, however, both male and female are completely human. Although it inhabits either a physically male/psychologically female or a physically female/psychologically male constitu-tion, the I that is the spiritual core of each person's being transcends sexuality. The more freely it learns to use the body and soul that it has been given, the more its activity assumes a character that is both personal and universally human.

25.4 Conversations with children and adolescents

A glimpse of a large family

When the last baby is on the way, the older siblings are five, eight, ten, and eleven years old. Their conversation often revolves around the new baby. Will it be a little brother or a little sister? What will his or her name be? When will we be able to take the baby for a walk for the first time? And so on. All of the children know that the growing baby is safe and sound in their mother's body and will be born only when it is really ready. Beyond that, their questions vary greatly. An important principle in all sex education conversations is to provide only the information that each child asks for and finds interesting. Unsought explanations are usually experienced only as emotional baggage that disrupts the thoughts and feelings children associate with their questions about their origins. In this instance, the oldest child will want to know exactly how the baby is going to get out of the mother's body and how it suddenly managed to start growing in there in the first place. The youngest, however, does not ask about physical details at all but is interested only in what the baby's soul does in heaven until the body is ready. The eight-year-old is fascinated by the thought that it might be twins but otherwise has no particular questions. The younger children reenact their conversations with their parents as they play with their dolls. Almost daily, someone gets married or gives birth — usually to twins, of course ...

One day, the ten-year-old surreptitiously shows his mother a pornographic drawing and poem that he brought home from school. His mother says calmly, "I don't think that's nice at all. I'm glad you showed me, but I hope you'll throw it away now." End of discussion. The boy is greatly relieved to find that his mother is not upset about the situation — unlike his teacher, who had gone red in the face and made the entire class stay after school. He understands that pornography is simply something to avoid, like anything else we don't like, and that the fuss in school was unnecessary. At supper, his father tells how he and their mother met and how they looked forward to having many children.

When preschoolers "play doctor"

A five-year-old discovers that adults get upset when he shows other children his penis. Or an appalled mother reports, "I walked into my son's room recently and found him lying on top of the little girl from across the street, and he announced proudly, 'We're playing man and woman in bed'." Usually, children who play games like this are between the ages of four and eight — that is, still in the age of imitation. When we hear about such behavior, we first ask the parents whether their children see examples of adult sexual acts in videos, on television, or in their daily surroundings. In most cases, the children are neither sexually precocious nor "perverted" in any way but are simply imitating what they see adults do. For this reason, the most important component of so-called sex education is the example of adults — that is, how they talk about sexual subjects and how they behave in their own relationships. Appropriate responses to a child's imitation of sexual behavior include humor, ignoring it, or dealing with it as the mother in

the previous section handled her ten-year-old's budding interest in pornography. One thing is certain, however: the more attention you pay to these incidents, the more frequently they will occur. Children enjoy attracting the attention of adults. If they don't get attention simply as a matter of course or at least for good behavior, they try out various types of provocation until they get the desired results.

What's the purpose of the stork?

The story of the stork provides an image of an unembodied soul wanting to incarnate on earth. Because everyday language that emphasizes sense-perceptible facts is inadequate for describing the events of life before birth, the people of earlier times talked about these events in images that everyone could understand immediately. These images were then passed on in the form of myths and legends. Even today, such images remain better suited to a child's preintellectual consciousness than abstract explanations, and they still serve a significant purpose if adults are convinced that the content of the images is true. If you yourself are uncertain about the truth of the image, however, it is best not to bring it up. Instead, tell your child honestly that you don't know anything about life before birth. But do you know someone who could answer your child's questions out of personal conviction? There is no basis in fact for stating that there is no life before birth; all we know is that we cannot see the human soul and spirit in the

25

body-free state, although we can approach this state through our thoughts and feelings. Purely biological explanations of the "facts of life" are depressing for young children. Either they sense that they are being told only part of the truth or they accept the details without being able to relate to them on any personal level. Their curiosity is satisfied for the moment, but their questions about their origins have not really been answered.

The delicate subject of birth control

When you discuss the pill and other contraceptive methods with adolescents, it is important for them to sense that they themselves must answer the related questions about human relationships and responsibility for others. For example, does your teenage son really want his sixteen-year-old girlfriend to manipulate her body with hormones, or would he rather make love to her in ways that mean she doesn't have to do that? In this connection, questions about life before birth as it relates to abortion will inevitably arise.

Often, however, children and teenagers are fully informed about sexuality long before you broach the subject. Their early experiences of love are often very idealistic and tender, in stark contrast to anything they read about sex in most popular magazines, and it is all the more comforting for them when adults make it clear where they stand. For example, on the way out of biology class, a sixteen-year-old boy casually asks his teacher, "What do you think? Is taking the pill actually O.K. for a woman's body?" "No" was her brief reply. "Hmm. Thanks." End of conversation. Exact information is available in any number of books on the subject. But what the boy was asking for — and got — was a respected adult's assessment of the facts.

Admittedly, adolescents' exposure to contradictory views on sexuality often lead them to wonder secretly whether they are really "normal," especially if they have friends of the same age who are already sexually active. They want to know whether it is abnormal at their age to not yet feel the need to "go all the way." Is it still normal to experience love on a more emotional and erotic or spiritual and idealistic level? In private conversations with sixteen- to eighteen-year-olds, we've experienced again and again that they are deeply relieved to know that we think they're "normal" even if they are not yet sexually active.

25.5 Do young children have sexual feelings?

Views differ on this subject. In our experience, whether or not young children exhibit sexual behavior depends largely on the adult behavior they see and imitate. From the purely biological perspective, sexual development is linked to maturation of the sex glands, which begins around age eight or nine. Before that age, children are totally receptive to their environment and crave "body experience" in a wider sense, not yet linked to specific erogenous zones. They don't want sexual stimulation; they want to be loved as whole children. If a young child engages in sexual behavior, it is usually provoked by examples set by adults or older children and encouraged by adult reactions. Such behavior usually disappears if ignored and if the child's contact with playmates who encourage it is reduced — or better yet, supervised. The situation is different when children are often left alone and are bored or anxious. In these instances, thumb sucking (see Section 21.5) or eating usually satisfies their need for enhanced self-perception, but in some cases excessive masturbation may develop (see Section 21.10).

25.6 Homosexuality

Those who equate homosexuality with deviance, perversion, pathology, or abnormality can rest assured that they are suffering from a bias that is totally unfounded in reality. Neither statistics nor everyday experiences confirm the notion that heterosexuals are less likely than homosexual men and women to indulge in sexual exploitation or perversions, criminality, or other social pathologies. On the contrary, some of the most significant figures in our cultural and intellectual life, such as the author Oscar Wilde and the composer Peter Tchaikovsky, were homosexuals.

It is true that the male and female bodies complement each other in the sexual act and that homosexual love remains unfruitful and thus "unnatural" from the perspective of the survival of the species — at least if we assume that procreation is the only purpose of sexual activity. In human beings, however, this is not the case, as is evident from the fact that sexual attraction between humans is not limited to procreative seasons and is

25

independent of the woman's fertility cycle. Physical tenderness and sexual love, in varying forms, are elements that shape human relationships. Each person's physical, emotional, and intellectual experience of love and sexuality is highly individualized and eludes any "norm."

The problem of pedophilia and seduction of minors must also not be associated with homosexuality. Now that sexual abuse of children and adolescents has become a topic of international discussion, it is well known that seduction and abuse of minors, far from being limited to homosexual lifestyles, is primarily the domain of heterosexual men and women. Even-handed treatment of homosexuality is also important, especially in school, where a teacher's brief, objective comments can make the two or three gay or lesbian students in a class feel accepted and understood. For example, the homosexuality of great artists or historical figures should not be concealed. Even the briefest unbiased mention of such facts can make these students feel accepted in their "differentness" and sets a positive precedent.

25.7 Sexual abuse

This theme must play an increasing role in sex education because much of what children and adolescents learn about it through magazines, media, and conversations with friends is difficult for them to digest and process on their own. In this area in particular, the most important goal of education is to develop the appropriate sense of injustice. In adolescence at the latest, it becomes obvious that sexuality is more than just a natural human possibility, a factor in love and relationships, and a private, individual matter that should not be forced upon anyone else. Sexual abuse is dangerous for perpetrators and victims alike and can become as addictive as any drug.

When children and teenagers ask questions about sexual abuse, it is important first of all to confirm that it occurs in all social classes and that it is caused by a deep-seated disturbance in the maturation of the perpetrator's personality. This maturational or developmental disorder affects primarily the person's will and emotions (for disorders in sensory development in preschoolers, see Section 12.4 and 13.8; for disturbances in emotional development in school-age children, see Section 17.3) rather than his or her intelligence.

Abused youngsters need help in the form of attentive interest and observation from adults who see many children and adolescents. Hence it is very important for adults, especially parents and teachers, to inform themselves adequately about how to recognize signs of abuse. We will summarize a few important perspectives here. For more detailed information, see the *Bibliography*.

The concept of abuse

An adult's relationship with a child becomes sexually abusive:

- when sexual arousal, regardless of how it is achieved, becomes the goal of the adult's actions;
- when the child cannot resist the adult's advances;
- when the child feels exploited;
- when the child is unable to get help by talking about his experiences with someone else.

Not only the child's body but also their trust and affection are abused by the adult (usually a close and trusted acquaintance or even a parent). The child feels torn between the desire to return the adult's affection and the sense that what is happening is wrong.

Possible signs of abuse in children

Physical symptoms:

Injuries (uncommon) in the genital area; bites or bruises on the chest, abdomen, buttocks, or thighs; recur-

rent inflammation of the genital organs; spots of blood on underwear.

Possible suspicious behavior

Playing at sexual behavior and sexual talk; masturbation or postures suggestive of intercourse; attempting to fondle children or adults; exaggerated shame; reluctance to get undressed. In infants and toddlers, unusual difficulties during diaper changes; later, auto-aggresive behavior such as pulling out hair, nail biting, self-mutilation; suicide attempts, addictive behavior, or descriptions of abuse in the child's drawings, paintings, or conversation. Depending on the child's vocabulary, abuse may be described either quite clearly or in symbolic or situational terms. For example, adults should always perk up their ears if a child says that a ghost touches her in strange ways at night or a teacher is acting funny, or that she suddenly says she doesn't want to go to someone's house any more.

Psychosomatic symptoms

Recurrent headaches, loss of appetite, vomiting, insomnia, wetting, soiling, attacks of anxiety or asphyxiation at night, asthma; speech, visual, and concentration disorders.

Psychological and behavioral symptoms

Feelings of inferiority or severe self-doubt, generalized anxiety, interpersonal difficulties, either withdrawal or lack of distancing and overfamiliarity (also with strangers), feelings of shame and guilt, either declining

25

performance or extreme motivation in school, helplessness or power plays; depression, phobias, or signs of mental illness.

With a few exceptions, the symptoms on this list are unspecific indicators that can also be observed when children are exposed to other conflicts, such as divorcing parents, the death of a close friend, or experiencing extreme violence or other trauma. For this reason, we urgently recommend that you observe the child carefully but do not attempt to talk with him yourself about your suspicions of abuse. Before doing anything, get expert advice on how you might proceed and what steps to take first. The first thing to do if you suspect sexual abuse of a child is to contact a family counseling center, social service or health department, or an experienced child or adolescent psychiatrist. Above all else, it is important to avoid causing the child further suffering by placing people under suspicion unnecessarily or through unprofessional sex education efforts.

Is subconscious behavior genetically predetermined?

What we now know about heredity, genetics, and medical manipulation of body functions has led to the prevailing view that psychological experiences are almost totally determined by the body. Very little is still attributed to the supersensory human being that is active in the body and its functions. This perspective is questioned only by people who have personally experi-

enced the degree to which physical and psychological malaise, up to and including clinical disorders, can be influenced by self-education. These people are alone in asking which activities of the soul-spiritual being stimulate the body's processes of growth and development and its potential for instincts, urges, and desires in healthy ways.

The purely genetic basis of behavior is called into question if we consider, for instance, the case of the identical twins Reginald and Ronald Kray who dominated the London underworld in the 1950s and 60s with their violent criminal activity. Although monozygotic twins with exactly the same genes, Reginald was heterosexual while Ronald was an active homosexual from an early age.

In his fourth lecture to teachers, Rudolf Steiner describes the development of different aspects of will in relationship to the human body and the members of the human constitution.[43] He shows that human *instinctive behavior* is directly bound to the physical body and especially to the sense organs. Thus cultivating and stimulating the senses through adequate experience is the essential prerequisite to developing healthy instinctive activity (see Section 12.4).

Just as the development of our instincts is based on dealing with the physical body, our *urges* are based on experiencing and managing the etheric body. Through the metamorphosis of growth forces into thought forces, the physical drives expressed in growth, development, and organ functions persist on the soul level as the urge to learn and acquire knowledge (see Section 15.4). If children's interest in the world and eagerness to learn are met only by "useful" information and abstract contents that encourage superficial knowledge rather than an active, enlivened understanding of reality, their developing emotional life will turn away from this type of thinking and seek satisfaction elsewhere. In the absence of thoughts that are true guiding images, children turn to bodily sensory experiences. As a result, their emotions remain at the juvenile stage of clinging to sense impressions and later fail to connect with thinking or to transform into motivating forces or enthusiasm for ideal goals and values. Thus subconscious activity is impoverished on the soul-spiritual level and intensified on the physical level.

The vehicle of our life of *desires,* which is significantly more conscious than our instincts and urges, is the astral or soul body (see page 130). Just as our sensory activity is totally dependent on the physical body and our thinking on the ether body, our emotional life is dependent on the astral body. In preschool children, soul activity is not yet clearly differentiated into thinking, feeling, and will. Thinking is only gradually emancipated from feeling and feeling from willing. The main task of education for school-age children, along with refining their likes and dislikes, is to emancipate feeling from will activity. During the preschool age,

personal experience and personal enjoyment of the world are the dominant factors in all of children's experiences. As modern marketing psychology knows all too well, discovering, "trying out," "having," and enjoying are the typical juvenile forms of experience and form the basis of the healthy self-centredness that is established (and expressed in immature innocence) during early childhood. If this infantile, body-bound, and egocentric emotional life persists, however, it lays the groundwork for many later developmental crises including a variety of problematic relationships. In people who have not learned to empathize with others or to take others just as seriously as they take themselves, emotions remain strongly body-oriented, sentimental, subjective and at risk for chronic self-pity. In contrast, educational techniques that free children's feelings from their bodies and redirect them toward thoughts about life and the world also free them from body-bound will activity (see also Section 17.4). This is the only way to transform our life of desires into conscious, body-free soul activity that wants to learn and is satisfied by learning. An emotional life that relates to the guiding power of good thoughts allows us to relinquish our desires when necessary, whereas self-control is almost impossible for an infantile, will-bound emotional life. Behavioral therapy and/or training are necessary if this situation is to change.

25

Therapies for victims of abuse

The central problem in damage due to sexual abuse is impairment of the young victim's developing I-function. On the bodily level, abuse disturbs children's natural identification with their own bodies to the point where they may even hate their bodies. As a Self, an abused child also no longer feels at home in his own soul life, since he cannot process or adequately explain to himself his own tolerance of abusive incidents, his longing for closeness and acceptance, and his abhorrence of the repeated abuse. Self-respect, self-confidence, and self-awareness are unable to develop because this development occurs on the boundary where the self interacts with other people, and this boundary has been breached repeatedly and violently. On the spiritual level, abused children may develop serious identity problems and personality disorders up to and including split personalities. Independent of the family or individual therapy indicated in any specific case, educational efforts (both in school and at home) for victims of abuse should concentrate on strengthening the I, the core of the child's personality. Stimulating and affirming the child's independent activity in all areas as much as possible can do a great deal to encourage healing.

In our experience, mothers whose children have been sexually abused need as much help as their children. Their situation is dominated by anxiety and concern about whether their children have suffered permanent damage. In addition, mothers feel guilty for failing to protect their children. The first step in such cases is to help them realize that their own anxiety also has negative effects on their children's development. For their own and for their children's sake, it is very important for these mothers to recognize their need for help in learning to deal with and process their guilt, disappointment, anger, pain, and sorrow and transform them into forgiveness, understanding, and trust in destiny. There is nothing in human life that cannot be transformed into good. No mistake or trauma is ever exclusively bad or tragic. It can also always be a starting point for a new, much more conscious understanding of life and personal development.

26. Understanding Addiction and Avoiding Drugs

26.1 Why do people turn to drugs?

Why do adults, teenagers, and — increasingly — children turn to drugs? Why would anyone deliberately ingest substances known to damage the body and shorten life? Among children and teenagers, the most common reasons are curiosity and peer pressure. They don't want to lose friends or feel excluded because they refuse drugs. Often, however, young people take drugs for the same clearly defined personal reasons as adults of all ages:

- to *escape* from a world that has become uncomfortable — an unpleasant home life full of arguments and parental conflicts, or worries and problems in school or at work;
- out of *fear of failure* — in a relationship, at work, or in school;
- out of *longing* to experience the warmth, light, pleasure, harmony, closeness and security that were missing in their childhood and adolescence, or as a way of gaining spiritual experience;
- out of *curiosity* to experience danger, adventure, or feeling special, or out of the desire to "get something out of life."

All of these longings, hopes, and desires are as natural as life itself. We might even say that a life without them is no life at all. The issue here is simply whether our upbringing and education strengthen our natural emotional and spiritual abilities so that we can satisfy these desires through inner work and independent activity or whether we resort to the artificial stimulation of passive drug consumption.

Our concern here is to make it clear that drug abuse is an understandable, even inevitable response to modern life, which emphasizes personal liberty and isolating self-reliance to such an extent that individuals are forced to confront themselves and their existential loneliness at a very early age. The modern human condition can easily become unbearable for anyone who does not discover strategies for overcoming the symptoms it produces. Thus drug abuse poses perhaps the single most important challenge to educators in the twenty-first century. As parents and teachers, we must first understand the experiences that different types of drugs convey and then ask ourselves how these experiences can be achieved in ways that support healthy development and constructive education. With this in mind, the most important experiences triggered by different drugs are listed below.

Alcohol

Desired effects: Feeling a sense of community, being able to speak freely with each other and leave daily cares behind, feeling happy and relaxed, creating a festive mood, finding relief from loneliness.

Possible health consequences: Brain damage, liver disease, kidney damage, muscle tremors, high blood pressure, insomnia, perspiration, nerve paralysis, pancreatic disease, alcohol embryopathy (damage to the baby *in utero).*

Nicotine

Desired effects: Improved concentration, calming down or distancing oneself from events, a fresh perspective or a short break to come to one's senses, avoiding eating or drinking (unnecessary calories!), enjoying pleasant company and conversation, staying awake longer and reducing the need to sleep.

Possible health consequences: Cardiac symptoms, headaches, respiratory diseases, increased risk of cancer, poor peripheral circulation.

Opium, morphine, heroin, and other opiates

Desired effects: Being able to rest, relax, feel warm, and sleep deeply in spite of pain and worries; feeling free, floating, and slightly out-of-body, like a being who can unite with the light, color, and other beings in the surroundings. Longing for eternal rest, warmth, sleep, darkness, and unconsciousness (the word *morphine* comes from Morpheus, the god of sleep). Experiencing euphoric pleasure and bliss unhindered by the body's heaviness or daily cares ("paradise" or life in a spiritual world as if after death). Longing for the "lightning strike" that frees one from life's narrow confines, the dullness and uniformity of everyday life, and sluggish bourgeois thinking.

Possible health consequences: Weakens the digestive system, inhibits sexual functioning. Muscle cramps, pale skin, weight loss, joint and limb stiffness. Ultimately, all body functions are destroyed. General weakness, hepatitis infections.

Cannabis, marijuana, and hashish (derived from the female hemp plant)

Desired effects: Sensing that all realities are relative. Escaping from the constraints of daily life with its habits, obligations, deadlines, stress, and aggravation. Feeling high, happy, free, and uninhibited; laughing uncontrollably. Experiencing thoughts, feelings, and perceptions (including space and time) in new ways unknown in everyday life (many impressions seem more elemental or enormously enlarged, extracted from their usual contexts and seen from new perspectives or in isolation). Consciously experiencing the dream state between waking and sleeping.

Possible health consequences: Unsafe driving, reduced concentration and ability to learn, reduced sperm count, irregular menstrual cycles, developmental disabilities in unborn children, weakened immune system, lack of initiative.

LSD / ergot alkaloids

Desired effects: Out-of-body experiences, colorful visions and hallucinations of light and warms, a panoramic view of one's life, reemergence of long-forgotten memories and experiences, feeling completely present and yet in a different world.

Possible health consequences: Temporary psychosis, delusions, kidney and/or liver damage, unreliability of sense impressions. Drug-induced experiences may recur months later in the form of flashbacks.

Cocaine and amphetamines

Desired effects: Feeling strong, capable, and unusually clear-thinking and intelligent; longing for mental challenges and stimulation and a special personal task; delusions of grandeur and feelings of superiority; orgiastic feeling of bliss; feeling alert and strong with total absence of physical constraints; being able to transcend the ordinary limits of fatigue.

Possible health consequences: Irritability, restlessness, sense of persecution, headaches, racing heart, anxiety, insomnia, abdominal cramps, dizziness.

Ecstasy (XTC) and designer drugs

Desired effects: Psychological changes (openness, being able to reveal feelings, reduced anxiety, increased interest in conversations and relationships). Intuitive understanding of how others feel; reduced inhibitions in every respect. (Designer drugs are combinations of amphetamines, ephedrine, caffeine and MDMA, a synthetic derivative of nutmeg.)

Possible health consequences: disorientation, hallucinations, anxiety, depression, exhaustion, insomnia, palpitations.

Health risks of all drugs: premature aging, increasing loss of I-function (physical, emotional, and mental self-control).

26

26.2 Prevention and treatment

In Place of the Self, a very worthwhile book by the Dutch psychologist and drug therapist Ron Dunselman, describes and differentiates the physical, emotional, and mental effects of drugs. As the overview above suggests, each drug displaces the I, taking the place of personal initiative and conveying certain experiences that would otherwise require the hard work of self-development. This phenomenon is also a problem for psychotherapy. It is so much easier to take a sleeping pill or a tranquilizer, for example, than it is to find peace by learning to pray or meditate. Taking drugs is much easier than meditating for those who want to see nature as spirit-imbued and their own thoughts and feelings as much more colorful and real. Taking pills that make us feel secure and mildly euphoric is also much easier than doing exercises that lead to inner stability and help us withstand whatever life brings. The decision to use drugs, however, is a very individual matter. We are repeatedly astonished to see the levels of suffering that some people are willing to tolerate and manage to process internally while others in similar circumstances soon turn to drugs.

As you read the following viewpoints on preventing and treating drug abuse, keep in mind that they are meaningful only in combination with real and supportive human relationships. People who seriously promise themselves or others that they will resist temptation (in other words, who decide that the I will control their thinking, feeling, and willing) are much more likely to resist drugs successfully. For individuals in recovery, the most effective helpers and therapists are people who have been close to turning to drugs or took them briefly but gave them up after realizing that they are nothing but a dead end. Without effective intervention, drug use and addiction lead to illness — the physical symptoms listed above. Taking drugs bypasses the I, as indicated by drug users' weakened will, empty emotional life, and undermined ability to think.

Disorientation, doubt, feelings of hatred for a bad and unjust world, and existential anxiety and worry are becoming endemic throughout the world, and children and teenagers are not exempt. No wonder a fifth to a third consume alcohol while up to one tenth give in to internal or external pressures to turn to other drugs. Under these circumstances, it is quite understandable that more and more people are calling for legalization of drugs, which would make their use a matter of individual responsibility. How can we legally and effectively forbid something that more and more people "need" and therefore consider normal? Today, drug use is assuming crisis proportions because social forces and religious traditions no longer offer effective support, but individuals have not yet developed enough personal stability and the new inner forces needed to resist drugs. But instead of resorting to redefining pathological habits as normal and healthy, we should do everything possible to insure that drugs are supplanted by an individual human I that actively contributes to its own development and that of its surroundings.

Alcohol and drug-dependent children and adolescents are often more sensitive than others, more receptive to beauty and idealism. As a result, they often have a revolutionary streak. But they are not adequately prepared to deal with the hard realities of everyday life. They either avoid problems or attempt to solve them through violence. It is difficult for them to summon enough persistence to deal with the same problems day after day until real solutions are found. Hence treatment tends to be effective only in individuals who apply a great deal of effort to their own recovery and are removed from surroundings that support drug use.

In this context, we can mention only the most basic steps that parents and teachers can take to prevent addiction in children:

- Breastfeeding instead of formula feeding in infancy
- The loving interest of parents and teachers in every developmental step the child takes (see Chapter 17)
- Appropriate sensory education
- Cultivating good daily habits, including regular meals. Satisfying the desire for sweets at mealtimes only (see Chapter 14).
- A balance between strictness and permissiveness in disciplining your child. Clear limits allow your child to feel secure and confident (see Section 20.2).
- Strengthening your child's independent imagination by telling fairy tales. Replace passive consumption of ready-made images with reading good stories, legends, and biographies (see next Chapter 27).
- Nondogmatic religious education.

26

27. Children and Multimedia

Television, videos, and CD and cassette players, along with telephones, fax machines, e-mail and the Internet, are becoming increasingly attractive as communication technologies merge. In many households, they now play a central role in personal life and recreation. As a result, the authors find themselves faced with the thankless task of delivering this piece of advice:

To the greatest extent possible, allow your children to grow up without media. Allow them to establish real, lasting, and supportive relationships based on perceiving their human and natural surroundings as they really are. Have conversations with your children, play with them, and do not allow machines to become their best friends and constant companions.

27.1 Why is television "not for children"?

Why does television in particular cause such lasting damage to the nervous system and sensory organs? Here are some contributing factors:

Unnatural visual processes and disintegration of sensory activities
When we watch television, our eyes are fixed on the screen while the images move over it. This phenomenon is used to good advantage in eye clinics, where several hours of television viewing are prescribed for patients who have just had eye surgery. Avoiding movement supports healing of muscles after surgery, and watching television is the *only* way to keep the eye muscles completely still. What does it mean, however, when countless children between the ages of three and twelve watch television for four to six hours every day? At a time when independent physical activity and movement are essential to normal development, these children are sitting immobilized in front of the television, since the eye muscles' lack of movement carries over to the rest of the body. This visual process is highly abnormal. (In normal seeing, the eye muscles move in all directions as the surface of the observed object is

explored.) Furthermore, since television reduces three-dimensional figures to two-dimensional images, none of the colors or proportions of television objects correspond to reality. When we watch television, only two of our senses (sight and hearing) interact. The others are barely stimulated at all, and their functions become dissociated.

Central nervous processing that stimulates passive reception

The processing televised images in the brain is not the same as in the normal, active process of seeing, in which the eyes move constantly and perceive subtle color variations and vision is supplemented with input from all the other senses. Furthermore, the flood of sensory information coming from the television screen overwhelms children's ability to process what they perceive. They take in bits and pieces and are often unable to establish any connection between what they see and what they hear. TV viewing stimulates fragmentary, associative thought processes and passive receptivity in the brain because there is no time for active perception. As a result, television stimulates intricate nerve connections (which are still developing in children) in ways that shape the brain into an instrument of passive, associative thinking that is poorly adapted to active, creative thinking.

Promotion of aggressive, restless behavior

After watching television, children often don't know what to do with themselves for a while and tend to be aggressive, annoying, and in a bad mood. This physical restlessness is just as unnatural as their lack of movement while looking at the screen. This reaction is due primarily to forced inactivity rather than to the *content* of the program (whether violent, silly, or meaningful); problematic content simply increases the effect.

We have observed other television-related symptoms in our pediatric practice:

- Children who watch television regularly:
  - approach other people with a lack of respect or appropriate reserve
  - have trouble establishing contact with others
  - tend to grimace and avoid eye contact
  - give superficial or stereotyped answers to questions and show little in-depth interest in objects
  - read less and prefer "shortcuts" to reading, such as comic books
  - have less ability to concentrate.
- Television supports the tendency to become addicted to alcohol, medications, and illegal drugs because it accustoms children to mental stimulation and contents that are available without personal effort — at the touch of a button, so to speak.
- Will development is fundamentally disturbed because sitting motionless in front of the TV replaces physical activity and imitation.
- Television viewing has been shown to cause delays in language development.[44]

Publications are now available to advise parents on which programs are appropriate or inappropriate for specific ages. If we look at the titles and descriptions of recommended programs, however, we find that most of them are fantasies that bear no relationship to real life. Their caricatures of reality work their way into children's souls, distancing them from real life before they have a chance to develop authentic relationships to human beings and natural objects.

It can't be that bad, can it?

Parents often object:

- I can't do anything about it; television is part of normal family life today. And I need the uninterrupted private time that I get when my children are watching television. Besides, it can't be that bad....
- If that's the case, why are there televisions in schools and television and computer programs aimed specifically at children?
- At least it is better to watch television at home than at the neighbours'....
- It is important for my kids to know what other children are talking about....

All we can tell you is that your children will thank you later for allowing them to grow up knowing how to entertain themselves and with their self-awareness intact. They will be glad that they learned to use electronic media when needed without being dependent on them and that their emo-

tional life is not full of caricatures and ersatz virtual experiences.

We should also mention the neurophysiological fact that a six-year-old's brain is only two-thirds the size of an adult's but has five to seven times more connections between neurons than the brain of either an eighteen-month-old or an adult. A six- or seven-year-old brain has the capacity for thousands and thousands of dendrite connections between neurons. At age ten or eleven, children lose most of these connections again when an enzyme produced in the nerve cells of the brain dissolves all minimally myelinized nerve connections.[45] In other words, the development of the nervous system is essentially complete at this age, and nerve connections disappear if they have not been activated by many different types of activity.

Children who don't watch TV are preferred playmates

What fosters the development of independence in a child more — being just like everyone else or having the courage to say, "We don't watch TV at home, we'd rather play games"? Children raised without television and videos are preferred playmates; parents are glad when they come over to play because it means their own children watch less television.

- Your neighbors may be glad when their children are invited to play at your house; they may even honor your request not to let your children watch television in their house.

27

- Are your children really missing out on anything if they learn about nature, other people, and social life through their own experience or through stories that leave them free to develop their own images and ideas instead of through cartoons and animated films? Active, physical play balanced by hearing fairy tales stimulates abilities that your children will value for their entire life.
- Furthermore, who finances and supports the entertainment industry (at your children's expense)?

How can I tell my child?

Convincing your children will take some effort on your part if the television disappears from your house or never appears in the first place. The mother in the example below sets a good example less through the strength of her argument than through her clear and decisive opinion on the subject.

Annie: *Why don't we have a TV set?*
Mother: *Because we don't have time to watch it.*
Annie: *But I do have time. And the kids in school talk about all the fun things they see. Besides, you already let Jason watch it twice at his friend's house.*
Mother: *But I don't want you to get started just yet.*
Annie: *Why not?*
Mother: *Because this television stuff wrecks your imagination. It is just as bad for children as cigarettes and alcohol. When you're grown up, none of those things do as much damage any more.*
Annie: *But why do other parents let their kids watch?*
Mother: *Because they don't know any better. If you want to make me really happy, don't watch TV at your friends' houses. Do me a favor and wait until you're twelve, like Jason was before he was allowed to watch it.*

The more convinced parents are about their decision, the more likely their children are to accept it. If you think your children are missing out on something by not knowing what their friends are talking, you will set yourselves up for endless debates and unnecessary compromises.

Ideally, television should play a part in children's lives only when their emotional and will development is complete — in other words, somewhere between the ages of twelve and fourteen. In any case, television should be taboo until the "crossing of Rubicon" at age nine (see also page 301). In the intervening years, decisions about TV watching should be based on individual circumstances.

Media education

How do children learn to deal with television and other audiovisual media? When you begin to allow your children to watch television, it is very important to watch it with them. This is the only way to insure that the TV will be switched on and off deliberately and consciously. Choosing programs together and discussing what you will watch, for how long, and why also help your children learn to manage their TV viewing independently. Discuss programs after watching them so that your children at least have to respond actively to what they have viewed passively. Once they are twelve years old, you should still be aware of what they are watching and ask them to tell you about it. Even at this age, help in processing the content is often still meaningful and/or necessary. After puberty, the situation looks somewhat different. If their independent activity has been adequately stimulated, teenagers will not be spellbound by television and will deal with it responsibly. Your children should not have free access to the room where you keep electronic media for your own use. Children accept the fact that some things are "just for grownups."

Many medical and educational statements about media use assume that the only appropriate approach is to accept current situations as given, correct extremes, and prevent children from increasing their media consumption. This attitude is not helpful for any child. It only covers up the problem, and existing habits and their consequences persist.

Since the 1960s, significant efforts to change the status quo (such as the environmental movement and the revival of breastfeeding) have been successfully initiated by amateurs. Media use is another consequence of civilization that will change only when individuals decide to act on their insights. We hope that the books, lectures and workshops by the American computer specialist and Internet founder Clifford Stoll will mark the beginning of a popular movement in support of humanly worthy dealings with our multimedia culture. We would like to quote a few of Stoll's challenging statements word-for-word:

The computer changes the ecology of the classroom. Predictably, kids love the new computers and the kindergarten increasingly looks and sounds like a video arcade. Meanwhile, the machine becomes the center of attention, pushing aside clay, crayon and teacher ...

Somehow computers are supposed to be "good" because they're interactive and non-commercial. Television is "bad" because it's passive and commercial. Videotapes on the whole are "good" because they don't have commercials. I'll bet that to a child there's not much difference. All provide big, colourful cathode-ray tubes. All show their favourite characters in fast-paced animated clips. All deliver long stretches of mental excitement with minimal muscular activity.

Suppose we wanted to encourage attention deficit syndrome. I can't think of a better way than to point youngsters at fast animated video clips. Give 'em electronic games with races, spaceship dogfights, shoot-'em-ups, and lots of explosive noises, garish colours, and disconnected information coming from diverse sources. Give them post-modern

27

hyper-linked media rather than simple story-telling. Encourage them to write programs with computerized Turtle graphics rather than touching a real turtle. In short, lock them in an electronic classroom ...

I can hardly think of a less appropriate place to put computers than kindergartens and preschools. Think of the things a three-year old most needs: love, affection, personal attention, human warmth and, mainly, care. Four- and five-year olds need to develop human skills ... how to get along with others. They should be playing with things, not images.[46]

27.2 Computer games aren't harmless, either

The most common subjects for computer games are sports, war, science fiction, chasing criminals, car races, and the like. All of them reduce encounters with human beings and objects to action and reaction; actions and so-called creativity are possible only within the game's (and the computer's) predetermined limits. When it occurs to a ten-year-old girl to tickle a dragon in the desert in a computer game, the makers of the game praise her "creative idea." How can positive learning occur in this setting? Of course computer games encourage attentiveness and quick reaction times, but what about the content? Does it make sense to practice these skills in the context of an extraterrestrial attack on our planet or by tracking down fictional criminals?

Computer games ensnare young children and teenagers in illusory, distorted worlds that have little in common with their real surroundings. These games foster feelings of superiority, manipulativeness and cynicism, encourage youngsters to enjoy making fun of others, and mobilize intelligent responses in a one-sided way that is closely linked to visual phenomena.

They suppress rather than encourage the emergence of imaginative or creative intelligence — that is, any intelligence not fixed on objects or ready-made images. This type of intelligence cannot develop in an environment characterized by pleasurable alienation from objects, humorous or gimmicky staging, spell-binding cruelty, or tension-filled battles. Its development requires moments of stillness, listening, and reflection on internalized impressions that we ourselves direct.

27.3 Comic books and the world of images

Comics leave a lasting imprint on children's mental images. When we ask children who have been exposed to comics to paint pictures in the waiting room while we talk with their mothers, the stereotyped images they produce — clouds with solid outlines and familiar cartoon figures and patterns — are shattering in their poverty of imagination and lack of originality. Even when they are told fairy tales, these children can no longer draw pictures of their own but simply reproduce ready-made caricatures. Why are children so spellbound by the sequences of images in comic books long before they understand the writing in the dialog balloons? Because their thinking is still saturated with images of the perceptible world and has not yet become abstract and image-free, young children are drawn to all pictures and images. In any book, they look for the illustrations first. With equal intensity, they absorb images from their surroundings or the bright colors and sharp outlines of comic-book figures. Such images, however, do not leave the human soul free as other sense impressions do. Our ability to form mental images is pinned down by their self-contained character and suggestive power.

Adults, who have learned to think abstractly, find it much easier to shake off television and comic-books. Children can't do that. Their developing imagination and emotional life are paralyzed and overwhelmed. In addition, the fact that ideals and morally valuable contents are often associated with cartoon characters inextricably links these pure concepts with this type of images in children's minds.

Why are cartoons and comics among the most widely seen and read products?

When we ask teenagers why they like cartoons and animated films, they say things like, "They make it easy to relax," or "They're so silly, they really make you laugh," or "Even though you know none of it is for real, you get totally involved and it is really entertaining."

Three prominent features stand out when we consider the story lines and contents of animated films and similar comics:

They reveal wishes, fantasies and fears that we hide from ourselves, including violent tendencies, making fun of others, and all sorts of cynicism. The heroes who chase, outsmart, destroy, attack, or love and help each other are usually animal-like figures. They are like caricatures of our subconscious, not yet fully humanized urges. When we watch them, it is as if we were instinctively trying to encounter the lower self, which psychology calls the *alter ego* or other self.[47]

They draw on a non-sensory reality.

27

Movement sequences, language, colors, proportions — none of these correspond to sense-perceptible reality, even if we disregard the fact that the heroes are often extraterrestrials transported from some known or unknown planet to the Earth. It is as if our subconscious longing to leave the sense-perceptible world behind and cross the threshold to the spiritual world were creating at least a caricature of other worlds in order to alert people to this other dimension of existence.

A connection to the "spirit of technology" (see also Section 18.2). In several chapters in this book where we talked about thinking and its relationship to reality (see especially Section 24.2), we pointed out that all thoughts are related to realities of some sort. What realities lie behind these monstrous products of human imagination? In animated films, movements are usually extremely abrupt and jerky and the sounds associated with them are faithful reproductions of technical processes. "Click", "boing", "pop," truncated gestures, unnatural transformations of beings or objects into other beings or objects — all of these standard features of animation suggest that these fantastical images (which are designed by — adult — cartoonists

and force their way into our consciousness) correspond to what Rudolf Steiner calls the domain of the elemental beings that are active in human technological inventions, just as the elemental beings (elves, sylphs, undines, and salamanders) that we know from ancient fairy tales and legends inhabit the kingdoms of nature. Rudolf Steiner describes how human beings who spend their days embedded in materialism and technological culture lose their nocturnal connection to the higher spiritual beings (angels, archangels, and time spirits) and begin to be influenced and inspired by these other elemental beings. In contrast, idealistic thinking directed toward the goals of spiritual development leads to nightly encounters with angelic beings, while loving, truthful speech leads to encounters with the archangels and actions oriented toward the ideal of goodness lead to the spirit of the age.[48] Today the appropriate response to our legitimate longing to consciously cross the threshold to the spiritual world is an active spiritual practice based on self-knowledge and self-education, which raise our unconscious instincts, urges, and inclinations to consciousness so that we can transform and humanize them.

27.4 Sensory overload — teaching superficiality

A small child looks through the transparent panels of an open-sided buggy or stroller and sees one fleeting impression after another without being able to focus on anything. This child is being trained to be inattentive.

In contrast, a baby riding in an old-fashioned high baby carriage sees mainly his mother's face. He unhurriedly takes in the subtleties of her changing expressions — her smile, her thoughtfulness, her pleasure when she sees something beautiful, and so on. All of his perceptions are related because they center on one person, his mother, who provides continuity through all the changing contents of his other perceptions.

The mother of a six-month-old leaves the radio on or puts on a tape for the baby, as recommended in modern books on parenting. Can this child relate the music in any way to her other perceptions of her surroundings?

In the first and third examples, sensory impressions are experienced out of context because the child is not moving independently and has no fixed point of reference to which to relate all of her other individual sense impressions. In contrast, a baby who hears her mother rattling the dishes or singing in the next room experiences the connection between these sounds and her mother's work or emotional expression. *What is most important for infants is not the quantity of their sense impressions but the fact that they occur in a real context.* Elsewhere in these observations on child development, we mentioned that it is easier for young children to focus their attention on a single thing that stands out — for example, Daddy coming through the door by himself — than on a large number of simultaneous impressions, especially against a chaotic background such as a shopping mall. Under these circumstances, impressions cancel each other out, and each single one becomes unimportant. This experience is very tiring for babies, who respond by establishing a protective boundary between themselves and the outside — that is, they suck their thumbs or fall asleep. But although sleeping offers some protection, the sleeping child still has to process — on the unconscious level — all of the blurry experiences of the waking state.

This type of training, which fosters superficiality and reduces the value and impact of individual sensory impressions, also affects how children learn to talk and think. Objects' names are applied to them like labels instead of expressing something of their essence. This alienation from reality paralyzes children's interest in the

27

world and encourages them to consider objects in terms of the pleasure they yield. Thinking then serves exclusively to satisfy personal desires, which are unfortunately addressed with increasing success by advertisements and propaganda.

27.5 Early intellectual stimulation

Early intellectual stimulation has become widely practiced and has now conquered the toy market. Broad-based popular faith in science speeds acceptance of the latest toys "based on cutting-edge science." We find the beginnings of this tendency in the work of the educationist Friedrich Froebel who developed toys intended to promote creativity in kindergartens. Having correctly ascertained that children grasp wholes before moving on to understand their individual parts, he presented first a sphere, then a cube, and finally cube consisting of eight smaller cubes. The thrust is obvious: to teach logical, mathematical thinking. Such "toys" give children nothing to do but extract the thoughts that adults have built into them. The same is true of toys that require arranging numbers in sequence, sorting shapes, or assembling blocks into predetermined pieces of furniture. Clearly, these are all examples of abstract thinking that is applied to producing "toys" that are meant to encourage creativity but actually defeat their own purpose. After all, creativity can never be achieved by following a diagram!

Sensory overload deprives the perceived world of its profundity, while comic-book and television images lead children's thinking into illusory realms. Early training in logic mistakenly links concepts that can be understood only through pure thinking to sensory perception. In these three ways, human consciousness is led astray in full view of the public. Millions of children bear the consequences — an absence of meaning and alienation from reality later in life.

28. Environmental Toxins and Environmental Protection

In their book, *Raising Children Toxic Free,* Needleman and Landrigan succinctly characterize the problem of environmental toxins and the task of environmental protection:

> The practice of pediatric medicine has changed steadily over the past two decades. It's focus is now what is referred to as "the new morbidity," meaning that the predominant diseases of children have shifted from brief and simple infections to complex, chronic, handicapping conditions of multiple origins ... Some of these conditions have at least part of their origins in environmental factors. Air pollutants clearly worsen and may initiate asthma and other respiratory disturbances. Metals, solvents, pesticides and other neurotoxins, by affecting the central nervous system, can contribute to the pool of learning disabilities, as well as attention deficit disorder and behavioral disturbances ...
>
> Awareness of environmental health issues is spreading, but there continues to be an excess of skepticism about the reality of these hazards. Parents who take steps to protect their children from unnecessary exposures to pesticides, metals, asbestos, or radiation may meet with disdain and occasional disbelief from officials, physicians, and even some of their fellow parents.[49]

Obviously, the environment affects everyone, regardless of skin color or social status. Through the air they breathe, the water they drink, and the food they eat every day, the children and senior citizens of any given region are affected by the state of the natural world and by the changes human intervention has inflicted on it.

We enthusiastically welcome the rise of the international environmental protection organizations that have come about through individual initiatives on the part of lay people and experts. Increasingly, these organizations are partnering effectively with government agencies and industries to keep the extent of environmental damage at acceptable levels. We hope that our comments in this chapter will help increase awareness of the fact that we are all co-affected by and co-responsible for environmental degradation. Our only chance for coping with the damage is for as many people as possible to work actively together to minimize it.

We human beings are more than just the cause of environmental damage and the only possible protectors of our biosphere. In comparison to plants and animals, we are also the living things best able to cope with environmental pollution. In recent history, thousands of plant and animal species have become extinct while the Earth's human population has increased exponentially. Although human illnesses and damage due to environmental pollution have also increased, it is nonetheless true that our chances of survival and adaptation are astonishingly high. This fact encourages our tendency to dismiss environmental damages as harmless in the short term. It is usually very difficult to trace individual cases of human illness to the complex, long-term effects of changing concentrations of different toxic compounds that also interact. Unlike lead poisoning, lung cancer due to smoking, or increases in asthma due to air pollution, not all physical and behavioral problems, especially those that appear during childhood and adolescence, are as easily traced to a specific cause.

In any case, it is consoling to know that the stabilizing and stimulating effects of good parenting and adequate attention can help children cope with harmful environmental influences. An upbringing that strengthens the immune system by stimulating all types independent activity is an effective means of protecting children from environmental damage "from the inside out." Thus in addition to the task of democratically applying individual possibilities to coping with environmental damage, we can also take advantage of the healing and moderating effects of our soul-spiritual environment.

28.1 Radioactive contamination of the environment

Artificial radioactivity refers to the ability of substances that are not naturally radioactive to become radioactive and destabilized when bombarded with high-energy rays (usually neutrons). When this happens to elements that play a role in body functions, they may develop life-threatening effects. The most familiar examples are radioactive iodine, which is stored in the thyroid gland, and strontium 90, which accumulates in bones.

Atom bomb testing, the bombs dropped on Hiroshima and Nagasaki, and so-called peaceful uses of atomic energy have all contributed to the radioactive contamination of our environment. (Fortunately, at least, above-ground atomic testing has mostly been discontinued.) The half-lives of radioactive elements range from eight days for iodine-131 through 33 years for caesium-137 to 24,390 years for plutonium-239, which is one of the most toxic products of nuclear fusion. Dispersed in the air, plutonium-239 causes lung cancer in quantities as low as .001 gram. It is important to note that plutonium, which is virtually non-existent in the natural world, was first produced through nuclear fission experiments. In contrast, living things on earth have always been exposed to low but omnipresent levels of cosmic radiation, which influenced their evolution very gradually over long periods of time.

How much radioactivity individuals can tolerate varies considerably, but children are significantly more sensitive than adults. Radiation damage occurs mainly on the cellular level. Direct radiation damage to a cell's genetic material can disrupt the cell's metabolism, cause malignant degeneration, and trigger the production of new chemical compounds. The current state of knowledge does not allow us to determine with certainty which levels of radiation have no effect on humans and animals. Any exposure to radiation has the potential to destabilize matter, weaken the body's forces of regeneration, and cause long-term damage.

In this connection, it is important to know that the tissues with the most rapidly dividing cells — for example, the intestinal mucosa, bone marrow, and gonads — are especially sensitive to radiation, while the brain is relatively insensitive. The growing bodies of children and embryos in particular are especially at risk.

Possibilities for counteracting radioactive damage

The radical step of banning nuclear energy would be the only lasting solution to the problem of radioactive pollution. Unless or until humankind takes this step, understanding the nature of the living body's regenerative processes, as we have attempted to present in various parts of this book, is perhaps the most important aid to preventing damage due to radioactivity. Inherent in the nature of the ether body (the vehicle of processes of both thinking and growth) is the fact that it can be supported and strengthened from two sides — its natural side (regeneration and growth) and its "cultural" side (the activity of thinking).

In this context, fostering rhythms and habits in childhood is especially effective, as are sensory education, nutrition, and religious education. Worthy of special mention is eurythmy, which is unique in its ability to activate the ether body directly through the I (see also Section 22.4). Although it cannot directly influence the physical effects of radiation on the body, it can do so indirectly, by strengthening the body's ability to regenerate and to counteract breakdown processes. All bodily processes, right down to the life processes of individual cells, occur in rhythms that can be supported and stimulated by the measures mentioned above. With regard to nutrition — aside from choosing foods exposed to the least radiation — we can attempt to support the body's vital processes through appropriate combinations of foods that stimulate all aspects of the body's vitality.

Clearly, coming to grips with the invisible forces of the atom requires equally emphatic efforts to come to grips with the invisible forces of the spirit, which include the formative forces of the ether body.

The Alliance for Childhood

In place of an afterword

The experiential world of children and adults underwent exceptionally dramatic changes during the last decades of the twentieth century. Computers made the interconnectedness of all human life on earth a matter of everyday experience. Pragmatic economic thinking took hold of almost all domains of work, and concepts such as "quality control" and "reorganization" began to play a role in research on the molecular structures of human genetic material and in the many related ethical issues.

As exciting as the breakthroughs in new fields of knowledge and technical methods may be, the possibilities of misusing them have nonetheless become burning issues. Regulation offers no lasting protection. In these areas, our only insurance is to strengthen individual human personalities and their awareness of the value and dignity of human existence and development. Novalis' saying, "The mysterious path leads inward" becomes ever more relevant as basic security and supportive values disappear from outer life.

Another aspect of newly emerging human qualities of thinking and feeling, however, is that increasing numbers of people are no longer willing to simply accept the fact that in spite of all the promises of scientists, politicians, and economists, three-quarters of the Earth's human population still live in poverty and children's rights to be cared for, fed, clothed, and educated are almost impossible to uphold. Ongoing initiatives ranging from the largest non-governmental organizations to school classes are promoting a worldwide network of practical assistance and sponsorships in India, Africa, South America, Eastern Europe, and Asia.

On the basis of this experience, the international Alliance for Childhood was established in February 1999 in New York, London, and Stuttgart. It is an independent association of individuals, institutions, and organizations who choose to join forces to protect children and recognize their right to childhood. The Alliance welcomes new members at any time. For information on partner organizations and projects all over the world, check the Alliance's web site at *www.allianceforchildhood.net.*

Appendix

External Treatments for Home Nursing

by Petra Lange

The following guidance has been thoroughly revised for this edition by Petra Lange, author of *Hausmittel für Kinder. Naturgemäß vorbeugen und heilen* (Home remedies for children: Natural prevention and treatment).

A useful website offering self-help guidance for different countries is found at: http://www.weleda.com

Compresses and poultices

For obtaining at least some of the following materials or products made from them, see Greenfibres of Totnes, UK, and Kids Nature of Santa Cruz, CA, both of which have websites.

Every compress or poultice consists of at least two cloths– an inner cloth of silk, linen, or cotton and a somewhat larger outer cloth for the outer covering. Wool is best for the outer cloth. For children who are sensitive to wool, wrap the woollen outer layer in a thin cotton or silk cloth so it doesn't scratch.

Silk: Ideally raw silk (a medium-weight, grainy, linen-like silk made from short waste fibers).
Linen: A dishtowel, for example.
Cotton: Gauze nappies or diapers, brushed cotton or flannel, handkerchiefs.
Wool: Scarves of soft virgin wool (you can knit one of merino wool in k1, p1 ribbing); felted, woven virgin wool fabrics; or combed, unspun fleece wool.

A

Choosing the inner cloth for compresses

Damp compresses

Fairly thick linen, brushed cotton or flannel, thick gauze nappies or diapers, or a double layer of raw silk.

Oil and ointment compresses

Thinner raw silk, thin gauze nappies or diapers, or handkerchiefs.

Quark poultices

A highly absorbent middle layer (such as brushed cotton or flannel or fleece wool) is absolutely necessary. Caution: Quark (fermented skimmed milk) causes matting of woollen fabrics.

Compress cloths should be as wrinkle-free as possible. As outer layers, woven wool felt and knit scarves make outer layers that are especially easy to handle. Secure the wrappings tightly so the compress doesn't shift when the child moves.

Chamomile bag

for earache

Place a handful of dried chamomile flowers in the center of a thin cloth and secure the cloth with thread to make a small bag. Knead the bag briefly to break the flower heads into smaller pieces so the bag will conform to the shape of the ear. Heat the bag between two plates placed like a lid on top of a pot of boiling water. This method of heating preserves the etheric oils, and the bag does not get wet.

When the bag is warmed through, place it on the child's ear, cover it with cotton or a piece of fleece wool, and secure it with a wool scarf or cap.

Duration: At least half an hour, or overnight.

Chamomile flowers have a pleasant smell and are very popular with children. The bag can be reused four or five times before the flowers lose their scent.

Onion bag

for severe earache

Finely chop a medium-sized onion and wrap it in a thin cloth to make a roll as thick as your finger. (Tip: If you pack the onion into a gauze tube bandage and knot the ends, the onion cubes will not fall out even if the child tosses and turns.) The roll should be at body temperature; apply it to the child's ear and the area behind the ear. Cover it with cotton or fleece wool to absorb excess onion juice, and fasten it securely in place with a wool scarf, a bandanna, or a thin wool cap.

Duration: Half an hour or longer, depending on skin sensitivity. May be applied several times a day.

Thirty minute treatments repeated at intervals of one to two hours throughout the day are especially effective. Onion bags reliably relieve pain and inhibit inflammation.

Throat poultice with eucalyptus

for lymph node inflammation

Spread eucalyptus paste on a **raw silk** or cotton cloth long enough to cover the throat but somewhat shorter than the circumference of the child's neck (the cloth should leave two finger-widths exposed on either side of the neck vertebrae). Cover the paste with another cloth of the same size (1). Roll the poultice up from both ends toward the middle (2, 3) and heat it between two plates as described for the chamomile bag on page 422.

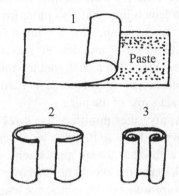

Test the temperature of the poultice on the inside of your lower arm. Press the poultice, still rolled up, briefly against your child's throat several times to make sure the temperature is comfortable, then unroll it in both directions, beginning at the larynx, and wrap it around your child's throat as smoothly as possible. Secure it with a woollen cloth, which will also prevent the poultice from cooling too quickly.

Duration: Overnight.

Throat poultice with angelica or onion ointment

*for lymph node inflammation
or swollen glands*
Apply a layer of ointment as thick as a knife blade to a **raw silk** or cotton cloth that is long enough to cover the throat but leave the neck vertebrae exposed. Apply the ointment side of the cloth directly to the skin and secure it firmly with a layer of woollen cloth. The cloth can be reused several times. Each day, add enough ointment to make the surface of the cloth greasy.

Duration: A poultice made with angelica ointment can be left in place all day or overnight unless skin irritation develops. Leave an onion ointment poultice in place for one to two hours unless skin irritation occurs sooner.

Cool lemon juice compress

for acute sore throat (with high fever)
Place half of an unsprayed (preferably organic) lemon in a small bowl, cover it with water, make a few cuts in it, and press the juice out with the bottom of a glass. If only sprayed lemons are available, use a citrus juicer and dilute the juice with water.

Cut or fold a thin raw silk or cotton cloth so that it is long enough to cover the throat but leave the neck vertebrae exposed. Roll the cloth up from both ends toward the middle and saturate it with the lemon water. Wring it out and unroll it as smoothly as possible around your child's throat, beginning at the larynx. Secure it firmly with a wool scarf.

Duration: One hour or longer, depending on skin sensitivity.

A

Hot lemon juice compress

for milder sore throat or hoarseness
Place half of an unsprayed (preferably organic) lemon in a small bowl, cover it with very hot water, make a few cuts in it, and hold it in place with a fork while you press the juice out using the bottom of a drinking glass. If you must use a sprayed lemon, extract the juice with a citrus juicer and dilute it with hot water.

wringing cloth

Cut or fold a raw silk or cotton cloth (not too thin) to the right size to cover the throat but leave the neck vertebrae exposed. Roll the cloth up from both ends toward the middle, wrap it in a longer piece of cloth and dip both cloths into the hot lemon water, leaving the ends of the longer cloth dry. Pick up the ends of the longer cloth, drape it around a water-faucet/tap, and twist the ends together to wring it out thoroughly. The drier the hot compress, the more comfortable it will be on the skin.

Remove the compress from the wringing cloth. Test the temperature before unrolling it onto your child's throat, beginning at the larynx. The compress should be as wrinkle-free as possible. Secure it firmly with a wool scarf.

Duration: At least five to ten minutes.

Throat poultice with lemon slices

for tonsillitis
More effective than compresses made with lemon juice but also more irritating to the skin. Cut an unsprayed (preferably organic) lemon into thin slices. Wrap it in a cloth (not too thick) as illustrated, and squeeze it hard to extract some of the juice.

Apply the poultice as directed above and secure it with a wool scarf. As with other throat applications, the neck vertebrae should not be covered.

Duration: Twenty minutes or longer, depending on skin sensitivity. Remove the poultice when it begins to itch.

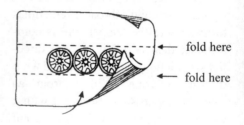

← fold here

← fold here

Throat poultice with Quark

for tonsillitis
Apply the Quark (fermented skimmed milk) to a **raw silk** or cotton cloth. Use a thinner or thicker layer of Quark depending on the patient's constitution. For a child who tends to feel cold, use a thinner layer; otherwise, use a layer

approximately five millimetres (one-quarter of an inch) thick. Fold the cloth into a packet. There should be only one layer of cloth on the side that will be applied to the skin.

Warm the poultice to room temperature between two hot water bottles (not too hot) and wrap it smoothly around the child's throat, leaving the neck vertebrae exposed. Secure it with a cotton or linen cloth, followed by an insulating layer of fleece wool wrapped in another cloth. Add another layer of wool cloth for the final covering.

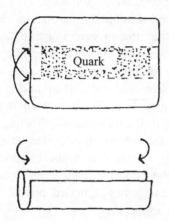

Duration: Three to five hours, until the Quark layer dries out.

This poultice is not suitable for eczema patients with allergies to cow's milk. After removing the poultice, keep the patient's throat covered for a while with a scarf or turtleneck.

A Quark poultice is very soothing for when your child has a sore, swollen throat, a bad taste in his mouth, and a high fever.

Chest poultice with ground mustard

for obstructive bronchitis, asthma, and pneumonia

N.B. Use only as directed by a physician! Prepare the poultice in a warm room. Lay a wool cloth and an intermediate layer on the bed where the child's back will be. Spread a layer of ground mustard seed on a thin cloth that corresponds to the size of the area to be treated. The layer should be as thick as the blade of a knife. Fold and roll the cloth as illustrated below. The ground mustard should not escape from the cloth.

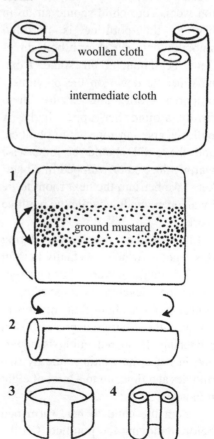

A

A mustard poultice can be applied to the shoulder blades, the chest, or both, but it is most effective if it wraps all the way around the patient's ribcage.

Immediately before applying the poultice, moisten it thoroughly with warm water (no hotter than 38°C/100°F). If the cloth spread with ground mustard is small, use a spray bottle to moisten it. If you're using a larger cloth, roll it up from both ends, submerge it briefly in lukewarm water, and carefully press out excess water with your hand (do not wring).

Protect the patient's nipples and armpits with petroleum jelly and cotton wool. Your child should sit up in bed as the poultice is unrolled smoothly onto her skin in both directions, beginning at the spine. Next, have her lie down on the previously prepared cloths and secure them firmly around her upper body. A pullover goes on top of the poultice, and the child should be otherwise warmly dressed or wrapped in a blanket. Take her into the next room to lie by an open window while the poultice works.

Little children usually cry during this process, which is actually helpful for their lungs. A warm, burning sensation soon develops over the ribcage. It usually takes about four minutes to produce the desired degree of skin reddening. If no reddening is apparent, increase the waiting time by two minutes at a time, up to a total of eight minutes.

Return the child to her warm bed before removing the poultice. Oil the treated area with a mild vegetable oil, making sure that no traces of ground mustard remain on the skin.

This poultice is usually applied once a day in the evening to help the child fall asleep. If her skin shows signs of pimples or is still reddened the next day, substitute an oil compress and do not repeat the mustard treatment until the following day.

A mustard poultice is a very powerful treatment that must be applied very carefully. *Never* use oil of mustard. Blistering will not occur unless the patient's skin is oversensitive or the poultice is left on too long.

If no skin reddening occurs, check whether the ground mustard is too old. Mustard freshly ground immediately before use is most effective. Mustard seed contains oil and is sensitive to heat. Do not grind it in a grain mill, and avoid overheating it if you use an electric coffee grinder. Using overly hot water to moisten the mustard also reduces its effect.

Make a new mustard poultice for each application.

Once you have experienced the beneficial effects of this poultice, you will find it well worth the effort to make it and to help your child through the few minutes of burning warmth.

Chest compress with ginger

for obstructive bronchitis,
persistent cough

Measure $^1/_4$ litre (one cup) of hot water. In a small bowl, mix two teaspoons of grated fresh ginger root or ground ginger thoroughly with four tablespoons of the water. Cover it and set aside to steep for ten minutes. Meanwhile, prepare the compress cloths:

A raw silk or cotton cloth large enough to completely cover the child's ribcage is rolled up from both ends toward the middle and wrapped in a larger cloth to make it easier to wring out (see illustration on page 424).

Pour the rest of the water over the ginger, dip the cloths into the ginger-water mixture, keeping the ends of the outer cloth dry. Loop the cloth over a faucet and twist hard to wring it out. Make sure the compress is not too hot before applying it.

Spread the outer woollen covering on the child's bed. With the child sitting in bed, roll the compress out smoothly from the spine in both directions to cover the entire ribcage. Have the child lie down on the wool cloth and use it to secure the compress firmly in place.

Duration: Five minutes for the first application. If no skin irritation occurs, increase the time by three minutes at each application, but do not exceed twenty minutes.

The patient should be in a warm bed when you remove the compress. Rub the treated area gently with a mild vegetable oil.

The ginger-water mixture should not be used more than once. Ground ginger may be available from a herbalist under the name *rhizoma zingiberis pulvis,* or from a general store.

Chest compress with etheric oils
(10% lavender, 10% eucalyptus or dwarf-pine)

for bronchitis, obstructive bronchitis, croup, pneumonia, or whooping cough
Warm a raw silk or cotton cloth on the radiator, and warm 5-10 ml (half to one tablespoon) of oil in a clean bottle in a hot water bath. Drop the oil on to the cloth until it is completely saturated. Wrap the cloth around the patient's ribcage, beginning at the back, and secure it firmly with a wool scarf.

If the patient's bedroom is unheated, saturate the cloth with oil, roll it up from the ends toward the middle, wrap it in a piece of aluminum foil and warm it in the child's bed between two hot water bottles. (Do not use plastic bags as etheric oils can dissolve them.) Have the wool cloth lying ready in the bed, too, so that it will also be well-warmed by the hot water bottles.

Duration: For at least half an hour if applied during the day, but overnight is better. The oil-saturated cloth can be reused as long as it still smells good (two weeks or longer). After each use, store it in a clean glass jar in a cool, dark place or in the used aluminum foil. Freshen it up with a little new oil before each use.

Chest compresses with etheric oils, especially lavender oil with its pleasant scent and calming effects, are great favorites with parents and children alike.

A

Chest rub with etheric oils

(10% lavender, 10% eucalyptus, or dwarf-pine)

as an alternative to a chest compress
A chest rub requires calm, concentrated movements with *warm* hands and *very small amounts* of oil. Rub the entire rib cage with the oil of your choice; wrap the child's upper body in a wool cloth when you have finished the rub. In NZ, Eucalyptus comp. chest paste or Eucalytus/Plantago comp. chest rub are available.

Chest rubs with damp compresses

for bronchitis, obstructive bronchitis, croup, pneumonia, or whooping cough
The effect of a chest rub can be enhanced by adding a damp compress. Use a piece of raw silk or cotton cloth as wide as the child's chest. Roll the cloth up from both sides toward the middle, place it inside a larger cloth (see illustration, page 424), and pour hot water over it. Grasping the larger cloth by the ends, sling it around a water-faucet/tap and twist firmly to wring it out. The drier the cloth, the more heat the skin can tolerate. Remove the compress from the outer cloth, place it on the treated skin and secure it firmly with a woollen cloth.

Duration: After half an hour, loosen the woollen wrappings just enough to remove the compress. Leave the wool cloth in place while the patient rests for an hour, or even overnight.

Chest compress with horsetail tea

for bronchitis with a great deal of phlegm but no high fever
To make the tea, pour half a litre (2 cups) of water over a handful of dried horsetail herb, bring it to a boil, and simmer for ten minutes. Remove from heat and allow the tea to steep, covered, for five minutes longer while you get the compress cloths ready. (This alternative method makes somewhat stringer tea: Soak a handful of dried horsetail herb in half a litre of water for ten hours, boil it for five minutes, and let it steep covered for five minutes longer.) Prepare the compress as above. (Use the tea instead of hot water and pour it through a strainer onto the cloth.) Spread the outer woollen cloth on the child's bed. With the child sitting up in bed, unroll the compress smoothly onto his back in both directions, ending in front. Have the child lie down on top of the wool cloth and use it to secure the compress in place.

Duration: After half an hour, loosen the wool wrapping slightly and quickly remove the compress. Leave the wool fabric in place while the patient rests for an hour (or overnight), as long as the patient's skin is not irritated by the wool. If it begins to itch, remove the woollen wrapper and put it back on again over a pajama top. Move quickly to avoid losing heat.

Chest poultice with Quark

for pneumonia and pleurisy
Spread Quark (fermented skimmed milk) on a raw silk or cotton cloth (see illustration, page 425). The layer of Quark should be about as thick as your little finger. The size of the cloth depends on whether the poultice will be applied all the way around the ribcage or only to the patient's chest. Warm the Quark poultice to skin temperature on a hot water bottle (not too hot, or the Quark will curdle). To apply a poultice that wraps all the way around the torso, spread the outer woollen cloth and an absorbent intermediate layer on the child's bed, with the poultice on top. With the child lying on her back on the entire package, wrap both sides of the poultice around to the front, secure it firmly with the absorbent layer, and cover it with the outer cloth.

Tip: A layer of fleece wool wrapped in a cotton cloth makes a very warm and absorbent intermediate layer for a Quark poultice, and a thinner cloth or even an undershirt can then be used for the outermost layer. Using fleece wool also avoids ruining a woollen cloth, which mats in contact with the liquid from Quark.

Duration: Leave the poultice in place until the layer of Quark dries out. How long this takes depends on the thickness of the Quark layer and also varies from patient to patient (anywhere from three to eight hours).

Quark poultices are not suited for eczema-prone patients allergic to cow's milk.

Abdominal compresses

Use for certain types of abdominal pain and vomiting (appendicitis should be ruled out first) and for insomnia
Abdominal compresses are a wonderful aid to falling asleep.

Abdominal compress with yarrow

To make the tea, cover a handful of yarrow with approximately half a litre (two cups) of hot water, cover it, and allow it to steep for at least ten minutes.

Meanwhile, fold a cloth to the desired size and wrap it in a larger cloth to make it easier to wring out (see illustration, page 424). Pour the tea through a strainer onto the cloths. Grasp the larger cloth by the corners, drape it over a water-faucet/tap, and twist the ends together firmly to wring it out.

Remove the compress from the outer cloth. It should be applied as hot as the child can tolerate. Secure it with a strip of cotton or linen long enough to wrap all the way around the body, and add a woollen cloth as the outer covering. These cloths should be much wider than the compress so that no cool spots develop along the edges.

Place a hot water bottle (not bulging full) on top of the compress and pull the child's pyjama bottoms up over it to secure it. The compress can remain in place for one hour.

A

Other external abdominal treatments

Chamomile compress
Prepare it in the same way as the yarrow compress.

Oxalis essence compress
Use one tablespoon of essence to approximately $1/4$ litre (1 cup) of hot water.

Caraway or lemon balm oil compress
Saturate a thin raw silk or cotton cloth with the oil, wrap it in foil, and warm it between two hot water bottles. Also warm a layer of fleece wool (cotton wool may be substituted); wrap it in a cloth first to prevent fuzz.

Apply and secure the compress like a yarrow compress.

Copper ointment (0.4%) compress
Spread the copper ointment thinly on a cloth, place it on the area to be treated, and secure it in the same way as a yarrow compress. The ointment-soaked cloth can be reused several times. Apply more ointment as needed (two or three times a week).

Dry abdominal compress
Place a dry, well-warmed cloth on the patient's abdomen and secure it firmly with a strip of wool cloth.

Liver compress with yarrow

Make the compress as described for an abdominal compress with yarrow. Apply it to the skin over the liver (on the right side, from the navel around to the back).

Kidney compress with copper ointment

for asthma, as directed by a physician
Apply the copper ointment thinly and very evenly to a raw silk or cotton cloth, staying away from the edges. Apply the cloth to the kidney area and secure it firmly with a woollen cloth that reaches all the way around the body.

Duration: as prescribed by your physician. Your doctor may also prescribe silver (Argentum) ointment to alternate with the copper ointment.

After removing the compress, clean the patient's skin with warm water and dry it thoroughly. Like all ointments made with metals, copper and silver ointments leave stains that are difficult to remove.

Bladder rub with 10% eucalyptus oil and moist compress

for early treatment of
urinary tract infections
With a *warm* hand and slow, careful movements, rub the bladder area with a very small amount of 10% eucalyptus oil.

Roll up a palm-sized piece of raw silk or cotton cloth from both sides toward the middle, wrap it in a larger cloth to make it easier to wring out, and pour hot water over it (see illustration, page 424). Grasp the larger cloth by the corners, drape it over a faucet, and twist the ends together firmly to wring it out. The drier the cloth, the hotter it can be applied to the skin. Remove the compress from the outer cloth, place it on the oiled area, and cover it with a woollen cloth or fleece wool. Hold the compress in place with a pair of snug-fitting underpants.

Duration: After half an hour, loosen the wool covering and remove the compress. Leave the wool in place for one hour while the patient rests.

Repeat this application several times during the first and second days of the infection, then continue the treatment with eucalyptus oil compresses.

Bladder compress with 10% eucalyptus oil

for urinary tract infections; follow-up treatment after eucalyptus bladder rubs

Pour about 5 ml (half a tablespoon) of oil into a clean medicine bottle and warm it in a hot water bath. Meanwhile, warm a palm-sized piece of raw silk or cotton cloth on the radiator. Apply the warmed oil to the cloth drop by drop. Place the oiled cloth over the patient's bladder and cover it with a woollen cloth or a layer of fleece wool. Pull the child's underpants over it to hold it in place.

Alternatively, apply unwarmed oil to the cloth and warm the compress between two plates as described for chamomile on page 422.

Duration: Several hours once a day at least until symptoms are gone.

The oil-saturated cloth may be reused as long as it still smells good (two weeks or longer). After use, store it in a clean glass jar in a cool, dark place. Freshen it up with a little additional oil before each application.

Your physician may prescribe bladder compresses with silver ointment (Weleda's Argentum metallicum preparatum 0.4%) to alternate with eucalyptus compresses.

Warm compresses with arnica essence

for rising fever if your child is restless, nauseous, has a headache or chills.

For this treatment, you will need four pieces of raw silk or cotton cloth of the right size to wrap around the child's wrists and ankles. Roll each cloth up individually from both ends toward the middle, and wrap two each in two larger cloths. Place both of the larger cloths in a bowl (see illustration, page 424) and pour over them a mixture of one tablespoon of arnica essence and approximately $1/4$ litre (one cup) of very hot water. Thoroughly wring out one set of cloths at a time by twisting the covering cloth around a water-faucet/ tap.

First apply the compresses to the inside of the wrists. Take one of the inner cloths out of the large cloth, wrap it over the wrist and fasten it firmly with a woollen cloth. Then do the second wrist and the ankles, removing the compress cloths from their covering one at a time.

These compresses can be repeated every ten minutes for three times, followed by a one-hour pause. In any case, remove all of the compresses as

A

soon as the period of rising fever is over; that is, as soon as your child's limbs feel hot.

Cool leg compresses

to reduce fever
If the patient has cold feet and/or cold legs, do not use these compresses even if her fever is high! In this case, apply a hot compress to the feet.

First, lay a thick cotton cloth such as a bath towel over the bed to protect the mattress. Pour two to three litres/quarts of water into a bowl. The water should be several degrees cooler than the patient's body temperature. You may add a tablespoon of lemon juice or apple cider vinegar to the water. Fold two cloths to a size that covers the child's leg from the ankle to just below the knee and wraps around the leg about one and a half times. Roll the cloths up from both ends and wet them thoroughly with the water. Before applying them, squeeze them out until they no longer drip. Wrap each leg from the ankle to the knee with one of the cloths, securing it with a large wool sock, a woollen scarf, or a thick cotton cloth. Do not use foil, plastic, or non-absorbent cloth. Keep the patient fully covered (including her legs) during the treatment; a light blanket or sheet is enough if her fever is high. After five or ten minutes, the cloths will be warmed through and must be replaced with new ones. After three repetitions, wait for half an hour before continuing. Discontinue treatment if the patient's feet get cold.

Cool calf compresses are a reliable fever-reducing treatment. Since they usually need to be applied at night, here are a few tips for making the process easier:

Prepare four cloths at once rather than two, so that two new ones are already at hand when it is time to change the compresses. Remove each used cloth from its wrapping and apply a fresh one immediately, while the leg is still a bit damp.

Linen works especially well for calf compresses. Unlike cotton fabrics, it is somewhat stiffer wet than dry and does not cause a constricting sensation as it dries.

If your child will not tolerate having compresses applied, you can rub down her calves with cool, damp cloths. Wrap one calf in a fairly thick damp cloth and rub gently from the ankle toward the knee. Repeat this stroke until the cloth becomes warm. Then rinse the cloth, squeeze out excess water, and apply it to the other leg, using the same rubbing motion. The leg not currently being treated should remain covered, as should the patient's abdomen.

Mustard footbath

for inflammation of the nose, sinuses, or throat; enlarged tonsils; migraine
Mix a handful or two of freshly ground mustard seed with a footbath measure of water warmed to 37 –39°C/98.5 –102°F. The patient's feet should stay in the bath for up to ten minutes. Wrap a bath towel around the

container and the patient's legs so the water does not cool down too fast.

Do not allow the bath mixture to come into contact with any mucous membranes. Wash your hands carefully after preparing the bath, and rinse the patient's legs thoroughly when the footbath is over.

This footbath produces significant skin reddening, although it may appear only after several applications. As a general rule, use no more than one footbath per day.

Conclude the treatment by rubbing the patient's legs with good-quality body oil.

Mustard poultices on the soles of the feet

an alternative to footbaths for children who are very young or very restless
For each poultice, tie a tablespoon or two of ground mustard in the center of a thin but densely woven handkerchief. Thoroughly moisten these little bags in lukewarm water and then squeeze them out. Apply one bag to the sole of each foot, holding it in place with a sock or a larger cloth. Remove the poultice when a burning sensation develops.

Duration: Until the skin reddens (varies from person to person – at least three minutes but no more than fifteen minutes). After removing the poultices, rub the patient's feet with a good grade vegetable oil. Warm wool socks intensify the effect.

Cool compress with arnica essence

for bruises, sprains, and strains
For this compress, saturate a fairly thick cloth (a double layer of raw silk or brushed cotton or flannel) with one tablespoon of arnica essence diluted with nine tablespoons of water. Squeeze out the cloth until it no longer drips, and apply it as smoothly as possible to the area to be treated. Fasten the compress with a woollen cloth or a thick cotton cloth. Use a spoon or a small jug to add more of the diluted essence to the compress as it dries.

Change the compress at least once a day. Do not apply arnica compresses to broken skin, and do not use them if the patient is allergic to arnica.

Quark poultice

for sunburn, bruises, sprains, and strains; also for mastitis and milk retention
Apply a thin layer (knife-blade thick) of skim-milk Quark to a thin raw silk or cotton cloth (see illustration, page 425). The size of the poultice cloth depends on the size of the area to be treated. For sunburn, bruises, sprains, and strains, use cool Quark for the poultice.

To secure the poultice, use an absorbent cotton cloth (better yet, a piece of fleece wool wrapped in cotton fabric). This intermediate layer reliably soaks up excess moisture, so you can use a thinner outer cover such as an undershirt.

In the case of a nursing mother with

A

mastitis or **milk retention,** warm the poultice to skin temperature on a hot water bottle (not too hot, or the Quark will curdle). Leave the nipple exposed when you apply the poultice. Remove the poultice approximately twenty minutes before nursing. Rubbing the breast gently with oil will warm it and stimulate milk flow.

Duration: Until the Quark dries (three to eight hours, depending on the amount used). Full-fat Quark will not dry out.

Poultices made with milk-products are not suitable for eczema-prone individuals with allergies to cow's milk. Treatment by physician may be necessary.

Cool compress with calendula essence

for scrapes and oozing wounds
See instructions for making an arnica compress, page 433. Calendula compresses are changed every hour. If possible, use freshly ironed inner cloths to help prevent infection. After several hours, stop applying compresses and let the wound air-dry.

This compress is also a painless way to remove bandages that have stuck to wounds.

Cool compress with Combudoron essence®

for burns, insect bite or sunburn
See instructions for making an arnica compress, page 433.

Tip: This compress is good for relieving pain on the way to the doc-tor. It also removes bandages that have stuck to wounds.

Combudoron compresses are changed at least once a day. If the skin is broken, use a freshly ironed inner cloth. Caution is advised in using Combudoron on patients with known allergies to arnica.

Warm compress with 10% calendula oil

for mumps
Warm a palm-sized piece of **raw silk** or cotton cloth on the radiator. Pour approximately 5 ml of calendula oil into a small, clean bottle and warm it in a hot water bath. Drip the oil onto the cloth until it is completely saturated. You can also saturate the cloth with unwarmed oil and heat the compress between two plates (see under chamomile on page 422).

The compress should be as warm as the patient can tolerate. Apply it to the swollen area, secure it with a bandanna, and cover it with a woollen scarf. Fleece wool is especially good for this type of compress; use a layer under the bandanna.

Duration: Several times a day for half an hour, or overnight.

The oil-saturated cloth may be reused as long as it smells good (approximately two weeks). After each use, store it in a clean glass jar in a cool, dark place. Freshen it up with a little additional oil before each application.

Compress with horsetail tea

for severely oozing eczema

To make the tea, cover a handful of dried horsetail herb (Equisetum) with one litre/quart of cold water, bring to the boil, and simmer for ten minutes. Cover the tea and allow it to steep for five minutes while you get the cloths ready. (Here's an alternative technique that makes somewhat more tea: Soak a handful of dried horsetail herb in one litre/quart of water for ten hours, then boil it for five minutes and allow it to steep for five minutes longer.)

Use a raw silk or cotton cloth of the right size to cover the affected area. Soak it in the tea (which should be at body temperature or slightly warmer), squeeze it out, and apply it as smoothly as possible. In this case, a wool wrapping is often not possible. Secure the compress with a larger cotton cloth (or better still, with a layer of fleece wool wrapped in a cotton cloth so that the wool is not in direct contact with the skin).

Duration: At least half an hour. If the compress is left on longer, it may be necessary to remoisten the inner cloth by carefully adding more tea with a spoon.

Cool washes with Rosemary bath milk® or concentrate®

to strengthen the immune system
Do not apply cool washes if your child's skin is not thoroughly warm. Washed body parts must be dried and covered immediately to prevent evaporative cooling.

This application is best done in the morning, in a bed still warm from the night. Have your child sit up and slip out of her pyjamas. Spread a large bath towel in the bed for her to lie on, and cover her warmly. In a basin, mix a teaspoon of rosemary concentrate with about two litres/quarts of cool water. The water should not be so cool that it feels unpleasant. Dip a wash mitt (not a washcloth) into the water and wring it out until it no longer drips. Wash your child's face first; a few strokes from the forehead to the neck are sufficient. Carefully pat her face dry. Rinse and wring the wash mitt, uncover your child's left arm, and wipe it with upward motions, moving from her fingers to her shoulder. Dry and cover the arm immediately. Wash and wring out the wash mitt and repeat the treatment on the right arm.

Next ask your child (carefully covered up to her neck) to stick one leg out from under the covers. Using large strokes, wipe it from her toes up to her hips. (To avoid getting the bed damp, you can spread an extra towel under her leg.) Finish the treatment by washing the other leg. The whole procedure should not take more than five minutes. When it is finished, have your child rest in bed, well covered, for half an hour.

Sweat packs

May be preceded by a warm bath, adding hot water gradually to increase the temperature, with a few drops of lemon added to the water.

A

Give your child hot linden-flower tea to drink. Have him put on a bathrobe if it seems necessary for warmth. Cover him very warmly in bed (up to his ears). After half an hour to two hours, when he has perspired freely – and perhaps slept a little – rub him down with a damp, cool wash-cloth and change his pyjamas.

Steam inhalation

Take any safety precautions appropriate to your child's age. For a toddler, place an open, wide-bottomed pot of hot chamomile tea on a narrow table between you. Hold both your child's hands across the table with the pot between your arms. It is even safer to put the pot in the sink and support your arms on the cool rim of the sink, which you should first cover with a towel. Make a game of it by blowing steam in each other's faces, then make a "circus tent" out of a big towel to cover both your heads. Challenge your child to see if he can breathe in through his nose and out through his mouth for longer than you can. For older children who can safely sit alone with their heads under the towel, an egg timer and a flashlight help pass the time. Stop the treatment when the steam subsides, after three to five minutes. After the steam treatment, apply calendula or Mercurialis ointment to your child's face (avoiding the eyes) and have him stay in a warm room for an hour.

We repeat: be careful to avoid scalds!

Bath with horsetail tea

for hives; eczema, especially itching forms and neurodermatitis; to stimulate skin metabolism
Soak 50 grams ($1^3/_4$ oz) of horsetail herb (Equisetum) in two to three litres/quarts of cold water for ten hours, then bring to a boil and simmer for ten minutes. (Faster alternative: Pour two litres/quarts of cold water over 100 grams/$3^1/_2$ oz of horsetail herb, bring to a boil, simmer for five minutes, and steep covered for fifteen minutes.) Strain the tea into the bath water.
Bath duration: five to ten minutes.
Bath water temperature: 35 –36°C/95 –97°F.
For hives, rinsing with cool water after the bath often feels good.

Baths with herbal essences

Use Wala or Weleda essences, which are made from fresh, biodynamically grown medicinal herbs. Add one tablespoon of essence to a full bath. Duration and temperature as for baths with horsetail tea.

Baths with Equisetum (horsetail) essence stimulate elimination via the kidneys and are good for eczema (including the itching forms) and poorly healing wounds.

Baths with seasalt

for adenoids and susceptibility to upper respiratory infections; not for use during feverish illnesses
Seasalt baths are administered two or

three times a week. Water temperature should be 35°C/95°F — check it with a thermometer. Do not use soap or shampoo during these baths and do not rinse the saltwater off. Simply dry the child quickly, or (better still) wrap her immediately in a big bathrobe and put her to bed. A one to two-hour rest after the bath is a necessary part of the treatment.

The amount of salt used depends on the child's age, and both the amount of salt and the duration of the bath are increased during the series of baths. For children three to twelve years old, begin with 3 kg seasalt in 200 litres of bath water ($6^1/_4$ lb seasalt to 50 US gallons); do not simply estimate the amount of water; measure it a ten-litre (2 gallon) bucket or the like. The first four baths should each last ten minutes. For baths 5 through 8, increase the amount of salt by one-third and the length of the bath to fifteen minutes. Beginning with bath 9, increase the *original* amount of salt by two-thirds and the length of the bath to twenty minutes. A complete saltwater cure includes fourteen baths.

You can use less salt for a smaller child who can be bathed in a smaller tub. The child must be able to lie comfortably in the tub, however, and be completely covered by the bath water.

Knitting instructions

Baby's woollen pants

Size given is for about four months to fourteen months. (They tend to grow with the child!) For a smaller size use thinner knitting needles.

Materials
70 g (2.5 oz) pure untreated wool, double knitting thickness.
One pair each of No. 8 (4 mm) (5 US) and No. 10 (3.25 mm) (3 US) knitting needles.
One set of No. 10 (3.25 mm) (3 US) knitting needles.

Front: Cast on 60 sts. on No. 10 needles.
Work 16 rows K2, P2.
Change to No. 8 needles and work 48 rows in garter (plain) stitch.
Change back to No. 10 needles and knit 8 rows K2, P2.
Next 16 rows: K together the first two and the last two sts. of every row keeping K2, P2 rib intact. 28 sts.
Knit 5 more rows in K2, P2 and cast off.

Back: Work as front.

A

Sew up side seams from waist down to where the ribbing starts.

Sew up seam between legs.

With set of No. 10 needles, pick up the end sts. around each leg (about 48 sts.).

Make a K2, P2 border of 6 rounds.

Cast off loosely.

Vest / Sleeveless sweater

Size given is for about 6 month to one year. (Larger size 4–6 years in parentheses.)

Materials

50 g (2 oz) (100 g, 4 oz) soft four-ply wool or silk.

One pair No. 9 (3.75 mm) (4 US) knitting needles.

Front: Cast on 50 (60) sts. and work 10 (14) rows in K2, P2.

Knit 40 (63) rows in st.st.

Work the next 18 (39) rows in K2, P2.

Next row, to shape neck opening:

Work 12 (14) sts. in K2, P2, cast off 26 (32) sts., work 12 (14) sts. in K2, P2.

Knit 6 (12) rows with the 12 (14) sts. on each side, keeping the K2, P2 ribbing intact.

Cast off.

Back: Work as front.

Press carefully. Join shoulder seams and side seams leaving an opening for the arms.

Baby's hood

Size given is for about birth to two months. (Larger size six to twelve months in parentheses.)

Materials

30 g (1 oz) of four-ply wool or cotton or silk.

One pair No. 11 (3 mm) (2 US) knitting needles. (Larger size: No. 8 (4 mm) (5 US) needles.

Cast on 60 (80) sts. and work 7 (8) rows in K1, P1.

Carry on knitting in st.st. until work measures 10 cm (4 in) (12.5 cm, 5 in), ending on a right-side row.

Start to decrease as follows:

First row: * sl. 1, K1, psso, K8 *. Repeat from * to * to end of row, 54 sts. (72 sts)

Next and every alt. row: purl

Third row: * sl. 1, K1, psso, K7 *. Repeat from * to * to end of row.

Fifth row: * sl. 1, K1, psso, K6 *. Repeat from * to * to end of row.

Continue in this way until you have 6 (8) sts. left.

Break the yarn and thread through left over sts. Sew up back seam from back of hat to row at which decreasing started. Crochet two lengths of string for tying bonnet and sew one on to each front corner.

alt.	alternate	rep.	repeat
k.	knit	sl.	slip
p.	purl	st(s).	stitch(es)
psso.	pass slip stitch over	st.st.	stocking stitch

One-piece suit for eczema sufferers

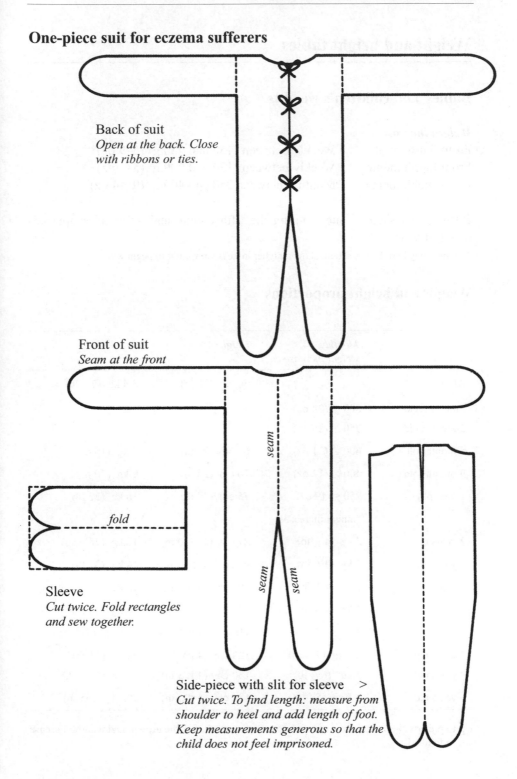

Back of suit
*Open at the back. Close
with ribbons or ties.*

Front of suit
Seam at the front

Sleeve
*Cut twice. Fold rectangles
and sew together.*

fold

seam

seam

seam

Side-piece with slit for sleeve   >
*Cut twice. To find length: measure from
shoulder to heel and add length of foot.
Keep measurements generous so that the
child does not feel imprisoned.*

A

Weight and height tables

Babies' and children's weights

Weight increase

From fourth week	Weekly between 150 and 250 g (5–9 oz)*
From fourth month	Weekly between 130 and 200 g (5–7 oz)
From eighth month	Monthly between 250 and 400 g (9–14 oz)

Birth weight should double during the fifth month, and treble after approximately 1 year.

* prematurely born babies should show a higher increase in weight to begin with.

Weight and height proportions

	Monthly weight increase	Height	Weight
At birth		50 cm (20 in)	3.4 kg (7½ lb)
First 4 weeks	800 g (28 oz)		
2 months old	750 g (26 oz)		
5 months old	600 g (21 oz)	64 cm (25 in)	7 kg (15 lb)
9 months old	400 g (14 oz)	70 cm (28 in)	9 kg (20 lb)
1 year old	250 g (9 oz)	75 cm (30 in)	10 kg (22 lb)
	Annual increase		
2 years old	2 kg (4½ lb)	87 cm (2 ft 10 in)	12 kg (26½ lb)
3 years old	2 kg (4½ lb)	95 cm (3 ft 1 in)	14 kg (31 lb)
4 years old	2 kg (4½ lb)	103 cm (3 ft 5 in)	16 kg (35½ lb)
5 years old	2 kg (4½ lb)	108 cm (3 ft 7 in)	18 kg (40 lb)
6 years old	3.5 kg (7½ lb)	116 cm (3 ft 10 in)	21.5 kg (47½ lb)
7 years old	2.5 kg (5½ lb)	123 cm (4 ft)	24 kg (53 lb)
8 years old	3 kg (6½ lb)	130 cm (4 ft 3 in)	27 kg (59½ lb)
9 years old	2.5 kg (5½ lb)	134 cm (4 ft 5 in)	29.5 kg (65 lb)

Up to puberty the increase is more or less constant, thereafter the growth and weight increase are individual.

Endnotes

1 Compare articles by F. Jauck, *Zeitschrift für Allgemeinmedizin,* 1985, Vol.3; and H. Hensel, Die Funktion des Fiebers, *Tempo Medical,* 1982, No.5. Also Barbara Styrt, and B. Sugerman, Antipyresis and Fever, *Archive Intern. Med.* 1990; 150, pp.1589–97.

2 R. Ader, D. Felten, N. Cohen, eds. *Psychoneuroimmunology,* Academic Press, New York 1991.

3 Compare P. Heusser., Das zentrale Dogma nach Watson und Crick und seine Widerlegung durch die moderne Genetik. *Verhandlungen der Naturforschende Gesellschaft Basel,* 1989, 99:1–14; J. Wirz / E. Lammerts, eds. *The Future of DNA.* Kluwer, Dordrecht 1997.

4 Compare H. Hensel, Die Funktion des Fiebers, *Tempo Medical* 1982, No.5.

5 Translated by George and Mary Adams, from Rudolf Steiner, *Verses and Meditations,* Rudolf Steiner Press, London 1972.

6 Witzenberg, B.C. Masernsterblichkeit und Therapie [Measles mortality and therapy]. *Beiträge zu einer Erweiterung der Heilkunst* 1975, 28.3:116. Also R. Goldberg. Childhood Infectious Illnesses. *SA Journal of Natural Medicine,* 2001, No.5.

7 Fanconi. *Lehrbuch der Pädiatrie,* Stuttgart 1960.

8 Compare Goebel, W. *Schutzimpfung selbst verantwortet* [Taking individual responsibility for immunization]. Urachhaus, Stuttgart 2002.

9 Steiner, R. *Course for Young Doctors,* Mercury Press, New York 1994.

10 See also Glöckler, M. (ed.,). *Gesundheit und Schule* [Health and school]. Dornach 1994, and *Das Schulkind* [The schoolchild]. Dornach.

11 Von Alm, J., and J. Swartz, Atopy in children of families with an anthroposophical lifestyle, *Lancet,* 1999. 353:1485–88.

12 Maslow, Abraham H. *Motivation and Personality,* Harper & Row, New York, 1987.

13 Antonovsky, A. *Health, Stress and Coping,* Jossey-Bass, San Francisco 1979, and *Unraveling the Mystery of Health.* Jossey-Bass, San Francisco 1987.

14 Opp, Fingerle, Freytag, (eds.). *Was Kinder stärkt. Erziehung zwischen Risiko und Resilience,* Munich 1999.

15 Steiner, R. *Verses and Meditations.* Steiner Press, London 1972.

16 Steiner, Rudolf. *Overcoming Nervousness* (Lecture of Jan 11, 1912). Anthroposophic Press, New York 1978, and *Practical Training in Thought,* Anthroposophic Press, New York 1978.

17 Endres, Klaus-Peter & Wolfgang Schad, *Moon Rhythms in Nature.* Floris Books, Edinburgh 2002.

18 For a thorough discussion, see Glöckler, Michaela (ed.) *Gesundheit und Schule.* Goetheanum, Dornach 1998.

19 These exercises for the days of the week are included in *Seelenübungen* Vol. 1, Dornach 1997.

20 Roos, A. *Kulturzerfall und Zahnverderbnis.* Bern/Stuttgart 1962. Roos' work is mentioned in Weston A. Price, *Nutrition and Physical Degeneration* Price-Pottenger Nutrition Foundation, California 1970. Price, also a dentist, did research similar to Roos' in different parts of the world.

21 Iyengar, G.V. Elemental Composition of Human and Animal Milk: A Review. Technical Document 269. International Atomic Energy Agency, Vienna 1982.

22 See also Wilhelm zur Linden's *A Child is Born. Pregnancy, Birth and First Childhood,* Rudolf Steiner Press, London 1973.

23 Miller, M.A. *et al.* Safety and Immunogenicity of PRP-T combined with DPT. *Pediatrics* 1995. 4.

24 For more information, see Goebel, Wolfgang. *Schutzimpfungen selbst verantwortet. Grundlagen für eigene Entscheidungen.* Urachhaus, Stuttgart 2001. Also R. Goldberg. Should I vaccinate my child? *SA Journal of Natural Medicine,* 2002 April.

25 Rare cases of severe tetanus are known to occur in men highly immunized through vaccinations. Three cases are reported in: Crone, E.N. & Reder, A.T. 1992. Severe tetanus in immunized patients with high anti-tetanus titers. *Neurology* 42:761–64.

26 See for instance Menkes, J.H. and M. Kinsbourne, Workshop on Neurological Complications of Pertussis and Pertussis Vaccination. *Neuropediatrie* 1990, 21:171–76.

27 Christie, C. *et al.* The 1993 epidemic of pertussis in Cincinnati: Resurgence of the disease in a highly immunized population of children. *New England Journal of Medicine* 1994. 331:16–21.

28 A study in Bavaria revealed that within an eleven-year period, the decrease in cases of measles encephalitis as a result of immunization was more than equalled by the increase in other forms of encephalitis; unfortunately, the total number of reported encephalitis cases actually increased. See Windorfer and Grüneweg, *Bundesgesetzblatt,* 1993, 3:87, and Windorfer, A. and M. Kruse, Zentralnervöse Infektionen im Kindesalter. *Sozialpädiatrie,* 1992, 15:690.

29 Compare Glöckler, M. *Begabung und Behinderung. Praktische Hinweise für Erziehungs- und Schicksalsfragen* [Talents and handicaps: Practical tips on issues of education and destiny]. Stuttgart 1997.

30 See Note 28.

31 Steiner, Rudolf. *Intuitive Thinking as a Spiritual Path: A Philosophy of Freedom,* Anthropsophic Press, New York 1995.

32 Steiner, Rudolf. Lecture given on Oct 11, 1913. In *Okkulte Untersuchungen über das Leben zwischen Tod und neuer Geburt.* Dornach 1990. Trans. C. Creeger. English published as *Links between the Living and the Dead,* Rudolf Stiner Press, London 1973.

33 Rudolf Steiner, *The Education of the Child,* Anthroposophic Press, New York 1996.

34 Martin Buber, *I and Thou,* Charles Scribner's Sons, New York 1970.

35 The results of animal experiments support the suspicion that heavy potato consumption in pregnancy is related to the appearance of malformations of the brain and back. See Renwick, J.H. et al. Neural-tube defects produced in Syrian hamsters by potato glycalcaloids, *Teratology* 1984. 30.

36 See also Karl König's *The First Three Years of the Child,* Floris Books, Edinburgh 1998.

37 Heckmann, Helle. *Nokken, a Garden for Children: A Danish Approach to Waldorf-Based Child Care.* Available from the Waldorf Early Childhood Association of North America.

38 Bauer, Michael. *Menschentum und Freiheit.* Stuttgart 1971.

39 Steiner, Rudolf. *Intuitive Thinking as a Spiritual Path: A Philosophy of Freedom,* Anthropsophic Press, New York 1995.

40 See Rudolf Steiner, *How to Know Higher Worlds,* Anthroposophic Press, New York 1994.

41 See Rudolf Steiner, *An Outline of Esoteric Science,* Anthroposophic Press, New York 1997.

42 Morgenstern, Christian. *Wir fanden einen Pfad.* Munich 1986. (Trans. Catherine Creeger.)

43 Lecture of August 25, 1919, in *Foundations of Human Experience,* Anthroposophic Press, New York 1996. This lecture also gives a brief but complete account of Rudolf Steiner's theory of the senses.

44 A resolution of the German Association for the Rehabilitation of the Disabled (December 2, 1994) on the alarming increase in speech problems in children, observes: "An interdisciplinary team of researchers including representatives from the fields of medicine, special education, speech therapy, and health insurance has concluded that this increase is not due primarily to organic causes but rather by inadequate linguistic stimulation related to altered communication behavior in families, such as hours of daily television viewing, which not only overwhelms children's senses but also has negative effects on communications in their everyday surroundings and on sensory integration (seeing, hearing feeling) and thus on their overall linguistic, mental, and emotional development."

45 Pearce, Joseph Chilton. *Evolution's End: Claiming the Potential of our Intelligence,* Harper, San Francisco 1992.

46 Clifford Stoll, *High-Tech Heretic,* pp. 66–68.

47 A famous depiction of the problem of the other self is found in Oscar Wilde's novel *The Picture of Dorian Gray.*

48 Steiner, Rudolf. *Die menschliche Seele in ihrem Zusammenhang mit göttlich-geistigen Individualitäten. Die Verinnerlichung der Jahresfeste.* Dornach 1992.

49 Needleman, H.L., and P.J. Landrigan. *Raising Children Toxic Free,* Farrar, Straus & Giroux, New York 1994.

Bibliography

Health and sickness

Arta (rehabilitation center) *Rock Bottom: Beyond Drug Addiction*, Hawthorn Press, Stroud.

Bass, Ellen / Davis, Laura. *The Courage to Heal: A Guide for Women Survivors of Child Sexual Abuse*, Harper & Row, New York 1994.

Bentheim, T, *Caring for the Sick at Home*, Floris Books, Edinburgh and Anthroposophic Press, New York.

Bos, Arie, *Aids: an Anthroposophical Art of Healing*, Hawthorn Press, Stroud.

Bott, Victor, *Anthroposophical Medicine*, Anthroposophic Press, New York.

Bühler, Walter, *Living with your Body: the Body as an Instrument of the Soul*, Rudolf Steiner Press, London.

Dumke, Klaus, *AIDS: The Deadly Seed*, Rudolf Steiner Press, Forest Row.

Dunselman, Ron. *In Place of the Self: How Drugs Work*. Hudson, NY: Anthroposophic Press, 1995.

Evans, Michael and Rodger, Iain, *Healing for Body, Soul: An Introduction to Anthroposophical Medicine*, Floris Books, Edinburgh 2000.

Holdrege, Craig, *A Question of Genes*, Floris Books, Edinburgh 1996.

Holtzapfel, Walter, *Children's Destinies: the Three Directions of Human Development*, Mercury Press, New York.

—, *Our Children's Illnesses*, Mercury Press, New York.

Husemann, Armin, *The Harmony of the Human Body*, Floris Books, Edinburgh 2002.

Husemann, F. and Otto Wolff (Ed.) The *Anthroposophical Approach to Medicine*, (3 vols) Anthroposophic Press, New York.

Julien, Robert M. *A Primer of Drug Action: A Concise, Nontechnical Guide to the Actions, Uses, and Side Effects of Psychoactive Drugs*, W. H. Freeman, New York 2001.

Leroi, Rita, *Illness and Healing*, Temple Lodge Press, London.

Leviton, Richard, *Anthroposophic Medicine Today*, Anthroposophic Press, New York.

Mees, L.F.S. *Blessed by Illness*, Anthroposophic Press, New York.

Steiner, Rudolf, *Health and Illness*, (2 vols) Anthroposophic Press, New York.

—, *Introducing Anthroposophical Medicine*, Anthroposophical Press, New York.

—, *Overcoming Nervousness*, Anthroposophic Press, New York.

Steiner, Rudolf, and Ita Wegman, *The Fundamentals of Therapy*, Rudolf Steiner Press, London.

Twentyman, Ralph, *The Science and Art of Healing*, Floris Books, Edinburgh 1992.

Vogt, Felicitas, *Addiction's Many Faces*, Hawthorn Press, Stroud.

Wolff, Otto, *Anthroposophically Orientated Medicine and its Remedies*, Mercury Press, New York.

—, *Home Remedies*, Floris Books, Edinburgh 2000.

Babies and toddlers

Gibson, Margaret, *Becoming a Mother*, Hale & Iremonger, Sydney.

Glas, Norbert, *Conception, Birth and Early Childhood*, Anthroposophic Press, New York.

Gotsch, Gwen and Judy Torgus, *The Womanly Art of Breastfeeding*. La Lèche League International, Illionois 1997.

König, Karl, *The First Three Years of the Child*, Floris Books, Edinburgh and Anthroposophic Press, New York 1998.

Mitchell, Ingrid, *Breastfeeding Together*. Seabury Press, New York 1978.

Linden, Wilhelm zur, *A Child is Born*, Rudolf Steiner Press, London.

Toys and activities

Berger, Petra, *Feltcraft*, Floris Books, Edinburgh 1994.

Berger, Thomas, *The Christmas Craft Book*, Floris Books, Edinburgh 1990.

Berger, Thomas & Petra, *The Easter Craft Book*, Floris Books, Edinburgh 1993.

—, *The Gnome Craft Book*, Floris Books, Edinburgh 1999.

—, *Crafts through the Year*, Floris Books, Edinburgh 2000.

Jaffke, Freya, *Toymaking with Children*, Floris Books, Edinburgh 2003.

Kraul, Walter, *Earth, Water, Fire and Air*, Floris Books, Edinburgh 1989.

Meyerbröker, Helga, *Rose Windows and how to Make them*, Floris Books, Edinburgh 1994.

Müller, Brunhild, *Painting with Children*, Floris Books, Edinburgh 2002.

Petrash, Carol, *Earthways*, Gryphon House, Maryland 1992. Published as *Earthwise: Environmental Crafts and Activities with Young Children*, Floris Books, Edinburgh 1993.

Reinckens, Sunnhild, *Making Dolls*, Floris Books, Edinburgh 2003.

Schmidt, Dagmar & Jaffke, Freya, *Magic Wool*, Floris Books, Edinburgh 2000.

Sealey, Maricristin, *Kinder Dolls*, Hawthorn Press, Stroud.

Thomas, Anne & Peter, *The Children's Party Book*, Floris Books, Edinburgh 1998.

Van Leeuwen, M. & Moeskops, J. *The Nature Corner*, Floris Books, Edinburgh 1990.

Wolk-Gerche, Angelika, *More Magic Wool*, Floris Books, Edinburgh 2001.

Fairy-tales and stories

Burnett, Francis Hodgson, *The Secret Garden*, Puffin, Harmondsworth.

Colum, Padraic, *The King of Ireland's Son*, Floris Books, Edinburgh 1986.

—, *Myths of the World*, Floris Books, Edinburgh 2002.

Grimm, *The Complete Grimm's Fairy Tales*, Routledge & Kegan Paul.

—, *Favourite Grimm's Tales* (Illustrated by Anastasiya Archipova) Floris Books, Edinburgh 2000.

Knijpenga, Siegwart, *Stories of the Saints*, Floris Books, Edinburgh 2000.

Lagerlöf, Selma, *The Emperor's Vision and Other Christ Legends*, Floris Books, Edinburgh 2002.

Mellon, Nancy, *Storytelling with Children*, '.

Meyer, Rudolf, *The Wisdom of Fairy Tales*, Floris Books, Edinburgh 1995.

Sehlin, Gunhild, *Mary's Little Donkey and the Flight to Egypt*, Floris Books, Edinburgh 1987.

Verschuren, Ineke, *The Christmas Story Book*, Floris Books, Edinburgh 1988.

—, *The Easter Story Book*, Floris Books, Edinburgh 2001.

Wyatt, Isabel, *King Beetle-Tamer*, Floris Books, Edinburgh 1994.

—, *The Seven-Year-Old Wonder Book*, Floris Books, Edinburgh 1994.

Young, Ella, *Celtic Wonder Tales and Other Stories*, Floris Books, Edinburgh 2001.

Festivals

Barz, Brigitte, *Festivals with Children,* Floris Books, Edinburgh 1987.

Bock, Emil, *The Rhythm of the Christian Year,* Floris Books, Edinburgh 2000.

Bryer, Estelle & Nicol, Janni, *Celebrating Christmas Together,* Hawthorn Press, Stroud.

Bryer, Estelle & Nicol, Janni, *Christmas Stories Together,* Hawthorn Press, Stroud.

Capel, Evelyn, *The Christian Year,* Floris Books, Edinburgh 1991.

Carey, D. and J. Large, *Festivals, Family and Food*, Hawthorn Press, Stroud.

Cooper, S., C. Fynes-Clinton and M. Rowling, *The Children's Year*, Hawthorn Press, Stroud.

Druitt, A., Fynes-Clinton, C. & Rowling, M. *All Year Round,* Hawthorn Press, Stroud.

Fitzjohn, S., Weston, M. & Large, J. *Festivals Together,* Hawthorn Press, Stroud.

Jones, Michael (Ed.) *Prayers and Graces,* Floris Books, Edinburgh.

Steiner, Rudolf, *The Festivals and their Meaning*, Rudolf Steiner Press, London.

Parenting & general education

Anschütz, Marieke, *Children and their Temperaments,* Floris Books, Edinburgh 1995.

Being a Parent, Parent Network, Hawthorn Press, Stroud.

Bishop, D.V.M. *Handedness and developmental disorders.* Oxford 1990.

Britz-Crecelius, *Heidi, Children at Play,* Inner Traditions, Vermont.

Dunn, Judy, and Robert Plomin. *Separate Lives: Why Siblings Are So Different.* Basic Books, 1990.

Elkind, David, *All Grown up and no Place to go*, Holt, New York.

—, *The Hurried Child: Growing up too Fast too Soon*, Holt, New York.

Finser, Torin M. *School Renewal.* Anthroposophical Press, New York 2002.

Gabert, Erich, *Educating the Adolescent*, Anthroposophic Press, New York.

—, *The Motherly and Fatherly Roles in Education*, Anthroposophic Press, New York.

Halloweel, Edward M. / Ratey, John J. *Driven to Distraction: Recognizing and Coping with Attention Deficit Disorder from Childhood through Adulthood,* Simon & Schuster, New York 1995.

Harwood, A.C. *The Way of a Child,* Sophia Books, Forest Row.

Kane, Franklin G. *Parents as People: the Family as a Creative Process*, Aurora, Edmonton.

König, Karl, *Brothers and Sisters: the Order of Birth in the Family*, Floris Books, Edinburgh and Anthroposophic Press, New York.

Large, Martin, *Who's Bringing them up? Television and Child Development*, Hawthorn Press, Stroud.

Mander, Jerry, *Four Arguments for the Elimination of Television.*

Needleman, H. L., and P. J. Landrigan. *Raising Children Toxic Free,* Farrar, Straus & Giroux, New York 1994.

Pearce, Joseph Chilton, *The Magical Child,* Bantam, New York.

Piaget, Jean. *The Origin of Intelligence in the Child.* London: Routledge and Paul, 1953.

Plomin, Robert and Dunn, Judy, *Separate Lives: Why Siblings Are So Different,* Basic Books.

Postman, Neil. *The Disappearance of Childhood.* New York: Vintage Books, 1994.

Rapp, Doris J., M. D. *Is this your child's world?* New York: Bantam, 1997.

Rawson, Martyn & Rose, Michael, *Ready to Learn,* Hawthorn Press, Stroud.

Salter, Joan, *The Incarnating Child*, Hawthorn Press, Stroud.

Stoll, Clifford, High Tech Heretic: *Why Computers Don't Belong in the Classroom, and Other Reflections by a Computer Contrarian*, Doubleday, New York 1999.

—, *Silicon Snake Oil: Second Thoughts on the Information Highway.* Anchor 1996.

Waldorf (Rudolf Steiner) education

Aeppli, Willi, *Biography in Waldorf Education*, Anthroposophic Press, New York.

—, *Rudolf Steiner Education and the Developing Child*, Anthroposophic Press, New York.

—, *Teacher, Child and Waldorf Education*, Anthroposophic Press, New York.

Barnes, H. and others, *Introduction to Waldorf Education*, Mercury, New York.

Childs, Gilbert, *Steiner Education In Theory and Practice,* Floris Books, Edinburgh 1992.

Clouder, Christopher & Rawson, Martyn, *Waldorf Education,* Floris Books, Edinburgh 2003.

Cusick, Lois, *Waldorf Parenting Handbook*, St George, New York.

Edmunds, Francis, *Rudolf Steiner Education*, Rudolf Steiner Press, London.

Heydebrand, Caroline von, *Childhood,* Anthroposophical Press, New York.

Koepke, Hermann, *Encountering the Self: Transformation and Destiny in the Ninth Year*, Anthroposophic Press, New York.

Nobel, Agnes, *Educating through Art,* Floris Books, Edinburgh 1996.

Petrash, Jack, *Understanding Waldorf Education,* Gryphon House, Maryland 2001 and Floris Books, Edinburgh 2003.

Richards, Mary Caroline, *Towards Wholeness: Rudolf Steiner Education in America.* Wesleyan University Press 1981.

Spock, Marjorie, *Teaching as a Lively Art*, Anthroposophic Press, New York.

Steiner, Rudolf, *The Child's Changing Consciousness and Waldorf Education*, Rudolf Steiner Press, London.

—, *Education as a Social Problem*, Anthroposophic Press, New York.

—, *The Education of the Child,* Anthroposophical Press, New York.

—, *The Essentials of Education*, Rudolf Steiner Press, London.

—, *The Four Temperaments*, Rudolf Steiner Press, London.

—, *An Introduction to Waldorf Education*, Anthroposophic Press, New York.

—, *The Kingdom of Childhood*, Rudolf Steiner Press, London.

—, *A Modern Art of Education*, Rudolf Steiner Press, London.

—, *The Renewal of Education,* Anthroposophical Press, New York 2002.

—, *Soul Economy and Waldorf Education,* Anthroposophic Press, 1986.

Strauss, Michaela, *Understanding Children's Drawings*, Rudolf Steiner Press, London.

Nutrition and biodynamics

Cook, Wendy, *Foodwise, Understanding what we Eat and How it Affects us*, Clairview Books, Forest Row.

Hauschka, Rudolf, *Nutrition*, Rudolf Steiner Press, London.

Koepf, Herbert, *Bio-Dynamic Agriculture: An Introduction*, Anthroposophic Press, New York.

—, *The Biodynamic Farm*, Anthroposophic Press, New York.

Philbrick, John & Helen, *Gardening for Health and Nutrition*, Steinerbooks, New York.

Podolinsky, Alex, *Bio Dynamic Agriculture: Introductory Lectures*, Gavemer Foundation, Sydney.

Schilthuis, Willy, *Biodynamic Agriculture,* Floris Books, Edinburgh 2003.

Schmidt, Gerhard, *The Essentials of Nutrition*, Biodynamic Literature, USA.
Steiner, Rudolf, *Nutrition and Health*, Anthroposophic Press, New York.
—, *Problems of Nutrition,* Anthroposophic Press, New York.
Thun, Maria, *Results from the Biodynamic Sowing and Planting Calendar,* Floris Books, Edinburgh 2003.
Thun, Maria & Matthias, *The Biodynamic Sowing and Planting Calendar,* Floris Books, Edinburgh annually.

—, *Questions of Destiny: Mental Retardation and Curative Education,* Anthroposophic Press, New York.
Steiner, Rudolf, *Curative Education,* Rudolf Steiner Press, London.
Weihs, Anke, Joan Tallo and Wain Farrants, *Camphill Villages*, Camphill Press, Botton.
Weihs, Thomas, *Children in Need of Special Care*, Souvenir, London.
Woodward, Bob and Hogenboom, Marga, *Autism, A Holistic Approach,* 2002.

Eurythmy

Dubach, Annemarie, *Principles of Eurythmy,* Rudolf Steiner Press, London.
Poplawski, Thomas, *Eurythmy: Rhythm, Dance,* Floris Books, Edinburgh 1998.
Spock, Marjorie, *Eurythmy*, Anthroposophic Press, New York.
Steiner, *Curative Eurythmy,* Rudolf Steiner Press, Forest Row.
—, *Eurythmy as Visible Speech*, Rudolf Steiner Press, London.
—, *An Introduction to Eurythmy,* Anthroposophic Press, New York.

Handicapped children and special needs education

Clarke, P., H. Kofsky and J. Lauruol, *To a Different Drumbeat: A Practical Guide to Parenting Children with Special Needs*, Hawthorn Press, Stroud.
Hansmann, Henning, *Education for Special Needs,* Floris Books, Edinburgh 1992.
König, Karl, *Being Human: Diagnosis in Curative Education*, Camphill Press, Botton., and Anthroposophic Press, New York.
—, *In Need of Special Understanding*, Camphill Press, Botton.
Luxford, Michael, *Children with Special Needs,* Floris Books, Edinburgh 2004.
Pietzner, Carlo, *Aspects of Curative Education*, Aberdeen University Press.

Phases of life

Bittleston, Adam, *Loneliness*, Floris Books, Edinburgh.
Burkhard, Gudrun, *Taking Charge, Your Life Patterns and their Meaning,* Floris Books, Edinburgh 1997.
Covey, Stephen R. *The Seven Habits of Highly Effective People.* Simon & Schuster, New York 1990.
Keller, Helen, *The Story of my Life*, New York.
König, Karl, *The Human Soul*, Floris Books, Edinburgh.
Lievegoed, Bernhard, *Man on the Threshold*, Hawthorn Press, Stroud.
—, *Phases: Crisis and Development in the Individual*, Rudolf Steiner Press, London.
—, *Phases of Childhood*, Floris Books, Edinburgh.
Lusseyran, Jacques, *And there was Light*, Floris Books, Edinburgh.
Mathews, M., S. Schaefer and B. Staley, *Ariadne's Awakening*, Hawthorn Press, Stroud.
Sleigh, Julian, *Crisis Points: Working through Personal Problems*, Floris Books, Edinburgh 1998.
—, *Friends and Lovers,* Floris Books, Edinburgh 1998.
—, *Thirteen to Nineteen: Discovering the Light*, Floris Books, Edinburgh 1998.
Staley, Betty,. *Between Form and Freedom: A Practical Guide to the Teenage Years,* Hawthorn Press, Stroud.

Treichler, Rudolf, *Soulways: The Developing Soul — Life Phases, Thresholds and Biography*, Hawthorn Press, Stroud.

Religious education

Bittleston, Adam, *Our Spiritual Companions,* Floris Books, Edinburgh 1983.
Anschütz, Marieke, *But who Made God? Religion and your Growing Child,* Floris Books, Edinburgh 2004.
Bittleston, Adam, *Meditative Prayers for Today*, Floris Books, Edinburgh.
Jones, Michael (editor), *Prayers and Graces,* Floris Books, Edinburgh 2004.
Rittelmeyer, Friedrich, *Meditation: Guidance of the Inner Life,* Floris Books, Edinburgh.
Steiner, Rudolf, *Calendar of the Soul,* Anthroposophic Press, New York.
—, *Prayers for Parents and Children*, Rudolf Steiner Press, Forest Row.
—, *Verses and Meditations*, Rudolf Steiner Press, London.

Pre-existence and reincarnation

Bock, Emil. 1996. *Wiederholte Erdenleben* [Repeated lives on earth]. Stuttgart: Urachhaus.
Capel, Evelyn, *Reincarnation within Christianity*, Temple Lodge Press, London.
Frieling, Rudolf, *Christianity and Reincarnation*, Floris Books, Edinburgh.
Rittelmeyer, Friedrich, *Reincarnation*, Floris Books, Edinburgh.
Steiner, Rudolf, *Between Death and Rebirth*, Rudolf Steiner Press, London.
—, *Life between Death and Rebirth*, Anthroposophic Press, New York.

Death and caring for the dying

Baum, John, *When Death Enters Life,* Floris Books, Edinburgh 2003.
Drake, Stanley, *Though You Die,* Floris Books, Edinburgh 2002.
Kübler-Ross, Elisabeth, *Death, the Final Stage of Growth*, Simon Schuster, New York.
—, *Living with Death and Dying,* Souvenir, London.
—, *On Children and Death*, Collier Macmillan, New York.
—, *On Death and Dying*, Tavistock Routledge, London, & Schribner, New York 1997.
—, *To Live until we say Good-bye,* Prentice Hall, London.
Moody, Raymond A. *Life after Life*. New York: Bantam, 1984.
Ritchie, George G., with Elizabeth Sherrill. *Return from Tomorrow*. Waco, TX: Chosen Books, 1978.
Roszell, Calvert, *The Near-Death Experience of George G. Ritchie,* Anthroposophical Press, New York.
Schilling, Karin von, *Where are You? Coming to Terms with the Death of my Child*, Anthroposophic Press, New York.

Social forms

Davy, Gudrun and Bons Voors, *Lifeways: Working with Family Questions*, Hawthorn Press, Stroud.
Lauer, H.E. *Aggression and Repression in the Individual and Society*, Rudolf Steiner Press, London.
Steiner, Rudolf, *The Renewal of the Social Organism*, Anthroposophic Press, New York.
—, *The Social Future*, Anthroposophic Press, New York.
—, *Towards Social Renewal*, Rudolf Steiner Press, London.
Voors, Tino and Chris Schaefer, *Vision in Action*, Hawthorn Press, Stroud.

Rudolf Steiner and Anthroposophy

Barnes, Henry, *Life for the Spirit,* Anthroposophical Press, New York.

Bockemühl, Jochen (ed.). *Toward a Phenomenology of the Etheric World.* Anthroposophic Press, New York.

Childs, Gilbert, *Rudolf Steiner: His Life and Work,* Floris Books, Edinburgh 2003.

Easton, Stewart, *Man and World in the Light of Anthroposophy,* Anthroposophic Press, New York.

—, *The Way of Anthroposophy,* Rudolf Steiner Press, London.

—, *Rudolf Steiner: Herald of a New Epoch,* Anthroposophic Press, New York.

Edmunds, Francis, *From Thinking to Living: the Work of Rudolf Steiner,* Element, Dorset.

Hemleben, Johannes, *Rudolf Steiner,* Sophia Books, Forest Row.

Lissau, Rudi, *Rudolf Steiner, Life work, inner path and social initiatives,* Hawthorn Press, Stroud.

A Man before Others, Rudolf Steiner Remembered. Rudolf Steiner Press, Forest Row.

Mcdermott, Robert, *The Essential Steiner,* Steinerbooks, New York 2005.

Nesfield-Cookson, Bernard, *Rudolf Steiner's Vision of Love,* Crucible, Wellingborough.

Rittelmeyer, Friedrich, *Rudolf Steiner enters my Life,* Floris Books, Edinburgh.

Seddon, Richard, *Rudolf Steiner, Essential Readings,* Crucible, Wellingborough.

Shepherd, A.P. *Scientist of the Invisible,* Floris Books, Edinburgh.

Steiner, Rudolf. 1994. *How to Know Higher Worlds.* Hudson, NY: Anthroposophic Press.

—, *An Outline of Esoteric Science,* Anthroposophic Press, New York.

—, *Intuitive Thinking as a Spiritual Path: A Philosophy of Freedom,* Anthroposophical Press, New York.

—. 1994. *Theosophy,* Anthroposophic Press, New York.

Wachsmuth, Günther, *The Life and Work of Rudolf Steiner,* Garber Books, New York.

Useful Organizations

Anthroposophical medicine

**Physicians Association for
Anthroposophic Medicine (PAAM)**
1923 Geddes Ave, Ann Arbor MI 48104-1797
Tel: (734) 930 9462   *Fax:* (734) 662 1727
Email: paam@anthroposophy.org
Web: www.paam.net

The Anthroposophical Medical Association
Park Attwood Clinic, Trimpley, Bewdley,
Worcs. DY12 1RE
Tel: 01299-861 444   *Fax:* 01299-861 375
Email: movementoffice@btinternet.com
Web: www.parkattwood.org

Weleda
Ilkeston , Derbyshire DE7 8DR, **UK**
Tel: 0115-944 8200   Fax: 0115-944 8210
Email: WeledaUK@compuserve.com
Web: www.weleda.co.uk

175 North Rte 9W, Congers, NY 10920 **US**
Tel: 1 800 241 1030
Email: info@weleda.com
Web: http://usa.weleda.com

PO Box 8132, Havelock North **NZ**
Tel. 0800-802 174   *Fax:* 0800-804 989
Email: help@weleda.co.nz
Web: www.weleda.co.nz

Australia. *Tel:.* (03) 9723 7278
Fax: +64 (6) 877 4989
Email: help@weleda.co.nz

Pharma Natura (South Africa)
Po Box 494, Bergvlei 2012
Tel: (011)445 6000   *Fax:* (011) 445 6089
Email healthcare@pharma.co.za
Web: www.pharma.co.za

International
Anthroposophical Society Medical Section
Goetheanum, 4143 Dornach, Switzerland
Tel: +41-61-706 4290 *Fax:* +41-61-706 4291
Email: med.sektion@goetheanum.ch
Web: www.goetheanum.ch/medicine

Childbirth, breastfeeding

La Lèche League International
1400 N. Meacham Road, Schaumburg
IL 60173–4808, **US**
Tel. (847) 519–7730
Web: www.lalecheleague.org.

National Childbirth Trust
Alexandra House, Oldham Terrace
London W3 6NH **UK**
Enquiry: 0870-444 8707
Breastfeeding Line: 0870-444 8708
Fax: 020-8992 5929
Web: www.nctpregnancyandbabycare.com

Therapies

Nordoff-Robbins Center for Music Therapy
New York University, 82 Washington
Square East, New York NY 10003, **US**
2 Lissenden Gardens, London NW5 1PP **UK**

Bothmer gymnasitcs
Martin Baker, 2 The Cheverils, Priory
Road, Forest Row, RH18 5HR **UK**
Jaimen McMillan, 129 Hayes Road,
Schuylerville, NY 12817, **US**

Association of Eurythmy Therapists
Park Attwood Clinic, Trumpley, Bewdly,
Worcs. DY12 1RE, **UK**

Waldorf (Steiner) education

**Association of Waldorf Schools
of North America**
3911 Bannister Road, Fair Oaks, CA 95628
Tel: 916-961 0927   *Fax:* 916-961 0715
Email: awsna@awsna.org
Web: www.awsna.org

The Steiner Schools Fellowship
Kidbrooke Park, Forest Row RH18 5JX **UK**
Tel: 01342-822 115   *Fax:* 01342-826 004
Email: mail@swsf.org.uk
Web: www.steinerwaldorf.org.uk

*Information for other countries can be
found through either of the above.*

Publications

Steinerbooks (Anthroposophic Press)
PO Box 799, Great Barrington, MA 01230
Tel: (413) 528-8233   *Fax:* (413) 528-8826
Email: service@steinerbooks.org
Web: www.steinerbooks.org

Rudolf Steiner Press
Hillside House, The Square, Forest Row
RH18 5ES **UK**
Tel: 01342-824 433   *Fax:* 01342-826 437
Email: editorial@rudolfsteinerpress.com
Web: www.rudolfsteinerpress.com

Floris Books
15 Harrison Gdns, Edinburgh EH11 1SH **UK**
Tel: 0131-337 2372   *Fax:* 0131-347 9919
Email: floris@florisbooks.co.uk
Web: www.florisbooks.co.uk

Anthroposophical Society

Anthroposophical Society in **America**
1923 Geddes Ave, Ann Arbor, MI 48104-1797
Tel: (734) 662-9355   *Fax:* (734) 662-1727
Email: information@anthroposophy.org
Web: www.anthroposophy.org

Anthroposophical Society in **Great Britain**
35 Park Road, London NW1 6XT
Tel: 020-7723 4400   *Fax:* 020-7724 4364
Email: rsh@cix.compulink.co.uk
Web: www.anth.org.uk/rsh

Anthroposophical Society in **Australia**
Tel: 08 8339 6407
Email: anthroposophy@bigpond.com
Web: www.anthroposophy.org.au

Anthroposophical Society in **Canada**
P.O.Box 38162, 550 Eglinton Avenue West,
Toronto, Ontario, M5N 3A8
Tel: (416) 488 2886   *Fax:* (416) 488 5546
Email: headoffice@colosseum.com
Web: www.anthroposophy.ca

Anthroposophical Society in **New Zealand**
18 Grants Road, Papanui, Christchurch
Tel: 03 354 4447
Email: hmulder@xtra.co.nz
Web: www.anthroposophy.org.nz

Anthroposophical Society in **South Africa**
P.O. Box 71925, ZA-Bryanston 2021
Tel: +27 11 706 85 44 5
Fax: +27 11 706 41 36

International
General Anthroposophical Society
PO Box, 4143 Dornach, Switzerland
Tel: +41-61-706 42 42
Fax: +41-61-706 43 14
Email: sekretariat@goetheanum.ch
Web: www.goetheanum.ch

Index